The Just and the Lively
The literary criticism of John Dryden

Michael Werth Gelber

Manchester University Press
Manchester and New York

distributed exclusively in the USA by St. Martin's Press

Published by Manchester University Press
Oxford Road, Manchester M13 9NR, UK
and Room 400, 175 Fifth Avenue, New York, NY 10010, USA
http://www.man.ac.uk/mup

Distributed exclusively in the USA by
St. Martin's Press, Inc., 175 Fifth Avenue, New York,
NY 10010, USA

Distributed exclusively in Canada by
UBC Press, University of British Columbia, 6344 Memorial Road,
Vancouver, BC, Canada V6T 1Z2

British Library Cataloguing-in-Publication Data
A catalogue record for this book is available from the British Library

Library of Congress Cataloging-in-Publication Data applied for

ISBN 0 7190 5414 1 hardback

First published 1999
05 04 03 02 01 00 99   10 9 8 7 6 5 4 3 2 1

Typeset by Special Edition Pre-press Services, London
Printed in Great Britain by Bookcraft (Bath) Ltd., Midsomer Norton

To my Mother
and to the memory
of my Father

Eugenius was going to continue this Discourse, when *Lisideius* told him that it was necessary, before they proceeded further, to take a standing measure of their Controversie; for how was it possible to be decided who writ the best Plays, before we know what a Play should be? but, this once agreed on by both Parties, each might have recourse to it, either to prove his own advantages, or to discover the failings of his Adversary.

He had no sooner said this, but all desir'd the favour of him to give the definition of a Play; and they were the more importunate, because neither *Aristotle*, nor *Horace*, nor any other, who had writ of that Subject, had ever done it.

Lisideius, after some modest denials, at last confess'd he had a rude Notion of it; indeed rather a Description then a Definition: but which serv'd to guide him in his private thoughts, when he was to make a judgment of what others writ: that he conceiv'd a Play ought to be, *A just and lively Image of Humane Nature, representing its Passions and Humours, and the Changes of Fortune to which it is subject; for the Delight and Instruction of Mankind.*

This Definition, though *Crites* rais'd a Logical Objection against it; that it was only *a genere & fine,* and so not altogether perfect; was yet well received by the rest…

        — John Dryden in *An Essay of Dramatick Poesie.*

Contents

Illustrations

Preface

In the writing of this book, I have incurred a number of happy obligations. To the work of previous scholars, including those with whom I continue to disagree, I remain permanently indebted: they have all challenged thought, encouraged speculation and helped me to define at the very least the direction of my own studies and investigation. I can only hope that I pay adequate acknowledgment to them in my footnotes and bibliography.

To colleagues, teachers, and other friends I owe many kindnesses, far too many to enumerate; but there are several I dare not fail to mention here. I began my studies in Dryden under the watchful eye of Professor Margaret Starkey. An early draft of the manuscript was read by Professors Gita May, John C. Nelson, Michael Seidel and John H. Middendorf. The discussion of Dryden's influence on Samuel Johnson was read by Professor Howard Weinbrot. The late Professor Howard Schless made valuable suggestions for the improvement of the text in almost all of its many permutations. I like to think that, in its present form, the book would have pleased him. Professor Steven N. Zwicker read the manuscript for the publisher and oversaw the final revision. For his having put at my disposal his learning and scholarship, I am extremely grateful. I owe many courtesies to the librarians of St Francis College, the City University of New York, St John's University, the New York Public Library and Columbia University. Many thanks are due to Professor Yvette Louria, who read each of the drafts and with each reading suggested how I might best improve a graceless expression or a not-very-convincing argument; and to the editorial staff of the Manchester University Press: in all my dealings with them they proved themselves unfailingly considerate and helpful, even indulgent. Fred Leise helped in preparing the index; and Corinne Orde carried out the tasks of copy-editor and compositor with good humour and a stunning grasp of detail.

My deepest debt of all, however, I owe to Professor Morton Irving Seiden. When it first occurred to me that I should like to undertake a study of Dryden's literary criticism, it was he who immediately urged me to do so. Afterwards, he discussed with me and clarified difficult matters of both fact and interpretation. He read and commented at length on each of the many visions and revisions through which the manuscript passed. At every stage of my research and composition he gave freely and patiently of his time, his encouragement and his moral support.

Portions of the book have already appeared in print: a part of Chapter Six has apeared in *Eighteenth-Century Studies*, 26:2 (Winter 1992–93); a part of Chapter Nine in *Papers on Language and Literature*, 29:3 (1993); and parts of Chapters Twelve and Thirteen in the *Huntington Library Quarterly*, 61:3 (1998). For permission to reprint this material, I wish to thank the editors. I also wish to thank the Regents of the University of California for permission to reprint material from *The Works of John Dryden* (ed. H. T. Swedenberg, Jr *et al.*, in progress, *c.* 1956–).

TEXTS, DATES AND FORMAT

Whenever possible, references to Dryden's works are based on the California edition. Since that edition is now incomplete, however, I occasionally make use of others: for the poems, the edition by George R. Noyes; for the prose criticism, the edition by Sir Walter Scott and George Saintsbury and that by George Watson.

When quoting from Dryden, or from his contemporaries, I follow the punctuation and spelling of the edition from which the passage comes, but with one slight exception. In the California edition, the editors follow, in their use of italics, the example of Dryden's compositors. I follow the same example, but not when an entire passage is set in italics: I then follow more or less modern practice. The date of a work is that of publication; when two dates are given, the first is that of composition or, for a play, that of first production.

I have in each chapter separated my units of discussion by means of roman numerals and asterisks. I place numbers between the larger units, in each of which I take up chronologically one of Dryden's works or some related problem or issue. I use the single asterisk between the smaller units, in which I take up in detail either an aspect of a larger unit or one or more of its buried implications.

Michael Werth Gelber

Introduction

John Dryden is the father of English literary criticism; but, despite the sheer volume of his criticism and its range and brilliance, these days he rarely if ever gets the tribute where tribute is due. Like many fathers, even the best of them, either he suffers neglect or he is misunderstood and severely condemned. It may perhaps be argued that, during the past two or three decades, there has been a resurgence of interest in his criticism: that it has been the subject of many articles (more than a hundred) in learned journals; that it has been the subject of two book-length studies, one by Robert D. Hume, the other by Edward Pechter; and that it has also been discussed, sometimes at length, in biographies by Charles E. Ward, Kenneth Young and James Anderson Winn and in a number of articles and books of a more or less general nature, including histories of English critical theory and practice. Nevertheless, when set historically in its proper context, and its excellence is fully granted, it continues to suffer neglect; and when not neglected it still receives inadequate treatment – very much so.

Dryden's criticism is again and again made subordinate to biographical study or to the cultural history – political or social, philosophical or religious – of the age during which he lived; to excursions into his wide reading and hence into his sources and analogues; to his unending concern with technical problems in which the modern reader is not likely to be interested; or to the most recent fashions in our literary creeds.[1] As in the past, so again in our own time, no attempt has been made to study the criticism both chronologically and textually in order to demonstrate not only its fundamental unity and coherence but also its consistency, its development within that consistency and, within its development, Dryden's abiding attempt to reconcile opposing strains in literature (the just and the lively), along with the mental faculties (judgment and imagination) in which they originate.[2] It was to fill in these many lacunae, while modifying and correcting failures in point of view and interpretation, that I undertook the study that follows.

Dryden is one of the great poet-critics in the language, initiating that line which includes Samuel Johnson, Samuel Taylor Coleridge, Matthew Arnold and T. S. Eliot. Generally, we denominate these men as poet-critics because they wrote both poetry and criticism and achieved distinction in each. In applying the term to Dryden, however, we must add a further detail: Dryden is a poet-critic in the additional sense that his poetry and his criticism are intimately related. Unlike Johnson and Coleridge, Dryden did not tend to give up poetry and then write criticism, inclining first to one discipline and then the other. Unlike Arnold and Eliot, he did not consider his own poetry merely in odd moments or comment upon it at great remove. Dryden was a critic as long as he was a poet; and for the entire time in which he was a critic he was avowedly a critic of himself. The primary task of his criticism was the explanation and justification of his own poetry, plays and translations.

1

The forms in which Dryden wrote as a critic are those which, not surprisingly, facilitate self-analysis. His customary vehicles were the dedication, the preface, the prologue and epilogue and a number of other forms that, no less easily and quickly, could be adapted to the text at hand. He was never inspired to write a treatise on some abstract theory or to compose an essay that had no immediate bearing on himself. Only once did he even appear to consider literary ideas for their own sake; and that single instance, the famous *Essay of Dramatick Poesie* (1668), is actually an oblique defence of his most recent experiments in the drama.

Throughout his career Dryden's criticism dealt with the pressing issues upon which the success or failure of his creative work might depend. Its common topics are those of literary source and genre, together with the Aristotelian categories of plot, character, subject, style and metre. Its larger aim is to reconcile the two native English traditions – one represented by William Shakespeare, the other by Ben Jonson – in which he worked. Dryden's criticism is often technical and detailed; nevertheless, its scope of reference is engagingly wide. Dryden always generalizes from his own practice; but his discussions, though centred on his own texts, move outwards in an ever-widening orbit. Out of the immense store of the literary past he selects a number of kindred spirits and then groups them into a school. He soon grants that school the status of a literary tradition; and upon that tradition he erects a theory. Interested initially in explaining his own work, Dryden ends by illuminating a broad expanse of Western literature.

The scope of Dryden's criticism and its depth would seem to compel our admiration. Yet the full significance of the criticism has never been recognized. Even during the eighteenth century, when Dryden's fame as a poet was at its height, his criticism was said to be a hotchpotch of insight and error. We mistakenly tend to equate Dryden's standing as a critic in the eighteenth century with the encomium by Johnson. But Johnson's tribute, where not stringently qualified, is not typical of the age. Far more representative is the judgment by Leonard Welsted, who thought it was Dryden's method 'to say every Thing that came into his Head', thus making his criticism 'a pretty amusing Mixture of Wit and Ribaldry, good Sense and Impropriety, Vanity and Modesty oddly jumbl'd together'.[3] Welsted attributed the motley of the criticism to a mercurial temper. An even more common explanation blamed the disorder on Dryden's prefatory habit. Dryden's criticism, complained Jonathan Swift and John Oldmixon, is not the handmaiden but the lackey of his art: it defends the work to which it is joined in complete disregard of fact, principle and system.

The unfavourable verdict on Dryden in the eighteenth century has enjoyed a remarkably long life. Reaffirmed by such nineteenth-century figures as Sir Walter Scott, it has survived to become an important aspect of our literary heritage. Critics today, like those of the past, regard Dryden's criticism as dangerously flawed by special pleading. A distrust of its alleged sophistries has either driven the twentieth-century scholar away or, at best, inhibited his generous engagement. Dryden's criticism as a whole, in any event, has never been the object of a detailed, chronological study. To examine it *in extenso* necessitates a sympathetic reading of the self-criticism, and that reading no one so far has been willing to give. It is the purpose of the present study to initiate the endeavour. But more immediately, the purpose of the present study is to examine year by year the criticism of the first period (1664–1672), since that is the formative stage in Dryden's thought, and then to trace how shifts in perspective led to the great essays of the next two periods, the middle (1673–1679) and the late (1680–1700).

I hold as my central thesis that Dryden's criticism offers the best guide to the rest of his canon; and I try to substantiate this view by considering all of the criticism, the minor as well as the major works: the prologues and epilogues no less than the many prefaces. Throughout, I have endeavoured to read the criticism as it was designed to be read, as a series of introductions to or comments on specific poems or plays. What others deplore as an absence of settled conviction, moreover, I look upon rather as Dryden's attempt to bring his theories into harmony with his art. His changes in critical judgment are neither radical nor perverse but are the fitting counterpart to a poetic career that constantly moved in new directions.

I argue, further, that the criticism, initially linked to specific occasions, gradually achieved an independent existence and has since enjoyed an independent life. All of Dryden's criticism was written for the moment. Its immediate goal was to placate contemporary audiences; and that task done, its primary function was at an end. Yet there is ample evidence that Dryden also aspired to leave a critical testament behind and to alter literary taste permanently. And these things are precisely what he did achieve. Long after his death, readers, oblivious of the quarrels that set him to writing, came to him to learn about literature. It was from him that they gleaned the meanings of literary terms, the nature of literary genres and the historical development of literature in England. They went to him as well to learn how to appreciate major poets from Homer and Virgil to Shakespeare and Jonson; and in this field of practical criticism none of his remarks have been more influential than those which he made on himself. For the last three hundred years our perspectives on Dryden's poetry have been precisely the ones that he established. To read through the centuries of Dryden criticism is to find echoes of Dryden's own criticism everywhere. His influence even extends, as I hope to prove, to those who reject virtually the whole of the criticism and to those who condemn it only when he writes about himself.

Despite the originality of his thought, Dryden the literary critic was not sufficient unto himself. He read widely in Renaissance literature, as well as in the literature of classical antiquity and the Middle Ages; and he knew remarkably well the modern heirs – mainly the Italian and the French – of Aristotle and Horace, Longinus and Quintilian: Vida, Scaliger, Castelvetro; Chapelain, Rapin, Bouhours, Le Bossu. My concern is not, however, with the sources and analogues of Dryden's thought, but rather with the manner in which, like the major poet-critics who had preceded him (Tasso, Jonson, Corneille), he would reconcile in his own behalf critical theory and literary practice and, in the very act of doing so, help define a new literary tradition, one which would have to be both ancient and modern, both national and cosmopolitan, both lively and just.

Of the political and social backgrounds of Dryden's criticism I speak intermittently, but only in passing. Aspects of the subject have already been dealt with
by George McFadden, Michael McKeon and Steven N. Zwicker. My own interest
and emphasis lie elsewhere. Although roughly half the book is of necessity centred
on the foundations of Dryden's criticism, the rest is concerned with his criticism
as a whole, with emphasis on the critical writing of the middle and later years:
its interconnections with the early work, its unifying themes, its principles of
development.

My discussion of the criticism thus unfolds chronologically; but the book has
another structure as well, one dictated – unexpectedly, I think – by the inner logic
of Dryden's very evolution as both theorist and poet. After a brief overview (in the
opening two chapters) of his lifelong commitment to theoretical and practical
criticism, I discuss in Chapter Three his interest, at the onset of his career, in a
general problem of the Restoration, that of literary tradition; in Chapter Four, his
more specific concerns, initially, with language and literary genre, as well as with
the purpose of literature and its subject matter; and in the next four chapters, the
beginnings of his critical theorizing about all literature, but mainly about the three
kinds of drama that he then favoured the most: first tragi-comedy, next mixed
comedy, and eventually the heroic play. In Chapter Nine I summarize the early
criticism in the light of the work to come. And I then turn to the middle criticism
(Chapter Ten) and the essays of the final years (Chapters Eleven to Fourteen). In
my concluding chapter, I consider Dryden's own final judgment on his total output as critic; and I take up briefly his later reputation and influence.

In what follows I generally restrict to the notes my comments on those scholars
whose works I may seem to echo, and who therefore may seem to have anticipated
my own first principles, and my disputation with those other scholars whose views
would in advance prove me wrong and with whom I disagree categorically. During
the last hundred years or so there has come into being in every discussion of
Dryden's criticism an elaborate web of the commonplace: in his lack of any formal
system Dryden initiated an English style of literary criticism; despite his commitment to the rules of classicism, whether English or French, he was remarkably
flexible; he turned always to authority and tradition – to Aristotle, Horace,
Shakespeare – for justification of his critical theory and practice.

During this same period, on the other hand, it has been argued – erroneously,
in my opinion – that to the modern reader Dryden's criticism is, and can only be,
a mere curiosity;[4] that between his pronouncements and the works to which they
are appended, especially his own, there is no connection or very little;[5] that the
pronouncements lack consistency;[6] and that the pronouncements, with few if any
exceptions, show little or no development or change.[7]

It has been argued – no less erroneously, in my opinion – that in his many
comments about *Annus Mirabilis* (1667) the criticism is centred not so much on
matters literary as on contemporary politics;[8] and that in the *Essay of Dramatick
Poesie* (1668) it dwells on and favours not tragi-comedy but the heroic play,[9] in
the 'Preface to *The Tempest*' (1670) it is without irony or reservation a tribute to

4

Sir William Davenant,[10] in the 'Preface to *An Evening's Love*' (1671) it denies the comic muse a moral purpose,[11] in 'Of Heroique Playes' (1672) it is either superficial or, as a statement of literary sources and background, profoundly misleading.[12] Mistakes in the interpretation of the early works, moreover, have produced concomitant errors in the interpretation of later essays: for example, the notion that 'The Grounds of Criticism in Tragedy' (1679) exhibits a rigidity of method;[13] the notion that the 'Preface to *Fables Ancient and Modern*' (1700) is riotous and exhibits no method at all.[14]

Upon my coadjutors, both those with whom I agree (more or less) and those with whom I clearly disagree, I have chosen on the whole to avoid direct comment in the text. Such comment would have lengthened the present study needlessly; and it would have required endless digression from the main lines of my endeavour and chief concern. It would have been, I believe, an act of violent and tedious supererogation.

At the risk of seeming repetitious, I must grant that, my sub-title notwithstanding, I give somewhat more attention to the early criticism than to what came later; but I do so for good reason. If one is to appreciate the tree, as William Blake suggests, one must concentrate on the roots and trunk first: only as one understands the matrix can one fully understand the miracle, the branches and all the leaves, to which it necessarily gives rise.

I must also grant that, in commenting on the late criticism, I consider at what might appear excessive length Dryden's growing preoccupation with classical and medieval scholarship and learning; and here too I must argue that the scale of treatment is wholly justified. The subject has generally been neglected; it has never been adequately identified, studied or appreciated. In raising the subject I have tried merely to give it the emphasis that Dryden himself gives it and that, in the overview of his criticism, it surely deserves. So I believe.

PART I
Themes and variations

CHAPTER ONE

The ends of criticism

I

With the exception of the *Essay of Dramatick Poesie,* written at the beginning of his career (1668), and the 'Preface to *Fables*', written at the end (1700), John Dryden's criticism (the early, the middle, the late) enjoys an indifferent fame. It is celebrated without enthusiasm and championed without being read. To know all of Dryden's criticism is to be distinguished, even in academic circles, by an odd accomplishment. Yet the criticism in its entirety is worth knowing for many reasons, not least of which is that a grasp of the whole helps to clarify the meaning of the parts. Hence, although each period of the criticism is complete unto itself, each may best be approached initially by a brief overview of forty years of thought.

For the neglect of the criticism both Dryden and his supporters must be held responsible. Dryden, for his part, frequently disappoints the modern reader: he does not often consider the ultimate problems in literature; he investigates issues now forgotten; he appears to confuse art with life. In addition to these deficiencies the criticism contains others. It consists, in the main, of short pieces that, individually, reach no final conclusions and that, collectively, are hard to digest. At the outset, then, the reader is offered many hurdles and is promised, so it appears, few rewards.

The difficulties inherent in Dryden have been compounded by his defenders. He has been praised in many ways, but always in a manner that dulls curiosity. One group praises him for his importance in the history of ideas. F. N. Lees finds Dryden's essays 'refreshing' and 'most informative', remarkably so, despite 'some remoteness, as they stand, from the concerns of modern critics'.[1] So too, Walter Jackson Bate, although more appreciative than Lees, tends to make Dryden's criticism as a body of work strangely unappealing. Dryden, according to Bate, is, '[w]ith the possible exception of Ben Jonson', 'the first great model of "the new classicism"'. His essays stand like a public monument, though one that enjoyed more homage in a past age than it enjoys in our own.[2]

Besides Bate and Lees, along with others in their camp, there exists a second group that has written in Dryden's favour. Its members – Frederick A. Pottle and J. W. H. Atkins and more recently Robert D. Hume and Edward Pechter – have ranged through Dryden's major critical works and noted, buried amidst what they see as arid stretches, occasional growths of genius. For Pottle, these remarkable plants are very few in number,[3] though Atkins has compiled a fairly extensive list:

> He decried bombast in the drama, for instance, conceits and 'false wit' in poetry, irrelevance and superfluity in prose; he called attention to the importance of dramatic characterization, whereas the ancient Chorus and the Unity of time he regarded as unnecessary features of English drama;

and besides commending a subtler form of satire, he noted also the emotional values of literature in general, and the relations existing between poetry and one of the sister arts.[4]

Pechter and Hume are a little more generous. They each emphasize what may be taken as an underlying pattern of the criticism. For Pechter, Dryden is the most catholic of English critics and the most flexible: he holds a number of divergent theories simultaneously and never prefers one to any of the others.[5] According to Hume, he is the most stable of English critics and the most constant: he holds a number of 'objective critical standards', no one of which he ever modifies significantly or abandons.[6] Like Pottle and Atkins, however, they are convinced that, whether in generalization or in minute particulars, most of the criticism is not worth considering.

The effect of the historical school of Lees and Bate, as well as of the judicial school represented by Atkins, Pottle and their more recent descendants, has been to increase understanding of Dryden and to diminish interest in his work. The first school relegates Dryden to literary manuals, the second to anthologies. Neither has spurred investigation into Dryden's criticism as a whole. For both approaches are ultimately based on the argument that the criticism exhibits no whole to be grasped. It is my purpose to refute that premise.

II

Dryden's criticism displays unity amidst diversity. To borrow a phrase from Johnson, who borrowed it from Dryden, the criticism is always 'another and the same'.[7] Throughout his criticism, as well as in the poems and plays on which it is based and which it tries both to explain and justify, Dryden attempts to reconcile two opposing literary traditions. For these traditions he has no clearly defined names; however, he appears to have thought of them occasionally as the Shakespearean and the Jonsonian, but more consistently and frequently as the early seventeenth-century English and the Continental French. We today, centuries later, would perhaps prefer to describe them as the romantic and the classical. In any event, in his attempt to reconcile the two traditions, he did hold to certain constants; and those constants, all of which were first defined between 1664 and 1672, are clearly recognizable.

In evaluating literature, Dryden always insists on the importance of genre and tradition, probability and decorum, as well as unity and variety, and the general and the particular. He insists no less on the importance of what, like a number of his contemporaries, he regards as the two principal mental faculties, judgment and imagination: the faculty that sees, imitates and recreates the order in nature as in fact it really is and so discovers differences among apparent similarities; and the faculty that discovers hidden similarities in the order of nature and so imbues the commonplace with wonder, the poet's self-expression and emotional intensity.

Throughout his criticism nothing is more constant or more important than his concern with and his attempts to resolve, though not always in the same way, what has been declared the 'key' problem of the Renaissance critic: how to reconcile 'the set of critical notions ... subsumed [during the Renaissance] under the conflict between the realistic and the marvelous ... in the ordering of the mass of detail'.[8] That the problem was indeed central in Renaissance criticism we may learn from Torquato Tasso:

> But now let us pursue our argument as to how the verisimilar may be combined with the marvellous ... The verisimilar and the marvellous are very different in nature ... , different almost to the point of being anti-thetical; yet both are necessary in a poem, though to join them takes the art of an excellent poet. And while many have done this well enough before now, no one, to my knowledge, teaches us how to do it.[9]

To Dryden, writing in the second half of the seventeenth century, the problem was essentially the same, though he preferred a different terminology.[10] The problem now was how to reconcile two opposing strains in literature, the 'lively' (or the life-like and the marvellous) and the 'just' (or the accurate and the true), each generally associated with one of the two chief mental faculties: the lively with the imagination and the just with the faculty of judgment. He gives us no systematic explanation of the terms; but he refers to them frequently enough so that, when his essays are read in the context of his other works, especially his plays, we may easily deduce both his meaning and his purpose.

We may also detect the extent to which Dryden never ceased to be a man very much of a specific time and a given place. After the turmoil of the Civil War and the Commonwealth, thoughtful men and women of the Restoration tried with great concern to reconcile extremes in matters both political and religious. They urged in the government a constitutional monarchy, in the established church a latitudinarianism.[11] The same tendency of the age – the same English flexibility – is reflected in Dryden's every attempt, throughout his criticism, to reconcile in the best possible way polarities that he found, and that troubled him, in both life and art.

III

Dryden's critical vocabulary is of course not ours; ours is not his; and the differences must be kept in mind. For example, we call a work realistic if, in its account of places and events, things and people, it is empirically valid. Dryden would not think in such terms; and he would never use the word 'realistic'. He would say of the work, instead, that it combines 'probability' (or 'verisimility') and 'plainness' of language with truth to '*Humane Nature*', including all its frailties; or he might very well explain and illustrate the precise ways by which it brings together the just in our experience with the lively.[12]

In Dryden's view, the just is centred in the faculty of judgment and hence, more or less, in the objective imitation of the external world. By the just in literature, which he associates with ancient and Renaissance classicism, and primarily with the works of Horace and Jonson, Racine and Corneille, he has in mind a tendency in literature or a mode of writing based mainly on long-established rules of composition: on those rules which define the several literary genres, characterize and distinguish among them, subordinate such lower forms as the ode or comedy to higher forms like tragedy and epic and, ultimately, govern every aspect of significant composition, whatever the genre. Plot or structure, especially in the drama, must conform to the unities of time, place and action and to the more specific principles of consistency and condensation, probability and verisimilitude. In a literature of the just, social classes are clearly distinguished from one another. Characters tend to belong to the upper classes or the aristocracy. With one odd exception, that of the humours (or eccentrics) in low comedy, they are idealized human types; and, the humours excepted, they are men and women who, on the whole, exhibit the highest moral values and embody the Christian belief that to be reasonable is to be virtuous. Plot is more important than character; and character and plot are more important than either style or metre. The language, which is always correct, is simple, clear, lucid and direct; and metre (preferably blank verse or the heroic couplet), however much it may be varied, never violates the rhythm of its basic measure or pattern.

In a literature of the just, Dryden believes, the subject is man in a state of grace. The pervasive theme is that universal harmony is maintained or restored and human nature fulfilled whenever, in the comedy or tragedy of life, the individual submits to the proper order of things: he subordinates passion to reason, and self-interest to the authority of state and church. The purpose, though never obtrusively didactic, and not without some emphasis on the pleasant or the agreeable, is always to define or illustrate moral absolutes and so present the reader or audience with a moral vision. To be just, every aspect of a work, from the ode or comedy to the epic and tragedy, must obey the strictures of decorum: that rule according to which what a poet says is appropriate to the way in which he says it and, simultaneously, accords with the best taste of a genuinely civilized – that is, aristocratic and Christian – audience.[13]

The lively is the other side of the coin. Dryden identifies the lively with the faculty of imagination (or fancy) and hence, more or less, with the subordination of the external world to the faculty that contemplates it. By the lively in literature, which he associates both with medieval and sixteenth-century romance and with Elizabethan drama, and primarily with the works of Boccaccio and Chaucer, Ariosto and Shakespeare, Dryden has in mind a body of literature in which the rules of classicism may be treated with flexibility or – through appeals to common sense and human nature and so to what people actually like – may be ignored totally. The literary genres may thus be combined, as he, for example, combines in his heroic plays the main features of Caroline drama with what he borrowed from the classical epic and the sixteenth-century romance, as well as from music, opera and ballet. Plot or structure, including that of the drama, may violate all three of the unities; it may rely heavily on the episodic and the discursive, the improbable and the marvellous. In the literature of the lively, social classes are not clearly distinguished from one another. The characters tend to come from all the social classes, from one end of the social scale to the other.

Whatever their social class, men and women tend to be highly individualized; and they are now presented in all their terrible human imperfections: they subordinate reason to passion; and, in their passion, they may surrender themselves to what in our time we call the pathological. Character is more important than plot; and both may be subordinated to language and metre. The language, which is emotionally charged, brings the external world vividly to life. It is complex, evocative, oblique; it draws heavily on elaborate rhetorical figures, on witticisms and on the pyrotechnics of a richly involved syntax. And metre – though free verse is necessarily to be avoided – may be as varied as the poet or playwright likes, and may even alternate with prose.

In a literature of the lively the subject is man in a state of sin. The theme or unifying idea is that disharmony results and human nature is unfulfilled when, in the tragedy or comedy of human life, the individual violates the proper order of things: reason is subordinated to passion and self-interest supersedes obedience to state and church. The purpose, though moral vision is not excluded, is centred in the giving of pleasure through variety of episode or language or through the evocation of the strange and the marvellous. And in every aspect of a work a poet, though without ever succumbing to obscenity or treason or blasphemy, may flout or completely ignore the rules of strict decorum. He need not make what he says conform either to how he says it or to the straitjacket of good taste. He may in the same work mix high and low life, the frivolous and the serious, the noble and the base.

Dryden's preoccupation with what he calls '*A just and lively Image of Humane Nature*' thus provides him with what generations of scholars have inevitably failed to see: the harmony and coherence of his criticism and its main lines of development. But throughout his criticism he is not so much concerned with the defining of his terms as he is with another issue entirely: chiefly, how the two opposing and conflicting '*Image[s] of Humane Nature*' – one based on judgment, imitation and the rules, the other centred in imagination, self-expression and artistic freedom – may best be integrated or synthesized. And that concern extends to how they are to be integrated in all of literature, but (as we shall see) specifically in the epic poem and in comic and serious drama.[14]

Dryden discovered at the start of his career that in seventeenth-century England there were two literary traditions, the Shakespearean and the Jonsonian. He also discovered that there were on the Continent two corresponding traditions, however defined; that on the Continent the traditions were thought to be in absolute variance with each other; and that consequently, in spite of attempts to the contrary by poet-critics like Tasso, Guarini and Corneille, the two were thought irreconcilable. A new age had dawned; the barbarism of medieval and Renaissance romance was to be avoided; a severe formalism was to shine forth pure and undefiled in all literary genres.

For such celebration of rule and measure Dryden had typical English disdain. By his growing insistence on the lively, and especially in matters of poetic language, he would stem – at least in England – an emphasis on the just. The just defines necessarily the laws by which all literature must be written and judged; but unless it is counterbalanced or interfused by the lively, it can produce, he believed, only the cold and lifeless excesses of French classicism.[15] The crowning achievement of his career, he genuinely hoped, was to be the complete synthesis or integration of the lively and the just; and at the end of his life he was convinced that he had achieved what forty years earlier he had set out to do, although it must be understood that, as he matured, as he read ever more widely in ancient and modern literature, and as he thought the entire matter over and over again, his mode of effecting that synthesis did occasionally undergo significant change.

*

In the essays of his first period (1664–1672) Dryden explains that the lively and the just may be brought together, and harmonized, by their being juxtaposed in ever shifting tensions: he starts out by insisting that the two contrasting '*Image[s] of Humane Nature*' must be held more or less in equal balance; however, as the years pass, he increasingly comes to prefer the flights of imagination to the rules of a strict decorum. In the essays of the second period (1673–1679), written after his discovery of Longinus, he argues that the lively and the just are not in fact two radically opposed modes of writing: they are different aspects or extensions of each other. Indeed, the lively may be seen as neither more nor less than the heightening of the just through the rules of rhetoric. And in his third and final period (1680–1700) Dryden attempts a compromise between his earlier views. He continues to insist that, by and large, the just and the lively are part of a single continuum; yet he also insists that, here and there, they are obviously unrelated and, under certain circumstances, may be effectively juxtaposed.

The three periods of Dryden's criticism, although they do occasionally overlap, are easily distinguishable from one another. Nevertheless, despite all the changes that his criticism undergoes, one clearly defined pattern does in fact emerge. In his criticism, from beginning to end, he gives increasing emphasis and priority to the importance of language over all other elements in literature; and as he does so, though perhaps not so much at the beginning of his career as afterwards, he increasingly argues that in all great literature a language of statement – simple, lucid, clear – is inextricably bound up with the imaginative in language or what, from time to time, he celebrates as the 'Magick' of poetry and its very 'Soul'.[16] Hence, though in many ways an excellent guide to Dryden, Mark Van Doren is surely wrong in insisting that Dryden regarded 'diction in poetry' 'as a splendid wash that is spread over the framework of the plot'.[17] Indeed, unless we reject Van Doren's view, we cannot make sense of the dynamic that impels Dryden gradually to prefer plays read to plays acted, later to prefer the style of the epic to that of the drama, and finally, once he became a translator, to discover the greatest pleasures of poetry in language alone.

At the end of his life Dryden was convinced that he had provided English poets with the 'Outlines' of their art;[18] but his success, as we may now see, was far greater than he could have possibly anticipated. Through his many syntheses of the just and the lively he defined, as Bate observes, that flexible classicism that was to dominate English literature – and specifically English critical theory – for the whole of the eighteenth century. And because of his concern with critical issues of permanent interest, he achieved something no less impressive: he helped set the context in which for the past two hundred years critics like Hazlitt and Arnold and poets like Yeats and Eliot have endeavoured to identify and integrate, as had Dryden before them, the just and the lively and therefore the two opposing strains in English literature. That these critics and poets have preferred to speak not about the just and the lively, or about the Jonsonian tradition and the Shakespearean, but about classicism and romanticism is obviously of no great importance. What is important is that their concerns were initially his; and that his solutions, or most of them, ultimately became theirs.

Dryden may have changed his mind, at different stages of his life, on how best to mingle the just and the lively; but he seldom altered his judgment, to any great extent, on what each of the terms signified. Nevertheless, as he moved from one stage of his development to another, from theories of literature to practical criticism, from one explanation of a literary principle or genre to another, and from the blanket approval of some genre or principle to disapproval, sometimes partial, sometimes absolute, he did now and again modify, in his own behalf, both his explanation of a fixed principle and his application of it. When approached in this way, all his so-called inconsistencies disappear. They now become nothing but a most intelligent critic's adjustment to the requirements of his own best poems and plays and hence to the exigencies of life and art. So, we are continually reminded, decorum has one meaning in tragi-comedy, another in the heroic play, another in mixed comedy, another in the heroic poem. So too, as we read the criticism, both theoretical and practical, we encounter necessarily ever-shifting imperatives on the meanings and the uses of wit and verisimilitude, on probability and metaphorical language and on the moral function of art.

IV

Of the many charges levelled against the criticism, the most damning is that, in the end, it is much too self-centred. Whether discoursing in the most general terms on the nature and function of literature, the theories and the rules, or expatiating on his own work, the poetry and the prose, or evaluating and passing judgment on other poets and critics, the great and the small, sooner or later Dryden gets around to what is, after all, his primary concern: the justification of himself to mankind. To complicate matters somewhat further, he really has no fixed principles: with every new problem he must invent for the occasion wholly new resolutions and precepts. Dryden as critic lacks integrity; and his work, taken as a whole, has neither unity nor truth and hence neither coherence nor genuine merit. So at least the argument goes; but the charges are not well founded, even when qualified, as they sometimes are. In the proper light, the theoretical criticism does have validity; and

15

in the same light, even when about his work, so too does the practical criticism, on which it is based and through which it is, in turn, fully realized.

In 1808 Sir Walter Scott published his eighteen-volume edition of Dryden's works; and as an introduction, he included a critical biography, which contains a comprehensive and detailed assessment of all the criticism. Like Johnson before him, though with greater sympathy and restraint, he approaches the criticism, both the theoretical and the practical, from two very different points of view. He admires the whole edifice; but he must distinguish between the failures and the achievements, between what is merely self-serving and what very clearly is not:

> The didactic criticism of Dryden is necessarily, at least naturally, mingled with that which he was obliged to pour forth in his own defence; and this may be one main cause of its irregular and miscellaneous form. What might otherwise have resembled the extended and elevated front of a regular palace, is deformed by barriers, ramparts, and bastions of defence; by cottages, mean additions, and offices necessary for personal accommodation.[19]

In 1962 George Watson published an edition of the criticism, along with extensive commentary and notes. It was well received and it has continually been much admired. But one wonders whether it was undertaken as a labour of love. Unlike Johnson and Scott, he finds in Dryden's work little that is not self-serving. He would therefore dismiss, unexpectedly, the larger portion of it as being 'studio-talk', that 'of a successful artist who knows how to give away a little, but not much, whose revelations are always likely to be self-recommendations artfully disguised, and who in debate never hesitates to evade or suppress'.[20] In the same year Watson also published a history of English criticism. Here, when he again discusses Dryden's essays, his dismissal is, if anything, even more complete:

> Much the greater part of his criticism, the prefaces to his plays and the essay *Of Dramatick Poesie,* represents a series of stages in his career as a dramatist; they are aspects of a continuing literary war that Dryden fought with his own critics, full of the bitter sound and fury of the Restoration theatres and coffee-houses; and his later critical essays ... are rather more reflective exercises in the same ephemeral vein.[21]

Scott and Watson disagree only in assessing the amount of self-justification in Dryden's work. Scott believes that the self-criticism amounts to no more than easily discardable additions to a structure of outstanding merit. Watson, on the other hand, does not think that the self-criticism can be so easily removed. He recognizes that Dryden's criticism is so largely self-centred that to dismiss that which deals with his own work is inevitably to dismiss the whole. Whatever their differences on this point, however, both place the same value on Dryden's statements about himself: they judge them to be entirely worthless.

The irony of their position is that, in seeking to assess his importance as a literary figure, they depend heavily on the very statements which they reject. Scott in particular is deeply indebted to the self-criticism. There is little in his estimate of the poems, the plays and the translations that does not accord with Dryden's own. Scott adds an extraordinary wealth of detail and a sharpened historical vision, but in essential matters he echoes Dryden's every position. As for Watson, the extent of his borrowing is limited by the range of his interests. Watson evaluates only the criticism; and the criticism seldom evaluates itself. Nevertheless, those few instances in which it does, Watson surprisingly enough cites with approval.[22]

Given that Scott and Watson depend so very much on Dryden's self-assessments, it is hard to account for their hostility. Perhaps the reason lies in disappointed expectations. Like so many others, they demand of the self-criticism the very qualities which it does not contain. Where they want order, Dryden provides variety. When they seek the grand abstraction, he deals resolutely with the particular case. Dryden's criticism is cast in forms that they can neither understand nor appreciate. Hence, although they do not ignore his statements, they deny him praise. Their one tribute is that of largely unacknowledged borrowing.

*

Contrary to popular belief, the fair hearing which Dryden extends to himself he frequently extends to others: he gives the principles that he deduces from his own works a broad application; and as a rule he does so with both detachment and integrity.[23] His statements about Shakespeare are the best illustration of his method and his success, and especially those statements made in *An Essay of Dramatick Poesie*. In a memorable passage in the *Essay* Dryden makes a balanced assessment of Shakespeare's plays. Although he finds egregious errors in style and taste, he celebrates the excellence to which he, in his own works, intermittently aspires:

> To begin then with *Shakespeare;* he was the man who of all Modern, and perhaps Ancient Poets, had the largest and most comprehensive soul. All the Images of Nature were still present to him, and he drew them not laboriously, but luckily: when he describes any thing, you more than see it, you feel it too. Those who accuse him to have wanted learning, give him the greater commendation: he was naturally learn'd; he needed not the spectacles of Books to read Nature; he look'd inwards, and found her there. I cannot say he is every where alike; were he so, I should do him injury to compare him with the greatest of Mankind. He is many times flat, insipid; his Comick wit degenerating into clenches, his serious swelling into Bombast. But he is always great, when some great occasion is presented to him...[24]

Samuel Johnson read this passage and, notwithstanding reservations about Dryden as a practical critic, found it perfectly poised in its presentation of Shakespeare's merits and limitations: 'The account of Shakespeare may stand as a perpetual model of encomiastick criticism; exact without minuteness, and lofty without exaggeration'.[25] And indeed the 'account' is as objective as Johnson asserts: Dryden is far less interested in advancing his own career than in paying proper tribute to his great predecessor.

17

Dryden's opinions, nevertheless, were both moulded by and compatible with self-interest. Having initially chosen Shakespeare as one of his models, Dryden felt impelled to celebrate him. At the same time, he could not allow him unqualified praise. If Shakespeare were shown to have exhausted every possibility in the drama there would be nothing left for him to do. Hence, Dryden emphasizes those weaknesses which, in his judgment, he would correct or modify in his own works. The errors of Shakespeare, however limited, created a field of action for him; and, once identified, they set a context for what he hoped would be, in his own plays, the achievements to come. Self-interest may indeed lie at the heart of the 'account'; but the 'account', for all its self-interest, is also a celebration of Shakespeare. And that celebration is both objective and sound.

*

It has sometimes been argued that, as a practical critic, Dryden was neither candid nor altogether fair in his studies of contemporary French literature: he would deny to himself, as well as to his reading public, his dependence on – and hence his borrowing from – that literature, including the criticism. David Bruce Kramer finds Dryden's handling of French authors 'strange and a little terrible'. According to Kramer, 'with the reopening of the theaters' in 1660, the 'French aesthetic … rushed into the dramatically barren England with all the force with which nature abhors a vacuum'. He then goes on to say that, unable to escape the influence of figures like Corneille, and unwilling to acknowledge their contribution to his essays or his plays, Dryden adopts elaborate subterfuge to hide his borrowings. He anoints himself, for example, the heir of Shakespeare, Jonson and Fletcher – from each of whom he took little – but 'suppresses … his substantial debt to the still-living writers in the French tradition'.[26]

Kramer makes Dryden's works, and not least his criticism, appear far more French than they in fact are. And his position is vulnerable to the same objections that have been made over the last seventy years to all those who argue for the French origin of Restoration literary culture: that they restrict foreign influence to a single country; that they ignore the importance of the native tradition; that they fail to distinguish adequately between the sources of a work and their transformation by a man of genius.[27]

*

Dryden wrote far more about himself than about anyone else; with the exception of Shakespeare and Ben Jonson, William Davenant and Thomas Rymer, far less about current or recent poets and critics than about many of his great forebears, both ancient and medieval, from Homer to Chaucer. He admires Virgil and Shakespeare, Milton and Congreve enormously. And he is convinced that with the restoration of the monarchy England and, in particular, English literature are about to enter a golden age. At the same time, in matters literary, as in every other human enterprise, he has little or no patience with dullness and mediocrity. And in much of the criticism, when it comes to what he genuinely believes in, he is quick to invite controversy. He loves a good fight, especially if he thinks himself under attack. He mans the ramparts fearlessly, even joyously; and when he does so, he exercises, as a rule, an impressive degree of self-control. He tries to be as tactful and polite as circumstance allows. His only weapon is a ridicule that always hits the mark.

On the other hand, there are instances – actually, very few – when his purpose is not to play the dispassionate judge. He has been deeply offended; and he must gratify a deeply felt desire for revenge. Once more his only weapon is ridicule, and this time it is devastating. In *Notes and Observations on 'The Empress of Morocco'* (1674) he lashes out against Elkanah Settle, an aspiring young playwright who has appropriated his literary principles and, through incompetence, has misunderstood and debased them; and in the 'Preface to *All for Love*' (1678), against the Earl of Rochester, who, among other insults, had once been Settle's patron.[28] In the 'Discourse concerning … Satire' (1693) and again in the 'Preface to *Fables*' (1700) he sets down a whole catalogue of those whom he takes to be his personal enemies, most of them scribblers of one sort or another, and he lashes out against all of them, one at a time: they would soil his good name and so do him irreparable harm. And there is *Mac Flecknoe* (1682), a mock epic, which is the most hilarious of his satires and the most biting.

The poem grew out of a long-standing debate with Thomas Shadwell on the nature of comedy. During much of the Restoration Shadwell was generally recognized as a playwright of some brilliance. Dryden thought otherwise: in his opinion Shadwell was without a doubt a better dramatist than Elkanah Settle, but not remarkably so. Nevertheless, he entered the debate quite willingly. Although we can never be certain, he seems not even to have been the one who initiated it; but for years he kept it going with the best of intentions. Shadwell then made a fatal error: he allowed himself to engage in personal invective. Finally, after several provocations, Dryden retaliated. And to posterity Shadwell has ever since been known ironically not so much because of his plays, good or bad, as because of Dryden's poem, which has granted him his niche in the history of English literature.[29]

On Dryden's part the debate was conducted mainly in three prose works: 'A Defence of *An Essay of Dramatick Poesie*' (1668), the 'Preface to *An Evening's Love*' (1671) and the 'Defence of the Epilogue' (1672).[30] But the poem, which seems to have been written during his middle period, perhaps sometime between 1676 and 1678, moves beyond the original terms of the quarrel, very much so. It presents a theory of comedy, but comedy reduced to bathos and lampoon. And it presents that theory through example, not explanation. During a festival in praise of dullness and bad taste tribute is paid to all the worst of contemporary writers: confetti and toilet paper have been made out of their unsold books. A parade is held; and speeches are delivered. Human waste flows obtrusively down the 'silver Thames'; and a mock coronation takes place. The eponymous hero – none other than Thomas Shadwell – occupies the place of honour, only to be stripped bare of his every pretence and disguise. He is revealed as a thoroughly comic figure, the butt of vulgar farce, who, in a state of complete torpor, is crowned monarch of dull poets everywhere.

Meanwhile, even as he would make us laugh, Dryden has another axe to grind. He does not for a moment forget or neglect his own role as dedicated poet and serious critic. The poem also reflects his growing interest in Longinus, whose essay *On the Sublime* he had first come upon in 1674 (that is, about two or three years before he could possibly have thought about the poem or begun to write it). And that work, along with the *Aeneid* and *Paradise Lost,* provides a touchstone against which Shadwell is now to be judged.[31]

With Longinus in mind, we can see more clearly that Shadwell is pointedly denied every qualification for sublime writing, whether innate or acquired: he is totally without any sort of literary excellence. And since his soul is completely governed by the pursuit of ease and low pleasure – for Longinus a cause of enervation in writing – even the false sublime is far beyond him. His plays are neither tumid nor frigid nor puerile: they are sheer 'Non-sense'. When Dryden wishes to name a work that Longinus might think it worth the trouble to condemn, he has to turn away from Shadwell and to the Nursery, a school for child actors, where one of his heroic plays, *Tyrannick Love* (1670), is oft performed:

> Near these a Nursery erects its head,
> Where Queens are form'd and future Hero's bred;
> Where unfledg'd Actors learn to laugh and cry,
> Where infant Punks their tender Voices try,
> And little *Maximins* the Gods defy.[32]

Shadwell is linked to the false sublime not through his verse or 'hungry...prose' but through the grossness of his person. His swollen body, like that of Longinus's 'man who has the dropsy', is the physical equivalent of the overblown style. He also resembles, though in grotesque distortion, the Pythian priestess, whom Longinus invokes to explain the importance of emulating great writers. She, we must remember, is 'impregnated' by 'divine vapour', he is 'big with Hymn' from a 'Celestial charge'. Her inspiration produces 'oracles'; his, 'Pang without birth'.

V

At this point it is reasonable to ask why Dryden bothered to justify himself at all. Is it not true, as Veronica Wedgwood says, that he 'over-shadows the last half of the seventeenth century as Ben Jonson did the Jacobean age'? Was he not for thirty years, as she points out, 'the established monarch of the literary world, ruling it from his seat in Will's coffee-house as Ben Jonson had done from his progression of taverns in the Strand'?[33] Who was it who had the temerity to attack him?

In our time, Dryden's position as a Restoration poet makes him seem invulnerable, and the more so owing to the powerful influence of his self-defence. By the end of his first decade in the theatre, however, attacking him came to enjoy the status of a national sport. 'More libels have been written against me', he declared in 1693, 'than almost any man now living...'[34] Many of the attacks grew out of political and religious debate; a number of others, out of personal tensions rife within the confines of a self-enclosed social world.[35]

But we are wrong if we think that he was not also attacked on carefully reasoned literary grounds. Many men were sincerely convinced that he was a misguided poet, leading English literature into ruin. He chose, for instance, not to follow in the footsteps of Jonson or Corneille, yet each of these authors had enthusiastic supporters. Every literary clique, with its varied membership of gentlemen, clergymen and professional authors, wrote criticism to interest the literate public in its own behalf. Dryden's own criticism is similarly aimed. It may be superior to that of his opponents; but it is not more loftily conceived. It is a frank bid for public favour.

George Watson regards Dryden's decision to enter into public discussion of his works as strikingly original: 'According to the accepted view of Dryden's day, the poet who explains himself condemns himself, and Dryden's decision to supply the run of his own works with critical prefaces was both novel and defiant.'[36] In support of his position, Watson cites the mockery that Dryden's criticism provoked, mockery initiated by the Duke of Buckingham (George Villiers) and elaborated by innumerable others, including Swift. But self-justification may always be greeted with mockery, no matter how common the practice; and among literary critics self-justification by Dryden's time was anything but new. Among the older poets, it can be found in the works of Edmund Spenser, George Chapman, Ben Jonson and a host of Continental writers.[37] Among Dryden's contemporaries, it is found in Davenant and Shadwell. Self-justification alone does not make Dryden's criticism either defiant or novel. What is novel, and perhaps defiant, is the disarming interplay of learned argument and autobiographical aside.

Almost alone among European poets, from his own day to the present, Dryden as a critic is extremely informal, even intimate. Whereas other poet-critics may imbue their judgments with the air of personal authority, Dryden speaks insistently with an all-too-human voice; and he turns writing about literature into autobiography, and autobiography into an engaging display of his inner life. His criticism, or at least that part of it which is written in prose, often reads like a diary, recording confessions, in a tentative voice, of his hopes and fears, his sense of victory and his awareness of failure. But the autobiographical element in the criticism consists far less in psychological detail than in the continual exhibition of creative powers.

Dryden's critical works reveal in fact the same qualities of mind, even the same perceptions, as those which inform his poems and plays. By exhibiting and explaining his artistic temper in the more transparent medium of his criticism he teaches us to recognize that temper in the more difficult forms – satire, epic, drama – in which the rest of his work is cast. Always he encourages the reader to make a silent reference from his literary performance to his creative abilities. He labours to make us regard his poetry not as an autonomous creation but as an embodiment of his mind and art. The criticism reaches out to the poems in order to bring us closer to the poet; or it delves into the poet in order to bring us closer to the poems. The movement back and forth never ceases, although the means by which it is achieved undergoes many changes.

CHAPTER TWO

From theory to practice
(1664)

I

Dryden's criticism, the theoretical and the practical, falls into three distinct periods, each of which has its unifying concerns and techniques. With but one minor exception, each has its appropriate manner and style. And both manner and style are always appropriate to and always reflect Dryden's changing conceptions of his role as poet and critic, as well as his changing attitudes toward the theories that he expounds and the judgments that he sets forth.

Dryden may reject in his critical theory what in his practical criticism he sometimes condones: the people must be satisfied; bills must be paid. The criticism remains nevertheless impressive for its coherence and consistency: despite shifts in emphasis and perspective, or even changes in judgment, he never once accepts or rejects a first principle merely to gratify a private whim or to curry public favour. Despite changes in personal fortune, or pressures and changes in external circumstance (political and religious, economic and social), he never once neglects, either as poet or as literary critic, his commitment to the Christian religion and (after 1660) to the requirements and demands of a well-ordered royalist government and state. The commitment is one which he takes for granted and on which he may occasionally insist. Throughout the criticism, however, he addresses his audience and the reading public – 'the Town [or the gentry and petty aristocracy], the City [or the professional and commercial classes], and the Court [or the royal family and their circle]'[1] – with an ever increasing confidence in his literary opinions and his art. And as confidence grows, so too does he gradually alter the very language of his criticism, both theoretical and practical, and his whole manner of public discourse. Under the pressure of changing circumstances, sometimes personal, sometimes public, he takes off one persona and adopts another.

The first manner begins in 1664 with the dedication of *The Rival Ladies;* it ends with the 'Preface to *Tyrannick Love*', which he published in 1670, two years before the end of the first period of his intellectual development. When he writes in his first manner Dryden addresses his criticism to the aristocracy. He adopts the stance of a courtier and conceives of his criticism as an amusement for the great. When he writes in his second manner, which covers the years from 1670 to about 1680, he assumes the mask of the professional author, zealous in pursuit of public fame and contemptuous of his rivals. Finally, when he writes in his last manner, which begins in 1680 and lasts until the year of his death, 1700, he assumes the mantle of an authoritative teacher of literary subjects; he is above and beyond all controversy: he has become a man of letters.

II

Dryden's ventures into literary criticism began when he appended to his first plays prologues and epilogues, each a verse essay in miniature. The practice was scarcely a new one. Throughout the Renaissance and during the early seventeenth century it was very much the custom for English playwrights to introduce their plays with prologues and to end them with epilogues. And in either prologue or epilogue the playwright might appeal to the goodwill of the audience, justify himself and his art, or make boasting or explanatory comments on the work to which the verses necessarily referred.

Playwrights could of course write their prologues in a variety of ways and for a variety of objectives. But it may be said in general that, before the Restoration, the seventeenth-century playwright tended to follow the pattern set by Shakespeare, whose ceremonious prologues served largely utilitarian ends. It is the function of the 'Prologue to *Romeo and Juliet*' (1597), for instance, to provide a brief summary of the intrigue that follows and to make a polite request for silence. With the Restoration, however, the whole conception of the prologue underwent a significant change; and with that change the entire manner of writing prologues was transformed radically. The playwright of what was thought to be a supremely witty age chose now to find his paradigm in Jonson, whose comic prologues, learned and demotic, were a source of entertainment in themselves. Jonson began a revolution in the writing of prologues. We can see the first hint of the passing away of the old manner and the birth of the new in the shift in style towards the middle of his 'Prologue to *Cynthias Reuells*' (1601):

> If gracious silence, sweet attention,
> Quicke sight, and quicker apprehension,
> (The lights of iudgements throne) shine any where;
> Our doubtfull authour hopes this is their sphere.
> And therefore opens he himselfe to those;
> To other weaker beames, his labours close:
> As loth to prostitute their virgin straine,
> To eu'rie vulgar, and adult'rate braine.
> In this alone, his MVSE her sweetnesse hath,
> Shee shunnes the print of any beaten path;
> And proues new wayes to come to learned eares:
> Pied ignorance she neither loues, nor feares.
> Nor hunts she after popular applause,
> Or fomie praise, that drops from common iawes ...[2]

Whatever his preference, as a rule, for the plays of Shakespeare over those of Jonson, it was the latter's combative prologues that Dryden followed in both his serious and his comic drama. And it was Dryden who, more than any other writer, helped to establish the new mode, the bravura of which he imitates, describes and, with broad humour, attacks in the 'Prologue to *The Rival Ladies*' (1664):

'Tis much Desir'd, you Judges of the Town
Would pass a Vote to put all Prologues down;
For who show me, since they first were Writ,
They e'r Converted one hard-hearted Wit?
Yet the World's mended well; in former Days
Good Prologues were as scarce, as now good Plays.
For the reforming Poets of our Age,
In this first Charge, spend their Poetique rage:
Expect no more when once the Prologue's done;
The Wit is ended e'r the Play's begun.[3]

The formula here is simple and effective. Give the audience what it expects; display your powers; delight the spectators into silence. With their energy and wit, their graceful and impeccable verse, Dryden's prologues and epilogues were soon regarded as the best of the period. At first, he composed them only for his own works; later, and increasingly (after 1680) as he wrote fewer plays, he composed them for the works of others. These commissioned pieces were much in demand. And as Samuel Johnson observes, 'a play was considered ... less likely to be well received if some of his verses did not introduce it'.[4]

In the prologues and epilogues, wherever they appear, Dryden speaks rarely if at all in his own person. Instead, he assumes a persona or mask, sometimes that of a character called Prologue or Epilogue, sometimes that of a character or that of an actor (at times an actress) in one of the plays; but whoever the speaker, we are made immediately aware of Dryden's presence and voice.

Between 1664 and 1700, Dryden wrote about one hundred prologues and epilogues. They may here and there take up affairs of state, but they comment, almost invariably, on his literary theory and practice. He also did occasionally allow the criticism, quite independently of the prologues and epilogues, to overflow into his other poems, especially those concerned with the praise or blame of contemporary writers. Apart from of course *Mac Flecknoe* (1682), the other poems include such relatively slight pieces as 'To ... Mr. Higden' (1687), 'To Mr. Southerne ...' (1692), and 'To Mr. Granville' (1698), along with splendid works like 'To the Memory of Mr. Oldham' (1684) and 'To My Dear Friend, Mr. Congreve ...' (1694).[5] In any event, one may draw some distinctions between the prologues and epilogues published in one period of his career and those published in either of the other two. But prologue and epilogue, whenever written, have far more in common with each other than, despite exceptions, with the prose criticism written at about the same time. They were conceived, of necessity, as brief and pungent divertissements for the stage; the prose essays, which are centred in technical detail, literary history and intellectual scuffling, were designed more for the library and (presumably) for very private contemplation. Hence, when published at the same time, and in the very same volume, prologue and epilogue on the one hand, and the prose criticism on the other, appear to have been set into a deliberate counterpoint, though that counterpoint must never be equated with a choice between pleasure and instruction.

Despite its technicalities and restraints, the prose criticism – dedication, preface, postscript – is fresh and engaging and enlivened with mental agility, good humour and felicity of phrase. For Dryden recognized that, if learning were to be disseminated, it would have to acquire a 'polish'd' mien. The critic had to leave his noisy quarrels behind him, acquire breeding, and become an agreeable man of the world. His writing was to be not crabbed, not frothy, but a 'mixing ... [of] solidity ... air ... and gayety'. He was, in short, to imitate that 'conversation', 'refin'd ... easy ... plyant', the recent development of which in England Dryden would explain in the 'Defence of the Epilogue' (1672):

> Now, if any ask me, whence it is that our conversation is so much refin'd?
> I must freely, and without flattery, ascribe it to the Court: and, in it,
> particularly to the King ... At his return, he found a Nation lost as much in
> Barbarism as in Rebellion: and as the excellency of his Nature forgave the
> one, so the excellency of his manners reform'd the other. The desire of
> imitating so great a pattern, first waken'd the dull and heavy spirits of the
> *English,* from their natural reserv'dness: loscn'd them, from their stiff
> forms of conversation; and made them easy and plyant to each other in
> discourse.[6]

Dryden's analysis of the new refinement in social discourse, however, does not explain or account for the style of all his prose criticism. For one thing, he never completely rid himself of the vituperation that often characterized seventeenth-century debate. When he wrote about contemporary authors he customarily expressed ridicule or even contempt. In the *Notes and Observations on 'The Empress of Morocco'* (1674), for instance, his remarks on Settle are quite insulting:

> [H]e's an Animal of a most deplor'd understanding, without Reading &
> Conversation: his being is in a twilight of Sence, and some glimmering of
> thought, which he can never fashion either into Wit or English. His Stile
> is Boisterous and Rough Hewen: his Rhyme incorrigibly lewd, and his
> numbers perpetually harsh and ill sounding.[7]

But when he discarded insult as a tool his ideal was always that of a man who had received 'a gallant and generous education',[8] though a man who throughout the criticism had a variety of rich disguises. When he wrote criticism in his first manner, for example, his ideal, and hence his persona, was specifically that of the Renaissance courtier, to whom openness and directness were quite foreign.

III

For the Renaissance courtier, indirectness and dissimulation were the soul of good conduct. Initially, this mode of behaviour was the product of the political climate in which the courtier moved. As a servant of a despotic prince, the courtier could not afford plain speaking. Trained to assume an independent position in civic life, the sixteenth-century courtier had to direct his verbal skills away from oratory and towards the service of royal entertainment, towards what has been defined as 'courtliness, politeness, tactful skill, culture that services, that becomes the refined instrument of a precise technique'.[9] But what followed from necessity soon became a virtue. The courtier came to prize obliquity of speech and manner as things worthy in themselves. Moreover, he came to see his deceptions as producing effects not only diverting but salutary. For by clothing truth in delightful fictions, he believed that he could make it impossible to resist.

Through his art the poet influenced and imitated the manner and the rhetoric of his aristocratic audience; through his rhetoric and manner the courtier in turn imitated the poet's art and influenced it. Throughout the Renaissance, according to Daniel Javitch, the dissembling of courtiers and the artifice of poets thus entered into a rich symbiotic relationship:

> Poets benefited from the fact that the artifices that characterized their art ['ornament, dissimulation, playfulness'] were deemed desirable in court conduct. Like the courtier, who cultivated these artifices to win the grace of his sovereign and his peers, the poet could use his mastery of similar devices as a means of securing favor and place at court ...[10]

In examining the courtly style, Javitch confines himself to the sixteenth century and the early seventeenth. But this theory, *mutatis mutandis,* also illumines the Restoration, the Court as well as the literature.

Although the practice of courtliness during the Commonwealth underwent first a decline and then a partial eclipse, it reasserted itself with the accession of Charles II. 'The Restoration of the monarchy ... meant, among other things,' writes one student of the period,

> the revival of the English court. In spite of the upheaval of the Civil War, the great courtly tradition of the Renaissance remained alive at White- hall ... The court of Charles II was the last English court to be a real centre of culture as well as of fashion.[11]

While the Restoration courtier did not aspire to the moral goodness of his Renaissance counterpart, he still valued, in however attenuated a form, the dichotomy between seeming and being, the effortless display of abilities and the gracefully diverting speech. A touch of coarseness might mar his elegance; but of his essential elegance, there can be no doubt. And what he admired in life the Restoration courtier also demanded from the arts over which he exercised considerable control. Music, painting and sculpture all mirrored his interests; but nowhere were his tastes more fully expressed than in the drama. 'The Restoration stage', as John Harold Wilson has pointed out, 'was owned and dominated by the Restoration Court'.[12] Although a playwright did not write to please only the Court, the Court was ever on his mind.

At the outset of his career, perhaps as early as 1654, when at the age of twenty-three he may have drifted to London, Dryden was committed, in all likelihood, to the Commonwealth. But with the restoration of the monarchy in 1660 he had a change of heart. With a change of heart came a change in allegiance. And with a change in allegiance he was no less interested than other aspiring young writers in serving the interests of the new age and the fashionable world. Of life at Court he knew little or nothing. He had come to London from the provinces, where he had grown up in the midst of the local gentry; and during his first half-dozen years or so in the capital he had held only a minor post in Cromwell's government.[13] But now, with the restoration of the monarchy, he had high hopes. In his poems and plays, as well as in his criticism, he would pay tribute where tribute was due and where he hoped he would gain tribute in return: he would gain fame and fortune: He would demonstrate that, in matters literary and aristocratic, the English were just as civilized as their counterparts elsewhere, and perhaps more so: they were resplendent.

At the same time, he did not rely on high hopes alone or, for that matter, on the vagaries of mere chance. Dryden had remarkable self-confidence; but he understood that, to get what he very much wanted, something else was required, something even beyond literary merit or genius. Through steady output, and a good deal of effort, he soon established a reputation for himself. With the help of powerful relatives and friends – a very close friend, Sir Robert Howard, was appointed Auditor of the King's Exchequer in 1660 – he made contact in high places. And with determination, as well as certainty, he took advantage of every occasion and circumstance. He provided what his audience (by which he meant his courtly audience) expected to hear. He submitted his works – both poems and plays – to Court figures for amendment. In 1662 he seems to have found a patron in Edward Hyde, Earl of Clarendon, the lord chancellor and virtual head of the government.[14] By 1667, with the publication of *Annus Mirabilis,* he defended Court policy in the war against the Dutch; and in the same year he demonstrated his usefulness yet again by lending the Crown what for him must have been an enormous sum of money, five hundred pounds. In 1668, having apparently made his wishes known, he was declared Poet Laureate and, shortly afterwards, Historiographer Royal.

Dryden of course attempted 'to delight the Age'.[15] He would be understood, nevertheless, to prefer 'glory ... receiv'd from a Soveraign Prince' and approbation from '[t]he Court, which is the best and surest judge of writing'.[16] But pleasing the Court, however eagerly one tried, was no easy task. The *Essay of Dramatick Poesie* (1668) makes eminently clear Court figures were divided in their tastes. One courtier championed one form of drama; a second championed another. Having to choose among competing possibilities, Dryden could not please everyone. He could, however, minimize the dangers of disagreement by adopting an ingratiating manner. Criticism that was amusing and deferential could do much to mollify resentment where sustained argument would only fail.[17]

The ingratiating manner of Dryden's early criticism is in fact central to his very purpose. He is a courtier-poet writing to courtiers.[18] His fundamental responsibility is not only to entertain but to wait upon the great and to pay homage. In his 'Preface to *The Tempest*' (1670), written towards the end of his first manner and the beginning of the second, he identifies the precise nature of his early criticism, though with unexpected mockery, even scorn:

The writing of Prefaces to Plays was probably invented by some very ambitious Poet, who never thought he had done enough: Perhaps by some Ape
of the French Eloquence, who uses to make a business of a Letter of gallantry...[19]

Here Dryden as courtier is the object of a later Dryden satire; but the courtier
manner is remarkably well defined. In his role as courtier Dryden is that 'ambitious
Poet' who, not content to delight in verse, must display his power – through
'Eloquence' and 'gallantry' – in 'Prefaces to Plays'. As for the 'Letter of gallantry',
or dedication, with all its tensions between epideictic praise and self-interest, it must
surely have been one of the important influences on the early criticism: he all but
tells us so himself.

Like Castiglione's *Book of the Courtier* (1528), in which every true courtier is
a poet, and every true poet is a courtier, Dryden's early criticism is set in a never-
never land, in which fact gives way to fantasy and political intrigue is displaced by
pastoral. Like *The Courtier,* the criticism treats 'Eloquence' and 'gallantry' as their
own excuse for being, and hides didactic intent under the guise of a courtly game.

Dryden never refers either to *The Courtier* or to Castiglione by name. But he
must have been familiar with the book; there is every reason to believe that, in his
excursions into fantasy and pastoral, he had Castiglione's paradigms clearly in
mind.[20] At first in the original Italian and later in a 1561 translation by Sir Thomas
Hoby, *The Courtier* had very much influenced English literature from Wyatt and
Surrey to Sidney, Spenser, and Shakespeare; and that influence was to continue into
the seventeenth century.[21] Despite a lull during the Civil War and the Commonwealth, it was to continue into the Restoration, when it seems to have been widespread among the aristocracy and men of letters.[22] Castiglione had conceived of
his book as a celebration of an Italian prince, Guidobaldo da Montefeltro. To
Dryden and his contemporaries it apparently had another dimension. It could be
read as a glorification, however fanciful, of their new king, Charles II, and of the
grace and splendour, the literature and courtliness that he was said to encourage.

Reading through Dryden's early criticism, one discovers its courtly bias on
almost every page. It is addressed, in the main, to members of the nobility, lords
flatteringly presented not only as patrons but as poets and critics as well. They
understand and practise the art of poetry, Dryden declares, better than he does himself. Since the novice cannot teach the master, he will make no pretensions to
authoritative learning. He will give them merely a diverting account of his unworthy
plays.

As courtier-poet, and as critic or playwright to courtiers, Dryden assumes the
pose of well-bred humility. He feigns indifference towards those of his works, both
plays and essays, which he in fact takes quite seriously; and he does so through the
commonplaces of affected modesty. His play *The Rival Ladies,* he tells his patron,
is but a 'worthless Present'; the *Essay of Dramatick Poesie,* he confesses, is just 'the
Relation of a dispute' overheard.[23] Dryden even goes so far as to boast, though
always with tongue in cheek, that he takes seriously neither the interconnections

between his theory and his art nor the several methods – defence, attack, self-justification, inquiry – by which he may set forth a critical position or theory. His opinions, however deeply held, are treated less often as statements of belief than as elements in a delightful ploy:

> Sometimes, like a Schollar in a Fencing-School I put forth my self, and show my own ill play, on purpose to be better taught. Sometimes I stand desperately to my Armes...But that I may decline some part of the encounter with my Adversaries, whom I am neither willing to combate, nor well able to resist; I will give...the Relation of a Dispute betwixt some of our Wits on the same subject...[24]

As he pokes gentle fun at his methods of criticism, so in the criticism itself he may allow for conflicting interpretations of his best work, but always playfully. In the 'Preface to *Secret Love*' (1668), he excuses a shocking instance of indecorum as a mere whim, or so he pretends:

> That which with more reason was objected as an indecorum, is the management of the last Scene of the Play, where *Celadon* and *Florimell* are treating too lightly of their marriage in the presence of the Queen, who likewise seems to stand idle while the great action of the *Drama* is still depending. This I cannot otherwise defend, then by telling you I so design'd it on purpose to make my Play go off more smartly...[25]

In the 'Preface to *Tyrannick Love*', Dryden justifies both himself and his art. He refutes the notion that, because it is altogether profane, the modern theatre must avoid sacred subjects and serve only the ends of entertainment. The drama critics are wrong; and so too are theologians and priests. *Tyrannick Love* has a worthwhile moral purpose, but it also entertains; the play entertains, but it also encourages religious faith:

> I considered that pleasure was not the only end of Poesie; and that even the instructions of Morality were not so wholly the business of a Poet, as that the Precepts and Examples of Piety were to be omitted...By the Harmony of our words we elevate the mind to a sense of Devotion, as our solemn Musick, which is inarticulate Poesie, does in Churches; and by the lively images of piety, adorned by action, through the senses allure the Soul...[26]

In the epilogue, spoken by the actress Nell Gwyn, who plays the role of Elveria, an exceptionally virtuous woman, and then steps miraculously out of character, Dryden sarcastically damns himself and denies that his 'Tragedy' has any merit. But if through his epilogue he would negate his preface, so he makes the epilogue undo itself. It is, after all, '[s]poken by Mrs. *Ellen,* when she was to be carried off dead by the Bearers'; and Mrs. Ellen somewhat good-naturedly refers to herself as 'a little harmless Devil' out of the pits of hell:

> *To the Audience.* I come, kind Gentlemen, strange news
>   to tell ye,
> I am the Ghost of poor departed Nelly.
> Sweet Ladies, be not frighted, I'le be civil,
> I'm what I was, a little harmless Devil.
>   ...
> O Poet, damn'd dull Poet, who could prove
> So sensless! to make Nelly dye for Love;
> Nay, what's yet worse, to kill me in the prime
> Of Easter-Term, in Tart and Cheese-cake time!
> I'le fit the Fopp; for I'le not one word say
> T' excuse his godly out-of-fashion Play:
> A Play which if you dare but twice sit out,
> You'l all be slander'd, and be thought devout.[27]

It has been argued that, in much of his criticism, Dryden held no fixed principles or judgments. Samuel Johnson complains that, whatever its excellences, the criticism often lacks scruple and caution.[28] And in our own century, though often with greater tolerance, the inconsistencies have been no less frequently observed.[29] It must nevertheless be allowed that, during a career of almost forty years, Dryden would have to modify some first principles and that, as he matured, he would have to give up old judgments for new ones. It must also be allowed that, in the whole of his early manner, he took himself seriously enough and still enjoyed his courtly game.[30]

When it does not mock and apparently negate, Dryden's playfulness may itself sometimes instruct: concealed within his flights of wit, one may find important critical ideas. Thus, as he playfully addresses a patron, he also teaches us the art of both character drawing and plot construction:

> Yet I wonder not your Lordship succeeds so well in this attempt [play-writing]; the Knowledge of Men is your daily practice in the World; to work and bend their stubborn Minds...Thus, my Lord,...the Poet [is] but subordinate to the States-man in you; you still govern Men with the same Address, and manage Business with the same Prudence; allowing it here (as in the World) the due Increase and Growth, till it comes to the just highth; and then turning it when it is fully Ripe, and Nature calls out, as it were, to be deliver'd...[31]

Finally, in handling the playful, Dryden may use it as a courtly diversion, or interlude, between stretches of solemn discourse. He sometimes lectures, but he never does so for long. As soon as he is fairly launched upon a subject, he reigns himself in, with the recognition that ''tis your Lordship to whom I speak; who have much better commended this way by your Writing in it, than I can do by Writing for it'.[32] In the next moment we are carried off playfully on the wings of compliment.

Through his prose criticism, as Johnson observes, Dryden always tries to mingle pleasure and truth:

[T]he criticism of Dryden is the criticism of a poet; not a dull collection of theorems, nor a rude detection of faults, which perhaps the censor was not able to have committed; but a gay and vigorous dissertation, where delight is mingled with instruction, and where the author proves his right of judgement by his power of performance.[33]

What is true of the whole of the criticism becomes in his early manner a mingling of the serious and the playful, each with a voice of its own. The serious voice analyses, illustrates and expounds; the playful voice entertains and tries to win favour. The two voices separate, alternate and fuse; but they always serve a common end: that of advancing, among the courtiers of the age, Dryden's reputation.

The aristocratic manner of Dryden's criticism lasts until the late 1660s, at which time he gradually ceases to be a poet-courtier and slowly becomes a poet-critic, a role that he then holds for the whole of the middle period (1673–1679). In this second role, which by contrast helps to define the essential qualities of the first, Dryden lays aside diffidence and reserve. Instead of recommending himself through flattery and subtle indirection, he now promotes his works explicitly and celebrates his virtues. Thus, in the 'Preface to *An Evening's Love*' (1671), he examines his play and, after admitting its many faults, finds it superior to the other comedies of the age:

> After all, it is to be acknowledg'd, that most of those Comedies, which have been lately written, have been ally'd too much to Farce ... While I say this I accuse my self as well as others: and this very play would rise up in judgment against me, if I would defend all things I have written to be natural ... Yet I think it no vanity to say that this Comedy has as much of entertainment in it as many other which have bin lately written: and, if I find my own errors in it, I am able at the same time to arraign all my Contemporaries for greater.[34]

Similarly, whereas he had insisted, before, that his plays were outshone by their models, he now claims to surpass even those from whom he borrows:

> 'Tis true, that where ever I have lik'd any story in a Romance, Novel, or forreign Play, I have made no difficulty, nor ever shall, to take the foundation of it, to build it up, and to make it proper for the English Stage. And I will be so vain to say it has lost nothing in my hands: But it alwayes cost me so much trouble to heighten it for our Theatre ... that when I had finish'd my Play, it was like the Hulk of *Sir Francis Drake,* so strangely alter'd, that there scarce remain'd any Plank of the Timber which first built it.[35]

Dryden may sometimes profess indifference to what his audience thinks of his work, but the indifference is not expressed until after he has refuted his critics point by point.

As he alters the style of his criticism, so too he looks beyond Town and Court. He no longer writes to a lord who, he assumes, knows everything. He writes for an unspecified 'Reader', untitled and perhaps unlettered, one whom he credits with understanding very little.[36] With this new audience in mind, Dryden becomes more confident. He is no longer willing to grant that the task of judging literature is the prerogative solely of the aristocracy. He instead claims that the privilege ought, in reason, to belong to someone like him. The professional poet is the true *arbiter elegantiae:*

> Poets themselves are the most proper, though I conclude not the only Critiques. But till some Genius as Universal, as *Aristotle,* shall arise, one who can penetrate into all Arts and Sciences, without the practice of them, I shall think it reasonable, that the Judgment of an Artificer in his own Art should be preferable to the opinion of another man...[37]

Aristocrats should be content with their estates. Poetry is the rightful province of poets.[38]

Dryden's role as a poet-critic lasts for a decade. By 1680 he is launched upon a third manner of critical writing, the last of his career; and at the same time there is a significant change or shift in the very subject and direction of his criticism. Up to 1680, he is primarily a dramatist, commenting upon his plays. Henceforth, he becomes ever more committed to the translation of ancient and medieval authors; and as he explains his chosen texts to the public, his criticism becomes of necessity more learned. One might expect that his immersion in the details of scholia and commentary would have an inhibiting effect upon him. In fact, the opposite is true. Despite the weight of the scholarship he now bears, he has never seemed more free. For the first time we hear Dryden's own voice, or at least the one which suits him best. No longer is he a courtier-poet soliciting the great, or a struggling writer demanding to be heard. He is an independent man of letters; and he has no doubt about either his powers or his achievements. The dissenters may think what they wish. His 'Poetry' he has 'wholly given up to the Criticks; let them use it, as they please'. If he has 'suffer'd in silence', he has at least 'possess'd [his] Soul in quiet'. He anticipates fame 'in another Age', when 'Interest and Passion...lye bury'd' and 'Partiality and Prejudice be forgotten'.[39]

The sense of freedom is enhanced, moreover, by a seeming artlessness and expansive ease. The essays are not cast in any rigid mould but follow the meanderings of Dryden's thought. The delight that he takes in his new role leads him constantly from one exploration to another. Like Plutarch and Montaigne, whose practice he admires, he loves to 'strike a little out of the common road', certain that where he goes is the right place to be. For 'the best quarry', he tells us, 'lies not always in the open field; And who would not be content to follow a good Huntsman over Hedges and Ditches when he knows the Game will reward his pains?'[40]

Dryden's sense of accomplishment raises him beyond debate. He has good evidence that his literary judgments are altogether sound. He may argue with the commentators on matters of fact or interpretation; but on questions of literary value he will explain his point of view, but engage in no disputation: his every statement must speak for itself. Or he asks that we accept him as our only authority and guide, that we make his taste our own, and that we take his every preference on trust. Why did he choose to translate certain passages in an author instead of others? His answer is that they 'most affected' him 'in the reading'. Do the critics cavil at his play? Then 'let them look a little deeper into the matter' and their every objection will be answered.[41]

Dryden's unconcern with literary argument or debate is matched by a style that grows indifferent to decorum. Instead of the aristocratic manner of the first period or the contentious manner of the second, we now encounter a style that is colloquial and racy, vigorous and abundant with homely detail. For an unusually fine example of the new manner, we can do no better than turn to the 'Preface to *Examen Poeticum*' (1693), where Dryden discusses two of Homer's characters, Hector and Andromache, as if they were an ordinary London couple:

> *Andromache* in the midst of her Concernment, and Fright for *Hector*, runs off her Biass, to tell him a Story of her Pedigree, and of the lamentable Death of her Father, her Mother, and her Seven Brothers. The Devil was in *Hector*, if he knew not all this matter, as well as she who told it him; for she had been his Bed-fellow for many Years together: And if he knew it, then it must be confess'd, that *Homer* in this long digression, has rather given us his own Character, than that of the Fair Lady whom he Paints. His Dear Friends the Commentators, who never fail him at a pinch, will needs excuse him, by making the present Sorrow of *Andromache*, to occasion the remembrance of all the past: But others think that she had enough to do with that Grief which now oppress'd her, without running for assistance to her Family.[42]

We have come a long way from the flourishes and trappings of Dryden's first period and the indignations of the second.[43]

IV

With *The Rival Ladies* (1664), his first tragi-comedy, Dryden established himself in the great world of Restoration drama.[44] With the prologue to the play, along with the dedication, he also declared himself, despite a playful indirection, the leading and most influential critic of the age.[45] In the prologue, a paradigm for all of the prologues and epilogues to follow, he at first assumes a single persona, that of the courtier-poet, albeit with a threefold aspect: he is author as poet-critic, personified abstraction and minor character in his own play. The prologue is a drama review before the event (that is, before the curtain goes up and the play begins); but he does not so much defend himself and his work as, through gentle ridicule, attack every possible or disgruntled adversary. He complains about 'the [new] reforming Poets' who write witty prologues as introductions to their own very bad plays; hence, 'The Wit is ended e'r the Play's begun.' He condemns, in the modern theatre, the total neglect of good writing and, in its place, the predilection for incidental effect and spectacle:

> You now have Habits, Dances, Scenes, and Rhymes;
> High Language often; I [aye], and Sense, sometimes;
> As for a clear Contrivance doubt it not;
> They blow out Candles to give Light to th' Plot.[46]

In the remaining portion (or last third) of the prologue he assumes two personae, each that of the courtier-poet, each with the same threefold aspect: as the first persona he is engaged in a dialogue with himself as the second. He now describes at length the playwright who looks for approbation from other playwrights, those as bad as he is, or from critics who are even worse:

> *A Second Prologue [or Speaker] Enters.*
>
> 2.   —Hold; Would you admit
> For Judges all you see within the Pit?
> 1. Whom would he then Except, or on what Score?
> 2. All, who (like him) have Writ ill Plays before:
>
>   …
>
> All that are Writing now he would disown;
> But then he must Except, ev'n all the Town:
> All Chol'rique, losing Gamesters, who in spight
> Will Damn to Day, because they lost last Night:
> All Servants whom their Mistress's scorn upbraids;
> All Maudlin Lovers, and all Slighted Maids:
> All who are out of Humour, or Severe;
> All, that want Wit, or hope to find it here.[47]

The prologue (in both of the two personae) is quite amusing. It sets before reader and audience Dryden's critical principles with simplicity and directness. And with disarming brevity it is a glorious example of quiet self-justification. Without quite saying so, Dryden makes it perfectly clear that he does like his play. He may even think that he alone is the best critic of the work; but he makes his appeal not to the Pit or to himself, but (as courtier-poet) to the one group he leaves unscathed, the aristocratic few. In any event, the prologue does have another dimension, not quite lost on those who first read the play or saw it performed, but scarcely noticed today, if noticed at all. The prologue, along with both dedication and play, is in fact an ironic commentary aimed specifically against a recent work, *The Adventures of Five Hours* (1663), by one of 'the [new] reforming Poets', Sir Samuel Tuke.[48]

*

Though now all but forgotten, Sir Samuel Tuke was, early in the Restoration, one of the most popular of playwrights. And for years, *The Adventures*, his only play, enjoyed an extraordinary vogue. Samuel Pepys attended the première and enjoyed it immensely:

> Dined at home; and there being the famous new play acted the first time today, which is call[ed] *The Adventures of five houres*…, I did long to see it and so made my wife to get her ready…And so we went…And the play,

in one word, is the best, for the variety and the most excellent continuance of the plot to the very end, that ever I saw or think ever shall.[49]

The Rival Ladies was probably written soon after the initial run of Tuke's work, and was produced and published the following year. Dryden mentions *The Adventures* in the *Essay of Dramatick Poesie,* but not in any way connected immediately with his play.[50] The omission is hardly important. The evidence does suggest that in the play, as well as in the prologue and dedication, he has *The Adventures* very much in mind; and the evidence is hard to refute or deny.

Dryden's prologue, which follows Tuke's rather closely, is intended both as a mockery of the original and as a highly polished (and entertaining) improvement on it. Tuke does his best in his prologue, which is entitled 'A New Play', to demonstrate his wit, and he does so rather pompously:

> Ne'r spare him [the playwright], Gentlemen, for to speak truth,
> He has a per'lous Cens'rer been in's Youth;
> And now grown Bald with Age, Doating on Praise,
> He thinks to get a Periwig of Bays.[51]

In his prologue, as we have seen, Dryden refers with contempt to the witty prologue that introduces a dull play. Tuke brags about the staging of his work and about those incidental devices which are part and parcel of his very design:

> Th'are i'the right, for I dare boldly say,
> The English Stage ne'r had so New a Play;
> The Dress, the Author, and the Scenes are New.[52]

Dryden (as we have also seen) condemns outright plays in which there is a proliferation of needless effect and spectacle. Tuke has no second speaker in his prologue, but he does add an epilogue in which he identifies the one group, the critics of the Pit, that he would have pass judgment on his work:

> You n'er can want such Writers, who aspire
> To please the Judges of that Upper Tire [Tier].
> The Knowing are his Peers, and for the rest
> Of the Illiterate Croud (though finely drest)
> The Author hopes, he never gave them cause
> To think, he'd waste his Time for their Applause.[53]

Towards the end of his prologue (again, as we have seen) Dryden introduces a second speaker; and his two speakers engage in delightful banter on the poet who seeks approbation from playwrights no better than he and from uninformed but friendly critics.[54]

In the dedication of his work, 'To the Right Honorable Henry Howard...', which is rather short, Tuke merely explains that he would bring something 'Delightful' and 'Natural' on to the English stage, points to his innovations and moral purpose and suggests that he be praised for his many accomplishments.[55] In his dedication, 'To Roger Earl of Orrery', which is relatively long, Dryden repudiates the one by Tuke. By contrast, as he echoes a half century of English literary theory,[56] he centres his attention not on himself and his play but on the specific rules and the general principles that (he says) every true-blooded English playwright must follow and, at the very same time, on the psychological faculties involved in the creative act itself.

Tuke's work, which is on a Spanish subject, is written in a traditional Spanish manner. The unexpected variety of its 'Spanish plot' has been aptly described by Allardyce Nicoll:

> *The Adventures of Five Hours* is an admixture of fun and seriousness. It is a regular intrigue play of love, revenge, and honor, alternating grave and gay, dignified Spanish manners with the ludicrous tomfooleries of serving men.[57]

Dryden's play, an answer to Tuke's, and a very much more successful work, is written in a thoroughly English manner even though it has a Spanish subject.[58] It is that manner which in his dedication he explains and defends.

*

The dedication is quite discursive, unabashedly so. As he turns from one subject to another, Dryden gives the impression that the entire essay is nothing more than a series of digressions from a point, or basic argument, with which he is never quite willing to come to terms. He praises things English, but with surprising reticence and tact. He takes up a number of matters literary, though rarely with the kind of openness or precision which, under the circumstances, they no doubt require. In his role as courtier-poet he pays frequent tribute to Lord Orrery, an early patron. With a humility that we can hardly accept as genuine, he complains (in his role once more as courtier-poet) about the difficulties of composition; he even admits the failure of his own best efforts. And he relies on a prose that sporadically verges (it will never do so again) on the metaphysical, even the fantastic, and never more so than when he turns to Orrery and speaks to him directly:

> Like an ill Swimmer, I have willingly staid long in my own Depth…For beyond your Poetry, my Lord, all is Ocean to me…I can only say in general, that the Souls of other Men shine out at little Cranies; they understand some one thing, perhaps, to Admiration, while they are Darkned on all the other Parts: But your Lordship's Soul is an intire Globe of Light, breaking out on every Side; and if I have only discover'd one Beam of it, 'tis not that the Light falls unequally, but because the Body which receives it, is of unequal parts.[59]

There are other problems in the essay. Dryden writes at some length about literary genre, which he never once pauses to define or explain, and about the one genre (tragi-comedy) that he favours and that he is more than willing to discuss and celebrate, but which, except on the title page, he never identifies or names: we must do so for him.

Oblique in its pronouncements though it may be, the dedication elaborates on the most important statements made in the prologue. Dryden sets before his reader the rules and principles which English playwrights ought to follow and by which he would have his own play judged. Prologue and dedication are each a commentary on the other (the prologue indicating what he dislikes, the dedication what he wholeheartedly approves of), although the dedication, which is obviously very much longer, sometimes reads as if, while writing it, he had Horace's *Art of Poetry* at his elbow.

In the kind of play Dryden has in mind, the action has both variety and unity, conflict and resolution. There is to be but a single plot; and all episodes are to conform to the dictates of probability and decorum. He who would write a successful drama must undertake

> to move so many Characters ... as are requisite in a Play, in those narrow Channels which are proper to each of them: To conduct his imaginary Persons, through so many various Intrigues and Chances, as the Labouring Audience shall think them lost under every Billow; and then at length to work them so natural[ly out of their Distresses, that when the whole Plot is laid open, the Spectators may rest satisfied, that every cause was powerfull enough to produce the effect it had; and that the whole Chain of them was with such due order Linck'd together, that the first Accident would naturally beget the second, till they all render'd the Conclusion necessary.[60]

Characters are both individuals and representative types. Each is to be based upon common human traits. Those traits, moreover, are to be so thoroughly particularized that the minds of the characters do not go 'all after the same Grain, but each of them so particular a way, that the same common Humours [or traits], in several Persons, must be wrought upon by several means'.[61]

The characters, in addition, are to bear the impress of both nature and art. As in the criticism of Cinthio and Mazzoni, Saint-Évremond and Corneille, the Aristotelian principle of imitation is once again challenged and modified; and characters may therefore be true not only to human nature (or representation) but also to art (or the poet's self-expression). On the one hand, they must be portrayed realistically: they must seem to be men and women 'in the World'. On the other hand, they must display some sign of their artistic origin: they must make us aware that they are 'imaginary Persons', the 'Creatures' of the dramatist. If we think that they appear 'to move freely, in all the Sallies of their Passions', we must know too that the playwright has made 'Destinies for them which they cannot shun'.[62]

Language is to be neither 'pedant[ic] ... nor affected'. Metre is to be preferred to prose; and blank verse, a kind of heightened prose (or '*Prose Mesurée*'), may alternate with rhyme. Dryden prizes rhyme chiefly because it has the twofold advantage of elevating both subject matter and character and of allowing the play both 'Sweetness' and restraint. He has not yet reached the position where rhyme demands a special kind of exalted drama, 'unmix'd with mirth'. But his insistence

that rhyme is most suitable for noble characters in great 'Scenes ... of Argu-
mentation and Discourse' does suggest that he has taken his first small step in
formulating the distinctive nature of the heroic play.[63]

Although he does not here name the specific genre that he must surely have in
mind, we do have his definition. A tragi-comedy is a play that begins happily, brings
the protagonists – presumably, young lovers – into a state of peril and then restores
them to prosperity and joy.[64] By way of example, as he suggests both here and in
the prologue, *The Rival Ladies* is the very best he has to offer. Yet here in the
dedication he also apologizes for its many failures. He has not been so 'carefull of
the Plot and Language' as he should have been. Indeed, when compared with his
own opinion, 'the Censures of ... the severest Critiques are Charitable'.[65] That (in
his role as courtier-poet) he speaks only with false modesty we may not doubt. He
reminds us that a perfect play – that is, the perfect tragi-comedy – has yet to be
written and perhaps may never be.

Even as he discusses the mechanics of a well-made play, Dryden takes up at
some length subjects and problems of a much more general sort. The playwright
gives pleasure; and he does so through his handling of plot and character, as well
as through the very 'Ease' and 'Grace' of his metre and language. He also gives
instruction: he gives 'Wisdome' to his audience or reader. What Dryden means by
wisdom he never says; but we may infer that, since he draws an analogy between
the 'States-man' and the 'Poet', he has in mind a knowledge of the 'Prudence' and
the 'conduct' which prevail in a Christian state.[66]

The poet has to exercise both imagination and judgment; and he may do so in
two quite different, but related, ways. He exercises both faculties when he is
mastering (and demonstrating his mastery of) mere technique, including rhyme,
which in turn makes their proper interaction possible:

> [T]hat benefit which I consider most in it [rhyme] ... is, that it Bounds and
> Circumscribes the Fancy. For Imagination in a Poet is a faculty so Wild
> and Lawless, that, like an High-ranging Spaniel it must have Cloggs tied
> to it, least it out-run the Judgment. The great easiness of Blanck Verse,
> renders the Poet too Luxuriant ...: But when the difficulty of Artfull
> Rhyming is interpos'd, where the Poet commonly confines his Sence to his
> Couplet, and must contrive that Sence into such Words, that the Rhyme
> shall naturally follow them, not they the Rhyme; the Fancy then gives
> leisure to the Judgment to come in; which seeing so heavy a Tax impos'd,
> is ready to cut off all unnecessary Expences.[67]

More significantly, the poet exercises both faculties when, as he draws upon
memory, he is engaged in the very act of creation. He avails himself of his two most
important faculties when, with the help of memory, he calls forth all the many
details and particulars he intends to synthesize (or harmonize) into a varied but
thoroughly unified (and thoroughly new) work of art. The task may be difficult,
even painful; but to the dedicated spirit it is always worthwhile:

> Plotting and Writing ... are certainly more troublesome employments than many which signifie more, and are of greater moment in the World: The Fancy, Memory, and Judgment, are then extended (like so many Limbs) upon the Rack; all of them Reaching with their utmost stress at Nature; a thing so almost Infinite and Boundless, as can never fully be Comprehended, but where the Images of all things are always present.[68]

In their proper interaction (or balance) the two faculties transform chaos into order. To achieve his necessary end, the poet must be especially alert and, in his choice of imagery and detail, unusually discriminating and selective:

> This ... Play ... was only a confus'd Mass of Thoughts, tumbling over one another in the Dark: When the Fancy [or imagination] was yet in its first Work, moving the Sleeping Images of things towards the Light, there to be Disguish'd, and then either chosen or rejected by the Judgment ...[69]

Poet and audience may then share in the same experience: that tranquillity and calm which only great works of literature allow and grant.

The poet has also to rely on originality and tradition. These last concepts are Dryden's own; but the terminology is not, although in any and every attempt to understand his method and purpose it is extremely convenient. It helps us to understand – perhaps the first major attempt in English literature – to define and propagate a distinctly English (or national) theatre. The poet must of course be original (or 'invent[ive]'). At the same time, he must not write as if nothing of importance had ever been written for any theatre prior to his birth. A dedicated playwright should know something about the works of his great predecessors; and in those works he may find either models of excellence that he may imitate or, better still, those from which he may derive inspiration. Hence, in England, the English playwright must abide by things English. He may always borrow subjects from poets and playwrights of other 'civiliz'd Nations'. But he must first purify his language of foreign words and phrases. If he uses rhyme, he must also rely on the metrical patterns established by the most polished of English poets since the outbreak of the Civil War (that is, from the 1640s to the present):

> Mr. *Waller* ... first made Writing easily an Art: First shew'd us to conclude the Sense, most commonly in Distichs ... The sweetness of Mr. *Wallers* Lyrick Poesie was afterwards follow'd in the Epick by Sir *John Denham*, in his *Coopers-Hill* ... But if we owe the Invention of it to Mr. *Waller*, we are acknowledging for the Noblest use of it to Sir *William D'avenant;* who at once brought it upon the Stage, and made it perfect, in the *Siege of Rhodes.*[70]

The poet should write mainly in that genre which is a peculiarly English invention and development: tragi-comedy. As he may not carry originality to excess, so the English playwright must escape no less from narrow-mindedness. Even the most English of English playwrights should have more than a little familiarity with the leading poets and critics of antiquity and with their modern avatars. He must not be guilty of the 'Brand which Barclay has ... laid upon the English: *Angli suos ac sua omnia impense mirantur; cæteras nationes despectui habent* [the English eagerly admire themselves and their own works; they despise other peoples]'.[71]

It was a commonplace in the Renaissance and the seventeenth century that, in every approach to literature, a critic must first keep in mind principles or rules that govern both genre and tradition; that ideally he must prefer narrative poetry, especially serious drama, to all other forms; and that, when writing about or evaluating a specific poem or play, he must focus attention not only on details of technique or method, as well as the author's subject and purpose, but also on the apparent tensions between two dominant forces in Western literature and culture: Greek and Roman classicism and medieval rhetoric and romance. Throughout the dedication Dryden is very much a man of his age: he never once steps outside it. Nevertheless, he does give the commonplace a new (and hence a novel) twist.

He discovers in every aspect of literature and therefore in every detail of individual works, especially the drama, a striking concatenation of paired opposites or contraries: unity and variety, nature and art, individual and type, sweetness and restraint. These contraries or opposites he then sets – casually, and perhaps even accidentally – in juxtaposition with a triad of others: originality and tradition, pleasure and instruction, imagination and judgment. And he arrives at the conclusion inevitably that, in every instance, the opposing elements must be held in complete or equal balance with each other. Here then is the groundwork on which, throughout the rest of his career as both playwright and critic, he will have to build. He will never quite be able to repudiate his past: he will always have to take it with him.

But no sooner does he complete the dedication than he has an epiphany: in what he has only recently said, even insisted upon, he will be obliged to make a number of significant changes, adjustments, modifications, additions, but mainly three. He will subsume all of his paired opposites under imagination and judgment. He will identify (or equate) imagination with originality, judgment with literary rules and tradition. And he will decide that, if it is to teach successfully, every poem or play must by necessity give more pleasure than instruction. There are then circumstances when, in every poem or play, imagination must take some priority over judgment and therefore – we may now use the terms he will shortly prefer – the lively over the just.

PART II
First principles

CHAPTER THREE

A French play
(1665–1668)

I

In the summer of 1665 there was an outbreak of plague in London. To escape the danger Dryden fled the capital for a stay at the country seat of his father-in-law, the Earl of Berkshire. There, in a period of some sixteen months, he read Aristotle and Horace, Homer and Virgil, and their modern imitators and followers; and he wrote his first major piece of criticism, *An Essay of Dramatick Poesie,* as well as a tragi-comedy, *Secret Love,* and a 'Historical Poem', *Annus Mirabilis.* All three works were designed to stand by themselves; and each was later published in a separate edition: *Annus Mirabilis* in January, 1667; *Secret Love* in January, 1668; and the *Essay* also in January, 1668.[1] No explicit statement links the *Essay* to either the poem or the play, yet all three are clearly related. With a slight change in perspective, *Annus Mirabilis* and *Secret Love* embody literary ideas set forth in the *Essay;* with a slight change in emphasis, the critical introductions that explain and justify the poem and the play appear to be a continuation of the *Essay,* the major themes of which they echo and reflect.

The *Essay* thus stands at the fountainhead of Dryden's labours; and as the most comprehensive statement of his early criticism, and the most detailed, it is no less the groundwork of things to come. We must therefore consider it first. Dryden all but urges us to do so. In the dedication, 'To the Right Honourable Charles Lord Buckhurst', the most recent of his many patrons, he grants that his 'judgment [is] not a little alter'd since the writing of it': 'I confess I find many things in this discourse which I do not now approve ...' But he is quick to add that, to 'dissent from the opinion of better Wits ... [and] to defend ... [his] own', he is like '*Homer* tell[ing] us the fight of the *Greeks* and *Trojans*'. 'I ... speak', he boasts, 'in the language of the Muses'; and dissent is transformed utterly: it becomes a prophecy of things not yet dreamed of or planned but soon realized and achieved.[2]

II

The *Essay* is cast in the form of a dialogue – actually, a courtly debate – which takes place against the background of a naval battle between the English and the Dutch. It is also set ultimately against the background of another and very different conflict, a major controversy of the century, the Quarrel of the Ancients and Moderns.[3] The three conflicts – the war, the quarrel, and the debate – all take place simultaneously; and we shall later discover that a victory in one corresponds (in the world of the *Essay*) to victories in the other two. As the sound of gunfire fades in

43

the distance, four Englishmen sailing down the Thames air their views on the drama. The major portion of the *Essay* – more than three-fourths – is concerned with the relative merits of ancient and modern drama and, in a long passage specifically on the modern theatre, with the competing merits of French classical drama and a native English drama, made up of Elizabethan, Jacobean and Restoration plays. The speakers, each under a pseudonym, are partially modelled on a contemporary author or patron of the arts. But the disguises are slight; and the identifications originally made in 1800 by Edmund Malone have never been questioned, at least successfully.[4] Each speaker advocates a somewhat different position, one based on opinions held theoretically by his living counterpart. Dryden's old friend, Sir Robert Howard (Crites), now his brother-in-law, argues the case of the Ancients.[5] Dryden's patron, Charles Sackville, Lord Buckhurst (Eugenius), defends the Moderns. The position in favour of the French is then stated by Sir Charles Sedley (Lisideius), a prominent Restoration wit, while Dryden himself (Neander) speaks in favour of the English. In the course of their debate, the disputants take up many issues important in the composition of a play, including those of plot and characterization, as well as of subject, purpose and style. Finally, in a long coda, two of the speakers consider whether blank verse or rhyme is the proper medium for serious plays.

The *Essay* is written in an oblique mode of discourse, one that was traditionally favoured by most English courtiers, at least in public.[6] It operates on two distinct levels of meaning, one apparent and one concealed. On the surface, the *Essay* mirrors the Restoration ideal of civilized behaviour. Four gentlemen, all aristocratic in bearing, are shown conversing – effortlessly, gracefully, unpedantically – on an important subject in the arts. In the spirit of free enquiry each is allowed to make a case for his position; and each position seems to have a claim on our support. It is this level or aspect of the *Essay* which has beguiled many modern readers.[7]

Beneath this world of seeming intellectual freedom, however, there exists another world, in which Dryden as narrator manipulates his characters like pawns in a game. In that aspect of the *Essay* which is immediately apparent Crites, Eugenius and Lisideius may seem to express only their own minds. But here Dryden gives them destinies which they cannot shun. They are forced to espouse arguments that, in the end, destroy their respective positions and pave the way, inexorably, for the victory of Neander and the English stage.[8]

In the dedication to Lord Buckhurst Dryden makes his readers continually aware of the two worlds within the *Essay*. Indeed, because of the tensions in the *Essay* between explicit and implicit meaning or purpose the dedication mirrors the strategy of the *Essay* itself. Explicitly, Dryden claims that in his *Essay* he has set down 'a Dispute betwixt some ... Wits', which he chanced to overhear. His *Essay*, he tells us, is a simple history; and he, a mere historian. Like Tacitus, he has set down everything '*Sine studio partium aut ira:* without Passion or Interest'.[9]

His statement, however, that he is without passion or interest, is undercut by a number of other remarks that appear in the dedication. He implies, for instance, that he loves to say one thing when he means another. He is a master of disguise, one who delights in hiding his true purpose, that of ardent self-defence, a defence waged (he says) in the best courtly manner:

> For my own part, if in treating of this subject I sometimes dissent from the opinion of better Wits, I declare it is not so much to combat their opinions, as to defend my own, which were first made publick. Sometimes, like a Schollar in a Fencing-School I put forth my self, and show my own ill play, on purpose to be better taught. Sometimes I stand desperately to my Armes, like the Foot when deserted by their Horse, not in hope to overcome, but onely to yield on more honourable termes.[10]

He speaks, moreover, of his 'Adversaries ... [and their] Arguments'; he hopes that 'this Essay ... might awaken' in Lord Buckhurst 'the desire of writing something, in whatever kind it be, which might be an honour to our Age and Country'; and he identifies himself at this point not so much with Homer and the Muses as with those rhetoricians who, like Cicero, may carry on a 'war of opinions', but always do so 'like Gentlemen, with candour [or absence of malice] and civility'. That he may further set everything straight, he provides an epigraph from Horace: '*fungar vice cotis, acutum/Reddere quæ ferrum valet, exors ipsa secandi* [I'll play a whetstone's part, which makes steel sharp, but of itself cannot cut]'. The meaning of the epigraph is glossed by the larger passage of which it forms a part:

> Though I write naught myself, I'll play a whetstone's part, which makes steel sharp, but of itself cannot cut. Though I write naught myself, I will teach the poet's office and duty; whence he draws his stores; what nurtures and fashions him; what befits him and what not; whither the right course leads and whither the wrong.[11]

The epigraph underscores Dryden's real intention, that of framing prescriptive literary rules. And lest we miss the whole point of the epigraph, or fail to recognize the irony in his dedication, he grants us an address, 'To the Reader', in which he makes the basic thesis of the *Essay* as clear as it can possibly be made:

> The drift of the ensuing Discourse was chiefly to vindicate the honour of our *English* Writers, from the censure of those who unjustly prefer the *French* before them.[12]

Dryden as omniscient author may not appear directly in the *Essay*. He may not magisterially dismiss opposing views. But, as narrator, he has so arranged the debate that, in the end, only Neander's position (his own) remains convincing.

III

The dialogue begins, innocently enough, as the four speakers survey the current literary scene. The sheer worthlessness of recent poetry becomes a target of their wit; and two poets, left unnamed, are singled out for scorn, each embodying one extreme of poetic failure. The first 'extremity of poetry' is a writer who violates all norms in the pursuit of such stylistic novelties as puns and conceits. The second, far from having too much imagination, has no imagination at all. As Crites describes him,

> he is the most calm, peaceable Writer you ever read: he never disquiets your passions with the least concernment, but still leaves you in as even a temper as he found you; he is a very Leveller in Poetry, he creeps along with ten little words in every line, and helps out his Numbers with *For to,* and *Unto,* and all the pretty Expletives he can find, till he draggs them to the end of another line...[13]

Imaginative vigour without rule and rule without imaginative vigour, these are extremes which the four speakers agree poetry must avoid. It seems only logical, therefore, that, in defining the ideal play, the speakers seek a standard that combines order and variety; 'and they were the more importunate, because neither *Aristotle,* nor *Horace,* nor any other, who had writ of that Subject, had ever done it'.

After some discussion, they frame a standard – 'rather a Description than a Definition' – of their own. A play, they conclude,

> ought to be, *A just and lively Image of Humane Nature, representing its Passions and Humours, and the Changes of Fortune to which it is subject; for the Delight and Instruction of Mankind.*[14]

This standard appears to be a middle course between the extremes just deplored. Actually, it serves to establish criteria which, as an informed reader would have known, the English stage was best equipped to meet. Ever since Stuart times the English had taken pride in what they at first called the 'judicious[ness]' and 'fire' of their drama and, during the Restoration, its 'regular[ity]' and 'liveli[ness]'.[15] Hence, once the standard is announced, we need no longer wonder who is going to win the debate; we are only to appreciate the masterly strokes by which, under cover of an impartial inquiry, a preordained victory takes place.

Dryden's initial strategy, as narrator, is to have the first speaker argue, by inadvertence, against himself. Crites appears to make a plausible case for the Ancients, but we soon find his very argument turned against him and employed to establish the rival claims of the Moderns. The crux of Crites's admiration of the Ancients is that, by dwelling always on 'some appearance of probability' or truth, they perfected the dramatic form which later playwrights first borrowed and then debased:

> Those Ancients have been faithful Imitators and wise Observers of that Nature which is so torn and ill represented in our Plays... But, that you may know how much you are indebted to those your Masters, and be ashamed to have so ill requited them: I must remember you that all the Rules by which we practise the *Drama* at this day... were delivered to us from the Observations which *Aristotle* made, of those Poets, who either liv'd before him, or were his Contemporaries...[16]

Crites attributes the success of the Ancients to the civilization in which they

46

wrote. He argues that 'every Age has a kind of Universal Genius, which inclines those that live in it to some particular Studies'.[17] He further insists that what is loved is cultivated, and that what is cultivated is necessarily improved. To substantiate these claims he cites the incontrovertible results of the modern passion for 'useful Experiments in Philosophy':

> Is it not evident, in these last hundred years (when the Study of Philosophy has been the business of all the *Virtuosi* in *Christendome*) that almost a new Nature has been reveal'd to us? that more errours of the School have been detected, more useful Experiments in Philosophy have been made, more Noble Secrets in Opticks, Medicine, Anatomy, Astronomy, discover'd, than in all those credulous and doting Ages from *Aristotle* to us?[18]

Crites reasons that the effort which the present age devotes to science, antiquity lavished on the drama; and the results in each case are clear: ancient drama is superior to modern drama to the same extent that modern science is superior to that of antiquity.

Crites bases his case upon a single principle: that benefits are derived solely from intensive and unremitting labour. Unfortunately, his choice of argument proves disastrous: for the effects of labour, as Eugenius now shows, are progressive. If much labour improves a discipline, a little more will obviously improve it still further. Crites's views, unexpectedly, endorse a belief in progress; and the idea of progress necessarily supports the Moderns. As Eugenius argues,

> I have observ'd in your Speech that the former part of it is convincing as to what the Moderns have profitted by the rules of the Ancients, but in the latter you are careful to conceal how much they have excell'd them: we own all the helps we have from them, and want neither veneration nor gratitude while we acknowledge that to overcome them we must make use of the advantages we have receiv'd from them; but to these assistances we have joyned our own industry; for (had we sate down with a dull imitation of them) we might then have lost somewhat of the old perfection, but never acquir'd any that was new. We draw not therefore after their lines, but those of Nature; and having the life before us, besides the experience of all they knew, it is no wonder if we hit some airs and features which they have miss'd ...[19]

To prove that playwriting has indeed advanced since ancient times, Eugenius has merely to correct the many blunders in Crites's history of the drama. He points out that the rules which Crites attributes to the Ancients were actually first promulgated in modern times. For instance, 'the Unity of Place, how ever it might be practised by them [the Ancients], was never any of their Rules: We neither find it in *Aristotle, Horace,* or any who have written of it, till in our age the *French* Poets first made it a Precept of the Stage'.[20] And the rules which the Ancients did know, such as the unities of time and action, were violated by their playwrights egregiously. They failed therefore in creating 'resemblance[s] of truth and nature'

47

and 'perfect images of humane life'. In theory and practice, then, the drama of the Ancients is based on their 'having rather a general indigested notion of a Play, then knowing how and where to bestow the particular graces of it'.[21] Admirers of the classical rules should prefer the new drama to the old.

Eugenius, however, is far better at showing the 'defects' of the Ancients than in pointing to the 'excellences' of the Moderns. The Moderns are held up to be masters of classical drama, as it were, by default. The overwhelming failure of the Ancients is made to prove that somehow the Moderns must be better. Of course, Eugenius does not entirely neglect the achievements of the Moderns. He often alludes or refers to what is praiseworthy in modern drama, particularly English drama, which he likes the best. For example, along with variety and richness in plot and character, he praises 'the excellent Scenes of Passion in *Shakespeare,* or in *Fletcher*'.[22] The problem is that none of the qualities he names has anything to do with the classical standard that he espouses. Rather, they reflect and embody an entirely different theory of the drama, a theory which he nowhere defines. Complaining that he has spoken too much already, he leaves the clarification of his position to his friend Neander, whose opinion of English plays, Eugenius admits, is the same as his own.[23] Meanwhile, Eugenius is content to leave a muddle. It is this confusion that gives Lisideius his chance.

The task of Lisideius is to point out the obvious. He argues that the dramatic principles and dramatic tastes of Eugenius are completely at odds. If Eugenius upholds classical standards, he ought logically, argues Lisideius, to prefer the French stage to the English: the French 'have so imitated the Ancients that they have sur-pass'd them'. The French playwright 'so interweaves Truth with probable Fiction, that he puts a pleasing Fallacy upon us'; 'For the Spirit of man cannot be satisfied but with truth, or at least verisimility...'

As for the unities, which Eugenius has condemned the Ancients for not observ-ing, they are embodied in French drama in their most exacting form. Many French dramatists, for instance, believe that unity of time is achieved by covering the period not of a natural day but of an 'artificial day', or the twelve-hour span from sunrise to sunset. And their interpretation of the unity of action is equally scrupulous. By design, they confine themselves to a single story, and in the telling they include only what is necessary. Some details they omit entirely; others they present in narrative summaries or 'relations'. Through these means – omission and relation – they keep stage business to a minimum and concentrate on the really essential subject of the drama, the mind of man. The French, Lisideius explains,

> by pursuing closely one argument, which is not cloy'd with many turns, ... have gain'd more liberty for verse, in which they write: they have leisure to dwell on a subject which deserves it; and to represent the passions (which we have acknowledg'd to be the Poets work) without being hurried from one thing to another...[24]

In brief, the French have perfected classical drama: they have 'reform'd their Theatre' and 'it now surpasses ... the rest of *Europe*'.[25]

Lisideius's discourse has a plausibility that almost compels assent: it appears to cap the debate that has so far run through the *Essay* from the very beginning. Thus, Crites proves that the rules were introduced by the Ancients; Eugenius, that they were improved by the Moderns; and Lisideius, that they were perfected by the French. The three speakers may appear to be rivals. But each actually provides one stage of an argument, leading inexorably to the conclusion held by Lisideius, that French drama is the most classical, and therefore the one great drama the world has so far known.

But the victory of Lisideius proves to be short lived. As Neander now reminds us, the debate is in fact not about the observance of rules, whether ancient or modern, but about what constitutes a good play. What the drama ought to be, Neander tells his friends, was decided at the beginning of their discussion when all agreed that, among other things, a play must contain a 'lively imitation of Nature'. And liveliness, according to Neander, is precisely what French drama lacks. French playwrights so concentrate upon 'their servile observations of the unities', and other structural niceties, that 'they have brought on themselves that dearth of Plot, and narrowness of Imagination, which may be observ'd in all their Playes'.[26] They have not perfected the drama of the Ancients: they have exacerbated its worst tendencies.

In his condemnation of the French, Neander repeats, though in harsher terms, the very complaints Eugenius levels at the Ancients. Whereas Eugenius complains that the Ancients imitated life too narrowly, 'as if they had imitated onely an Eye or an Hand, and did not dare to venture on the lines of a Face, or the Proportion of a Body', Neander insists that, because of their inflexibility, the French do not capture life at all. Their plays have 'the Beauties of a Statue, but not of a Man, because not animated with the Soul of Poesie'. Similarly, whereas Eugenius compares the plots of the Ancients to a house you can 'see thorow all at once', the comparison by Neander is even more damning: French plots are likened to an 'ill Riddle', which is 'found out e're it be half propos'd'.[27] What was bad in antiquity the French have made worse.

Neander's own choice for a truly distinguished drama lies, at least initially, outside the classical tradition. At the beginning of his argument he champions a genre long popular in England, tragi-comedy, 'a more pleasant way of writing for the Stage than was ever known to the Ancients or Moderns of any Nation'. In tragi-comedy, which in large measure they 'have invented, increas'd and perfected', the English do not unify their plots by following a method of rigid exclusion.[28] They do not concentrate on a single action and admit only such characters and incidents as bear directly upon the denouement. An English tragi-comedy, argues Neander, is conceived on a grand scale. It aims at including as many characters and incidents as can be made to cohere and 'agree'. Hence, while French plots are 'single', carrying on 'one design which is push'd forward by all the Actors, every Scene in the Play contributing and moving towards it', the plots in English tragi-comedy are multiple:

> Our Playes [or tragi-comedies], besides the main design, have under plots
> or by-concernments, of less considerable Persons, and Intrigues, which

are carried on with the motion of the main Plot: as they say the Orb of
the fix'd Stars, and those of the Planets, though they have motions of
their own, are whirl'd about by the motion of the *primum mobile,* in
which they are contained …[29]

In attributing to tragi-comedy the unity-in-variety of the physical universe,
Neander is of course speaking in ideal terms; and in doing so he allows himself,
after celebrating the English stage, what we shall have to regard as a slight
reservation. The perfect tragi-comedy would indeed reflect cosmic plenitude and
harmony. The tragi-comedies thus far written in England do not. In attempting
to raise 'quick turns and counterturns of Plot', English playwrights have failed to
give their work sufficient unity. English plays are extraordinarily lively; but they are
not adequately just.

It would seem, then, that a good play has to be based upon a fusion of French
and English practice, the French providing the element of the just, while the
English provide whatever constitutes the lively. But no sooner does Neander
advance toward this conclusion than suddenly he changes his point of view. He
declares that the English possess, in addition to their tragi-comedies, an impressive body of classical plays. Borrowings from the French are superfluous. All the
elements required for a perfect play lie within native shores:

> I dare boldly affirm these two things of the *English Drama:* First, That we
> have many Playes of ours as regular as any of theirs; and which, besides,
> have more variety of Plot and Characters: And secondly, that in most of
> the irregular Playes of *Shakespeare* or *Fletcher* (for *Ben. Johnson's* are for
> the most part regular) there is a more masculine fancy and greater spirit in
> the writing, then there is in any of the *French*.[30]

To substantiate his claims for the self-sufficiency of English drama, Neander
provides brief sketches of four major English playwrights, each sketch a carefully
delineated study in literary character. These studies have often been detached from
their context by anthologists and admired as superb examples of practical criticism.
But Neander's purpose is less to describe the particular qualities of Shakespeare,
Beaumont and Fletcher, or Jonson, than to reveal the indigenous resources available
to future English playwrights.

Each of these authors is marshalled forth to display whatever service to the new
drama his works can provide. Appropriately, Neander begins with Shakespeare, the
'Father of our Dramatick Poets'. According to Neander, Shakespeare is a vast storehouse of invention. His plays are filled with 'All the Images of Nature' and, because
of his 'masculine fancy', nature in him enjoys a second and better life: 'when he
describes any thing, you more than see it, you feel it too'. As Shakespeare is the
English Homer, so in Jonson the English possess another Virgil. Jonson lacks
Shakespeare's imagination; but as Neander's analysis of *The Silent Women* – what
he calls an '*Examen*' – makes clear, his plays are more 'exactly form'd'. Indeed,
Jonson is 'the most learned and judicious Writer which any Theatre ever had'; and
from him English playwrights can best learn how to fashion their plots after the

true classical manner. Moreover, Jonson is an excellent model in another 'Sphere'. He is the supreme master in 'Humour', or the accurate representation of 'some extravagant habit, passion, or affection; particular...to some one person'.[31]

Shakespeare and Jonson represent, for Neander, epitomes of the lively in literature and the just. He thinks, however, that the opposing traditions which they represent have been at least partially reconciled in the works of their successors, Francis Beaumont and John Fletcher.[32] Beaumont and Fletcher had 'with the advantage of *Shakespeare's* wit [or genius], which was their precedent, great natural gifts, improv'd by study'. As a consequence, their plots, while they have Shakespeare's 'spirit', are 'generally more regular'. It is true that they have only a modest interest in humour; but no poet, not even Shakespeare, can match their 'gayety' and 'quickness of wit in reparties'. Beaumont and Fletcher left much work to be done: 'through carelessness [they] made many faults'. But on account of their many achievements, not least of which is that 'the *English* Language in them arriv'd to its highest perfection', their comedies and their more 'serious Playes', or tragi-comedies, 'are now the most pleasant and frequent entertainments of the Stage'.[33]

Neander's 'Character[s]' reveal the extraordinary richness of English drama. Not only do the English possess – in the comedies of Jonson – plays as 'regular' as the French; they also possess – in the tragi-comedies of Shakespeare – an 'irregular' drama, which is as lively as a drama can be. Two distinct literary traditions, however, are not the same thing as – and they should not be confused with – single plays that are both lively and just. Consequently, in the new drama of the new age, playwrights will go to school to Shakespeare and Jonson, and to Beaumont and Fletcher, but especially Fletcher. Fletcher was the first great synthesizer in English letters.[34] In his entirely comic plays he fused two forms of comedy (that of wit and that of humour) and, at the same time, two native literary traditions (that of Shakespeare and that of Jonson); and in the more important of his works, his tragi-comedies, he fused, however imperfectly, two kinds of comedy, two native literary traditions and two very different literary genres.

By the time he has completed his brief survey of the English stage and his character sketches of its four leading playwrights, Neander has delivered the central argument in what is tantamount to a manifesto – and one that is as important in the history and development of English literary theory and practice as Wordsworth's famous 'Preface to *Lyrical Ballads*' (1800). In the new age, one considerably more civilized than the last, the new playwrights will have to borrow from their predecessors; but they will obey more fully all the graces and rules of English decorum and so improve on what they borrow. They will take their inspiration from Fletcher, specifically his tragi-comedies. But Fletcher constructed his tragi-comedies out of single plots, in which opposing elements are inappropriately mingled. The playwrights of the modern age will henceforth construct their tragi-comedies out of separate but parallel plots. The serious action will be confined to the major plot, in which the lively ('high concernments', 'greatness of characters', 'spirit in the writing') will prevail over the just ('probability', 'decorum', 'correct[ness]'); and comedy, both that of wit and that of humour, will be confined to the minor plot, in which the just, 'or the imitation of what is natural', will prevail over the lively, the lively manifesting itself here and there through wit. In the play as a whole, furthermore, 'the greatest beauty...[and] magnificence', as well as 'variety and copiousness' and 'pleasure to the audience', take a slight precedence over 'instruction', 'the old Rule[s] of Logick', and 'verisimility' (or 'the nearest imitation of Nature').

Neander does not discuss these several matters in detail. He says nothing about the exact proportions of the lively and the just in major and minor plots or about the precise relationship – in importance – of parallel plots to each other. He is concerned not with the minutiae of literary rules but with a historical vision. He wants to convince his friends (and us) that, in England, new and better times are about to dawn:

> And though the fury of a Civil War, and Power, for twenty years together, abandon'd to a barbarous race of men, Enemies of all good Learning, had buried the Muses under the ruines of Monarchy; yet with the restoration of our happiness, we see reviv'd Poesie lifting up its head, & already shaking off the rubbish which lay so heavy on it. We have seen since His Majesties return, many Dramatick Poems which yield not to those of any forreign Nation, and which deserve all Lawrels but the *English*. I will set aside Flattery and Envy: it cannot be deny'd but we have had some little blemish either in the Plot or writing of all those Playes which have been made within these seven years ... And if I do not venture upon any particular judgment of our late Playes, 'tis out of the consideration which an Ancient Writer gives me; *Vivorum, ut magna admiratio ita censura difficilis:* betwixt the extreams of admiration and malice, 'tis hard to judge uprightly of the living.[35]

Neander refuses to name the 'present Poets' upon whose 'many and great beauties' his judgment is based. But are we not to assume that in their number he would include Dryden, whose first tragi-comedy, *The Rival Ladies* (1664), suffers from perhaps 'some slight, and little imperfections' and whose second tragi-comedy, *Secret Love* (1668), more nearly, though still imperfectly, reflects Neander's principles? The intimation, however, is somewhat obscured by the comic moment in which the passage ends. At the close of his peroration, Neander is so overcome by his own eloquence that he turns at breakneck speed from prophecy to history: from an expression of high hopes for Restoration drama to a grandiloquent claim of achievements already made. We are encouraged to laugh at his sudden transformation of wishes into facts. But as we laugh at him we gain only a renewed respect for the man he represents. Clearly, someone who, like Dryden, can provoke amusement at his own expense has a detachment that Neander lacks. In any event, Neander's manifesto puts forth a number of ideas which, as the years passed, Dryden was to modify or reject; but as an introduction to his first poems and plays, and as an overview of his early theory and practice, it is an extraordinary statement of first principles and a remarkable celebration of ideals and purpose.

IV

Neander's remarks on the ambitions of his contemporaries close the larger debate on national dramas; and he is left, though tacitly, in possession of the field. The first debate, however, is no sooner concluded than a second begins. Its subject is whether blank verse or rhyme is the more suitable medium for serious plays; its disputants are Crites and Neander. This second debate is sometimes regarded as a blemish in the *Essay:* Dryden, his critics say, diminished the interest of his work by ending with an issue both ephemeral and irrelevant.[36] But a discussion of verse is not unimportant in itself; nor is it unrelated to the earlier discussion. It is related in a number of ways, all of them quite significant, each a further demonstration that in matters literary Neander is always right.

At two junctures in the first debate the subject of rhyme is considered. Lisideius, for example, offhandedly asserts his preference for the rhymed verse of the French to the blank verse of the English:

> I should now speak of the beauty of their Rhime, and the just reason I have to prefer that way of writing in Tragedies before ours in Blanck-verse; but because it is partly receiv'd by us, and therefore not altogether peculiar to them, I will say no more of it in relation to their Playes.[37]

Neander also prefers rhyme, though he dwells on its indigenous development in England rather than on its intrinsic merit. '[We] have', he tells his friends,

> English Presidents of elder date then any of *Corneille*'s Playes: (not to name our old Comedies before *Shakespeare,* which were all writ in verse of six feet, or *Alexandrin's,* such as the French now use) I can show in *Shakespeare,* many Scenes of rhyme together, and the like in *Ben. Johnsons* Tragedies ...[38]

The evasiveness of Lisideius and Neander troubles Crites; and he finally complains that they 'have concluded, without any reason given for it, that Rhyme is proper for the Stage'. Their statements about rhyme, he contends, simply skirt the issues. 'I will not dispute', he says,

> how ancient it hath been among us to write this way; perhaps our Ancestours knew no better till *Shakespeare's* time. I will grant it was not altogether left by him, and that *Fletcher* and *Ben. Johnson* us'd it frequently in their Pastorals, and sometimes in other Playes. Farther, I will not argue whether we receiv'd it originally from our own Countrymen, or from the *French*; for that is an inquiry of as little benefit, as theirs who in the midst of the late Plague were not so sollicitous to provide against it, as to know whether we had it from the malignity of our own air, or by transportation from *Holland*.[39]

Lisideius and Neander provide no real defence of rhyme for the simple reason that, apparently, nothing can be said in its favour.

But the evasiveness of Lisideius and Neander has more to do with Dryden's strategy as narrator than with the merits of their case: rhymed dramatic verse was a long-standing convention in France but not in England; by postponing the discussion of rhyme until after the superiority of the English stage has been established, Dryden avoids having to make a damaging concession to the French. Moreover, by placing the debate on rhyme at the end of the *Essay*, Dryden (now as omniscient author) is able to shift the focus of Neander's argument and manifesto from one kind of drama, tragi-comedy, to one that he identifies as a slight modification of it, although he is to change his mind in the 'Preface to *Tyrannick Love*' (1670). When Neander defends rhyme, he speaks of what he still regards as tragi-comedy but now unexpectedly redefines. With his eye on some recent experiments in the drama (Davenant's *Seige of Rhodes*, Orrery's *Mustapha* and Dryden's own *Indian Queen* and *Indian Emperour*), he no longer refers to tragi-comedies as a synthesis of two dramatic forms: they are instead 'serious Playes', which, despite having happy endings, are 'unmix't with mirth'.[40] The shift in Neander's definition of tragi-comedy undoubtedly violates, from our perspective, the intellectual coherence of the *Essay*. But it enabled Dryden to refer to a dramatic form that, as the years passed, was increasingly to dominate his interest. That form is the heroic play, which he had at first assumed to be tragi-comedy in a new dress, but which he later regarded as another form entirely.[41]

The debate on rhyme hinges on the word 'natural' and two of its many meanings. For Crites naturalness in the drama is identified with 'probability' and, hence, with realistic imitation. That verse is natural which most closely approximates human speech. Since experience shows that 'no man, without premeditation speaks in Rhyme', rhyme 'on the Stage' must be judged absurd.[42] Crites concedes that, since a play is an imitation of life and not life itself, it need not mirror the external world exactly. Nevertheless, poetic licence must be strictly limited. The poet is to bind himself to the everyday world as closely as he can:

> For a Play is still an imitation of Nature; we know we are to be deceiv'd, and we desire to be so; but no man ever was deceiv'd but with a probability of truth ... Thus we sufficiently understand that the Scenes which represent Cities and Countries to us, are not really such, but onely painted on boards and Canvass: But shall that excuse the ill Painture or designment of them; Nay rather ought they not to be labour'd with so much the more diligence and exactness to help the imagination? since the mind of man does naturally tend to Truth; and therefore the nearer any thing comes to the imitation of it, the more it pleases.[43]

Hence, the proper form of verse in serious plays is blank verse, the form which is closest to 'ordinary discourse'.

Crites's defence of blank verse suffers the same unhappy fate as his earlier defence of the Ancients: the principles upon which he bases his argument are seized by his opponent and turned against him. As Neander wastes no time in showing, it is arbitrary, even illogical, for Crites to hold that 'a Play is the imitation of

Nature', hence distinct from it, and then to equate nature solely with what is probable and commonplace. If nature and the drama occupy separate and distinct realms, then, paradoxically, what is natural in the world may be deemed unnatural in a play; conversely, what is natural in a play may be deemed unnatural in the world. A play is an imitation of nature; but the definition of the term 'nature' is relative: it denotes at times 'a probability of truth', at other times the presence of decorum (or appropriateness) in the handling of a given subject or genre. What is appropriate or natural in one type of play may not be so in another:

> It has been formerly urg'd by you, and confess'd by me, that since no man spoke any kind of verse *ex tempore,* that which was nearest Nature was to be preferr'd. I answer you therefore, by distinguishing betwixt what is nearest to the nature of Comedy, which is the imitation of common persons and ordinary speaking, and what is nearest the nature of a serious Play: this last is indeed the representation of Nature, but 'tis Nature wrought up to an higher pitch. The Plot, the Characters, the Wit, the Passions, the Descriptions, are all exalted above the level of common converse, as high as the imagination of the Poet can carry them, with proportion to verisimility [or the probable]. Tragedy we know is wont to image to us the minds and fortunes of noble persons, and to portray these exactly...[44]

Under such circumstances, though to an extent Neander otherwise condemns, the lively has again some priority over the just, imagination over judgment. And it therefore must follow that, in 'a serious Play', 'Heroick Rhime is nearest Nature [or what is most appropriate], as being the noblest kind of modern verse'.[45]

In the very simplicity of his argument and its every detail, Neander's defence of rhyme is as effective as his earlier defence of the English stage and, more specifically, tragi-comedy. Again, no one takes notice of his skill in argument, neither Neander himself nor Dryden as omniscient author and narrator. Nevertheless, Neander's final opponent lies defeated before him; he is, once again, victorious in debate. Some commentators have suggested that Dryden intends a close parallel to be drawn between Neander's fortunes and those of the English sailors in the offstage engagement.[46] But if there is a parallel, it must surely be ironic. Unlike the battles of the English navy, those in which Neander takes part contain no real conflict. Indeed, despite the military trappings of their argument, and their ardent self-confidence, his adversaries actually help to facilitate his success. Neander convinces us of the superior wisdom of his position because he cannot do otherwise. The *Essay* is arranged to bring his victories about.

The *Essay,* then, does more than defend the Moderns against the Ancients, the English against the French, and Dryden's own works – tragi-comedies or heroic plays – against all others. The *Essay* also – through its critical theory and its mode of argument – demonstrates Dryden's achievement not only as playwright and critic but as rhetorician as well.

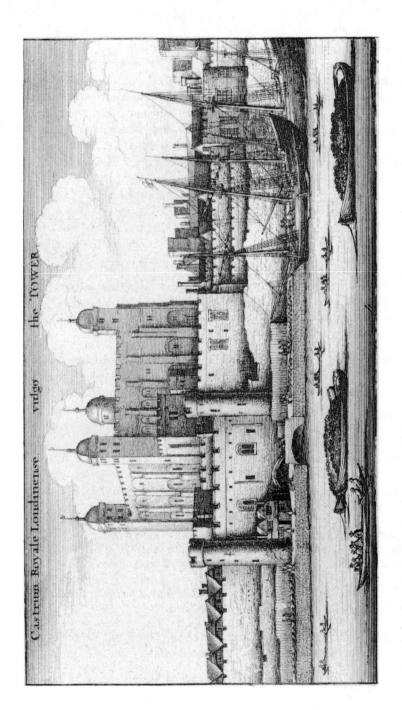

Castrum Royale Londinense   vulgo   the TOWER

Opposite page: The Battle of Lowestoft. Engraving by an unknown artist (*c.* 1665)
(By permission of the Rijksmuseum, Amsterdam)

This page: The Tower of London as viewed from the River Thames. Etching by Wenceslaus Hollar (*c.* 1662)
(Courtesy of Dr and Mrs Howard A. Fox)

V

Since there is no effective opposition to Neander and nowhere a rigorous exchange of ideas, it seems pointless – though many have tried – to regard the *Essay* as a philosophical dialogue. Indeed, every attempt to classify Dryden's dialogue in such terms ends in failure. The *Essay* has not convincingly been shown to resemble any of the dialogues of Plato or Cicero. To argue, as does one modern editor, that the *Essay,* while greatly indebted to the dialogues of no single author, bears minor resemblances to those of a great many, is to beg the whole question of form.[47] But the *Essay,* when properly understood, is not a philosophical dialogue at all: it resembles far too many variants of the form, and it resembles them only tangentially. To define and classify it, and to do so with any degree of exactness, we must look elsewhere: we must look in a new direction entirely.

A hint of where we are to look is provided by the *Essay* itself. At the end of his speech, as he excuses himself from talking further, Eugenius alludes to himself and Crites as comic actors:

> I will commit this cause to my friend's management; his opinion of our Plays is the same with mine: and besides, there is no reason, that *Crites* and I, who have now left the Stage, should re-enter so suddenly upon it; which is against the Laws of Comedie.[48]

Eugenius's allusion to the drama is more than the throwaway line of a witty man: his remark actually offers a clue to the form of the *Essay.* As the reference to strict 'Laws' clearly suggests, Dryden's work is a kind of French play, albeit one seen not in the glowing terms of Lisideius but through the jaundiced eye of Neander.

Lisideius, it should be remembered, celebrates French drama for restricting external action in order to dwell on the minds of the characters. Action in French plays is psychological. The aim is to 'represent the passions'; the method is the long, revelatory speech.[49] Neander too sees the long speech as the salient characteristic of French plays. But he denies that it has a psychological dimension. 'I confess', he declares,

> their verses are to me the coldest I have ever read: Neither indeed is it possible for them, in the way they take, so to express passion, as that the effects of it should appear in the concernment of an Audience: their Speeches being so many declamations, which tire us with the length ... Look upon the *Cinna* and the *Pompey,* they are not so properly to be called Playes, as long discourses of reason of State ...[50]

French plays, according to Neander, are not really plays at all. He calls them 'discourses'. But in the dedication Dryden refers to the *Essay* itself as a 'discourse'; and in the 'Defence of *An Essay of Dramatick Poesie*', published several months later, he is to refer to the *Essay* as 'a little discourse in dialogue'.[51] Without doing violence to Neander's meaning, cannot we therefore substitute the term 'dialogues' for his 'discourses'? It is that very word 'dialogues' that Thomas Sprat uses in describing French plays, in a passage alluded to in the *Essay:*

> The *French* for the most part take only One or Two Great Men, and
> chiefly insist on some one Remarkable Accident of their Story; to this End
> they admit no more Persons than will [barely] serve to adorn that: And
> they manage all in Rime, with long Speeches, almost in the Way of
> Dialogues ...[52]

The *Essay* is written in the form not of a philosophical dialogue but of a French
play. It is an imitation (or near parody) of what, according to Neander, makes up
the distinctive character and failing of the contemporary French theatre: 'long
discourses' without 'too much of the action' or 'variety of Plot', '[lengthy]
Speeches ... [and] declamations' without 'beautifull accidents', 'maturity of design',
or 'a gust of passion'.

We can establish the connection between Dryden's work and French drama by
analysing the *Essay* 'according to the rules which the *French* observe'. Like an
accomplished French dramatist, Dryden scrupulously follows the unities of action,
place and time: the *Essay* treats one subject, literature, and but one aspect of that
subject, namely the drama; the setting is a boat and two proximate landing points;
the time represented is exactly equal to the time in which the *Essay* can be read.
As the French, unlike the English, concentrate upon the workings of the mind and
'dwell on a subject', so too does Dryden: his characters do not enact 'quick turns
and counterturns of Plot'; they deliver 'declamations'. '[C]ombats & other objects
of horrour' are kept hidden from our view and occur only in the offstage battle,
which we learn about through 'Relations'. Never are we asked to witness anything
that might shock us. On the contrary, 'like Swallows in a Chimney', we find our
senses strangely denied. Afloat upon an empty stretch of water, and 'disingag'd'
from the noisy battle at sea, the ensuing English victory and the busy London
scene, we are encased in the minds of the characters. Not until the disputants land
at '*Somerset*-Stairs' and then encounter 'people ... merrily dancing', do we realize
how much of human life we have missed. The *Essay* carries distaste for dramatic
representation as far as it can go. Dryden's dialogue is a French play reduced to
absurdity. It is a closet drama; it is never to be performed.

Once the *Essay* is seen in these terms, we can understand better why Neander
dominates the work so completely. Partly, of course, Dryden wants to emphasize
Neander's points of view. But the extraordinary length of Neander's speeches can
be fully explained only on satiric grounds. In the course of his argument, Lisideius
mentions that the French make one character the *primus inter pares* and employ
all others to set him off. Lisideius denies that this 'exalting of one character' creates
an imbalance in a play.[53] But Dryden disagrees. Neander's tendency to lose himself in dramatic monologue is his dismissive commentary on the practice.[54]

But if Dryden reduces the typical French drama to an essay, or mere dialogue,
he simultaneously elevates his essay to an engaging play. And while enjoying this
double coup, he demonstrates further his skill as dialectician and critic, and incidentally as a playwright even in the new classical manner. The *Essay of Dramatick*

Poesie, by its very form, reveals the achievement and limitations of French drama. We are shown that that drama is not so much an imitation of an action as a vehicle for declamation and sermon. It analyses life; it does not represent it. For real drama we must look to England; and for the best of English drama, we can only conclude, we must turn to Dryden.

The drama and more generally the poetry that Neander advocates, Dryden will never write. In allowing his spokesman to give only a slight emphasis to the lively, Dryden was forgetting his own nature: his strong preference for the lively over the just, for pleasure over instruction and for language over both character and plot and almost everything else. That preference will be made apparent in his next two critical works: his detailed analysis of the tragi-comedy *Secret Love* and of the historical poem *Annus Mirabilis*, which perhaps more than any of his other works was to encourage his first preoccupation with the marvellous and the wonderful in narrative poetry and eventually in the drama as well.

VI

We have next to consider Dryden's analyses of *Annus Mirabilis* and *Secret Love*, analyses that are linked inextricably to *An Essay of Dramatick Poesie;* but a word more must first be said about the role or persona that he adopts in the dedication of the *Essay* and that which he adopts in the *Essay* itself.

In the dedication Dryden adopts unmistakably a single role or persona: that of a courtier-poet. In the Essay, strictly speaking, he adopts a double role or persona: that of a courtier-poet who is the narrator and that of the courtier-poet Neander, who is the narrator's *alter ego* and spokesman. With regard to the *Essay*, however, the term 'persona' seems best reserved for Neander alone. As courtier-poet, the narrator is present in the *Essay* far less as a voice (he speaks but rarely) than as a manipulator of character, dialogue and scene. Of the John Dryden who, as author, stands above and beyond both the dedication and the *Essay* it seems best to say nothing: the two works speak for him, and they leave nothing to add.[55]

In the dedication to Lord Buckhurst, a Court wit, Dryden's persona is that of an accomplished courtier-poet, one who is himself a wit and the cause of wit in others. He plays the role with ease, humour and grace. And he does so with great flourish, as he compares himself first to one of 'the Muses', then to '*Homer*', next to someone inferior to 'better Wits', then to 'a Schollar in a Fencing-School', next to a soldier 'stand[ing] desperately to [his] Armes', then to one of those 'Gentlemen' who argue, but do so 'with candour and civility', and finally to '[e]ven *Tully*', who 'had a controversie with his dear *Atticus*'.

Dryden's persona in the *Essay* is quite different. As Neander, he is still the courtier-poet. But since (as Neander) he is engaged in a debate with actual aristocrats, though under 'borrowed names', he restrains himself for the occasion: he forgoes wit and witticism altogether. As Neander, moreover, he is very much concerned with the first principles of his literary career and, among other things, with his founding of an English school of literary criticism. Under such circumstances playfulness of any kind would be self-defeating.

It may perhaps be argued not only that, as narrator of 'a wide dispute', Dryden parodies contemporary French drama but that, in the very act of doing so (in the very act of having Neander embody unknowingly what is being parodied) he ultimately makes Neander (his persona) an object of ridicule. Neander is exceptionally talkative, even long-winded. At the end of his 'Discourse', which he has been 'pursuing ... so eagerly', he takes no 'notice' of what is going on around him. He fails to 'notice that the Barge [on which he and his friends have spent a 'memorable day'] ... st[ands] still, and that they [are] at the foot of *Somerset*-Stairs, where they ... appointed it to land'. He fails to 'notice' anything at all until '*Eugenius* ... call[s] him twice or thrice'.[56] But no ridicule need be intended: as Dryden's persona, Neander is genuinely involved in his 'Discourse'. If there is ridicule, it is directed against the new French drama, a drama which relies presumably on little action and long speeches. Where the ridicule is perhaps directed against Neander, it is quite innocent. It is not to be taken seriously. It is the mock humility of Dryden as narrator: it is the mock humility of a courtier-poet who has created the world of the *Essay* and who is committed absolutely, for the time being, to Neander's point of view.

In the *Essay* Dryden is very much the courtier-poet, indeed more so than elsewhere in the early criticism. As narrator, he addresses, writes about and celebrates the aristocracy, members of which – the poet-courtiers – he tends to idealize. He does so the more easily since, by virtue of the form he uses – that of a debate – he allows actual aristocrats, all men of letters, to speak for themselves: Sir Robert Howard as Crites, Charles Lord Buckhurst as Eugenius, Sir Charles Sedley as Lisideius. As Neander, the fourth member of 'the company', Dryden of course wins every argument. Despite any appearance to the contrary, he completely vindicates the English stage, but with the utmost tact and restraint. As narrator, he delineates his 'Adversaries' with bold and clear strokes. But since '[the] three ... [are] persons whom their witt and Quality have made known to all the Town', he once again avoids the playfulness characteristic of his early manner; and he does so not only in Neander's 'Discourse' but, as narrator, in his own 'ill ... relation' as well. As his persona, moreover, Neander claims no victory for himself, and Dryden (as narrator) grants none: each behaves as if the entire debate has ended in a draw. In the world of the *Essay* the ruse works: no one is offended; but it has since worked unusually well outside the world of the *Essay*. Even the best of critics have been taken in by it. According to Samuel Johnson, 'It will not be easy to find in all the opulence of our language a treatise so artfully variegated with successive representations of opposite probabilities ...'[57]

We may now turn to Dryden's analyses of the historical poem *Annus Mirabilis* and the tragi-comedy *Secret Love*.

CHAPTER FOUR

The new imbalance
(1667–1668)

I

In *An Essay of Dramatick Poesie* Neander and his friends all agree that what in general they say about a good play is equally true about the whole of literature, whatever the genre: every poem, if successful, is a just and lively imitation of nature, and it gives both pleasure and instruction. Neander interprets the general principle in his own way; but he could not, on the whole, agree with it more; and he goes even so far as to suggest that in 'the representation of Nature' there can be no significant difference between the two most important genres, the epic and the drama: absurdities in the drama are not less so when repeated in the epic poem.[1] Once he had completed the *Essay,* however, Dryden felt himself impelled increasingly towards 'the lively imitation of Nature', 'the Soul of Poesie', 'quick turns and graces', 'Nature wrought up to an higher pitch', 'the imagination of the Poet', the 'beautiful ... and the hand of Art', 'the liberty of Fancy' and far more than Neander would ever allow.

In search of authority to justify what in any event he now preferred or believed, Dryden read (or re-read) not his favourite playwrights but the great epic poets of antiquity, poets of the imagination and fancy: Homer and Virgil, Ovid and Statius. He turned again to Aristotle, who sanctions for the epic – and perhaps for the drama – 'probable impossibilities' and who reminded him that '[t]he irrational, on which the wonderful depends for its chief effects, has wider scope in Epic poetry, because there the person acting is not seen'. Aristotle reminded him of what even Neander seems to forget or ignore: in both the epic and the drama 'the wonderful is pleasing', and 'absurdity is veiled by the poetic charm with which the poet invests it'. Aristotle also reminded him that 'That diction ... is lofty and raised above the commonplace which employs unusual words', and 'to have a command of metaphor ... is the mark of genius', although among 'various kinds' of style that of the epic is 'the stateliest and the most massive; and hence it most readily admits rare words and metaphors, which is another point in which the narrative form of imitation stands alone'.[2]

At the same time, he had to confront a problem about which, as the years passed, he was to complain. Hostile readers too frequently turned his criticism against him;[3] but he had eventually to admit that the responsibility was entirely his own. He had provided them with the only standards of excellence which they had: they had no other.[4] In addition, from the very outset he complained that, unable to grasp or cope with his subtleties, they misunderstood not only his criticism but also his poems and plays, on which it was based.[5] Both complaints are no less valid in our time than they were in his. We too may demonstrate that, for example, *Annus Mirabilis* does not live up to all the standards which Dryden set for 'An Historical Poem'; but we should also ask whether he merely set impossible standards for himself and whether or not, without his standards before us, we might recognize where he in fact nodded and failed. The preface and the first prologue to *Secret Love* damn the play in the most outrageous terms; but we should also ask whether Dryden would have us take the damnation seriously and whether or not, behind and beyond all the playfulness of a courtly game, he is in fact celebrating the play and demanding that his achievement be recognized and not left in doubt.

II

Dryden published *Annus Mirabilis* (1667) with a dedication to the city of London, 'To the Metropolis of Great Britain', and with a relatively long preface, 'An account of the ensuing Poem', in the form of 'a Letter to the Honourable, Sir Robert Howard', an old friend and now one of his patrons. He published *Secret Love* (1668) with a preface and two prologues; the volume also included an epilogue, which is quite amusing, but which has little if any relevance to his play or his critical theory.[6] In the critical comments on both works he once again assumes the courtly manner: he speaks with exaggerated courtesy and politeness; he pays more than adequate tribute to the King; and he argues that, in judging excellence in literature, the peers of the realm have no equal. But with a confidence no doubt born of recent achievements he gives his mask of the courtier-poet several new contours.

Just as the Castiglione courtier, or his Restoration counterpart, would and must forsake his amusements in order to serve the public good, so Dryden, in the statements attached to *Annus Mirabilis,* occasionally forsakes reticence and pleasantry for his own ends. He rises now and again to high argument, even solemnity, as he defends his political and religious opinions and inevitably his art, though never without 'candour and civility'. As he says, 'I detest arrogance, but there is some difference betwixt that and a just defence'.[7] And in his introductory remarks on *Secret Love* he so envelops himself, though playfully, with paradox and irony that we wonder whether he is in fact saying what he seems to be saying. Is the play a remarkable imitation of Corneille and French classicism or is it something very different? Is it the worst play that has ever been written or is it the major accomplishment of a new playwright and a new age?

In his critical observations on both the poem and the play he draws continually on Neander's manifesto. He is, in each instance, very much concerned with the counterpoint of imagination and judgment, of pleasure and instruction, of the lively and the just; and in his analyses of *Secret Love* he comments specifically on the fusion of the just and the lively in his major and minor plots, one serious and centred in 'rage and tenderness', the other comic and centred in 'impudence and raillery'.[8] But there is a shift in his perspective and emphasis; and because of that shift he approaches both works, and his critical theories, not only with a new sense of the pleasurable in art and perhaps the wonderful and not only (like Pope after him) with a new understanding that there are graces beyond the touch of rules. He also explains that the intelligent critic excuses minor faults in works of imaginative power; he justifies variety at the expense of order; he would elevate poetry above the commonplace and the ordinary. In the '[A]ccount' of *Annus Mirabilis* he gives to language and self-expression – to poetic language as opposed to historic fact – an importance that in his criticism so far it has never had. In his comments on *Secret Love* he declares himself – despite all the poses of mock humility – not only the leading playwright of the age and the best critic. He is now the only reliable critic of his works, and he is very much more: he is the only reliable critic of the poems and plays of his contemporaries. And apart from all of his other roles, he is the only reliable critic of critics.

III

Dryden toys with critical ideas throughout his early dramatic criticism, partly to display his powers but partly to suggest, in the best courtly mode, that he regards the drama as something unworthy of genuine concern. The example he follows appears to be that of King Charles, who (we are reminded) treats the drama as a small diversion from 'the hours which he is daily giving to the peace and settlement of his people'.[9] Kings, however, must often be serious, as must poets who take up matters of importance to kings. Hence, it is not surprising that, in the dedication and preface to *Annus Mirabilis,* Dryden temporarily lays aside his accustomed levity.

Annus Mirabilis, a long narrative poem, is a work of sacred history. It purports to explain the relationship between God's redemptive plan and those momentous events of 1666, the Second Dutch War and the Fire of London.[10] There was a widespread belief that the war and the fire constituted God's judgment against England for the sin of restoring the monarchy. Dryden's aim was to allay the anti-monarchal sentiment implicit in this view by pre-empting the theological argument and pressing it into the service of the royalist cause. As Michael McKeon points out, *Annus Mirabilis* is 'an ideological attack on sedition whose rhetorical strategy requires a complete and unquestioning acceptance of eschatological prophecy'.[11] The poem argues that the nation's difficulties are not manifestations of divine wrath but trials that God has designed as a prelude to national renewal and prosperity. However, in thus isolating religious and political themes, we must remember that *Annus Mirabilis* is not a tract but a work of art; and as Dryden so often tells us throughout his criticism, the immediate purpose of all great literature is not to teach but to please. *Annus Mirabilis* is avowedly an imitation of Virgil. But in explaining what he had in mind when he wrote the poem, and in justifying himself, Dryden suggests that pleasure is far more important to him than instruction; and he demonstrates a concern not so much with Virgil's subject and purpose, or with his design and theme, as with his language and style. He is concerned far more with the splendours of rhetoric, Virgilian though they may be, than with the wonders of God's redemptive plan.

As we read *Annus Mirabilis,* we may ask ourselves whether it ever occurred to Dryden, before he presented his interpretation of events to the public, that his poem might not enjoy an easy and wide acceptance. By 1667 he was known among his contemporaries as, in many ways, one of the 'wits of the town'.[12] Among the artisans and merchants of London, because of his having ridiculed them and their Puritanism in *Astrea Redux* as far back as 1660, and again in the first production of *The Wild Gallant* in 1663, he was known as a poet and playwright who did not and could not take them very seriously. How could he, we may ask ourselves, hope to address the people of London and be heard? How could he possibly get respectable men of commerce and dissent – anywhere in the city of London – to listen to him and to accept his judgments?

Whether such matters had occurred to him before he wrote the poem, we can have no way of knowing. It is not likely that they ever did. But if they had occurred to him, undoubtedly, he would have treated his past as he in fact did. He would have treated it with characteristic grace and ease. He would have treated it, unobtrusively, as if it had never been and as if, from the very beginning, he and his London audience had enjoyed a splendid understanding and rapport.[13]

In his dedication, 'To the Metropolis of Great Britain', Dryden presents himself as a man who has always been committed to high spiritual values. He conceives of life not as an elegant game, but as an agon, the participants in which can win the favour of God and the substantial emoluments that God can bestow. Elsewhere he may attack London citizens for their materialism and hypocrisy, but no slight is intended here. The inhabitants of London, with their worldly religion, are now conceived of as 'a great emblem of the suffering Deity'. No city in history, he tells us, has earned a reputation for virtue at so great a cost:

> As perhaps I am the first who ever presented a work of this nature to the Metropolis of any Nation, so is it likewise consonant to Justice, that he who was to give the first Example of such a Dedication should begin it with that City, which has set a pattern to all others of true Loyalty, invincible Courage and unshaken Constancy ... To submit your selves with that humility to the Judgments of Heaven, and at the same time to raise your selves with that vigour above all humane Enemies; to be combated at once from above and from below, to be struck down and to triumph; I know not whether such trials have been ever parallel'd in any Nation, the resolution and successes of them never can be.[14]

The moral fervour of the dedication is maintained in the '[A]ccount'; but here Dryden turns his attention more directly upon himself and his work.

In the '[A]ccount' Dryden informs his readers that the writing of *Annus Mirabilis* was a kind of public service. Some men aid their country with their swords; others, with their pens. Both deserve praise.[15] Public service provides its own rewards. His reward is that he was able to write a poem above his 'ordinary level'. In treating other subjects he had earlier been hampered by the necessity of elevating his thoughts entirely through his own exertions. But the topic of the war was, in itself, marvellously buoyant. In 'celebrating the praises of military men', the equal of epic heroes, he wrote 'much better' than he had ever written before:

> I have been forc'd to help out other Arguments, but this has been bountiful to me; they have been low and barren of praise, and I have exalted them, and made them fruitful: but here – *Omnia sponte suâ reddit justissima tellus* [The most righteous earth returns all of its own free will].[16]

In any event, Dryden is now a changed man. And his transformation helps to justify him in assuming the role of spokesman to the nation: he is properly qualified to write about national events and Divine Providence. There remains, however, another possible objection to his work, the belief that no poem can be an adequate source of either truth or instruction.

*

Dryden takes up, and considers at some length, an issue of importance through-out the century not only to poets and critics but to scientists and Puritans alike: the issue of poetic truth. Scientists and Puritans disagreed on just about everything; but there was one matter on which they were, more or less, odd bedfellows: they were convinced that, on the whole, poets tended to be liars. According to the scientist, poets give pleasure, but they do not advance knowledge: through their inventions they distort language and, however delightfully, the laws of Nature. The charge was stated most forcefully early in the century by Sir Francis Bacon. During the Restoration the charge was repeated by Bacon's latter-day descendants, members of the Royal Society, of whom Thomas Sprat was perhaps the most out-spoken. According to Bacon, poetry may 'give some shadow of satisfaction to the mind of man in those points wherein the nature of things doth deny it'; but at its best it is only '*feigned history*' and is therefore never to be accepted as truth.[17] According to Sprat, whatever the pleasure it may in fact give, poetry, with its '*Tropes* and *Figures*', is too frequently 'in open defiance against *Reason*'; and he therefore wonders, if only for a moment, whether it 'ought to be banished out of all *civil societies*'.[18]

Similar charges were made by the Puritans, though with a slight shift in empha-sis. According to the Puritan, not only do poets violate the rules of language and the laws of Nature; they also tend, unfortunately, to violate God's word and His work. But they are not then to be sent, without exception, into exile or be forced into silence. They may be permitted to remain in a Christian society; and they may be allowed (even encouraged) to write, but only if they are faithful to both Holy Writ and human experience and, in their very language, reveal all Heavenly Glory. Like the scientist, the Puritan thus took on the mantle of literary critic. As literary critic, he too had first principles; and he too was outspoken. But nowhere are those principles stated with greater directness and fervour than in a few lines of verse (a mere half-dozen) in the preamble to John Bunyan's *Pilgrim's Progress* (1678). Bunyan, a 'mechanick preacher', is concerned not so much with literature or poetry in general as with the matter and the manner of his own work; nevertheless, generalization is clearly intended:

> My dark and cloudy words they do but hold
> The Truth, as Cabinets inclose the Gold.
> The Prophets used much by Metaphors
> To set forth Truth; Yea, who so considers
> Christ, his Apostles too, shall plainly see,
> That Truths to this day in such Mantles be.[19]

Poets may write whenever they like. They may write whatever they like, however they like; and they may do so in any language or style they choose, whether plain or metaphorical or perhaps both.[20] But they must always 'assert Eternal Providence' and 'justify the ways of God to men'.

The scepticism with which scientist and Puritan, each in his own way, regarded poetry was wholly absent in Dryden. In his judgment of poetry, he was, as Louis I. Bredvold observed long ago, 'still, in some respects, in the afterglow of the Renaissance'.[21] He believed that the poet was the individual most able to distinguish truth from error and to guide the moral judgment of a nation. Not only did the poet possess a powerful imagination and rhetorical skill, he was also endowed with a ripe judgment and a strong memory. 'A man', Dryden declared,

> should be learn'd in severall Sciences, and should have a reasonable *Philosophicall*, and in some measure a *Mathematicall head;* to be a compleat and excellent Poet: And besides this should have experience in all sorts of humours and manners of men: should be throughly skil'd in conversation, and should have a great Knowledge of mankind in generall.[22]

If a poet can create a faerie kingdom and people it with monsters, he can no less give a clear and exact picture of national events. That a careful and exact narration of the war and the fire is contained in *Annus Mirabilis,* it is the purpose of the '[A]ccount' to demonstrate to both scientist and Puritan. And it does so, more or less, through a single argument.

The '[A]ccount' launches into this task almost at once. After some preliminary compliments to Sir Robert Howard, Dryden explains the subject of his poem. *Annus Mirabilis* does not contain a mere 'story', a profitless fiction. Rather, it relates the history of the fire and the war that have just befallen England:

> For I have chosen the most heroick Subject which any Poet could desire: I have taken upon me to describe the motives, the beginning, progress and successes of a most just and necessary War; in it, the care, management and prudence of our King; the conduct and valour of a Royal Admiral, and of two incomparable Generals; the invincible courage of our Captains and Seamen, and three glorious Victories, the result of all. After this I have, in the Fire, the most deplorable, but withall the greatest Argument that can be imagin'd …[23]

Dryden's overview recalls the descriptive summaries that were commonly used in the seventeenth century on the title pages of political and historical works, and thereby further encourages the reader to think of *Annus Mirabilis* in historical terms.[24] But if Dryden places his poem in the world of fact, he also takes pains to distinguish it simultaneously from the world of fiction. *Annus Mirabilis* is a true history, not a feigned one. No fiction is present because none is required. Life itself furnished 'the greatest Argument that can be imagin'd'. The events that he narrates are inherently imbued with that rareness and variety which poets, not blessed with such inspiring matter, have had to invent for themselves.

To represent historical facts with exactness, he tells us that he has infused into his poem a substratum of denotative language, including a sampling of nautical terms. If we would get close to things, he says, we must employ the very technical words designed to represent them. In thus affirming the importance of 'terms of Arts', he appears to reflect the position of the Royal Society, which urged writers in all 'parts of Learning', as well as in natural philosophy, to abandon 'the colours of Rhetorick' and 'the devices of Fancy' and to adopt the language of 'Artizans, Countrymen, and Merchants'.[25] His authority, however, is not the Royal Society. He relies instead, as he says, on classical literature: (for his inspiration and critical theory) on Horace's *Art of Poetry* and (for his model and practice) on 'Lucan in the … *Pharsalia*'. And that authority is more than fifteen hundred years old.[26]

It is politic of Dryden not to mention the Royal Society, since he honours their rules of correct usage more in the breach than in the observance. Despite his enthusiasm for technical terms, his use of them is slight. In *Annus Mirabilis* they are found only in a few stanzas in the battle scenes; throughout the rest of the poem, including those portions in which he dwells on historical fact, he employs those very poetic devices – simile, metaphor and allusion – which the Society deplored. *Annus Mirabilis,* in the main, glows with the colours of rhetoric. And because in its language it is more lush than severe, it imposes on Dryden, throughout the '[A]ccount', a double obligation. To the scientist he must prove that he has not 'overwhelm'd' his subject with '*Tropes* and *Figures*'. To the Puritan, he must prove by the same argument that his '*Tropes* and *Figures*' are not a display of vanity but a source of truth. But he must first deal with an objection from another quarter: he must prove to the literary critic that a historical poem is not a contradiction in terms.

*

Unlike the Puritan or scientist, the literary critics of the age did not want historical accuracy in poetry. Far from condemning poetic fictions, they demanded them. They held that only by creating a fictional world or by heightening and improving nature did a writer earn the title of poet. Thus, Sir William Davenant demotes Lucan to the position of a mere historian, since he chose 'to write the greatest actions that ever were allowed to be true' and did not 'mend the intrigues of Fortune by more delightful conveiances of probable fictions'. Davenant would not have a poet 'fetter his feet in the shackles of an Historian', an opinion that Thomas

Hobbes endorses in an even more extreme form.[27] According to Hobbes, adherence to history or brute fact is not the ruin but the death of poetry. By his definition, poetry demands an invented story, so that historical poetry, as well as philosophical or scientific poetry, cannot exist. They err, writes Hobbes, who

> reckon *Empedocles* and *Lucretius* (natural Philosophers) for Poets, and the moral precepts of *Phocylides, Theognis,* and the Quatraines of *Pybrach* and the History of *Lucan,* and others of that kind amongst Poems, bestowing on such Writers for honor the name of Poets rather then of Historians or Philosophers. But the subject of a Poem is the manners of men, not natural causes; manners presented, not dictated; and manners feigned, as the name of Poesy imports, not found in men.[28]

As the leading critics of the early Restoration, Davenant and Hobbes had to be answered, if Dryden, as author of *Annus Mirabilis,* was to enjoy the title both of public spokesman and poet.

Dryden's refutation is spare and economical, merely making a distinction between ends and means. Like his opponents, Dryden affirms that poetry must delight and instruct by creating a new vision of human life. He denies, however, that fiction is the only vehicle by which this vision can be achieved. It can, he believes, be achieved also by language. Through the artful choice of word and phrase, of trope and all manner of rhetorical device, the poet achieves the ends of fiction without departing from the world of fact. He transforms the commonplace: he imbues the stubborn facts of human experience with beauty and wonder. In presenting this theory, Dryden is not systematic at all; and some details are implied rather than stated. Nevertheless, the main outlines of his thought are clear.

Unlike Hobbes, Dryden does not regard fiction as the essence of poetry. Fiction is not an invariable concomitant of poems. It may be present or absent. And its presence is merely one of the differentiae by which we distinguish among genres. Thus, a fictional narrative may be an epic; but a true history cannot be. For that reason, because they are 'ti'd too severely to the Laws of History', as well as because their actions are 'broken', 'not properly one', Dryden labels his own work and that of Lucan not epics but historical poems.[29]

Poetry, Dryden tells us, differs from all other forms of discourse in a number of ways. But contrary to the general opinion, he goes on to explain, it differs not only through its invention (or what 'it designs to represent') and its disposition (or its arrangement of details) but also through the dominant qualities of its language. And to lend authority to so bold and original a pronouncement, he assumes throughout the '[A]ccount' the role of both master rhetorician and self-declared poet-philosopher. That he employs his philosophical terms with occasional vagueness need not trouble us; nor need we be troubled by the fact that here and there his usage differs, however slightly, from usage elsewhere in his criticism: the odd distinction he occasionally now makes between imagination and fancy; and the more odd, and perplexing, connections he occasionally makes between wit and imagination (or fancy) or between fancy and judgment. The gist of his meaning is perfectly clear:

> The composition of all Poems is or ought to be of wit, and wit in the poet ... is no other then the faculty of imagination in the writer, which, like a nimble Spaniel, beats over and ranges through the field of Memory, till it springs the Quarry it hunted after; or, without metaphor, which searches over all the memory for the species or Idea's of those things which it designs to represent ... So then, the first happiness of the Poet's imagination is properly Invention, or finding of the thought; the second is Fancy, or the variation, deriving or moulding of that thought, as the judgment represents it proper to the subject; the third is Elocution, or the Art of clothing and adorning that thought so found and varied, in apt, significant and sounding words: the quickness of the Imagination is seen in the Invention, the fertility in the Fancy, and the accuracy in the Expression.[30]

As the language of poetry differs radically from all other forms of discourse, so there is a language or style appropriate to every genre; and what is fitting, for example, in the epigram or the moral epistle would therefore not be fitting in an epic or historical poem. The 'Heroick or Historical Poem' is not to be characterized by surprising turns of argument or by 'grave sentence[s]'; nor is it to be filled needlessly with 'Epigram', 'Antithesis', and '*Paranomasia*' (or pun). The language of the epic is to consist 'chiefly' in the 'delightful imaging of persons, actions, passions, or things', 'some lively and apt description', and 'such colours of speech, that [set] before your eyes the absent object, as perfectly and more delightfully then nature'.[31] History 'in Verse' is transmuted into historical poetry when, 'chiefly' through a language which is 'lively and apt', the poet transmutes what he 'designs to represent', or things as indeed they are, into a powerful and immediate experience.[32] And this very transformation, Dryden insists, is found in *Annus Mirabilis*.

*

Throughout the '[A]ccount' Dryden's first concern, very clearly, is with the language appropriate to an epic or historical poem. He is also concerned, though briefly, with the language appropriate to a number of other genres, and especially the drama, including (it seems) all of its principal sub-types (comedy, tragi-comedy, tragedy), but not the heroic play. The language of the heroic play is a world apart, and he will not be able to define it for another few years. In any event, he would have us understand that in every genre there must be a balance of the language of statement (or the just) and the language of transport (or the lively); and that the balance must necessarily shift and change from one genre to another. And to illustrate his point, he emphasizes in particular the significant differences between the kind of language that is permissible and hence required in the drama and the language that is required and hence permissible in the historical poem or epic. In drama, for instance, 'where all that is said is to be suppos'd the effect of sudden thought', the poet must in all matters restrain himself. He must not engage in 'a too curious election of words, too frequent allusions, or use of Tropes, or, in fine, any thing that showes remoteness of thought, or labour in the Writer'. But in a narrative poem like *Annus Mirabilis*, since he addresses us directly, the poet 'gains more liberty ... to express his thoughts with all the graces of elocution, to write more figuratively, and to confess, as well the labour as the force of his imagination'.[33]

Dryden's model for this elaborate style, as he goes on to explain, is Virgil. So potent is the language of the Roman poet that his choice of subject is unimportant. Virgil is equally stirring whether he recounts events great or small, invented or merely observed. He illustrates in his best work a doctrine to which Dryden became increasingly committed, that in the masterpieces of literature a poet interweaves an objective imitation of the external world with varieties of self-expression:

> But when Action or Persons are to be describ'd, when any such Image is to be set before us, how bold, how masterly are the strokes of *Virgil!* we see the objects he represents us with in their native figures, in their proper motions; but we so see them, as our own eyes could never have beheld them so beautiful in themselves. We see the Soul of the Poet, like that universal one of which he speaks, informing and moving through all his Pictures ...
> See his Tempest, his Funeral Sports, his Combat of *Turnus* and *Æneas,* and in his *Georgicks,* which I esteem the Divinest part of all his writings, the Plague, the Country, the Battel of Bulls, the labour of the Bees, and those many other excellent Images of Nature, most of which are neither great in themselves, nor have any natural ornament to bear them up: but the words wherewith he describes them are so excellent, that it might be well appli'd to him which was said by *Ovid, Materiam superabat opus* [The workmanship surpassed the material]: the very sound of his words has often somewhat that is connatural to the subject, and while we read him, we sit, as in a Play, beholding the Scenes of what he represents.[34]

Virgil's descriptions consistently disclose within themselves a kind of movement more beguiling than any formal action on which he may dwell. His descriptions transport us from the mere sight of things to the glorious visions of art. In Virgil's poetry one first sees the phenomenal world as in fact it really is; yet one is also inspired to see it as being more beautiful than one ever thought possible. Virgil's language gives us a new but undistorted vision of nature and is a form of creation in itself. When he wrote poetry Virgil required no fictions: he is a poet of fact. He may not be a historical poet; but his example demonstrates that poetry and history are not incompatible, that through a language of evocation verifiable fact – whether history or not – may be transformed into poetry.

In suggesting that a composition may be a poem by virtue of its verbal artifice, Dryden harks back to the writing of such Renaissance theorists as Sperone Speroni, who tended to equate poetry with rhetoric.[35] But Dryden's statements also look forward, surprisingly enough, to Wordsworth. I do not mean the Wordsworth of the 'Preface to *Lyrical Ballads*', who condemned poetic speech and demanded a language of men speaking to men. I mean the youthful Wordsworth, whose delights in feats of rhetoric the mature Wordsworth remembered:

> Visionary power
> Attends the motions of the viewless winds,
> Embodied in the mystery of words:
> There, darkness makes abode, and all the host
> Of shadowy things works endless changes there,
> As in a mansion like their proper home.
> Even forms and substances are circumfused
> By that transparent veil with light divine,
> And, through the turnings intricate of verse,
> Present themselves as objects recognized,
> In flashes, and with glory not their own.[36]

Here Wordsworth defines, in so far as definition is possible, the effect that a certain kind of poetry once had upon him. Dryden's statements about Virgil, however, are far less personal and much more immediate. Through Virgil, he not only attempts to prove that historical poetry can be written but also tries to establish the specific model by which his historical poem should be judged.

*

When speaking about Virgil, Dryden quite openly declares both his intentions in *Annus Mirabilis* and his methods:

> I must own the vanity to tell you ... that he has been my Master in this Poem: I have followed him every where, I know not with what success, but I am sure with diligence enough: my Images are many of them copied from him, and the rest are imitations of him. My expressions also are as near as the Idioms of the two Languages would admit of in translation.[37]

Given his professed dependence upon Virgil, it is well to consider how intelligently he understood his master and how closely he followed him.

In his interpretation of Virgil, Dryden enjoys an unqualified success. His criticism is far more perceptive than the appreciations by such earlier writers as Spenser, Peacham or Davenant; and he may be said to establish English criticism of Virgil on a sound foundation.[38] Even the 'discovery' by Brooks Otis that Virgil invented a subjective form of narration to replace the objective mode of Homer turns out not to be so very new.[39] It but substantiates Dryden's assertion that Virgil 'relates all things from himself', infusing his own sensibility and values into the objects that he describes.

Dryden understood Virgil remarkably well; but his understanding does not inform his poem as fully as he claims or hopes. The criteria which he sets down for the historical poem may be arbitrary; and it may be that, according to criteria other than his own, the poem is a resounding success. But when measured or judged against the *Aeneid*, or his rule that in the historical poem metaphysical tropes are not entirely appropriate, *Annus Mirabilis* is not the major achievement he would have liked it to be. It does not measure up to those standards on which, through its many failings and its many excellences, it sheds a good deal of light. No less relevant and striking is the fact that, like Samuel Johnson, many who have praised the poem or condemned it have done so, inevitably and tacitly, on the same principles that, throughout the '[A]ccount', Dryden himself defends. When all is said and done, *Annus Mirabilis* is not entirely Virgilian because ultimately Dryden is not Virgil.

It may be argued that particular lines are memorable, though not the poem as a whole. As D. W. Jefferson has said, 'It is the minute parts of the work – the individual strokes of wit and fancy, and the descriptive touches ... – that exercise our attention at the expense of the total design'.[40] Dryden's 'strokes of wit and fancy', however, have nothing in common with anything in Virgil. Virgil's vivid and heightened descriptions are another matter. They may be Dryden's professed model and standard; but they are a model and standard to which he does not always conform. In the end, Dryden would capture the clarity or vividness of Virgil's language; and *Annus Mirabilis* is replete with Virgilian echoes and hence with highly effective descriptions of persons, actions, places and things. The stanzas on the repair of the English ships, for instance, are models of clear and vivid exposition. The fear and despair of the survivors of the Fire of London are finely captured and re-created. He is faultless when he records, however selectively, historical events and, at the same time, heightens them through a bare but emotionally charged language. His problems arise when he attempts to heighten not events but his language and puts on display ingenuity or mere rhetoric.[41]

Dryden's tropes do not give the 'adequate delight' that is promised in the '[A]ccount'. Virgil's figures of speech are always appropriate; Dryden's rarely are. We do not see through the poet's eyes: we see only the poet. His images tend to be far too bold, even far-fetched. Though delightful in themselves, they spirit us away from the historical action into a world of the poet's own making. They distract from the scene rather than illuminate it. Ironically, it is only when he writes plainly that he succeeds in that lucid portrayal of events that his theory of historical poetry demands. Allusions and comparisons, similes and metaphors are not generally a source of strength in the work. His history is poetry, by definition, because of his language; it is good poetry or great when, by his own standards, his language is simple and plain, impassioned and noble.

Whether or not *Annus Mirabilis* is the poem Dryden thought it was, or wanted it to be, is not as immediately relevant as the specific principles which helped to bring it into being – to which it in turn gave birth and, in large measure, justification – and which helped to determine how during the next few years his critical theory was going to develop. Works of literature must be judged by standards or rules of excellence; and the best standards are derived from works that, like the *Aeneid*, have best stood the test of time. Works of literature must be defined with regard to genre; and the genres must be distinguished from one another, as epic is distinguished from tragedy. What a poet says is not quite as important as the manner or the language in which he says it: language must be suited to subject,

First principles

but it is language and not subject that constitutes the art of literature. The ultimate purpose of literature is always moral. The immediate purpose is always to grant pleasure; and it does so through a new and decided imbalance of the lively and the just. Imagination takes a marked precedence over judgment. In its flight, although it never leaves judgment far behind, imagination recreates experience through beautiful and vivid 'Images' and, simultaneously, heightens experience through the wonderful, the marvellous, the improbable.

IV

Dryden's criticism sheds light on the more complex of his works, as it does remarkably well on *Annus Mirabilis*. That it should also provide the criteria by which, as he so often observed, the best of his endeavours were condemned is one of the many ironies in his career. But in the whole of his career no irony is greater than that, when he speaks with irony of himself and his works, the poetry and the plays, he should be construed as declaring settled convictions and absolute truth; and his irony is never greater than when in his 'Prologue to *Secret Love*' he would have us believe that his play observes 'Th' exactest Rules'. The misunderstanding of that prologue has indeed had some odd results. Among other things, it has led to a gross misunderstanding of the play and, unexpectedly, of the preface. Having decided that the prologue means what it appears to mean, generations of scholars and critics have ignored the second prologue and misread the preface, by both of which it is savagely undercut; and they have misunderstood completely the very play to which it is appended. If we would not accuse the criticism of dishonesty or, conversely, search in the play for signs of 'Johnsons humour' and 'Corneilles rhyme', we must enter into the spirit of Dryden's joke.[42]

*

In the first prologue, which W. P. Ker considers an unofficial epilogue to the *Essay of Dramatick Poesie* and takes literally,[43] Dryden stands before his audience, analyses his play in some detail, apologizes for what he insists is a total failure, bows his head in shame and hopes that he can be forgiven. He names the traditions in which he wrote, the rules that he obeyed and the authors whom he followed. And he then confesses that, for all his 'pains and thought', he has produced a dull and lifeless work:

> He who writ this, not without pains and thought
> From French and English Theaters has brought
> Th' exactest Rules by which a Play is wrought:
>
> The Unities of Action, Place, and Time;
> The Scenes unbroken; and a mingled chime
> Of Johnsons humour, with Corneilles rhyme.
>
> But while dead colours he with care did lay,
> He fears his Wit, or Plot he did not weigh
> Which are the living Beauties of a Play.[44]

Next, he compares *Secret Love* to a badly built fortress, the point being that in obedience to the rules of structure it has failed, and failed miserably, though he hopes that he can still be respected as a playwright and be forgiven:

> Plays are like Towns, which howe're fortifi'd
> By Engineers, have still some weaker side
> By the o'reseen Defendant unespy'd.
>
> And with that Art you make approaches now;
> Such skilful fury in Assaults you show,
> That every Poet without shame may bow.
>
> Ours therefore humbly would attend your doom,
> If Souldier-like, he may have termes to come
> With flying colours, and with beat of Drum.[45]

As Ker insists, the prologue is in many ways an epilogue to the *Essay of Dramatick Poesie;* but one wonders whether one is in fact to take it seriously. In the context of the *Essay,* the prologue would seem to damn the play; and with its direct references to 'Rules' and 'Unities', 'Johnsons humour' and 'Corneilles rhyme', 'colours' and 'living Beauties', it seems to do so without reservation. The play follows but violates the classical rules as set down by Crites, Eugenius and Lisideius; it violates and hence does not demonstrate what in his manifesto Neander justifies as a fine imbalance of the lively and the just. We must proceed, nevertheless, with the utmost caution. Neander's point of view alone matters; his general rules are not moral absolutes or, in the noble art of the drama, categorical imperatives; he argues for a flexibility which in every respect the prologue denies.

In the context of the *Essay,* and the manifesto on which the *Essay* is centred, Dryden's prologue is thus much too severe, outrageously so; and in the context of the play, to which it stands as a strangely grim introduction, it makes little or no sense: there is no meaningful connection between the two. Moreover, without a touch of irony Dryden would never announce to any audience, including peers of the realm, that what they were about to see would offend the rules of art and dull the human spirit. Besides, *Secret Love* was one of the best of his plays, as he well knew at the time, and one of the most successful.

The second prologue, which has generally been ignored, is not so much an independent work as a continuation, or second half, of the first. It too can be read in the context of the *Essay of Dramatick Poesie;* it too can be read, literally, as a statement of fact. In the first prologue Dryden considers classical drama in general and his own play in particular. In the second prologue he considers classical theory in general and, in particular, his own and Neander's views on the fine imbalance. So, Dryden attacks the classical critics:

> I had forgot one half I do protest,
> And now am sent again to speak the rest.
> He bowes to every great and noble Wit,
> But to the little Hectors of the Pit
> Our Poet's sturdy, and will not submit.

He'll be before-hand with 'em, and not stay
To see each peevish Critick stab his Play:
Each Puny Censor, who his skill to boast,
Is cheapily witty on the Poets cost.
No Criticks verdict, should, of right, stand good,
They are excepted all as men of blood:
And the same Law should shield him from their fury
Which has excluded Butchers from a Jury.[46]

He attacks even his own critical position:

But what a Pox keep I so much ado
To save our Poet? he is one of you;
A Brother Judgment, and as I hear say,
A cursed Critick as e're damn'd a Play.
Good salvage Gentlemen your own kind spare,
He is, like you, a very Wolf, or Bear;
Yet think not he'll your ancient rights invade,
Or stop the course of your free damning trade:
For he, (he vows) at no friends Play can sit
But he must needs find fault to shew his Wit...[47]

Dryden's attacks against classical critics are so outrageous that we are inclined not to take them seriously; but in the context of the *Essay,* and of Neander's manifesto, we must: Dryden means what he says. His attack against both himself and his own position on the drama is so outrageous that we are inclined to believe what he says; but in the context of the *Essay,* and of Neander's manifesto, we do not: he denies what he says. Except when he defends the classical rules, the serious prologue is not to be taken seriously: it is a joke. Except when he attacks his fine imbalance of the lively and the just, the jesting prologue is not to be taken as a jest: it is quite serious.

Moreover, the argument against taking seriously his attacks against his play in the first prologue can and must be made against taking seriously the attacks against his critical theories in the second: it is not likely that, before an aristocratic audience, and perhaps royalty, Dryden would publicly denounce the very foundations of his critical theories and his art. Besides, in the opening lines of the prologue he declares himself at one with the·great and noble wits of the age.

*

When placed in juxtaposition with each other, and read or heard in the context of Neander's manifesto, the two prologues are the halves of a typical English tragi-comedy. In the first prologue, which is the serious major plot, Dryden explains that *Secret Love* is a French play, but one which fails on two accounts: because he has not sufficiently emphasized the lively, he has neglected 'the living Beauties of a Play'; and because he has been much too careless with 'Th' exactest Rules by which a Play is wrought', he has failed in handling properly 'The Unities of Action, Place, and Time'. In the second prologue, which is the comic underplot, he celebrates those critics who have 'great and noble Wit' but ridicules everyone else ('the little Hectors of the Pit'), including, unexpectedly, himself: he too is 'A cursed Critick as e're damn'd a Play'.

The two prologues are the two halves of a tragi-comedy in yet another way, but with shifts ironically in overtone and meaning. Tensions between the lively and the just in a tragi-comedy – and hence between imagination and judgment – become in each prologue an ironic counterpoint between what the poet says and what he actually means. Dryden now assumes the courtly manner: in each of the prologues he condemns what he praises, praises what he condemns, and all but loses himself and us in a vast labyrinth of some courtly game, though one which ultimately allows no victory but his own.

In tragi-comedies of the new age, according to Neander, the lively and the just are balanced in a variety of tensions with each other: the lively prevails over the just in the major plot; the just prevails over the lively in the minor plot; and in the play as a whole 'the hand of Art' takes precedence over 'imitation[s] of Nature' and the 'Rule[s] of Logick'. In the lively conceits of the first prologue, Dryden compares the lively in the play to a painting, and the play to 'Towns ... fortifi'd / By Engineers'; he grants that in each instance – first as artist, then as engineer – he has failed miserably; and he urges 'humbly' that he be allowed some honour in defeat: that 'Souldier-like, he may have termes to come / With flying colours, and with beat of Drum'. He also makes it clear, though by tone and trope, that sense and judgment dictate a completely different point of view: the play that he attacks – a play written under the influence of the French theatre, 'Th' exactest Rules', and 'Corneilles rhyme' – is not *Secret Love*. It is the kind of drama which he does not like and in fact would never write.

In the just and straightforward language of the second prologue he turns his attention from his play to his critics, the 'men of blood'; he 'bowes to every great and noble Wit'; and he attacks outrageously the rule-choppers, the 'little Hectors' who would damn his play not so much because it lacks 'living Beauties' as because it has perhaps violated 'Th' exactest Rules'. He also makes it clear, through witticism and paradox, obscenities and far-fetched conceits, that against all critics, the 'great' and the 'puny', his own fancy and judgment stand unabashed, unafraid and altogether correct and sound: if he 'Bowes' to anyone, he bows only to those critics who accept his opinions as their own.

In the juxtaposition of the two prologues – in the two prologues taken as a whole – 'the hand of Art' prevails over any and every 'appearance of truth'. Witticism and conceit, paradox and solemnity, insult and praise, vulgarity and decorum, laughter and tears, the lively and the just follow one another in rich profusion. Dryden's concern is centred entirely on 'the greatest pleasure of the audience', but not without his paying arch tribute again and again to his 'smart Prologues', and of course to his 'Play'. *Secret Love* is a far better play than anyone, except 'every great and noble Wit', can possibly understand or enjoy. As in the two prologues which introduce it, and which are a tragi-comedy in miniature, so in the play itself

Dryden has obeyed the rules of logic and decorum, but subordinated them decidedly to 'a more pleasant way of writing' and 'the quick turns and graces of the *English* stage'.

*

In the preface to the play Dryden pretty much repeats the substance of his two prologues, with pretty much the same kind of irony, though in a considerably more straightforward language. The significance and value of the preface lies in the fact that it precedes the two prologues and very much clarifies their meaning and purpose. One might surmise that, having read the preface before reading the prologues, neither critics nor scholars would ever have misunderstood them; but the preface has, unfortunately, gone unheeded.

The preface, which is relatively short, is both a commentary on the two prologues and their gloss: it takes up the same subjects and themes; it abounds in the same kind of irony, though without a corresponding banter and solemnity; and in its every explanation of literature and critical theory, it is straightforward and direct. All good poetry, Dryden tells us, must be based on 'the strictest of… Laws'; and what is true of literature in general is especially true of the drama. A good play must, for the sake of verisimilitude, obey the three unities, especially the unity of action. The characters must be 'absolute pattern[s] of honour': they must obey the moral and social code of the world in which they live; and if or when they do not, they are to be either punished or redeemed.[48] When he wrote *Secret Love,* he did so therefore with all the best of literary rules in mind. But having said so much, and having suggested that – like Corneille and the contemporary French – he is committed to the most exacting formalism, Dryden makes an about-face, though not unexpectedly, once we have read either the play or the two prologues.

When measured against the standards that he set for himself, he admits, his play is a failure: he has violated the very 'Rules' to which he feels committed. *Secret Love* has not one plot, but two: one serious, the other comic; and the plots mingle and collide. Comic and serious characters meet on the stage; and in moments of great occasion comic characters behave with a boisterous lack of restraint. The failures are admitted, identified and then blithely defended. Dryden wrote his play according to the classical rules; but the play is full of blemishes. The play is indeed full of blemishes; but in defiance of the 'over-wise Censors', every blemish is now allowed. Through his two plots, as well as through every violation of decorum, not only has he achieved in his tragi-comedy a higher unity than the French would allow; through his twists and turnings (the 'pleasing Labyrinth of errors') he has introduced into his play a 'variety of Images'; and the variety serves the primary aim of all good poetry: to give not moral instruction to the audience but entertainment and delight. What is declared a failure is thus declared a remarkable success.[49]

It is moreover a success not only because Dryden says that it is but also because he can at last provide the critical theory that justifies it. The play follows the rules, but with great flexibility; and where it does not follow the rules but gives pleasure, it obeys the highest and first aim of all good poetry. And in each circumstance –

both where the rules are obeyed and where they are properly ignored – he alone must pass the final judgment. His declaration could not be clearer. Like every good poet, every good critic must know and obey literary rules. But neither critic nor poet may be a slave to dull formulae. The purpose of a good poem, and especially of a good play, is not to teach moral values or to illustrate the mechanics of form. However much it ought to be centred in the rules of genre and decorum, a good play must also have variety: it must reflect the twists and turns of actual human experience, in which the comic and the serious do in fact mingle and collide. It must primarily entertain; and just as the poet must submit his judgment to the requirements of his imagination, so must the critic subordinate both rules and standards to the ends which the poet, who alone 'may infallibly judg of the frame and contexture of [his] Works', has set for himself.[50]

The play and the theory on which it is based Dryden thus defends without reservation, in each instance declaring that he alone, as poet and critic in one, is the best authority. But he goes a step further. He calls to his aid and rescue the noblest and most sacred authority in the land: King Charles II. The King attended a performance of *Secret Love,* liked the work tremendously, though with one slight qualification, and 'grac'd it with the Title of His Play'. And Dryden can do no better than to 'seek protection' for his work from the man who, in the most civilized of ages, has become the ruling arbiter of taste – with perhaps the one exception, John Dryden himself:

> That which with more reason was objected as an indecorum, is the management of the last Scene of the Play…This I cannot otherwise defend, then by telling you I so design'd it on purpose to make my Play go off more smartly; that Scene, being in the opinion of the best judges, the most divertising of the whole Comedy. But though the Artifice succeeded, I am willing to acknowledg it as a fault, since it pleas'd His Majesty, the best Judg, to think it so.[51]

The irony is recognizable. Dryden is not merely the leading poet and playwright of the age; the King notwithstanding, he is the leading critic as well, and (we must conclude) the only one who, as both critic and poet, is best qualified to pass a correct judgment on *Secret Love,* on poetry in general and on the exactest rules by which a new English drama – or poetry in general – is to be conceived, enjoyed and ultimately judged.

V

In his statements about *Annus Mirabilis* and *Secret Love* Dryden continues his courtly manner, but with a vigour and conviction – and undercurrents of irony – that suggest a self-confidence he only recently developed and that are obvious indications of his newly felt powers and realizations of success. He continues to write about his own works, and specifically his favourite genres – epic and tragicomedy – while inevitably making it perfectly clear not only that good poetry and good criticism require each other but also that, as his own works are the foundations of his theory, so his theory is to be the foundation of a new (or renewed) tradition in English criticism and literature.

The *Essay of Dramatick Poesie* is firmly established as the context in which he and his successors must think of poetry and pass judgment on it. The *Essay* is echoed throughout his statements about his epic and his play, and it will continue to echo throughout his work until the end of his life; but once we examine the '[A]ccount' and the preface closely we understand that, if he echoes Neander, and if at the same time he ignores to a surprising extent much of Neander's obsessions with metre and rhyme, his contempt for foreign poets and his concerns with spectacle and staging, he is in a number of important details far more flexible than Neander. He will to a greater extent subordinate unity in poetry to variety, instruction and the just to the lively and pleasure, judgment to imagination, the rules to whatever delights or whatever purpose a poet may choose for himself and his work, and of course critics to poets. He is more flexible than Neander in considering decorum and, by implication, the subject and theme of both epic and drama; and he is far more flexible both in construing art as an imitation of life and in coping with problems of mimesis (or imitation and probability). And while he is equally concerned with excellence in language (it is language, he begins to understand, that truly distinguishes poetry from other forms of discourse), he now argues that poetic language ('more various and bizarre … then … any other kind') is itself a form of self-expression.[52]

With the completion of *Annus Mirabilis* and *Secret Love,* Dryden now thinks of himself as the leading poet and critic of the age; and he is prepared to charter for himself new freedoms as both critic and poet, but never in violation of his first principles: English poets must imitate nature but write in an English tradition; they must read ancient and Continental authors but imitate English models; poetry requires rules but also flexibility; and the ends of a good poem are pleasure, decorum and language that is both beautiful and correct. And as we shall soon observe, his fixed principles are quite compatible with bold experiments in literary form.

CHAPTER FIVE

A charter of freedom
(1668–1670)

I

From the very beginning Dryden was his own most perceptive critic. Throughout his life, he wrote critical essays that explained his achievements and failures, his contributions to English letters and his literary debts. In these studies Dryden always displayed an acute understanding of his own works, but often he did not do so until long after their date of publication.

Of all the genres which he struggled to master none seems to have presented him with greater intellectual problems than the heroic play. *The Indian Queen,* his first heroic play, was published in 1665; but not until 1672, when he published *The Conquest of Granada,* did he offer a mature analysis of the form. Of course, it might be argued that he understood the genre at once and, for a time, merely begrudged his insights to the public. The evidence of his criticism suggests, however, that his grasp of the heroic play developed at a slow and erratic pace. And that development can be traced in the three essays in which his early manner, that of the courtier-poet, underwent its first significant change: 'A Defence of *An Essay of Dramatick Poesie*', which was published (in a new edition of one of his heroic plays, *The Indian Emperour*) in the summer of 1668; the 'Preface to *The Tempest*', published in the winter of 1670; and the 'Preface to *Tyrannick Love*', published in November of the same year.

As he fashioned a theory of the heroic play, Dryden gradually modified his early manner. The persona of the courtier remained, but somewhat diminished. No doubt encouraged by his appointment as Poet Laureate in April 1668, he ceased to aim his criticism exclusively at an elegant coterie. He now began to write for a wider audience; and as he did so, he made his language far more clear and direct, so that it would be accessible to the whole of the reading public. The 'Defence' and the two prefaces may lack the clarity and directness, as well as the full combativeness, which were to characterize his middle style. But in all three works he is obviously shedding the manner of the poet-courtier and adopting that of the poet-critic.

II

The transitional nature of the criticism is evident in 'A Defence of *An Essay of Dramatick Poesie*', in which forms of aristocratic politeness acquire a sardonic edge, and a feigned indifference to fame alternates with a strong desire for self-justification. The 'Defence' was written to refute an attack on the *Essay of Dramatick Poesie* (1668) in Sir Robert Howard's preface to his play *The Duke of*

Lerma (1668).[1] Howard's attack and Dryden's rebuttal represent the last phase of a literary debate – a debate initiated with Dryden's dedication of *The Rival Ladies* (1664) and continued in Howard's 'Preface to *Four Plays*' (1665) and Dryden's *Essay*.[2] Generally, it has been assumed that Howard, who lost his temper in his preface of 1668, was angered at being portrayed in the *Essay* under the character of Crites, the die-hard classicist. But according to Howard's own statements, his outburst was prompted by Dryden's argumentative tactics.[3] He realized that the *Essay* was not what it seemed to be. It was not a dispassionate inquiry into competing theories of the drama, but Dryden's attempt to construct a new orthodoxy based on his own literary views. The *Essay*, he argued, was a piece of legislative criticism; and that kind of criticism he must condemn.

For poetry, as Howard conceives of it, is not susceptible to regulation. He more than rejects Dryden's rules. He condemns totally and absolutely the very idea and principle of literary authority. In place of established canons, he advocates the unrestricted application of private 'Taste' as the only sure basis of literary judgment. A poet must be left free, to compose his works 'as his fancy best approves'.[4] Similarly, his audience must be left equally free to judge those works solely in terms of its own preferences. What pleases a poet or an audience is good simply because it pleases. In the republic of letters, it would seem, 'nothing … [is] a ruder folly than to censure the satisfaction of others'.[5]

Howard attacks all literary rules on the ground that they 'infringe the liberty of opinion'.[6] However, he further argues that specific rules, notably the rules concerning time and place, as set forth in the *Essay*, are not only illiberal in their effect but also absurd in their nature. It is ridiculous to permit the stage to represent two houses but not two kingdoms, to allow the action of a play to take up twenty-four hours but not a thousand years: 'all being impossible, they are none of them nearest the truth or nature of what they present. For impossibilities are all equal, and admit no degrees'.[7]

In dismissing literary authority, Howard is convinced that he is sweeping aside the accumulated rubbish of the past. But his own position is less defensible than any he attacks. For one thing, he is blithely unaware that all human activity, not least the writing of poetry, must be based on some organizing principle. He appears not to understand that artistic choices are necessarily self-limiting, that the poet who ignores established rules must still subordinate himself to the demands inherent in his medium and art. In addition, Howard's preface is hardly the radical manifesto which he would have us believe it is. He casts himself as the foe of all literary authority. Yet, despite his protestations, he would be a literary dictator himself. He may condemn Dryden for attempting to establish rules in the *Essay*, but he does so only to promulgate another set of directives. Howard has his own orthodoxy to advance, and it is one that is no less self-serving than Dryden's. The ultimate purpose of his criticism is to justify and celebrate *The Duke of Lerma*.

In general, Howard's statements as a critic are in accord with his own dramatic practice. There is one point on which essay and play disagree: as critic, he derides the unity of place, which as playwright he scrupulously observes. But in all other details, a fairly conventional essay merely transforms into abstract principles the many devices that in one way or another are embodied in the play to which it is appended. So, as both critic and playwright, Howard has no interest in the unity of time. He urges, if not verisimilitude in character, the creation of characters who, like his own, are devoid of excesses in thought or feeling. And he would give all playwrights the licence he has taken and allow them to write in a variety of styles.[8] Of all statements, however, his most extended remarks are devoted to matters of prosody and, especially, to his preference for blank verse over rhyme.

Howard's theory of dramatic language, given his hatred of rules, is perversely restrictive. It insists upon the literal application of the idea that a play is an imitation of life or, as he puts it, 'a composition of several persons speaking *ex tempore*'.[9] Taking a close correspondence between life and art as the sole criterion for the language of drama, he insists that playwrights approximate as much as possible the way men actually speak. He is dismissive of Dryden's contention, stated in the *Essay,* that rhyme is the most proper medium for serious drama. 'For 'tis not the question', he insists, 'whether rhyme or not rhyme be best or most natural for a grave and serious subject, but what is nearest the nature of that which it presents'.[10] That prose and not blank verse best satisfies this formula, he never once considers.

The chief failing of the preface, however, is due not to inconsistency or omission but to outrageous pomposity of tone. Howard writes as if he alone in human history has arrived at a judicious conception of the drama. Others may have written on the subject; but the drama is 'no such thing as what they all pretend'.[11] Needless to say, his monumental conceit becomes a target for Dryden's satire.

Writing as the professed champion of '*Aristotle, Horace, Ben. Johnson,* and *Corneille*', Dryden relentlessly assaults each of Howard's several positions. He quotes a passage from Howard's preface; he ridicules it savagely; and through a malicious and witty reply he reduces it to absurdity. The pattern of statement and counterstatement gives the impression of a dialogue; and this impression, in turn, suggests that the technique itself, whatever its ultimate origins in a literature of controversy, was profoundly influenced by Dryden's close study of the drama. Indeed, the technique can best be viewed as an adaptation of a topos very common in seventeenth-century plays: the encounter between a bumptious lord and a polished courtier. The pages of Shakespeare and Jonson afford many examples of such scenes. But it is Molière who is the great storehouse of such material. In *The School of Women Criticised* (1663), for example, he presents us with two adversaries, a *chevalier* and a *marquis,* the one a fit companion for princes, the other a high-born fool. The two engage in a literary debate, in the course of which the Chevalier, who is clearly the author's mouthpiece, holds the Marquis up to ridicule:

> I hate to see People make themselves ridiculous, notwithstanding their Quality; those who always pass a decisive Sentence, and speak positively of every thing, without knowing anything of the Matter; who at a Play will exclaim against the ill Passages, and not be moved at those that are

good ... Pray, Gentlemen, hold your Tongues when God has not given
you any Knowledge in a thing; don't give those that hear you Cause of
Laughter; and consider that if you say nothing, you may perhaps be taken
for Men of Skill.[12]

It is in this spirit of intelligence disposing of stupidity that Dryden's work is cast.

Much of the 'Defence' is devoted to a thoroughly personal attack on Howard
for his failings in grammar, syntax and translation. Some ten days after the publication of the preface, Howard tried to forestall such criticism by blaming some of
his errors on his printer. But his *errata,* added to cover his most serious mistakes,
served only to inspire Dryden's scorn. It is wonderfully convenient, Dryden mock-
ingly contends, to have printers serve as the 'Proxies of every Gentleman
Author, ... to be chastis'd for him, when he is not pleas'd to own an Errour'. He
is sorry, however, that Howard did not extend the ruse a little further:

Yet since he has given the *Errata,* I wish he would have inlarged them
only a few sheets more ...: for this cursed Printer is so given to mistakes,
that there is scarce a sentence in the Preface, without some false
Grammar, or hard sence in it: which will all be charg'd upon the Poet,
because he is so good natur'd as to lay but three Errours to the Printers
account ...[13]

The remaining errors, which Howard inadvertently leaves to himself, Dryden then
cheerfully exposes. He devotes his major attention, however, to revealing Howard's
intellectual failings as both playwright and thinker.

*

Against Howard's contention that the drama must be governed by individual taste,
whether that of the playwright or that of the audience, Dryden asserts the dignity
and importance of literary theory. He does not dispute the right of an audience to
express its preferences or the power of an audience to impose its tastes on a playwright. But although an audience can set the fashion, he denies that it can
determine true literary merit:

The liking or disliking of the people gives the Play the denomination of
good or bad, but does not really make, or constitute it such. To please
the people ought to be the Poets aim, because Plays are made for their
delight; but it does not follow that they are always pleas'd with good
Plays, or that the Plays which please them are always good.[14]

Literary value must be decided by objective rules, based upon the definition of the
drama as an 'imitation of Nature'. And if plays are an imitation of nature, then there
must necessarily be an authoritative method of achieving that imitation; 'otherwise
there may be an end, and no means conducing to it'.[15]

That rules exist Dryden is certain; but here, it must be noted, his dogmatism
ends. He carefully distinguishes between the existence of rules, which he believes
is demonstrable, and the content of specific rules, which can be inferred but never

proved.[16] In clarification of his position he draws an analogy between theology and literary theory: as the existence of an ordered world demonstrates the existence of a deity to be worshipped but does not reveal the proper forms of worship, so too the existence of an order to be imitated proves the existence of literary rules but not the specific rules themselves.[17] Our knowledge of what these rules should be, consequently, must remain forever uncertain; and this uncertainty requires that literary theories be advanced with due scepticism and caution. As an example of the proper method in criticism, Dryden offers his own *Essay of Dramatick Poesie,* in which (he again claims) rules for the drama are tentatively set forth and not dogmatically asserted.[18] But even if we admit that the *Essay* conveys an appearance of open inquiry, we can hardly say the same for the 'Defence'. Here Dryden displays as much intellectual certainty in outlining a theory of the drama as the subject allows.

Dryden accepts the basic Renaissance definition of the drama as an 'imitation of Nature'.[19] The drama, he further holds, is divided into a number of genres, the chief of which are tragedy and comedy. Tragedy he defines as a play with nobility of action, character and language; comedy, as a play in which the constituent elements are more common.[20] Although he considers both forms, his main attention is devoted to tragedy, which he often places under the general heading of the 'serious Play'.[21] But when he speaks of the 'serious Play', he would have us apply his remarks not only to tragedy proper but also to a related form, tragi-comedy, and to a new kind of 'serious Play', which he had already begun to write, the heroic play, but to which he had not yet given a name.

Throughout the 'Defence' Dryden centres his entire analysis – of art as an 'imitation of Nature' – on a further premise: that the purpose of the drama, as of all literature, is to please and instruct. However, as he considers pleasure and instruction, he involves himself in a slight ambiguity or paradox. When he considers the pleasure evoked by the drama, he clearly distinguishes it from instruction, whether ethical or philosophical or both. In this respect, he resembles Sidney, who makes a sharp distinction between the two. When he deals with instruction alone, however, he becomes a thoroughgoing Aristotelian: he holds that instruction itself is a form of pleasure. Dryden's theory has two aspects. It is not two theories presented as one, but one theory considered from two different points of view, each with quite another emphasis.

Literature, then, gives pleasure in two very different ways: it appeals to our emotions and sentiments; and it appeals to our human desire to know and hence to the life of reason and contemplation. In the best poetry the two kinds of pleasure are of course interrelated: neither can nor should be separated absolutely from the other. Yet distinctions can and occasionally must be made. Early in the 'Defence', and before going on to discuss in elaborate detail such matters as imitation and probability, representation and literary rules, taste and ethical truth, Dryden considers for a moment only that pleasure which has nothing to do immediately with instruction and which a poet, in defining his purpose, must elect as his main concern and emphasis. '[D]elight', he says, 'is the chief, if not the only end of

Poesie'; and he goes on to add, significantly, that 'instruction can be admitted but in second place, for Poesie only instructs as it delights'.[22]

He had once argued that the end of poetry is to be lively and just and that it must please and instruct. He is now on the verge of arguing – or so it seems – that good poetry must be only lively and give only pleasure. The position is unexpected and in many respects startling. He is on the verge of making a break, however slight, however tentative, not only with the notions of imbalance that he had so far been holding between imagination and judgment but also with the main tenets of the whole of Renaissance literary theory. He now prefigures, by more than a century, ideals of the English Romantics and, in particular, of Wordsworth and Coleridge; and he does so never more than when he explains the interconnections between the pleasurable and the beautiful. Once he commits his critical theory to an emphasis on pleasure as opposed to instruction, though never of course to moral truth, he explains that the chief source of the pleasurable is the beautiful; that the beautiful is achieved when the poetic imagination heightens what it imitates or 'represents'; that the imagination heightens what it represents when, through study and care, it heightens language; and finally that a heightened language – the source of what is ultimately pleasurable and beautiful in poetry – depends entirely on metre, rhyme, metaphor and whatever else in language 'hides the deformities' in both nature and human life.[23]

In speaking as he does about such matters as pleasure and the beautiful, imagination and representation, Dryden may not always be very easy to follow. He never really defines any of his terms, however much he discusses the ideas or problems with which they are associated. But from his usage – both in the 'Defence' and in all the rest of his criticism – we may deduce his meaning and his intention: a copy or representation results when we merely accumulate sense impressions; imagination discovers their interconnections and evokes the wonderful; pleasure (as opposed to instruction) gives delight (or joy or transport) to one's emotions; beauty is a revelation, through language, of a cosmic or divine harmony. As a significant means of heightening language, and hence imitations of nature, metaphor is mentioned several times in the essay, though it is also discussed in several of his other important early prose works, including the '[A]ccount' of *Annus Mirabilis* (1667), but never with the importance that it now receives.[24] Dryden does not define 'metaphor' any more than he defines his several other key terms; but once again we may deduce his meaning from his usage. He apparently has in mind an implied comparison that is unexpected and emotionally charged, suggestive and pleasurable, and that appeals somehow to our love for not only the beautiful but also the true and the good.[25]

As poets attempt to achieve the beautiful, the various devices – the many 'Arts and Ornaments' – which they employ are determined largely by their choice of literary form: serious plays and the various types of comedy, and of course each of the many other genres, all demand distinct styles.[26] The only invariable rule, even as the rules of structure are suspended or ignored, is that the language of poetry must never be, and can never be, what Howard's theory implies: it can never be the ordinary prose of everyday human speech, unvarnished and plain. As Dryden wisely points out, and from time to time repeats, literature, whatever the genre, can never be a merely exact or literal representation of what it imitates. Even in the 'Lowest' genres, among which he singles out the prose comedies of Ben Jonson, art is inevitably and necessarily set above life:

> In *Bartholomew-Fair,* or the Lowest kind of Comedy, that degree of heightning is used, which is proper to set off that Subject: 'tis true the Author was not there to go out of Prose, as he does in his higher Arguments of Comedy, *The Fox* and *Alchymist;* yet he does so raise his matter in that Prose, as to render it delightful; which he could never have performed, had he only said or done those very things that are daily spoken or practised in the Fair ...[27]

Dryden would allow poets to 'heighten' speech to render it 'delightful', but that is not the only privilege which he grants. He would also allow them considerable freedom – but not Howard's licence – in the handling of such classical rules as the unities of time and place. He would not compel a poet to set his play on only one spot of ground, or make him represent only so much time in his play as actually transpires in the performance. The poet may have the stage represent now one imagined place and now another; similarly, the poet may represent a larger degree of 'imaginary' time within a smaller compass of 'real' time:

> I grant it to be impossible, that the greater part of time should be comprehended in the less, that twenty four hours should be crowded into three: but there is no necessity of that Supposition. For as *Place,* so *Time* relating to a Play, is either imaginary or real: The real is comprehended in those three hours, more or less, in the space of which the Play is represented: The Imaginary is that which is supposed to be taken up in the Representation, as twenty four hours more or less.[28]

The justification for creating imaginary time and for multiplying imaginary places, moreover, is the same as that which sanctions the heightening of speech: our pleasure is increased by an additional appeal to our imagination or fancy. The appetite of fancy for make-believe is keen and unlimited; there is no degree of fiction that it cannot allow. Nevertheless, he would have us understand, the pleasures of the imagination must indeed be limited and, at the same time, they must be counterbalanced by the pleasures that reason derives from 'Moral Truth', which is 'the Mistress of the Poet', and 'Natural Truth', which 'must *be* Ethical. Indeed the Poet dresses Truth, and adorns Nature, but does not alter them'. What is attractive to fancy is not acceptable to the whole man: man is a reasonable creature, and reason delights far less in fiction or mere rhetoric than in philosophical and moral instruction.[29]

By instruction, Dryden does not mean a leaden didacticism or a dull sermon. Instruction in art signifies, rather, a vital correspondence of literature with both verifiable fact and ethical law. Reason demands and delights in this correspondence;

but, as the experience of English playgoers attests, it does not demand of poetry that it delineate the physical and moral world with the kind of exactness found in philosophy and empirical science. In the contemplation of a drama, reason permits its demands to blend with those of fancy. It will accept a measure of fiction, so long as the fiction is not based upon an impossibility and remains within hailing distance of probability and of truth, whether moral or natural or both. For fancy or imagination in man

> is supposed to participate of reason, and when that governs, as it does in the belief of fiction, reason is not destroyed, but misled, or blinded: that can prescribe to the reason, during the time of the representation, somewhat like a weak belief of what it sees and hears; and reason suffers it self to be so hoodwink'd, that it may better enjoy the pleasures of the fiction: but it is never so wholly made a captive, as to be drawn head-long into a perswasion of those things which are most remote from probability...[30]

The structure of the human mind itself demands that limits be set to a poet's freedom. What some of those limits are Dryden next considers in detail.

With respect to unity of time he insists, unlike Howard, that the poet pay due regard to probability. Imaginary time must contain a resemblance of truth: it must be based upon the observance of proportion. A three-hour play, hence, may extend the time it represents beyond three hours, but not more than is strictly required by 'the nature of the Plot, the quality of the Persons, and the variety of the Accidents'.[31] In handling the unity of place, by the same token, the poet must steer a course between the unlimited scope given to fancy by Howard and the complete authority granted to reason by the French. Such a middle course is achieved when the stage is allowed to represent more than one place, as long as the imaginary places represented are not too numerous and the distance between them is not too great.[32]

As in the plot there must be some kind of balance between fancy and judgment or between imaginative freedom and classical rules, so in the handling of the language there must be a corresponding balance between fact and fiction. For the sake of appealing to fancy, the poet 'dresses Truth and adorns Nature'. But further liberties he must not take. Only a bad poet will attempt to please by making comparisons which are not objectively sound or by constructing arguments which are more suggestive than true:

> False Reasonings and colours of Speech, are the certain marks of one who does not understand the Stage: For Moral Truth is the Mistress of the Poet as much as of the Philosopher: Poesie must resemble Natural Truth, but it must *be* Ethical...Therefore that is not the best Poesie which resembles notions of things that are not, to things that are: though the fancy may be great and the words flowing, yet the Soul is but half satisfied when there is not Truth in the foundation.[33]

It is because Virgil rejected all unwarrantable appeals to fancy that Dryden judges his severe Muse to be preferable to the more elaborate productions of Ovid.[34]

Throughout the 'Defence' Dryden touches upon a variety of other subjects, none of which he discusses at any great length, but all of which are important in the development of his criticism. English poets must imitate English models, but now they must also study the great writers, both poets and critics, of other nations. Literary rules, and especially those defined by principles of unity and harmony, are ultimately translations of divine law and cosmic order into principles of art. Specific rules have their own validity, which is determined first by the test of time and then by their presence – in one way or another – in the works of major critics and poets from antiquity to the present, from '*Aristotle* and *Horace*... [to] Ben. Johnson and *Corneille*'. The literary genres must be distinguished from one another, but it is also possible for them to be fused, as for example in English tragi-comedy or, as he will later explain, in mixed comedy and the heroic play (or epic drama).

*

In presenting his dramatic theory, Dryden insists that his purpose is to explain the *Essay of Dramatick Poesie* and to refute Howard's misinterpretations. To this end he quotes from his own work and clarifies its underlying assumptions. The 'Defence', however, is more than a work of ordinary exegesis: it alters what it expounds and, by doing so, shifts Dryden's thought on the drama out of its accustomed channels. What we are shown is not so much a new theory as an old theory in the process of transformation: a theory originally applied to one genre, tragi-comedy, in which there is a fine imbalance of the lively and the just, is now being redefined; and it is being redefined, if unconsciously, for eventual application to another but related genre, the heroic play, in which, as in *The Indian Emperour,* the lively will take precedence all but completely over the just.[35]

In the light of his later development, it is clear that Dryden's changes all tend to the same end: they lighten the restraints or 'Cloggs' on the poet's imagination. A new charter of freedom is in effect, and we can see its influence at work in his discussion of the unity of time. In the *Essay* he had argued that an absolute limit be set to the time which may be represented in tragedy. A tragedy, he had argued, may cover the events of up to three days. Flexible as he was in interpreting the rules, there is no evidence that he would allow a poet to go further.[36] However, when he purportedly reaffirms this position in the 'Defence', he actually substitutes a very different and much more liberal view. He now defines unity of time merely as a principle of economy: the plot of a tragedy is to take up the least amount of time that its events require. An extremely complex play, it would seem, might represent weeks, months or even years. This deduction may not appear explicitly in the 'Defence'. But it is a deduction which he will encourage when, two years later, he actually boasts – now almost echoing Howard – that in one of his plays he has not observed any of the unities, as conventionally defined.[37]

Just as Dryden moves, in his theory of the drama, towards the acceptance of a more imaginatively constructed plot, so too he increases the permissible range of dramatic language or style. In his earlier essays he had insisted that the language of the drama be less intricate, less self-consciously wrought than that of the epic. In order that characters might not appear to speak beyond their abilities, the dialogue is to be, if not plain, at least unassuming. Its artifice is to be hidden in shadows and do its work unseen.[38] Now, however, he bids the playwright emerge from behind the curtain, and make it apparent that characters have had their speeches written for them and placed into their mouths. The writer of poetic drama is to follow the example of the epic poet: he is to arouse admiration in his audience by the open display of rhetorical power.[39]

In its conflation of dramatic and epic styles the 'Defence' anticipates Dryden's later theory of the kind of language that is to be used in the heroic play. Further, in a more subtle manner, the 'Defence' helps to provide the intellectual framework for that theory. Previously, in the *Essay of Dramatick Poesie,* and even more so in the '[A]ccount' of *Annus Mirabilis,* he had pointed to an indissoluble link between language and truth. In these two essays, the pleasure of language is identified with the joy of intellectual discovery: rhetoric is said to please because it reveals most fully the nature of the world.[40] In the 'Defence' the bonds between truth and language are in part severed. Dryden now distinguishes between the pleasures solely of language and the very different pleasures of a language linked inextricably to truth, however defined. He may insist that the very finest poetry requires the joining of the two, but such a position is not essential to his thought. Having once separated or distinguished between truth and language, he will not find it difficult to justify a form of poetry that is based, to a significant degree, on the pleasures of language alone.

III

In 1667 Dryden and his friend Sir William Davenant made an adaptation of Shakespeare's *Tempest.* Two years later Dryden published the play and included in the volume both a preface and the original prologue. In the preface one may detect a further cooling of his interest in the just and hence in that kind of tragi-comedy in which, as he had explained in the *Essay of Dramatick Poesie,* classical rules must be given almost as much emphasis as flights of the imagination. His disaffection in no way amounts to a rejection of tragi-comedy: his objections are slight, faint and easy to miss. But for all the vagueness with which it is stated, the change in his opinion of and regard for tragi-comedy is no less real and, as an index of his drift towards the heroic play, no less significant.

In the prologue Dryden discusses the play in the context of early seventeenth-century literary history and ideas of literary progress. First he takes up all the major subjects that he had considered in the *Essay of Dramatick Poesie,* but he now gives them a new and unexpected interpretation. In the *Essay* he explains that there are two traditions in English drama: the lively, which he associates with Shakespeare; and the just, which he associates with Jonson and, in particular, his low comedy (or comedy of 'humour').[41] And he further explains that the two traditions were partially synthesized by Fletcher, who in his tragi-comedies sometimes added to the synthesis an intellectual or high comedy of 'wit'. In the prologue Dryden makes an about-face. He now argues that the two traditions and their synthesis, along with both high and low comedy, have their origins in Shakespeare alone. Like 'a Tree['s] … secret root', from which 'new Branches shoot', Shakespeare is the hidden source from which not only Dryden's 'new reviving Play' but the whole of modern drama ultimately 'Springs'. 'Monarch-like', he 'gave … his subjects law'; like 'Nature' itself, he is that which other playwrights imitate or 'paint'.[42] In addition, while in the *Essay* Dryden insists that Shakespeare, Jonson and Fletcher are more or less of equal stature, he now argues that Jonson and Fletcher are not only imitators of Shakespeare but his inferiors as well:

> If they have since out-writ all other men,
> 'Tis with the drops which fell from Shakespear's Pen.
>   …
> … Shakespear's Magick could not copy'd be …
> … Shakespear's pow'r is sacred as a King's.[43]

The criticism of Jonson and Fletcher, though hardly severe, is obviously (and surprisingly) negative; and it can perhaps be explained by his now feeling unusually sure of himself. After his success with *Secret Love*, he looked upon Jonson and Fletcher in a new light: he saw them no longer as masters but as mere rivals and, therefore, as appropriate objects of playful irreverence. And he would now have himself thought of as Shakespeare's only true disciple and hence the leading playwright of the age.

After examining the development of English drama Dryden goes on to justify the fact that in his and Davenant's redaction Prospero's 'Magick' – but not Shakespeare's – has deliberately been given a new treatment and definition: Shakespeare's play was based on 'Those Legends' which 'from old Priest-hood were receiv'd'; and what was once suited to the barbarism of the early seventeenth century – Shakespeare 'then writ, as people then believ'd' – is hardly suitable for the very much more civilized present.[44] The prologue then concludes with an amusing coda. His own version of Shakespeare's play, he boasts, is obviously superior to Fletcher's adaptation (*The Sea Voyage*), which had recently been revived on the London stage; but in the bizarre staging of his play, his own 'Theatre' has indulged in a bit of 'Magick', which violates even the minimal requirements of probability and verisimilitude:

> But, if for Shakespear we your grace implore,
> We for our Theatre shall want it more:
> Who by our dearth of Youths are forc'd t'employ
> One of our Women to present a Boy.
> And that's a transformation you will say
> Exceeding all the Magick in the Play.[45]

*

In the preface Dryden is far less concerned with literary history and ideas of literary progress than with the play itself. Throughout he attempts to distance himself from the adaptation and to insist that – in its design, execution and purpose – *The*

Tempest ought to be considered far more Davenant's play than his own. In so pressing the claims of Davenant's authorship, he insists that his motives are solely those of honesty and fairness. But it is hard not to think that he goes far beyond what decency requires. His disowning of *The Tempest*, some two years after its first performance, does not in fact reflect his moral scruples so much as his desire to have his name linked with a more ambitious kind of drama.

In the development of his argument, Dryden moves from irony to irony, of which the first is the most disarming. The preface begins with an attack on the writing of prefaces. Our surprise deepens as it becomes apparent that he is not rejecting the preface as a literary form but urging that its customary flattery be entirely replaced by tough-minded criticism. His work thus begins with an attack, indirectly, on his earliest critical manner:

> The writing of Prefaces to Plays was probably invented by…some Ape
> of the *French* Eloquence…We may satisfie our selves with surmounting
> them in the Scene, and safely leave them those trappings of writing, and
> flourishes of the Pen, with which they adorn the borders of their Plays,
> and which are indeed no more than good Landskips to a very indiffer-
> ent Picture.[46]

In a farewell gesture to his role as courtier-poet, Dryden aligns himself with the blunt Saxon character. No longer will he follow the French dramatists who write elaborate prefaces to atone for their dull plays. If he now offers another preface, this one contains no self-advertisements or 'flourishes of the Pen'.[47]

Yet having dispensed with one kind of 'Eloquence', he immediately proceeds to adopt another which, despite its apparent plainness, is neither blunt nor direct. In the rest of the preface he condemns in order to praise and praises in order to condemn. He speaks of Shakespeare's weaknesses, but only so that he may emphasize his genius (or 'Magick'). He celebrates Davenant's achievements in the redaction of Shakespeare's play, but only so that he may emphasize Davenant's limitations as a playwright and his blunders. He explains in minute detail his collaboration with Davenant, but only so that he may distance himself from it: he would absolve himself of any responsibility for the failure of the play and set himself up again as the major critic of the age and its leading playwright.

The preface, the ultimate purpose of which is to celebrate Shakespeare and one of his finest plays, begins with the praise of Davenant. Davenant had died before the revision was published, and Dryden wants to render public thanks for the opportunity of having worked on the project. The terms of the collaboration do not appear to have been very attractive: Dryden was not allowed to make any alterations of his own; and his writing was amended 'daily'. But if he chafed under these restrictions, he keeps his resentments to himself and, in this funerary tribute, says only the right things. His collaboration with Davenant was an 'honour'.[48]

Dryden grants that he joined in the revision only after Davenant had already decided on the form the new play was to take. What this form was we are never told; but if we examine his remarks closely in the context of the finished work,

Davenant's aim becomes clear: it was to turn a drama traditionally regarded as a romance into a tragi-comedy based upon the new classical rules. The result was a play that does surpass the original in probability of action, correctness of language, and symmetry or balance of structure.[49] Dryden is vague about how Davenant dampened the legends of priests and similarly vague about how he turned much of the lively in Shakespeare's language – the vivid handling of concrete detail, the flights of metaphor – into what is essentially a language of statement. But his remarks about Davenant's improvement of Shakespeare's faulty 'Design' are richly detailed. We learn that Davenant created better balance between the imaginative heightening of the major plot and the comic realism of the minor plot by building up '[t]he Comical parts of the Saylors'. Further, we learn that he established more clearly defined parallels and contrasts both between the two actions and within each of them by adding characters and episodes: for instance, juxtaposed with Miranda, a woman who had never seen a man, is Hippolito, 'a Man who had never seen a Woman'. These changes, we are then told, were the work of a 'quick and piercing imagination', and their invention 'put the last hand' to 'the Design of Shakespear'.[50]

That Davenant succeeded in doing what he had set out to do – that he brought the play into closer accord with the rules of composition – Dryden is only too willing to admit; and he pays tribute where tribute is due. Yet he no sooner praises Davenant's triumph than, with complete disregard for the prologue, he lets us know his thorough dissatisfaction with the play, though without offending the memory of his friend. The revision is an artistic success, but an aesthetic failure. It does bring into slight imbalance the lively and the just; but in spite of that imbalance, or rather on account of it, *The Tempest* in its new version fails to delight. Because of the literal-mindedness (the emphasis on balance and symmetry, probability and verisimilitude), he complains, Davenant has removed from the play not only Prospero's magic but Shakespeare's as well.[51] Davenant's 'thoughts', which are 'extreamly pleasant and surprizing', are a poor substitute for Shakespeare's insights; and 'imaginations' that cannot 'easily enter into any other man' do not adequately replace the legends of priests.[52]

The condemnation of Davenant, kindly worded though it may be, reflects an important stage in Dryden's critical thinking. In his first essays on the drama, he had preferred the kind of play that Davenant was to write, a tragi-comedy, in which according to a clearly stated principle the lively was to have a very slight imbalance over the just. And in his own plays, as he continually said, he might perhaps violate the principle and ignore or violate the rules flagrantly, but (he was quick to add) he never really sanctioned his lapses: at best he regarded them as 'slight, and little imperfections'.[53] By the time of the '[A]ccount' of *Annus Mirabilis,* however, he had made it perfectly clear that there were genres in which the lively might prevail more than slightly in both language and fable; and that, if the playwright was careful, it might also prevail more than slightly in the theatre.

In short, the whole drift of Dryden's development had been away from the just in literature and hence from that form, tragi-comedy, which by his own definition requires its abundant presence. As a result, by the time he passes judgment on Davenant's play, he equates our delight in great literature, and especially the drama, chiefly with the lively. With hindsight, we can say that his criticism is beginning to align itself with new forms. In comedy, it is moving towards what he is soon to call 'mixed ... Comedy'; and in serious drama, towards the heroic play: towards a theory and practice that will allow for all but complete submergence of the just in literature to the marvellous and the wonderful. That in the development of heroic drama he will turn for his inspiration not to Shakespeare – to romances like the original *Tempest* – but elsewhere (to Ariosto), is merely one of the oddities of his art and, it may be added, of literary history.

IV

By 1670 tragi-comedy had lost a considerable measure of Dryden's favour; and in his criticism he registered that change by centring his attention on other forms. In the dedication of *Tyrannick Love,* generally considered his most extravagant play, he identified one of the forms – an original contribution to the English stage – and for the first time he gave it a name: the work before us is 'an Heroick Play'. In the 'Preface to *Tyrannick Love*' he, moreover, gave the new form its first truly helpful commentary. The preface was purportedly designed to defend *Tyrannick Love* against charges of plagiarism and immorality; and in a spirit of anger and resentment, he appears to be almost totally immersed in establishing both the originality of his play and its high moral purpose. However, in the course of making his defence, he does a great deal more. He manages to set forth, though incidentally and unobtrusively, the chief characteristics of the heroic play and to elevate them into literary principles. He says nothing about their sources and analogues in ancient epic, Renaissance epic or romance, and seventeenth-century tragi-comedy; nevertheless, the preface contains his theory of heroic drama at its final moment of gestation.

A central idea in the preface is that the heroic play is a species of the epic; and because of its affinities with the epic, it is largely exempt from all the rules customarily imposed on the drama. A playwright may, for instance, incorporate the unities of time, place and action, as rigidly defined by the French, into a heroic play; and with equal authority, though he may never abandon them completely, he may treat them as loosely as he likes. The choice lies entirely within his discretion.[54] Similarly, in selecting characters and episodes he may, to a considerable degree, either follow or ignore the rules of probability. For just as the epic can represent the activities of supernatural beings, so too can heroic plays, 'which are of the same Nature with the Epick', represent anything within 'the extremest bounds of what is credible'.[55]

It has been said that the heroic play was produced 'essentially in consequence of the inevitable drift of epic critical theory and practice in the Renaissance and the early neoclassical period'.[56] But it would be truer to say that the heroic play represented an attempt to buck the tide. In England and on the Continent the drift of critical theory was not in the direction of turning dramas into epics but of turning epics into plays. For example, Sir William Davenant, a writer in both forms, thought that the epic ought to embody the structure and techniques of the 'regular species' of 'English ... drama'. In his influential 'Preface to *Gondibert*' (1650) he claims that his poem (an epic) is nothing less than a five-act play in narration:

> I cannot discerne ... that any Nation hath in representment of great actions, either by *Heroicks* or *Dramaticks,* digested Story into so pleasant and instructive a method as the English by their *Drama;* and by that regular species, though narratively and not in Dialogue, I have drawn the body of an Heroick Poem[57]

For Davenant, however, the ultimate lesson that epic poets are to glean from the drama does not involve matters of structure or style. Dramatists are chiefly valuable for teaching the importance of verisimilitude in the handling of plot. The 'best Dramaticks' know that 'Story, where ever it seems most likely, growes most pleasant'. Consequently, they 'lay the Scene at home [on the Earth]' and 'avoid the remote Regions of Heaven and Hell', the 'descending of Gods in gay Clouds', and 'the rising of Ghosts in Smoke'.[58] As a dramatist himself, Davenant may not have always followed these rules of the stage. But as a serious epic poet he tried to follow them to the letter.[59]

Davenant's ambition was to replace the fantastic marvels of Homer with the 'natural probabilities' that he associated with the best drama. His programme for the epic is one that was echoed by critics throughout the period, though decidedly not by Dryden. While Davenant and others regarded the marvellous as a discardable blemish in the epic and by implication in the drama, Dryden thought of the epic largely in terms of the marvellous. Not only did he want to keep the marvellous in the epic but he also wanted to create a new form of drama, the heroic play, which would embody all those aspects of the marvellous which he so much admired in the epic: the astonishing actions, the superhuman characters, and the extraordinary or hyperbolic speeches.

To establish authority for his position, he drew upon Aristotle, whose thought, through modification or careful selection, he made to serve his own ends. In the *Poetics*, after declaring that the marvellous has a place in poetry – though more of a place in epic than in drama – Aristotle subjects the use of the marvellous to strict limitations. For the marvellous – in the sense of the strange or the supernatural – to be admitted into poetry, Aristotle's main requirement is that it satisfy one of two conditions. First, the marvellous may be admitted when it conforms, if not to empirical reality, at least to common beliefs about the nature of the world.[60] Aristotle does not work out in any detail the implications of this rule, but his position can be glossed by a passage in Tasso, where the use of the supernatural in Christian epic is considered:

> The poet ought to attribute actions that far exceed human power to God, to his angels, to demons, or to those granted power by God or by

demons ... Such actions, if considered in themselves, will seem marvellous; nay, they are commonly called miracles. But if regarded in terms of their agent's efficacy and power, they will seem verisimilar. For men having drunk in this notion along with their milk from the time they were in swaddling clothes ... will not think unlikely what they believe not only is possible but has often occurred and can occur often again.[61]

Second, according to Aristotle, the marvellous may be introduced into poetry if it is so handled by the poet as to seem credible or real.[62] What this procedure entails is explained by S. H. Butcher in his commentary upon the *Poetics*. The poet, Butcher writes,

> feigns certain imaginary persons, strange situations, incredible adventures. By vividness of narrative and minuteness of detail, and, above all, by the natural sequence of incident and motive, things are made to happen exactly as they would have happened had the fundamental fiction been fact ... By artistic treatment things incredible in real life wear an air of probability. The impossible not only becomes possible, but natural and even inevitable.[63]

In other words, Aristotle would admit the marvellous into poetry after it is made an aspect or extension of the actual world, after it is tamed.

Dryden, on the other hand, has no interest in domesticating the marvellous. He wants it wholly to retain its wonderful character. He may defend the admission of supernatural beings into his play by reference to the Aristotelian doctrine of traditional belief. But in his hands, Aristotle's precept is almost completely shorn of its restrictions:

> As for what I have said of Astral or Aerial Spirits it is no invention of mine, but taken from those who have written on that Subject. Whether there are such Beings or not, it concerns not me; 'tis sufficient for my purpose, that many have believed the affirmative: and that these Heroick Representations ... are not limited, but with the extremest bounds of what is credible.[64]

It is not necessary that the audience believe in astral spirits: that men once believed in them he finds sufficient grounds for their admission into poetry.

Indeed, questions of belief or verisimilitude are quite irrelevant to Dryden's discussion. The audience of a heroic play need not be duped into accepting as true what is enacted on the stage: it cannot choose to do otherwise. The language of the heroic drama raises the spectators out of their rational selves. They are charmed, elevated, transported; and in that state they spontaneously believe in the marvellous and accept it. 'By the Harmony of words', playwrights inspire both faith and morals. They 'elevate the mind to a sense of Devotion, as our solemn Musick, which is inarticulate Poesie, does in Churches; and by the lively images of piety, adorned by action, through the senses allure the Soul ...'[65] Language, then, secures that acceptance of the marvellous which Aristotle believed could be won only by appeals to traditional belief or by the skilful articulation of plot. As for *Tyrannick Love,* not only does it arouse faith through the supernatural but through the supernatural it justifies God's ways to men. The hand of God is everywhere: the wicked are punished and the virtuous are properly rewarded, in this world or the next.[66]

*

In his preface, Dryden considers only the advantages of glittering rhetoric. However, in his prologue, also published in 1670 but written one year earlier, he attempts to assess its cost. A language of transport, and especially one not rooted in a language of statement, has (he recognizes) its very heavy price. It runs the risk always of falling into bathos:

> Poets, like Lovers, should be bold and dare,
> They spoil their business with an over-care.
> And he who servilely creeps after sence,
> Is safe, but ne're will reach an Excellence.
> Hence 'tis, our Poet in his conjuring,
> Allow'd his Fancy the full scope and swing.
> But when a Tyrant for his Theme he had,
> He loos'd the Reins, and bid his Muse run mad:
> And though he stumbles in a full career;
> Yet rashness is a better fault than fear.[67]

He nevertheless judges these failings to be unimportant and incidental and playfully chides those critics who, for such minor imperfections, 'whole plays decry'.[68] His patience, however, with 'the holy Criticks' was running low; and the anger that occasionally surfaces in both the 'Preface to *Tyrannick Love*' and his next two essays – one on comedy, one on the heroic play – becomes for some years his dominant tone.

In 1672, for the second edition of *Tyrannick Love,* Dryden added a final paragraph to his preface. Here he defends the soundness of individual lines of his prologue and play against the petty objections of his critics. What is of interest in that paragraph is a new severity of tone. Gone completely are the light touch and insouciant manner which dominate so very much of his early criticism. By 1672 Dryden no longer surveys his writing with the studied indifference of a man showing off a small possession. Poetry has become a serious business. He is willing to argue about it with confidence; and he is not beyond addressing 'the little Critiques' with indignation and contempt:

> For the little Critiques who pleas'd themselves with thinking they have found a flaw in that line of the Prologue, (*And he who servilely creeps after sence, is safe,* &c.) as if I patroniz'd my own nonsence, I may reasonably suppose they have never read *Horace. Serpit humi tutus,* &c. are his words: He who creeps after plaine, dull, common sence, is safe from committing absurdities; but, can never reach any heighth, or excellence of wit: and sure I could not meane that any excellence were to be found in nonsence ... Some foole before them had charg'd me in the *Indian*

Emperour with nonsence in these words, *And follow fate which does too fast pursue;* which was borrow'd from *Virgil* in the *XIth* of his *Æneids*, *Eludit gyro interior, sequiturque sequentem* [She eludes him, wheels inward and pursues the pursuer]. I quote not these to prove that I never writ Nonsence, but onely to show that they are so unfortunate as not to have found it.[69]

With the new conclusion to his essay we have fully entered into Dryden's middle style.

CHAPTER SIX

Varieties of comic experience
(1671)

I

In London, where he had arrived some years before the Restoration, Dryden began his literary career by turning out occasionally poems on affairs of state. But by the early 1660s, to achieve the fame and fortune he desired, he had also begun to compose for that favoured resort of Court and Town, the public stage. When he wrote his first plays he decided to do the safe and wise thing and to imitate the works of established authors: in *The Wild Gallant* (1663; 1669), a low comedy, he followed the example of Jonson; in *The Rival Ladies* (1664), a tragi-comedy, he followed the example of Fletcher; and in *The Indian Queen* (1665), a heroic play, he again followed the example of Fletcher, or so he thought at the time. Although only *The Wild Gallant* failed in performance, none of the three plays especially pleased him. Each lacks the variety of incident, the depth of characterization and the magic of language that he associated with the 'Soul' of English drama and, in particular, with Shakespeare.

Dryden's response to his disappointment was a programme of experimentation. Having initially failed to meet his own expectations in heroic play, tragi-comedy and comedy, he tried his hand at each again but this time employed somewhat different methods. In his second heroic play, *The Indian Emperour* (1667), a continuation of the first, he added complications to the plot, heightened the imagery, and, according to Derek Hughes, realized 'much of the promise [intermittently] shown in ... *The Indian Queen*'.[1] In his second tragi-comedy, *Secret Love* (1668), he also made advances. He abandoned the single-plot formula of Fletcher and grouped the serious and the comic actions into separate plots. He was at first enthusiastic about the results, but after a while grew disenchanted. Tragi-comedy, however constructed, demanded a closer imitation of the everyday world than eventually was to his liking; but at least he had found a type of tragi-comedy which he could somehow accept. Even non-dramatic poetry yielded to his touch. With good justification, he was far prouder of *Annus Mirabilis* (1667) than he was of his other political verse. Only one genre proved intractable: comedy. In *Secret Love* he had managed to write a brilliant comic underplot and to bring nearly to perfection the main characters of high comedy, the gay couple. But plays that were entirely comic and that properly mingled high comedy and low, he could not yet deal with, though he tried to do so many times.

II

After its initial failure Dryden rewrote *The Wild Gallant,* staged it again in 1667 and published it, along with two prologues, two epilogues and a preface, in 1669.

99

The original play has been lost. But as the second prologue makes clear, he thought that the play, a low comedy, had failed because it lacked sufficiently the roguishness of high comedy to please the Town. That fault he tried to correct in the revision by adding a scene of rakish intrigue, which includes, as objects of his gallant's wit, 'three Wenches more':

> One unfletch'd Author, writ a *Wild Gallant*.
> He thought him monstrous leud (I'l lay my life)
> Because suspected with his Landlords Wife:
> But since his knowledge of the Town began,
> He thinks him now a very civil man:
> And, much asham'd of what he was before,
> Has fairly play'd him at three Wenches more.[2]

Through the added scene he did increase to some extent the elements of high comedy demanded by the Town, yet the revision also failed because, as the second epilogue makes clear, he had not corrected another fault in the original: a serious violation of probability and decorum. Still ignorant in the ways of his craft, he persisted in giving his most polished lines and the wittiest to his 'fooles':

> But fooles grow wary now; and when they see
> A Poet eyeing round the Company,
> Straight each man for himself begins to doubt;
> They shrink like Seamen when a Press comes out.
> Few of e'm will be found for Publick use,
> Except you charge an Oph upon each house,
> Like the Traind-Bands, and every man ingage
> For a sufficient Foole to serve the Stage.
> And, when with much adoe you get him there,
> Where he in all his glory shou'd appear,
> Your Poets make him such rare things to say,
> That he's more wit than any Man ith' Play...[3]

Having twice failed to integrate properly high and low comedy in *The Wild Gallant*, he next attempted the unexpected: he tried to woo fame by removing high comedy or witticism all but entirely from his next work. In 1667, in collaboration with the Duke of Newcastle, he wrote *Sir Martin Mar-all*, a low comedy in which he mingles humour not with wit but with farce; and, with a prologue and an epilogue, he published it the following year. Samuel Pepys, who saw it in its initial run, called it 'an entire piece of mirth, a complete farce';[4] and its riotous good fun is an adequate explanation of the enormous popularity it enjoyed. But while audiences delighted in the play, it gave its author little satisfaction. Dryden came very quickly to regret that his play contained so much farce and so little wit that the 'Gallants' who came to see it, as he complains in the prologue, brought more wit into the theatre than they found on the stage:

> For, Gallants, you your selves have found the wit.
> To bid you welcome would your bounty wrong,
> None welcome those who bring their chear along.[5]

Despite the acclaim it enjoyed, Dryden liked *Sir Martin Mar-all* no better than he had liked *The Wild Gallant*. The experiment was, from his point of view, a failure: with his emphasis on low comedy and mere horseplay, he had neglected far too much the intellectual or high comedy which, he realized, he obviously preferred. By the mid-1660s he had decided on the importance of the lively in practically all forms of literature, but especially in both epic poem and serious drama. Through the disparagement of *Sir Martin Mar-all* in the prologue, he would now argue that the lively as wit – or what he will later call 'sharpness of conceit' – is essential in all really good comedy, though he says nothing about a proper regard for decorum: about his theory, soon to be developed, that wit and humour must each be confined to a separate plot. However, he does suggest the importance and the emphasis he will soon give to the lively as comic wit in a very different kind of drama, one which perhaps he had already planned to write. That drama, which he is to call 'mixt ... Comedy', he will explain at some length and hence justify in his 'Preface to *An Evening's Love*' (1671).[6]

III

Except for a single essay on the epic and the historical poem, Dryden's criticism, until the end of 1670, centres entirely on tragi-comedy; and that criticism, therefore, gives an inadequate picture of his range as playwright. His plays until then are fairly evenly divided among tragi-comedies (three), comedies (two) and heroic plays (three), but tragi-comedy dominates the criticism.[7] He did not write about his comedies, except in the most cursory way, because he found them disappointing. He wrote even less about his heroic plays because he did not believe they required analysis: heroic drama, he initially thought, was just a variant form of tragi-comedy. But his reluctance to comment on the two forms was soon to end. By November 1670 he had come to understand that the heroic play was a genre distinct unto itself; and slightly later, in 1671, he at last published his mixed comedy, *An Evening's Love,* which he felt worthy of analysis and reflection. As he had learned how to inspire wonder and awe in serious literature through a complete subordination of the just to the lively, so through a corresponding subordination in comedy he eventually learned how to provoke all the kinds and degrees of laughter he required.

By the time he published *An Essay of Dramatick Poesie* in 1668, Dryden had defined three different kinds of tragi-comedy. In one, which he initially traced to Fletcher but later to William Davenant, and which he was to develop in his first heroic plays (*The Indian Queen, The Indian Emperour* and *Tyrannick Love*), there is a single plot; and that plot, whether it ends unhappily or not, is (as he said) 'unmix'd with mirth'. In a second, of which (he thought) Fletcher had written the best examples, and which he had already imitated in *The Rival Ladies,* there is a single plot, in which the comic episodes alternate with the serious. In a third, which he hoped to develop by himself, and which he eventually did in *Secret Love,* serious and comic episodes again alternate, but they are now separated into parallel or contrasting plots.

Of the precise origins of *An Evening's Love,* a mixed comedy, or of its relation to tragi-comedy of any kind, it is all but impossible to speak with certainty. How he came to write *An Evening's Love* Dryden never says. Perhaps the germ of his inspiration was the commingling of wit and humour in the comedies and the tragi-comedies of Fletcher, as well as in the comedies of Jonson and perhaps even Shakespeare.[8] Perhaps Sir George Etherege's *Comical Revenge* (1664) with its separate and parallel love intrigues – the noble, the genteel, the common – also provided some of the inspiration.[9] It is more likely, however, that Dryden conceived of the play by analogy with *Secret Love* (1668). That tragi-comedy is the first of his plays to set a major plot, in which the lively supersedes the just, against an underplot, in which the just supersedes the lively; and *An Evening's Love* is a comedy with a similar counterpoint, notwithstanding additions and deletions, unexpected reversals in technique, style and theme, and radical shifts in emphasis.

In the major action of both works elements of the just – unity and decorum, probability and verisimilitude, moral truth and instruction – are more or less the same, though in the later work they are handled with extreme flexibility, even at times with abandon. And what is lively in the major plot of *Secret Love* – heroic character and action, noble language and theme – now becomes something very different: it becomes a language centred almost entirely in the pleasures of word-play and wit. The lively in the minor plot – the witticisms of the gay couple – is replaced by what is 'unnatural' and 'monstrous', the lively as mere farce; and the just, which is kept at a minimum, is equated once again with regularity of plot construction, but with a far greater prominence given to comic realism and especially Jonsonian humours. Wit in the minor action of one kind of drama dominates completely the major action of another kind; and the place it leaves vacant is occupied by something else altogether. In Dryden's new or mixed comedy wit thus prevails as high comedy in the main plot; and in juxtaposition with farce, humour prevails in the sub-plot as low comedy.

Dryden's mixed comedy and his heroic drama both developed ultimately out of tragi-comedy, albeit of different kinds: one 'having the allay of Comedy to depress it', one 'unmix'd with mirth'. And since they were further conceived under that charter of freedom which, beginning with the 'Defence' (1668), he would allow poets and playwrights alike, the two forms are in many respects obverse sides of each other. He allows that same charter of freedom in one kind of mixed genre, mixed comedy, which he had already begun to justify in another, heroic drama, though in very different terms. He would allow flights of the imagination and violations of literary rule; he would divorce, as much as decorum allows, pleasure from instruction, and beauty from moral truth. But he would encourage not emulation but laughter, demonstrate not the heroism or grandeur of life and events but their absurdity and evoke the marvellous or the wonderful not through noble discourse or the supernatural but through farce and outrageous wit.

An Evening's Love proved to be the only 'mixt ... Comedy' Dryden ever wrote. Temperamentally, although he had a fine sense of humour, he was not very much interested in writing comedy of any kind and wanted to give it up for 'serious Plot and Verse'.[10] Practically, he soon found that 'mixt ... Comedy' had been pre-empted by younger playwrights with whose works he could not compete.[11] But short-lived as it was, his interest in the form was immensely fruitful: it led him to write a play that helped to establish the conventions of what we know today as the comedy of manners; and it inspired him to write the first essay we have on mixed comedy and, in particular, on the element of wit (or liveliness of language) in high comedy,[12] an essay the manner of argument and the history of which are interesting in themselves.

IV

The 'Preface to *An Evening's Love*' perfects the combative style of criticism that Dryden had been developing since 1668 and that he would follow for the next eight years. Moreover, it marks a permanent shift in his criticism away from the Court and the Town and towards a larger, less exclusive audience. Henceforth, whenever he writes in his courtier manner he does so in his dedications alone, these directed always to a peer of the realm. He directs his prefaces to the untutored 'Reader', whose literary education he now undertakes, sometimes through the most detailed of critical analyses. In the dedications he continues to speak of literary matters;[13] but in his prefaces and miscellaneous other prose he ignores the aristocracy entirely: his only tributes are those to great writers, among whom he increasingly counts himself.

The 'Preface to *An Evening's Love*' provides a fascinating glimpse of how Dryden's new intended audience exerted an influence on his criticism. In its original conception, as he tells us, the preface was to be almost as far-ranging as the *Essay of Dramatick Poesie*. It was to deal with the comparative merits of Elizabethan and Restoration poets and specifically to take up three separate topics: serious drama, comic drama and correct English usage. In treating each of these subjects he had intended to prove, though with some reservations, that the Restoration had fulfilled its promise: except in 'humour' and 'contrivance' of plot, it was producing literary works superior to those of the last age. As his opening remarks in the preface make clear, he had also intended to conduct his argument boldly and even with a touch of defiance – in short, without what in a later essay he was to call a 'veneration for the past':

> I had thought, Reader, in this Preface to have written somewhat concerning the difference betwixt the Playes of our Age, and those of our Predecessors on the English Stage: to have shewn in what parts of Dramatick Poesie we were excell'd by *Ben. Johnson,* I mean, humour, and contrivance of Comedy; and in what we may justly claim precedence of *Shakespear* and *Fletcher,* namely in *Heroick Playes:* but this design I have wav'd on second considerations; at least deferr'd it till I publish the *Conquest of Granada,* where the discourse will be more proper. I had also prepar'd to treat of the improvement of our Language since *Fletcher's* and *Johnson's* dayes, and consequently of our refining the Courtship, Raillery, and Conversation of Playes ...[14]

What started out as a single essay, however, quickly became three: a considerably shortened preface to *An Evenings' Love* (1671), which deals mainly with comedy; and two essays published with *The Conquest of Granada* (1672): a preface, 'Of Heroique Playes', which explains heroic drama, and a postscript, 'Defence of the Epilogue', which fulfils his promise 'to treat of the improvement of our Language since *Fletcher's* and *Johnson's* dayes'. Like Dryden's original 'Reader', we must be grateful for the change in plan, since it allowed a fuller and clearer treatment of each subject and permitted him to join the essays to plays which best illustrate his statements and which, in turn, are best explained by them.

V

In the 'Preface to *An Evening's Love*' Dryden considers two kinds of comedy – 'Comedy ... [of] wit' (or high comedy) and 'low Comedy' (the inversion of high comedy) – and 'Farce', a separate and 'different' kind of drama altogether; the subject, nature and function of the three kinds; and the miscellaneous techniques – wit, humour, horseplay – by which the three achieve their respective ends. His overriding concern, however, is to explain what in his opinion is a thoroughly new development in the Restoration theatre: a form of comedy that he may in part have borrowed both from Jonson, whose low comedy contains some wit, and from Fletcher, whose comedy of wit contains some humour, but (as he boasts) a form that he has brought – despite some lapses – to near perfection. The form he has in mind brings together what, for the sake of convenience, may now be described as the two strands of all comedy – the high and the low; each strand sets the other into a complete and sharp relief; and the two together encourage as much laughter as, in their juxtaposition with each other and with farce, imagination and judgment will allow. Dryden celebrates his achievement as 'mixt ... Comedy', though it is neither a mixed form nor, strictly speaking, a new genre.

The preface is designed so as to refute the series of attacks by Thomas Shadwell, rival playwright, old irritant and eventually archenemy.[15] In his prefaces to *The Sullen Lovers* (1668) and *The Royal Shepherdess* (1669) Shadwell accuses Dryden of lacking sufficient reverence for Ben Jonson, whom (according to Shadwell) 'all Drammatick *Poets* ought to imitate'.[16] Dryden's statement, in the *Essay of Dramatick Poesie* (1668), that Jonson is 'frugal of [wit]', or the witticisms and therefore the conceits of high comedy, Shadwell misunderstands;[17] and he is then offended by what he takes to be Dryden's assertion that Jonson in fact 'wrote his best *Playes* without Wit' (that is, with none at all). From Shadwell's point of view, Dryden thus committed a twofold blunder: he condemned Jonson for not engaging in what is to Shadwell a literary vice, the indecencies of 'Jests' and 'Repartie', and at the same time for lacking what everyone admits to be his supreme virtue, poetic genius and hence a fine sense of literary decorum or 'Correct[ness]'.[18]

Ostensibly, Shadwell condemns witticisms in the name of Jonson, but his objections are actually made in support of his own comic theory. For Shadwell, comedy ought to be a heavily underscored exemplum, a satire strictly devoted to the punishment of vice and the exaltation of virtue. Consequently, light banter offends him by its apparent lack of seriousness and by its tendency to link arms with the bawdy and the profane. Not entirely without reason, he identifies the protagonists in Dryden's comedies with 'a Swearing, Drinking, Whoring Ruffian for a Lover, and an impudent, ill-bred *tomrig* for a Mistress'. The wit of this fine couple, Shadwell declares, disgusts even the 'most dissolute of Men'.[19]

It took Dryden almost two years to answer Shadwell's charges, but when he did so, in the 'Preface to *An Evening's Love*', they were remarkably fresh in his mind. Although it may appear to be rambling and digressive, the preface is a carefully organized refutation of Shadwell's propositions: that English dramatists ought to imitate only Jonson, that comic wit ought to signify only decorum, and that the end of comedy ought to be only the punishment of vice and the celebration of virtue. Throughout his preface Dryden demonstrates that Shadwell not only fails to understand the *Essay of Dramatick Poesie* but also fails to make the sharp distinctions upon which intellectual discussion depends. Here mistaking the part for the whole, there mistaking the accidental for the essential, Shadwell understands nothing with clarity. But of all his errors, Shadwell's most serious blunder, Dryden leads us to believe, is contained in his estimate of Jonson.

Shadwell identifies excellence in the drama solely with a close imitation of Jonson. It is for this reason that he regards himself as the pre-eminent Restoration dramatist, since he has laboured to follow Jonson while his contemporaries have not.[20] But, as Dryden argues, only a zealot would turn Jonson into the '*ipse dixit*' of the stage. For his own part, Dryden is willing to 'admire ... him where [he] ought', as master in plot construction ('contrivance') and as the creator of a new basis for dramatic character – the humour.[21] He will not follow Jonson blindly, and he will not, *pace* Shadwell, attempt to imitate him alone. To do so would be to forsake the imaginative vitality and rich diversity within the English traditions.

In order to determine Jonson's possible role as a model for the contemporary playwright, Dryden briefly surveys his limitations or failures in the drama and his achievements. In tragedy, where 'the Actions and Persons are great, and the crimes horrid', Jonson never achieves, in Dryden's view, the first rank. Rather, his talent lies in comedy, a humbler form, where the characters 'are of a lower quality, the action is little, and the faults and vices are but the sallies of youth, and the frailties of humane nature'. But even in this genre, in which he is an undisputed master, Jonson cannot serve later playwrights as their sole guide. There are two types of comedy, according to Dryden; and Jonson achieved his greatness only in one. He excelled in 'Comedy ... [of] humour' or what Dryden also calls 'low Comedy'. Except sporadically and with no great success, he never attempted what Dryden calls 'Comedy ... [of] wit', or what we know today as high comedy.[22]

It is in the preface that Dryden first explicitly considers the two strands of comedy, the high and the low; but they are surely adumbrated in both the *Essay of Dramatick Poesie* and other early works. Throughout his early criticism, whenever he mentions comedy, he has both strands in mind. And when he mentions the two, he always associates high comedy with Fletcher and low comedy with

Jonson; he does so even in the 'Prologue to *The Tempest*' (1670), where for the first time he states that whatever merits Jonson and Fletcher may have in comedy they derived from the 'heights' of Shakespeare and the depths:

> Shakespear, who (taught by none) did first impart
> To *Fletcher* Wit, to labouring *Johnson* Art.
> He Monarch-like gave those his subjects law,
> And is that Nature which they paint and draw.
> *Fletcher* reach'd that which on his heights did grow,
> Whilst *Johnson* crept and gather'd all below.
> This did his Love, and this his Mirth digest:
> One imitates him most, the other best.[23]

It is upon the distinctions suggested here – those between the accomplishments of Fletcher and those of Jonson and, by implication, between plays based on wit and plays based on humour – that Dryden in the preface constructs his theory of comedy.

Throughout the preface Dryden claims to distinguish between comedy of wit and comedy of humour on merely descriptive grounds. He insists that by comedy of wit (or high comedy) he means not superior comedy but comedy that depicts superior or eminently polished characters. Similarly, by comedy of humour (or low comedy) he means not inferior comedy but comedy that depicts inferior or socially 'vulgar' characters. If he prefers the former to the latter, he hastens to point out that he does so on thoroughly subjective grounds: '[M]y disgust of low Comedy proceeds not so much from my judgement as from my temper'.[24] As his analysis proceeds, however, it becomes clear that his categories are actually evaluative in nature. For Dryden, low comedy, or the comedy of humour, is the inferior form, its composition requiring little imagination in the poet, its effects providing only middling pleasure to an audience.

The subject of low comedy is folly and vice presented through actions of base intrigue ('cozenage' and 'cheat'); its characters are petty criminals, as well as men and women – the humours – labouring under a congenital madness or an acquired affectation. Ben Jonson, the master in low comedy, chose to draw his characters from the bottom of the social scale. However, the depiction of 'Mechanick people',[25] in Dryden's view, is an accidental, not an essential aspect of the form: the dangers of unreason can as effectually be shown through the follies and eccentricities of gentlemen.[26] What truly distinguishes low comedy is not the provenance of its characters but its means of creating 'satisfaction' and 'pleasure'. Low comedy works predominantly through the 'judgement' and aims at 'natural imitation'. The playwright 'observes only what is ridiculous, and pleasant folly [or madness], and by judging exactly what is so, he pleases in the representation of it'. Since low comedy is so tightly bound to the world of fact, it contains few imaginative elements. But if the lively is only residually present, its presence is unmistakably felt. For the poet records verifiable details, but not precisely: he heightens his materials. Natural actions are ingeniously arranged; characters are fashioned, not copied; and language is more striking than that which we hear daily about us. Hence, low comedy conveys both an accurate and a 'lively representation of … corruption', and 'works on the judgment and fancy'. We respond to low comedy not merely with detached acceptance but also with delight and peals of laughter.[27]

Low comedy pleases; but high comedy – the 'Comedy … [of] wit' – inspires what Dryden refers to as 'a pleasure that is more noble'. The subject of high comedy is 'the sallies of youth', presented through 'adventures' in 'love'. Characters are necessarily 'ingenious' '[ladies and] Gentlemen'. Their 'Courtship, Raillery, and Conversation' are never ill-bred or mean, but in general exhibit the 'excell[ence]' and 'refin[ement]' 'of … [the] Age'. They may at times have 'ridiculous … manners'. But the 'folly' which the characters illustrate, and which may flout the moral code of both church and state, is produced by 'small imperfections' and the 'frailties of [their] humane nature', and not by 'deformity' or 'premeditated crimes', 'corruption' or the 'extravagances of *Bedlam*'; and eventually, 'when they resolve to marry', they are 'reclaim[ed] … from vice', 'forgiven' and made 'happy, but only as heaven makes sinners so'.[28] However, the identifying mark of high comedy is the presence, in the dialogue, of that intensely imaginative element which Dryden calls 'wit'. 'Wit' is thus a key to unlocking the distinction he draws between low and high comedy. Moreover, to understand the term is to perceive, in yet another context, the importance he assigns to heightened language in all significant literature.

VI

In the Renaissance and throughout the Restoration 'wit' was a term to conjure with.[29] In the late Middle Ages 'wit' (from Anglo-Saxon *'witan'*, 'to know') occasionally meant 'a bodily sense' or 'the five senses', although throughout the period the word signified primarily 'mind' and hence 'understanding', meanings which the word has held, more or less, down to our own time. In the sixteenth century the humanists Roger Ascham and John Lyly, by analogy with the Latin word *'ingenium'* ('talent', 'genius') defined 'wit' as 'genius' or 'wisdom'. The first significant application of the word to literature, and to literary theory, appears to have been made by Sir Philip Sidney. In his *Defence of Poesie* (1580; 1595), Sidney defines 'wit' specifically as an aptitude for poetry and, by implication, as skill in handling any of the major literary genres, meanings which Sidney did not invent but which seem to have been in the air for some time, since they are found in so minor a work as the prologue to Alexander Barclay's *Certain Eclogues* (1570):

> The famous poets with the muses nine,
> With wit inspired, fresh, pregnant, and divine,
> Say, 'Boldly indite in style substantial!'
> Some in poems high and heroical,
> Some them delight in heavy tragedies,
> And some in wanton or merry comedies;
> Some in satires against vices dare carp,
> Some in sweet songs accordant with the harp;
> And each of these all had laud and excellence
> After their reason and style of eloquence.[30]

In the seventeenth century 'wit' acquired a new and narrower meaning. Given the esteem in which the new poetry of irony and paradox was held, the word increasingly came to stand not for broad intellectual gifts or skill in the major literary genres but for a talent of a different order: a capacity for ingenuity, an ability to make unexpected unions or contrasts of generally diverse ideas. We may see that shift beginning to take place in Jonson's *Everyman Out of His Humour* (1600), in which the major characters all speak at some length about wit; but how differently they use the term! For Asper and Macilente, men of old-fashioned tastes who lament the 'monstrousnesse' of the times, 'wit' retains its older meanings: it stands for mind, wisdom and correct writing. But for Carlo Buffone and Fastidius Briske, two inveterate lovers of the verbal jest, the word signifies quite different things: it is equated with what they call *'simile's'*, 'choice figures' and 'conceit[s]'.[31]

Briske is an object of ridicule, but the forms of speech which Jonson had dismissed as merely absurd in 1600 were half a century later taken quite seriously by Thomas Hobbes. In one of his early works, *Human Nature, or the Fundamental Elements of Policy* (1640; 1650), Hobbes can still equate 'wit' with *ingenium*. To have wit, he tells us, is to possess the chief intellectual faculties, both fancy and judgment. Hence, it is to find 'unexpected *similitude* [among] things otherwise much unlike' and to discern *'dissimilitude* in things that appear otherwise the same'.[32] Within a decade, however, he feels compelled to alter his definition: he would bring it into accord with, and so accommodate, new patterns of usage. In the *Leviathan* (1651) he notes that in popular speech, while 'wit' may still denote all the '*Virtues* INTELLECTUALL', it has also come to signify 'Fancy, without ... Judgment'.[33] Almost a quarter of a century later, in the 'Preface to Homer' (1675), he finally observes, though with severe disapproval, that for most men 'wit' now signifies 'Fancie ... alone': the new meaning has completely replaced the old.[34]

In his concern with the shifts in meaning of the word Hobbes was not alone. The concern was widespread: it preoccupied not only men of letters but also members of the Royal Society, churchmen and scientists alike. For all of them a mistaken sense of the intellectual virtues did more than produce bad poems. Love of false eloquence made men vulnerable to forms of unreason of every kind: the deceits of orators, the blandishments of Rome, the ravings of the sects.[35] And the mischief might lead, as it had in the past, to social unrest and even to civil war. Hence, early in the Restoration, there was a movement to restore 'wit' to its association with judgment and, therefore, with trained, gentlemanly intelligence and with respect for and obedience to the established political and moral order of things.

As 'wit', during the second half of the century, was increasingly defined as idiosyncratic statement, a reaction set in, one to which Thomas Sprat, in his *History of the Royal Society* (1667), gave characteristic expression. Sprat attacked the prevailing definition by advancing what was essentially its opposite. True, he equated wit not with judgment but with fancy; but he argued and insisted that fancy, and hence wit, must be grounded in judgment alone. It must be grounded not in '*Fictions*' or in '[t]he *Sciences* ['*Logical, Metaphysical, Grammatical,* nay even ... *Mathemat-*

ical'] of mens brains', but in 'the use of *Experiments*', in the '*Works of Nature*', and in 'those Ornaments ['the *Arts* of mens hands'] which are *Tru* and *Real* in themselves'.[36] With its emphasis on empirical evidence and verifiable fact, Sprat's definition helped to establish the meaning of 'wit' which would prevail in the eighteenth century. However, during the Restoration that definition was itself challenged by Dryden's usage, which pointed not forward to the strict canons of the next century but backward to the Renaissance conception of 'wit' as a comprehensive literary term.

As Hobbes treats 'wit' as a term that must denote preferably all the 'virtues intellectual', so too does Dryden; but throughout his criticism he also uses the word, as did Sidney, to signify not only poetic genius but also – indeed primarily – excellence in all kinds of writing. By thus taking 'wit' to mean specifically the inner harmony of a poem or the suitability of words and thoughts to subject, he is then able, again like Sidney, to affirm that 'the composition of all Poems is or ought to be of wit', each genre now possessing its own distinctive genius, its own poetic *ingenium*, its own peculiar requirements and proprieties.[37]

Hence, in the '[A]ccount' prefatory to *Annus Mirabilis* (1667), he does not establish, as one might expect, fixed categories of true and false wit. He distinguishes rather between what is appropriate to the epic ('delightful imaging', 'lively and apt description') and what is less appropriate ('grave sentence[s]') and entirely inappropriate ('Antithesis' and '*Paranomasia*', or pun). And he is quick to add that what is more or less inappropriate in the epic may always find a place in other genres.[38] Later in the essay, when he would further clarify his argument, he makes another distinction. He contrasts the 'proper wit' of the drama, 'where all that is said is to be suppos'd the effect of sudden thought', with the 'labour[ed]' wit – the 'curious ... words', the 'Tropes', the 'frequent allusions' – demanded in the epic, in which the poet is 'to express his thoughts with all the graces of elocution' and 'to write more figuratively'.[39]

The '[A]ccount' tells us nothing about the wit appropriate to comedy. Comic wit is, however, explained by Eugenius in the *Essay of Dramatick Poesie;* and that discussion helps set the context for Dryden's remarks on the subject in the 'Preface to *An Evening's Love*'. According to Eugenius, there are three distinct kinds of wit. One kind is 'independent of ... words'. It is based on 'a great thought', but clearly he does not mean that all 'great' or 'deep thoughts' are witty. As his many examples illustrate, all taken from either Latin or Commonwealth poetry, a witty thought involves the making of a 'bold' comparison, and hence the drawing of far-fetched analogies, between things thoroughly remote from each other: the ancient and the modern, as when John Cleveland equates Cain with 'the *Rebel* Scot'; the trivial and the significant, as when Terence compares a '*totum triduum* [all three days]' to a '*universum triduum* [three whole days]'; and the divine with the very human, as when Ovid 'call[s] the Court of *Jupiter* by the name of *Augustus* his palace'.[40]

Eugenius also believes that there is a kind of wit that is 'independent' not so much of 'expression or words' as of 'thought'. As the witty idea is not univocal but binds together disparate things, so too there is a kind of wit which is based on tensions in language itself: a severely correct style, like that of Horace, is punctuated by 'little accidents' or '*Catachresis*', 'elegancy' or 'coyning [of] words', but never so much as 'to obtrude a new word on … Readers', to violate 'custom and common use', or 'to express a thing hard and unnaturally … [in a] new way of Elocution'.[41]

In a third type of wit, and the one which Eugenius prefers, there is a disjunction unexpectedly between a 'great thought', one which is 'highly Metaphorical', and the 'common' or 'easie language' through which it is expressed. Although not without adding that he 'gives us many times a hard Nut to break our Teeth, without a Kernel for our pains', Eugenius now turns for illustration once again to the works of John Cleveland:

> For Beauty like White-powder makes no noise,
> And yet the silent Hypocrite destroyes.

'You see', he goes on to explain, 'the last line is highly Metaphorical, but it is so soft and gentle, that it does not shock us as we read it'. Therefore, he concludes, 'wit is best convey'd to us in the most easie language; and is most to be admir'd when a great thought comes drest in words so commonly receiv'd that it is understood by the meanest apprehensions, as the best meat is the most easily digested'.[42]

Any uncertainties we may have in deducing the argument Dryden expresses through Eugenius are resolved by the 'Preface to *An Evening's Love*'. Nothing in the preface, however, illuminates that argument better than the network of quotation and reference which links his views on wit with views set forth in Quintilian's *Institutio Oratoria*. For ultimately Quintilian on the '[verbal] jest' is the apparent source of Eugenius's statements on wit, or most of them; and he is explicit where Eugenius is either elliptical or vague. According to Quintilian, a 'jest' or witticism is the means through which pleaders in a court of law seek to raise laughter;[43] but more significantly, at least from Dryden's point of view, he goes on to explain, in some detail, that there are in fact four very different kinds of wit or jest: *urbanitas* (an urbane or learned wit), *venustus* (a graceful or charming wit), *facetia* (a polished or gentle wit) and *salsus* (a salty or sharp wit).[44] The accomplished or best jest, according to Quintilian, is effortless, spontaneous and brief and involves skill in both invention and language.[45] Quintilian concedes that it is possible for an unlettered man or even a rustic to stumble upon a jest, but he associates witticisms with gentlemen (*'viri boni'*), since 'all that is incongruous, coarse, unpolished, and exotic … in thought, language, voice, or gesture' blunts the comic effect.[46]

On the moral and intellectual character of what Eugenius calls 'a great thought', Quintilian is again instructive. The jests employed by orators, he insists, must always be harmless in intent; they must never be designed to wound or to make light of matters inherently grave.[47] Further, and more to Dryden's point, Quintilian identifies jests (or wit) with an element of falseness: jests are 'generally untrue'. They create odd fictions, seize upon chance resemblances or exploit latent ambiguities in the meanings of words.[48] Among the rhetorical devices that are most likely to produce jests, Quintilian names such figures of speech as hyperbole, metaphor, irony and pun.[49]

In his long discussion of jests Quintilian insists on never defining the thing of which he speaks. He explains that jests are too multiform in nature, too much buried in the mystery of human thought and feeling, to be anatomized in a phrase.[50] Dryden, however, steps beyond Quintilian. Having equated 'jest' and '[comic] wit', he insists on defining the thing of which he speaks, but in a strangely circuitous manner. Following the practice abhorred by lexicographers of glossing one complex term with another, he tells us that '[comic] wit' is 'sharpness of conceit', and then leaves us to work out the puzzle for ourselves.[51] The task is far from easy; but our understanding is enhanced by our pains.

In the seventeenth century 'conceit' had two dominant meanings. It maintained its original reference to a mental image or concept; but, under the influence of the Italian *concetto* and the Spanish *concepto*, it also came to stand for a trope or figure based, like wit, upon a comparison of dissimilar things.[52] In Jonson's *Bartholomew Fair* (1631), for example, John Little-wit speaks of a conceit as a 'deuice', or rhetorical figure, which he then equates solely with the pun, an identification of entirely unrelated words, based on a chance similarity of their respective sounds:

> *Little-wit [with a {marriage} licence in his hand.]*
> A Pretty conceit, and worth the finding! I ha' such luck to spinne out these fine things still, and like a Silke-worme, out of my selfe. Her<e>'s Master *Bartholomew Cokes,* of Harrow o' th' Hill, i' th' County of *Middlesex*, Esquire, takes forth his Licence to marry mistress Grace Welborne, of the said place and County: and when do's hee take it foorth? to-day! the foure and twentieth of August! *Bartholomew*-day! *Bartholomew* vpon Bartholomew! there's the deuice! who would haue mark'd such a leap-frogge chance now! A very ... lesse then *Ames-ace*, on two Dice! well, goe thy wayes, Iohn *Little-wit*: Proctor Iohn *Little-wit:* One o' the pretty wits o' *Paul's,* the *Little wit* of London, (so thou art call'd), and some thing beside.[53]

Given his intellectual capacity, Little-wit cannot think of the conceit as anything much more than a mere play on words. For Dryden, however, there are many different kinds of conceits. He never works out a system of classification as complex as those found in such seventeenth-century theorists as Baltazar Gracián and Emanuele Tesauro.[54] But in his early criticism he does informally distinguish, as a rule, among the 'thin conceit' (a feeble joke), the 'odd conceit' (a crude joke), the 'miserable conceit' (a conventional metaphor or paradox) and the type of conceit suitable to high comedy.[55] This last type is characterized by what he alternately calls 'sharpness' or 'acumen': it exhibits both intellectual subtlety and epigrammatic terseness of expression.[56]

In defining 'wit' in terms of the conceit, Dryden may appear to align comedy with metaphysical poetry. But the conceits which he advocates are not only less 'hard' or 'shock[ing]' than those in a poet like John Donne, they also have a different nature and purpose. Donne's conceits reflect his belief in a divine harmony which, through endless analogies and correspondences, links together every level in the Chain of Being; his conceits are part of a dialectic through which he argues, however darkly, for the congruity of the disparate objects he compares.[57] When he declares that 'She is all States, and all Princes, I',[58] he is asserting that there is a sense, metaphysical or spiritual, in which a pair of lovers reflects the temporal order. Hence, Donne's statement, though shocking, is true, and its apparent incongruities are reconciled. On the other hand, in Dryden's comedies the conceits (or witticisms) reflect not the harmonies of God but the disharmonies or incongruities by which imperfect or unreasonable human beings violate the temporal order and, consequently, the social norms. In the frailty of their youth, hero and heroine may defiantly compare themselves wittily to this or that; and quite apart from the identities which they insist upon, the playwright reveals what is actually so: the stated comparison is false; the implied incongruity is true; and in the context of the social and moral order, hero and heroine are laughable and absurd.

An Evening's Love, to which Dryden's preface is appended as guide, abounds with conceits or witticisms the tenor and vehicle of which remain forever disjoined. One example, both learned and urbane, is the following exchange between Jacinta and Wildblood:

> *Jac.* One of the Ladies in the Masque to night has taken a liking to you; and sent you by me this purse of gold, in recompence of that she saw you lose.
>
> *Wild.* And she expects in return of it, that I should wait on her; I'll do't. Where lives she? I am desperately in love with her.
>
> *Jac.* Why, Can you love her unknown?
>
> *Wild.* I have a Banque of Love, to supply every ones occasions; some for her, some for another, and some for you; charge what you will upon me, I pay all at sight, and without questioning who brought the Bill.
>
> *Jac.* Heyday, You dispatch your Mistresses as fast, as if you meant to o're-run all Woman-kind: sure you aime at the Universal-Monarchy.[59]

In the treatment of love as both commercial transaction and political intrigue the wit here is obviously urbane. But like the play as a whole, it does lack those very 'ornaments' of style – effortlessness, spontaneity, brevity, refinement – which, according to Quintilian, are essential to '[verbal] jests' and which, according to Dryden, are essential to the best witticisms or 'sharpness of conceit'.

For an example of Dryden's conceits or witticisms at their best, and most urbane and charming, we must turn paradoxically to a scene in *Marriage à-la-Mode* (1673), a tragi-comedy, where Rhodophil and Doralice vie with each other in expressing dissatisfaction with their marriage, and where they do so through brief statement and pithy reply (or 'repartie'), which Dryden calls 'the greatest grace of Comedy':

> *Dor.* I see you are in the Husbands fashion; you reserve all your good humours for your Mistresses, and keep your ill for your wives.
>
> *Rho.* Prethee leave me to my own cogitations; I am thinking over all

my sins, to find for which of them it was I marry'd thee.

Dor. Whatever your sin was, mine's the punishment.

Rho. My comfort is, thou art not immortal; and when that blessed, that divine day comes, of thy departure, I'm resolv'd I'll make one Holy-day more in the Almanack, for thy sake.

Dor. Ay, you had need make a Holy-day for me, for I am sure you have made me a Martyr.[60]

The language of this scene – the language of witty 'repartie' – is polished, correct and pellucidly clear. But thoroughly permeating this language of statement are surprising and wonderful comparisons: the sharp conceits of which Dryden speaks. What is inventive in the imagery enters into a reciprocal, though discordant, relationship with the civility and restraint of the style: the sharpness or boldness of conceit heightens completely with intellectual force the severe plainness of statement; the plainness of statement renders quite incongruous the boldness of conceit. Language is far more important than either action or character; wit is at the very centre of language; and the tensions between the lively and the just, even as the one overwhelms the other, excite the imagination and, in doing so, gratify judgment.

The religious metaphors in the exchange between Rhodophil and Doralice do not then serve, as they would in Donne, to establish a real link between the human and the divine. Nor are they, as Jeremy Collier takes them to be, a hellish outpouring of irreligion.[61] Grandiloquent and therefore innocent, they but give expression to a momentary discord within the contentment of a well-ordered marriage. By the end of the drama, while recognizing each other's faults, as well as their own, they realize what the audience already knows: they are truly in love.[62]

VII

Dryden's definition of 'wit' is ideally suited to the requirements of high comedy; but it does leave him open to an easy misinterpretation. By defining 'wit' in terms that can be applied only to high comedy, he now seems to reach the very same conclusion which Shadwell had found, though quite mistakenly, in the *Essay of Dramatick Poesie*: that there is and can be no wit at all in Jonson's comedy of humour. But what may seem to be Dryden's error, or even inconsistency, is more apparent than real. When in the preface he speaks about the presence or absence of wit in comedy, high or low, he forgets the definition and in fact uses the word, as in the *Essay*, in two very different senses. He would have us understand that, if low comedy lacks wit as 'sharpness of conceit', it yet has a kind of comic wit, or poetic *ingenium*, appropriate to its nature. And in the 'Defence of the Epilogue' (1672), for the benefit of his 'Friends' who may have misunderstood him, he will repeat the distinction, simplify it, and make it considerably more explicit: low comedy, he points out, may indeed lack 'Wit, in the stricter sense, that is, Sharpness of Conceit'; but in low comedy, he insists, 'even folly it self, well represented, is Wit in a larger signification'.[63]

In the preface, meanwhile, even as he denies low comedy 'sharpness of conceit', he does not deny its value. On the contrary, he takes its value for granted; and he distinguishes between comedy of wit and comedy of humour only so that he may propose and justify their fusion. We are at the intellectual centre of the preface when, with one more backward glance not only at Fletcher but also at Jonson, he declares,

> I will not deny but that I approve most the mixt way of Comedy; that which is neither all wit, nor all humour, but the result of both: neither so little of humour as *Fletcher* shews, nor so little of love and wit, as *Johnson:* neither all cheat, with which the best Playes of the one are fill'd, nor all adventure, which is the common practice of the other.[64]

With tragi-comedy in mind – or what the Italians called *tragedia mista*, 'mixed tragedy' – he refers to the form as 'mixt', though he does so only in a special sense. It is not so much a mingling of two different genres as in fact a mingling of two different kinds of the same one: it is 'neither all wit [or high comedy], nor all humour [or low comedy], but the result of both'. As at the very beginning of his career, so now Dryden champions a dramatic form that offers a double vision of human life: whereas tragi-comedy transports us up from the 'conversation of Gentlemen' to the deliberations of kings, so 'mixt ... Comedy' plunges us down from the 'conversation of Gentlemen' to the 'follies and extravagances of *Bedlam*'.[65] Together, the two mixed forms encompass a vast range of human experience.

Dryden is convinced that *An Evening's Love* represents an important advance over the entirely inadequate attempts of Jonson and Fletcher to combine humour and wit. Nevertheless, his work does not entirely please him, for it is 'ally'd too much to Farce'.[66] Modern commentators have assumed that Dryden identifies farce exclusively with French comedy and English adaptations of French plays.[67] In his criticism, however, the genre has a considerably broader range. It extends from what we may call 'high farce', or plays based upon a fantastic distortion of men and events, to what we may call 'low farce', or such forms as the *commedia dell'arte* and circus entertainment. To understand the full meaning of farce to Dryden, we need turn to the 'Epilogue to the University of Oxford' (1673), where the entire range of farcical entertainments is listed, both 'high' and 'low':

> Heaven for our Sins this Summer has thought fit
> To visit us with all the Plagues of Wit.
> A *French* Troop first swept all things in its way,
> But those Hot *Monsieurs* were too quick to stay;
> Yet, to our Cost in that short time, we find
> They left their Itch of Novelty behind.
> Th' *Italian* Merry-Andrews took their place,
> And quite Debauch'd the Stage with lewd Grimace;
> Instead of Wit, and Humours, your Delight
> Was there to see two Hobby-horses Fight,

Stout *Scaramoucha* with Rush Lance rode in,
And ran a Tilt at Centaure *Arlequin*.
For Love you heard how amorous Asses bray'd,
And Cats in Gutters gave their Serenade.[68]

Dryden's distaste for all farce is perhaps in part that of a disappointed rival who has found that 'the Artist is often unsuccessful, while the Mountebank succeeds'.[69] But his distaste is founded much less on box-office considerations or envy than on sound literary and ethical grounds. He condemns and rejects farce because in farce, which he defines as a distinct genre, the lively (or imagination) is divorced from truth, both moral and natural, and is reduced therefore to sheer nonsense; and the just (or sound judgment) ceases to exist all but completely. The subject of farce is the 'monstruous and chimerical'. Its plot is a collection of 'unnatural events'; its characters are 'forc'd humours'; and it communicates chiefly through gesture and face-making ('Grimaces').[70] Farce is enjoyed only by that inferior man who, when he scornfully laughs at 'an impossible adventure', conceives of himself as an admirable fellow and becomes confirmed in his miserable habits.[71] Farce is both bad in its nature and bad in its effects. By introducing it into *An Evening's Love*, he has 'given [in] too much to the people', so much so in fact that the 'very play' may 'rise up in judgment against [him]'. He is 'asham'd' both of himself and his audience, and he hopes that, for everyone's sake, farce will be completely supplanted on the stage by comedy: comedy alone occasions a 'kind of laughter' which gives true 'satisfaction' and, 'by exposing them to publick view', 'a cure on folly, and the small imperfections in mankind'.[72]

For Dryden, although its immediate and perhaps exclusive aim is 'divertisement and delight', the laughter produced by comedy must be grounded always in moral truth, however indirectly. If comedy is to instruct, then it instructs best through laughter and not by precept or 'example'. He dismisses Shadwell's contention that it is the comic poet's business to punish vice and reward virtue: if there is to be poetic justice anywhere in the theatre, it belongs in serious drama, and perhaps not even there. Similarly, he does not believe that it is the comic poet's task to propel his protagonists through an arc of continual self-discovery and illumination. Hero and heroine persist in their frailties until, in the very last scene, judgment prevails and they are reformed.[73] If scenes of moral conversion do take place prior to the last scene, they occur not upon the stage but in the minds and hearts of the spectators. The spectators 'are mov'd to laugh', and 'the shame of that laughter' teaches them to amend what is unseemly in their conduct.[74] Whatever immediate pleasure it gives, laughter is in the end a means of regeneration. It converts vice into virtue or, more accurately, reveals the good that is already there: a good to be found not only in the audience but in the poet's sub-text as well. As a speaker declares in Eliot's 'Dialogue on Dramatic Poetry',

> The morality of our Restoration drama cannot be impugned. It assumes orthodox Christian Morality, and laughs (in its comedy) at human nature for not living up to it. It retains its respect for the divine by show-

ing the failure of the human ... Our Restoration drama is all virtue. It
depends upon virtue for its existence.[75]

The preface concludes with Dryden's defence of his plays against the charge of
plagiarism, a charge typified by – though [not confined to – Shadwell's reference
to poets who, 'by continual Thieving, reckon their stolne goods their own'.[76] The
defence may not at first appear to have very much to do with Dryden's theory of
comedy. But as Dryden proceeds with his discussion of originality in literature, he
manages to touch upon the major principles which he has so far been developing
in both his essay on comedy and his other early criticism and to which he will give
increased emphasis through the rest of his career. Moreover, the passage represents
a significant break with the Aristotelianism of the Renaissance and is hence an
important moment in both English and Continental literary theory.

The defence rests upon the premise that, as poetry is an imitation of nature, so
literary works are part of the nature which poets imitate. Some poets imitate life;
others imitate art. In either case, whether a poet bases his plot on what he has seen
or on what he has read, his work must be accounted his own if through his judgment he reshapes what he borrows. A poet is not a 'maker', according to Dryden,
by virtue of his creating an entirely new action: he is a maker if, upon the 'foundation' of an old story – through 'add[ing]' and 'reject[ing]', 'height[ening]' and
'modell[ing]' – he 'build[s]' a plot which is 'almost ... new'.[77] By this standard,
Tasso is accounted an original poet, although he 'has taken both from *Homer* many
admirable things which were left untouch'd by *Virgil*, and from *Virgil* himself
where *Homer* cou'd not furnish him'. So too, by this same standard, Dryden
accounts himself an original poet, although he has never hesitated to appropriate
any story he 'lik'd ... in a Romance, Novel, or forreign Play', 'to build it up, and
to make it proper for the *English Stage*'.[78]

Dryden's defence of the poet's right to borrow is classical in both its premise
and conclusion. Nevertheless, the general drift of the argument is thoroughly
modern and, in particular, contrary to Aristotelian thought. His contemptuous dismissal of the charge of plagiarism ultimately rests on his conviction that what a poet
says – his subject, his theme, his plot – is never so important as how he says it: his
words and style (the 'Ornaments of language and elocution') are what constitute
the essence of his art, and it is in language rather than in the 'contrivance' of an
action that he chiefly displays his 'invention'.[79]

In discussing language, Dryden pays little attention to the role of judgment and
its demands for clarity and decorum. He insists that language must be correct, but
his emphasis falls elsewhere. Throughout he insists upon the superior role of fancy
('the principall quality requir'd in [the poet]') and on the imaginative leaps that
provide a poem with its 'life touches'. '[T]he work of a Poet' lies in the creation
of 'descriptions', 'similitudes' and 'wit'. For it is by such means that a poet
'heighten[s]' and 'beautyf[ies]' his subject, adds 'secret graces' to that of which he
speaks, and transmutes a dull story into a source of 'laughter' or 'concernments'.[80]
Unlike the Aristotelians, who subordinate language to content or literary form,

Dryden insists that through his imagination a poet creates a language by which audience or reader is given a new and vivid experience in life itself. And unlike the Aristotelians, he would also have us understand that the immediate purpose of all literature is to provide audience or reader with beauty through language, and pleasure through the beautiful, although the ultimate purpose is to provide or communicate some moral or philosophical truth.

In thus making language more important than subject or plot, and in thus preferring the pleasures of the imagination to philosophical or moral truth in art, Dryden makes a complete break with the Aristotelianism of his age and in fact initiates a new beginning in English criticism, a beginning that has influenced – both directly and indirectly – literary theory and practice to our own time. In his theory of comedy no less than in his theory of the epic and of the historical poem Dryden leaves the door ajar for Coleridge, who will later define poetry as 'the *best* words in the best order' or, more abstractly, as that which excites 'emotion for the immediate purpose of pleasure through the medium of beauty'.[81]

The 'Preface to *An Evening's Love*' is the most immediately useful of Dryden's early essays. By defining key terms, analysing literary genres and establishing a hierarchy of dramatic forms, it offers us a brilliant introduction to his comedies. But from a broader perspective – that of the English theatre as a whole – it is less important as a prolegomenon to his comedies than as a statement of a persistent pattern in English literature. Whereas the *Essay of Dramatick Poesie* teaches us that, in English serious drama, tears are never far removed from laughter, the preface teaches us that, in English comedy, wit is never far removed from humour. The preface establishes a perspective that enables us to see Dryden as a forebear of Oscar Wilde and George Bernard Shaw.

CHAPTER SEVEN

The heroic play
(1672)

I

By 1672 Dryden had come to regard his heroic plays as indeed his finest achievement. In his view, the heroic play was not an established form that he had newly embellished; it was a genre which, to a significant degree, he had brought into being. He remained justifiably proud of his accomplishments in comedy and tragi-comedy.[1] Yet he always seems to have been aware that his contributions to both forms were of far less importance than the specific literary traditions in which he wrote. He looked upon himself, when he composed comedy and tragi-comedy, as one who merely refined and synthesized. He would search out the golden bits and pieces that lay buried in the plays of older dramatists, polish them with care and join them artfully together. As a consequence, he realized that the excellence of such plays as *Secret Love* (1668) and *An Evening's Love* (1671) was necessarily bound up with the excellence of his sources, and the general praise of these works was attendant upon a corresponding praise of Shakespeare, Jonson and Fletcher. He knew that, if he was a successful writer of comedy and tragi-comedy, it was because he was heir to the riches of the past.

Dryden looked upon the heroic play, however, as being less his inheritance than his creation. He was convinced that he had taken it from its crude beginnings and brought it to its final and ideal form. To develop something entirely new in literature is an act of extraordinary genius. New genres have generally been regarded not as the work of individuals but as the collective accomplishment of an entire civilization. They are said to come into being not at once but, as Aristotle observed of tragedy, through slow and successive stages of growth. In the seventeenth century it was believed that Homer was the only man in history both to initiate a new genre and then to perfect it. That he could rival even a modest portion of Homer's achievement filled Dryden with a joy that imparts to 'Of Heroique Playes' (1672) its special brio.

The essay, though in part a defence of *The Conquest of Granada,* is concerned primarily with the heroic play as a literary form. Dryden examines its sources and development; explains its subject, theme and purpose; and sets forth the rules or principles by which (as a mixed genre) it is to be written. In addition, he shows in what way it brings to its fullest realization that charter of poetic freedom to which he had already committed himself and his art. In *The Conquest of Granada* and other heroic plays the lively all but overwhelms the just, which abides only incidentally in plot, character, language and spectacle. Their main – in some respects their only – purpose is to give pleasure through the beautiful, which is now linked inextricably to the wonderful, the admirable, the marvellous, though of course never once without its roots in a divine order and hence in the True and the Good.

II

Dryden was not alone in attaching special importance to the heroic play. According to Moody Prior, many of his contemporaries also judged it to be a most important contribution to the drama and thought that 'it increased the potentialities of serious plays even above those of antiquity'.[2] Absent from all seventeenth-century commentary, however, is any awareness of the fundamental nature of the genre, especially as conceived by Dryden, its major exponent. During the first decade of the Restoration, when the heroic play enjoyed its greatest success, those who admired it pointed to its exalted subjects and elevated language, but to little else. They did not go much beyond Mary Evelyn, who, after attending an early performance of *The Conquest of Granada* in the winter of 1670/71, found it quite ennobling: '[It is] a play so full of ideas that the most refined romance I ever read is not to compare with it: love is made so pure, and valor so nice, that one would imagine it designed for an Utopia rather than our stage'.[3]

Detractors found somewhat more to say. In discussing heroic drama they noted its loose episodic plot, its ranting heroes, its fondness for dialectical debate and its 'fantastical language'.[4] Yet they had not the slightest understanding of how the disparate parts were integrated into a whole: the conventions of the heroic play escaped them entirely. To Buckingham the genre is an elaborate hoax. It consists of 'plays without head or tail', and thus of works which a man of sense will greet with derision and dismiss with contempt. As he writes in the 'Epilogue to *The Rehearsal*' (1672):

> The Play is at an end, but where's the Plot?
> That circumstance our *Poet Bayes* forgot.
> And we can boast, tho 'tis a plotting Age,
> No place is freer from it than the Stage.
> The Ancients plotted, tho, and strove to please
> With sence that might be understood with ease;
> They every Scene with so much wit did store,
> That who brought any in, went out with more:
> But this new way of wit does so surprise,
> Men lose their wits in wondring where it lyes.[5]

Modern responses to heroic drama, though more learned than those in Dryden's day, often reflect seventeenth-century judgments.[6] The school of Mrs Evelyn is still with us. One of its distinguished proponents, Eugene Waith, regards the heroic play in essence as a 'celebration of greatness, where the conflicts of tragedy are replaced by ritual exaltation'.[7] So too, the school of sense is much in evidence. Those who dismiss Dryden's heroic strain as 'thick porridge sprinkled with phosphorescent confetti' may be said to speak in Buckingham's name.[8] As was true three hundred years ago, so today there is little sign of any willingness to listen

to an artificer on his own craft. Dryden's account of the heroic play as a mixed form
– a fusion of the drama with the epic or romance – has not sufficiently won the
understanding or acceptance which it fully deserves.[9]

That 'Of Heroique Playes' has not yet won the approbation of the critics is
owing, in no small measure, to its method of argument. The essay was designed
to serve as the preface to *The Conquest of Granada* (1672); and structurally at least,
in its movement from literary theory to practical criticism, it resembles many of
Dryden's other prefaces: for instance, the 'Preface to *An Evening's Love*' (1671).
But what sets 'Of Heroique Playes' apart is its extraordinary economy of statement.
While he does finally manage to tell us a great deal about heroic drama, Dryden
makes his points so very succinctly and elliptically that it is easy to misunderstand
them or even to pass them by. Indeed, we cannot profit from 'Of Heroique Playes'
unless we first realize that it is the kind of work which Aristotle calls 'acroamatic':
a work that cannot be understood in isolation but only in the light of other and
related works.

III

Before he could write 'Of Heroique Playes' Dryden had to improve his understanding of the major literary forms. On the one hand, he had to make a clearer
distinction between heroic drama and tragi-comedy. On the other, he had to
recognize fully and completely that the epic poem was radically unlike tragedy in
its subject, characters and style. Neither task was easy, for the age had a pre-
disposition to conflate the one genre with the other, so that, when taking up the
heroic play, he inherited a critical tradition that led him astray.

The poets who developed the heroic drama before Dryden had little sense of
being innovators. They rarely engaged in criticism; but when they did speak of their
works, they regarded them as tragi-comedies that differed in degree but not in kind
from the tragi-comedies of Fletcher. They recognized that their plays did not mix
'mirth and killing' – a requirement for one type of tragi-comedy. But since their
own plays contained a potentially tragic action which ended happily, writers such
as the Earl of Orrery and William Davenant believed that their plays fell well within
Fletcher's definition of the kind of tragi-comedy with which he was generally
associated:

> A tragie-comedie is not so called in respect of mirth and killing, but in
> respect it wants deaths, which is inough to make it no tragedie, yet brings
> some neere it, which is inough to make it no comedie: which must be a
> representation of familiar people, with such kinde of trouble as no life be
> questiond, so that a God is as lawfull in this as in a tragedie, and meane
> people as in a comedie.[10]

Hence, though generally reticent about his own works, Orrery called *The Generall*
(1664), the first heroic play to be written during the Restoration, a 'Trage-Comedi,
All in Ten Feet Verse, & Rhyme'.[11] And Davenant had similarly been content to

pour his new wine into old bottles. In prefatory remarks to *The Siege of Rhodes* (1656), often accounted the first heroic play in England, he complains that events forced him to omit 'the chief ornaments belonging to a History Dramatically digested into turns and counter-turns, to double Walks, and interweavings of design'.[12] That is, he apologizes for being unable to give his play the required structure of a genuine or fully developed tragi-comedy.

Unlike Orrery, Davenant did at least make one contribution to the defining of a new kind of drama: he coined the term '*Heroique Plays*'.[13] But his very usage only serves to underscore the wholly conventional nature of his thought. He speaks of '*Heroique Plays*' for much the same reason that Orrery was to mention rhyme: to point out precisely where there had been a refinement upon the coarser methods of Fletcher. Whereas Fletcher represents the affairs of 'familiar people', Davenant chooses a noble action and, more importantly for him, heightens his characters 'to render the *Ideas* of Greatness & Vertue pleasing and familiar'.[14] It seems never to have entered his mind that his work constitutes a far more radical departure from earlier drama and that it is not in fact a play with a romantic subject, but another form entirely: a romance – episodic, static, declamatory – in dramatic form.

With the precedents of Orrery and Davenant before him, Dryden at first also failed to grasp the distinctive nature of the heroic play – his own or that of other dramatists. In his earliest reference to the form, made in the dedication of *The Rival Ladies* (1664), he echoed Orrery and wrote of 'the New way ... of writing Scenes in Verse [rhyme]'. And in his second reference, made in the *Essay of Dramatick Poesie* (1668), he echoed Davenant and wrote of 'serious Playes where the subject and characters are great, and the Plot unmix't with mirth'.[15] Not surprisingly, in each instance, his statements were preceded by a discussion of tragi-comedy: in his mind, as in Orrery's and Davenant's, the two forms were intimately related.

Perhaps Dryden would not have found so convincing the contemporary theory of the heroic play – that it was a form of tragi-comedy – if he had not also accepted a then fashionable theory of the epic. Like many critics of the seventeenth century, including Thomas Hobbes, he believed, at least initially, that – except for the presence or absence of a narrator (or the poet's voice) – there can be no essential difference between the two principal forms of narrative verse, the epic and the drama; that they must both obey the strict rules of decorum and verisimilitude; and that contrary to ancient and medieval tradition the playwright must set the patterns which the epic poet is to imitate.[16]

The entire matter – the equation of epic poem and drama – is taken up at some length in the *Essay of Dramatick Poesie*. It is taken up specifically when Neander, having discussed the rules and principles which must govern a good play, goes on to explain that between tragedy and epic poetry there is 'a great affinity':

> The Genus of them [epic and tragedy] is the same, a just and lively Image of humane nature, in its Actions, Passions, and traverses of Fortune: so is the end, namely for the delight and benefit of Mankind. The Characters and Persons are still the same, *viz.* the greatest of both sorts, only the manner of acquainting us with those Actions, Passions and Fortunes is

> different. Tragedy performs it *viva voce,* or by Action, in Dialogue,
> wherein it excels the Epique Poem which does it chiefly by narration...[17]

Having been so completely identified with tragedy, and having at the same time
been stripped of many of its traditional features (supernatural machines, improbable
actions, heightened language), the pale epic of seventeenth-century theory did not
appear to have much in common with the heroic play, especially with its ghosts and
spectres, its bewildering plots and its glittering rhetoric. As long as he accepted the
commonplaces on the epic, Dryden could not counter Orrery's and Davenant's
views on the relationship of heroic drama to tragi-comedy.

There is always, however, an appeal from theory to practice. As he reread the
major epic poets in preparation for writing *Annus Mirabilis* (1667), Dryden began
to perceive the inadequacies in current literary theory. In later years, he would
credit a chance perusal of Ariosto's *Orlando Furioso* (1532) with first opening his
eyes to the true nature of the heroic play, and state that the experience took place
even before he himself had begun work in the genre.[18] But this explanation, found
in 'Of Heroique Playes', has the ring of fiction. It is much more likely that the event
which sparked his new understanding did not take place until after he had published
The Indian Queen (1665), and that event involved not Ariosto but Virgil. It is in
his discussion of Virgil, in the '[A]ccount' of *Annus Mirabilis,* that he took the cru-
cial step of disentangling the epic from tragedy and of insisting upon the distinctive aspects of each form. As he points out, whereas the end of the drama is to
arouse 'concernment', the purpose of the epic is to arouse 'admiration' or wonder.
The drama imitates probable action; the epic imitates actions which are marvellous
or strange. Lastly, the style of the epic and the style of the drama are entirely dissimilar. Since the dialogue of his characters must appear to be 'the effect of sudden
thought', the dramatist is self-effacing. He shuns 'a too curious election of words,
too frequent allusions, or ... any thing that showes ... labour in the writer'. On the
contrary, since as narrator he is present throughout his work, the epic poet is under
no requirement to disguise his art. He is free to delight in artifice and to make his
style 'confess, as well the labour as the force of his imagination'.[19]

Immediately after he had drawn the several distinctions, however, Dryden began
to return to his original position. He perceived that his earliest experiments in tragi-
comedy were essentially epic in nature; and with these plays in mind, he started to
insist again that, apart from the presence or absence of the poet's voice, there must
be no distinction between the story-telling of the epic poet and that of the serious
playwright. But the old position was now set in a totally new context, one predetermined by his charter of freedom for poet and playwright alike. The epic poet
was not to follow the rules of the contemporary theatre, a theatre committed
increasingly to French rules and logic. Rather, the playwright was to set his
imagination free; and provided he never abandoned absolutely the dictates of reason
and sound judgment, he was to bring onto the stage – in language and fable, in
subject and theme – the wonders of traditional epic and romance. In the 'Defence
of *An Essay of Dramatick Poesie*' (1668) he urged the playwright 'to move

admiration' and to do so 'with all the Arts and Ornaments of Poesie'. In the 'Preface to *Tyrannick Love*' (1670), he took it for granted that the 'Representations' in the drama can be 'of the same Nature with [those in] the Epick'.[20] And from this point on, it was an easy matter for him to work out further parallels and then to build a general theory of heroic drama upon them.

IV

When examining the origins of heroic drama, Dryden acknowledges, in 'Of Heroique Playes', that 'the first light' of the form in England came from Sir William Davenant, who in *The Siege of Rhodes* set 'that excellent ground-work' for its development.[21] His account has occasioned any number of polite dismissals, the most forceful of which is to be found in Alfred Harbage's *Cavalier Drama*. According to Harbage, the heroic play did not arise out of a single work. It was the culmination of an entire drama – the Cavalier drama – of the Caroline and Commonwealth stage. Harbage describes Cavalier drama as 'a schematic dramatization of the action of Greek romance'. Its characters are 'Platonics who deliver themselves of undramatic essays'; its language is a 'florid cadenced prose, feministic in tendency, grave and refined in tone'. In claiming to have borrowed not from the Cavalier tradition as a whole but from a single Cavalier play, 'Dryden', Harbage insists, 'was guilty, unconsciously perhaps, of suppressing evidence...'[22]

But Harbage does Dryden a grave injustice. Dryden was more than the leading poet and critic of the Restoration: he was the best informed of its literary historians. Far more than has been recognized, he was profoundly interested in the development and evolution of literary tradition and genre and in the literary models – the sources and analogues – inevitably present and echoed in every work of excellence.[23] The poet imitates nature. He also imitates proper models; and he does so whether he is aware of doing so or not. When he refers to *The Siege of Rhodes* as the inspiration of his first heroic plays, Dryden thinks of the work not so much as a part of Caroline drama, and hence an early tradition, but as a prefiguration – through metre, rhyme, spectacle, recitative – of new possibilities for the stage; and these possibilities alone interest him. What Davenant did he did incompletely, inadequately, badly. Through his own heroic plays, Dryden has for years been trying to bring to some perfection what was perhaps an original idea, though an idea which in Davenant's presentation was undoubtedly a failure. As 'Of Heroique Playes' demonstrates, he has finally succeeded.

Every discussion of heroic drama must lead eventually to Dryden, the most ardent of its champions; but, as he would have been the first to admit, it must begin always with William Davenant. By the summer of 1650 Davenant had completed the first half of an epic poem, *Gondibert*, the subjects of which were the tensions between love and war, political intrigue, and the losing and founding of great empires. Shortly afterwards he published a long commentary on the poem, the 'Preface to *Gondibert*', though the poem itself was not to be published until the following year. In the preface, which is part literary theory, part self-justification, he asserts the commonplace, later accepted by Dryden, that there can and must be no essential difference between the two major kinds of narrative verse, the epic and the drama: they both – the non-dramatic and the dramatic – must conform to a strict verisimilitude and the rules of classical decorum.

Gondibert, in its unfinished state, appeared in 1651. Five years later Davenant published a play, *The Siege of Rhodes,* the subject of which was very much like that of his epic poem, with which it had more than a little in common. In 1663 the play, minimally 'Enlarg'd', was republished with a sequel, *The Siege of Rhodes: The Second Part.* The new edition contained, moreover, a brief dedication, in which (with some emphasis) he spoke about '*Heroique Playes*'. The term, which was entirely of his own invention, referred not to a new dramatic genre but to plays of an established type in which, however, there was a 'heightening [of] the Characters'. As he further explained,

> I hope you will not be unwilling to receive (in this Poetical dress) neither the Besieg'd nor the Besiegers, since they come without their vices: for as others have purg'd the Stage from corruptions of the Art of the Drama, so I have endeavour'd to cleanse it from the corruptions of manners; nor have I wanted care to render the *Ideas* of Greatness & Vertue pleasing and familiar.[24]

The Siege of Rhodes was at once recognized as a novelty, the precise nature and origins of which have preoccupied critics and academic scholars into our own time. Davenant had earlier insisted that the two major kinds of narrative verse were essentially the same; he had called *The Siege of Rhodes* a heroic play; and for more than half a century it has been argued that it must have been Davenant's purpose to bring together and fuse in a single work or genre two different literary forms. Thus, according to John Harrington Smith and Dougald MacMillan,

> Davenant's *Gondibert,* with its plan for an epic or heroic poem…in five books, avowedly in imitation of drama, brought the two genres very close together…It would seem most logical, then, that Davenant should try to express the spirit of the heroic poem in a work for the stage…
>
> In fact, the intention to achieve an epic effect gives the play novelty in all, or nearly all, its salient features.[25]

Cornell March Dowlin goes so far as to identify *The Siege of Rhodes* largely, if not completely, with Davenant's own theory and practice of the epic:

> The *Siege of Rhodes* very plainly carries on the sentiments found in *Gondibert*…Anyone who was acquainted with the preface to *Gondibert* with its often expressed desire to promote virtue, its approval of conjugal love, its avoidance of vice, and with *Gondibert* itself with its viceless characters, its 'patterns' and 'ideas', could not help associating the 'heroique play' with the heroic poem…[26]

Dryden makes no such errors. Not only is he the father of English literary criticism: he is also the first of our literary historians. In considering the sources and analogues of Davenant's play, he presents us with a wealth of detail; and as he sets the work in the context of history, both English and Continental, his argument is sometimes circuitous; but it is never difficult to follow. And it is altogether convincing.

V

'Of Heroique Playes' starts out with a formal announcement, which Dryden takes as incontrovertible and which is without the slightest trace of his earlier Cavalier manner. It is almost pugnacious: 'Whether Heroique verse ought to be admitted into serious Playes, is not now to be disputed: 'tis already in possession of the Stage: and I dare confidently affirm, that very few Tragedies, in this Age, shall be receiv'd without it'.[27] Then, after a brief tribute to himself, and indirectly to his own recent achievement in the new form, *The Conquest of Granada,* he goes on to discuss 'the first light' of the new drama, Davenant's *Siege of Rhodes,* and in particular those details or aspects of the play which he considers innovative. And he does so with verve.

The Siege of Rhodes impressed him, apparently, by its manner of handling spectacle and song. Davenant was not the first to bring music, painting and dance upon the stage, but he was the first, Dryden recognized, to integrate them so completely into speech and action that it was difficult to tell where the non-dramatic elements ended and where the play itself began.[28] Half-singing their lines to an elaborate score, moving in front of realistically painted 'scenes', which turned the stage into a kind of talking picture, Davenant's cast achieved a heightened unity of effect that astonished contemporaries. They were so startled that many of them thought they had witnessed not a play at all but (as John Evelyn observed) 'an opera after the Italian way'.[29] Dryden, however, did not lose his perspective. For all its novelty, *The Siege of Rhodes* remained for him a 'Drama', albeit one which pointed in an entirely new direction.

In insisting that at the heart of the work there lay 'Action', 'Characters' and above all 'verse', Dryden may have been heeding some of Davenant's own suggestions. Whether *The Siege of Rhodes* is, as Philip Parsons denies, 'a makeshift freak, devised purely to avoid the Commonwealth ban on stage-plays' or, as he affirms, 'the culmination of... plans for lyric theatre',[30] Davenant clearly thought language, metre and rhyme its key elements. As a character declares in the *Entertainment at Rutland House* (1656; 1657), a series of declamations which Davenant wrote to advertise his forthcoming play, 'Vertue, in those Images of the *Heroes,* adorn'd with that Musick, and these Scenes, is to be enliven'd with Poetry. Poetry is the subtle Engine by which the wonderful Body of the *Opera* must move'.[31] In *The Play-house to be Lett* (1663; 1673), another of his plays, there is a passage in which a character insists on the centrality of 'language' and 'Poetry' in 'Heroique story in *Stilo Recitativo*':

> Recitative Musick is not compos'd
> Of matter so familiar, as may serve
> For every low occasion of discourse.
> In Tragedy, the language of the Stage
> Is rais'd above the common dialect,
> Our passions rising with the height of Verse;
> And Vocal Musick adds new wings to all
> The flights of Poetry.[32]

Dryden too thought that, with or without music, the poetry in *The Siege of Rhodes* had wings, but he was not so much interested in the language, which did not impress him, as in the metre and rhyme. In 1664, in the dedication of *The Rival Ladies,* he had celebrated the play not for its language or its spectacle but for its rhymed verse: for bringing rhyme upon the stage and for making rhyme noble or perfect. In later years, having carried this revolution in prosody a step further by substituting the heroic couplet for Davenant's irregular lines, he lost even that enthusiasm which he had originally had.[33] However, he rightly never altered his opinion of the historical importance of Davenant's experiment. After several generations of drama in prose or in increasingly etiolated blank verse, Davenant reminded his age not only that rhyme might be used upon the stage but that dramatic language requires tightness of form.

Even today, more than three hundred years later, we can experience something of the shock with which contemporaries read or viewed his drama by simply juxtaposing two passages, one taken from perhaps the most successful Caroline play, William Cartwright's *The Royal Slave* (1639), and one from *The Siege of Rhodes.* The following is from Cartwright:

> *Crat[ander]* Most vertuous Queen, you make me search my self,
> To find the worth which you do so far prize;
> As thus to hazard for one man, whose life
> Is under value, that which others would not
> For a whole Kingdome, Reputation.[34]

Here is Davenant:

> *Must[apha]* This is *Ianthe,* the *Sicilian* Flower,
> Sweeter than Buds unfolded in a shower,
> Bride to *Alphonso,* who in *Rhodes* so long
> The Theme has been of each Heroick Song;
> And she for his relief those Gallies fraught;
> Both stow'd with what her Dow'r and Jewels brought.[35]

For the florid impotence of Cartwright, Davenant substituted, in Dryden's words, a style 'writ in verse [rhyme], and perform'd in Recitative Musique'.[36] Though austere and plain, his dialogue does lack, to be sure, the beauty demanded in a noble play. Nevertheless, when spoken by heightened characters and delivered in a modulating voice, it suggests the style 'not so near conversation' which Dryden would exploit in his heroic verse. At one point, Harbage concedes that in *The Siege of Rhodes* 'we may observe the tone and materials of the Caroline mode in the process of mutation…'.[37] His remark may stand as an accurate (if unintended) gloss on Dryden's observation that Davenant, while writing *The Siege*, 'turn[ed] his thoughts another way'.

VI

Dryden hails Davenant for discovering – or, more accurately, stumbling upon – the heroic play. Yet he is certain that his predecessor left the genre in a very imperfect state. Like most men, Davenant did not 'have the happiness to begin and finish' a new project. *The Siege of Rhodes* shadows forth the heroic play, but it does so 'as first Discoverers draw their Maps, with headlands, and Promontories, and some few outlines of somewhat taken at a distance, and which the designer saw not clearly'.[38]

According to Dryden, the weaknesses in Davenant's play are of two very distinct kinds. There is, first of all, a failure in execution. As he learned from the preface to *The Siege of Rhodes*, Davenant regarded his work as an unhappy compromise between intention and circumstance. He had wanted to write a play that was filled with characters, diversified with incidents and adorned with lavish scenes. But faced with the exigencies imposed by a minuscule stage, he pared down his play to a 'contracted trifle':

> It has been often wisht that our Scenes … had not been confined to eleven
> foot in height, and about fifteen in depth, including the places of passage
> reserv'd for the Musick. This is so narrow an allowance for the fleet of
> Solyman the Magnificent, his army, the Island of Rhodes, and the varieties
> attending the Siege of the City, that I fear you will think we invite you to
> such a contracted trifle as that of the Caesars carved upon a nut.[39]

But what circumstance takes away circumstance can restore. Davenant believed that, under more propitious conditions, he could have composed a more substantial play. And Dryden takes him at his word. He generously admits that Davenant would have fulfilled his plans 'with more exactness had he pleas'd to give us another work of the same nature'.[40]

There is, however, a second weakness in *The Siege of Rhodes* which Dryden thinks Davenant could never have corrected, for it involves not the execution of the plan but the very plan itself. In writing his play, Davenant attempted to embody in dramatic form a theory of the epic that he had first developed and published as a preface to his epic poem, *Gondibert*. The distinctive aspect of the theory is a thoroughgoing hostility to the entire epic tradition of the West. Virgil, Tasso, Spenser – none of the major poets please him.[41] For they make the mistake of basing their works upon the 'Errors' of Homer, 'Errors which the natural humour of imitation hath made so like in all … as the accusations against the first appear but little more then repetition in every process against the rest'.[42] Davenant is all for a new beginning; and he hopes that, when it is published, *Gondibert* will change the direction of European letters. He regards himself, in brief, as a new and better Homer: a Homer so thoroughly conscious of his art that he publishes an account of his poem one year in advance of the poem itself.

The crux of the 'Preface to *Gondibert*' is that heroic poetry must be made increasingly useful, doctrinal and morally instructive. History shows that military leaders, judges, and statesmen have all failed to maintain public order; but they will not continue to fail if they have at their disposal 'some collateral help' which Davenant 'safely presume[s] to consist in Poesy'. They will not fail, that is, if poets cease to imitate Homer and, for the moral instruction of mankind, follow Davenant's precepts and example.[43]

One of Davenant's key principles, both as poet and as critic, is that heroic characters must be limited to patterns of virtue. Unlike Homer, he does not allow for the juxtaposition of a Thersites and an Achilles: base characters have no place in a heroic poem. Similarly, he does not countenance the creation of 'unequal Characters', those in whom vice is intermixed with virtue. Heroic characters must be all of a piece. In their nature there is to be no unsightly blemish; in their behaviour, nothing unseemly or untoward. They are all to pursue the noble passions of love and honour (or 'Ambition'). The worst failing allowed them is the occasional pursuit of love or honour to excess.[44]

If Davenant's demand seems to be conventional preciosity, in one detail it is distinctive. He takes pains to point out that his ideals of behaviour are founded upon observation. His heroes and heroines are not poetic fictions created to serve a didactic purpose: they are based upon individuals whom he has seen and met in 'Courts and Camps'.[45] When he asserts that his characters are based upon living men and women, he is neither angling for patrons nor paying amusing compliments. He is stating a fact in which he profoundly believes.

It is important that we take his claim seriously if we are to give proper weight to his second major principle: his insistence that in the epic an author must rely on a probable fiction. Davenant is an extreme instance of a critic who would remove from the higher forms of poetry every vestige of the marvellous. Believing that poetry is most useful 'where ever it seems most likely', he urges writers of heroic poems to give us 'a familiar and easie view of our selves' and to avoid those supernatural regions which are 'lifted above the Eyes of Nature'. Not unlike Hobbes, Davenant thinks that, while a poet must be left free to invent, adherence to probability defines the limits of his freedom.[46]

As proponents of what J. E. Spingarn called the 'new aesthetics', both Davenant and Hobbes agree that the epic must be redefined, though they disagree on the best method of doing so. Hobbes wants to redefine the genre through extra-literary means: he would base the heroic poem on the principles of his atomistic philosophy.[47] Davenant, on the contrary, would redefine it in terms of another literary genre. His plan for a new epic tradition is based upon the Caroline drama, to which he had contributed a number of plays and which, in any event, seems to have appealed to him because it contained those aspects of the sixteenth-century romance he could live with: rarefied characters, occasional probability in action, moral introspection. Hence, when he selected a model for *Gondibert*, he turned neither to the epic poets of antiquity – Homer, Virgil, Statius – nor to the Renaissance writers of romance – Ariosto, Tasso, Spenser. He decided to follow the 'wisdom of the best Dramaticks'.[48] As modern scholarship has shown, *Gondibert* was based upon Davenant's own play *Love and Honour* (1649) and other works for the Caroline stage.[49]

Cornell March Dowlin believes that, having modelled his epic, *Gondibert,* after the Caroline drama, Davenant next sought to model a drama, *The Siege of Rhodes,* after his epic. But Dryden's point of view is very different. *The Siege of Rhodes,* he explains, does resemble *Gondibert;* but where it resembles *Gondibert,* itself in part an imitation of Caroline drama, *The Siege of Rhodes* is a very ordinary and not very impressive tragi-comedy. Where it differs from the poem – and differs significantly – it has nevertheless an epic dimension, and a thoroughly disarming one, albeit one which Davenant never recognized or understood. Davenant's reference to the play as a heroic drama was indeed apt, but far more than he knew. When he wrote the play, Oliver Cromwell and the Commonwealth were at the height of their power; and Puritan sensibility had passed and approved stringent laws against the writing and production of plays. To have a play produced, Davenant had therefore to disguise it. It could not appear to be what in fact it was: it would have to look like something very different.

To that end, according to Dryden, he borrowed from a potpourri or miscel-lany of sources, some of them literary and some of them not, and welded them all into an impressive whole. Of Davenant's use or intermingling of dance, declama-tion and the episodic plot, all of which had been characteristic of the Caroline stage, and of their possible sources and analogues, he says nothing. From Italian opera, he tells us, Davenant borrowed music, moveable scenery, recitative; from classical drama, and especially the plays of Corneille, he took over-impassioned characters. As Dryden explains,

> It being forbidden him in the Rebellious times to act Tragedies and Comedies, because they contain'd some matter of Scandal to those good people, who could more easily dispossess their lawful Sovereign than endure a wanton jeast; he was forc'd to turn his thoughts another way: and to introduce the examples of moral vertue, writ in verse [rhyme], and perform'd in Recitative Musique. The Original of this musick and of the Scenes which adorn'd his work, he had from the *Italian* Opera's: but he heighth'd his Characters (as I may probably imagine) from the example of *Corneille* and some *French* Poets.[50]

But Italian opera and French classicism, including Corneille's tragedies, have their recognizable origins in sixteenth-century French and Italian romance.[51] Without knowing what he was doing, Davenant created – inadvertently, accidentally – a new kind of English drama: a new kind of mixed genre, the heroic play. When he described his play as 'Heroique', Davenant used the correct word; but he gave it the wrong meaning.

Dryden speaks of *The Siege of Rhodes* as an epic drama and he traces it to the sixteenth-century romance. But he is not using his terms carelessly. It was another commonplace of both the sixteenth century and the seventeenth that, under certain circumstances (and these were spelled out), the romance might be considered an epic poem. As Bernard Weinberg establishes in *A History of Literary Criticism in the Italian Renaissance,* critics of the seicento often argued that epic and romance were forms essentially alike.[52] And in England, critics as different as Sidney, Alexander and Davenant followed their precedent.[53] In accepting the romance as a variety of the epic or heroic poem (the terms were synonymous), Dryden was in accord with the critical opinions of his age.

In commenting on Davenant's contribution to the English stage Dryden finds a number of limitations and failures; but he never once forgets the importance of the contribution or his indebtedness to it. In the *Essay of Dramatick Poesie* he had emphasized his debt to Fletcher's tragi-comedies. Those of his tragi-comedies which contain some 'mirth' he had based on those of Fletcher's plays in which the serious and the comic alternate with each other, though he had preferred to confine the opposing elements, the serious and the comic, not to different episodes but, to avoid 'the fits of *Bedlam*', to separate plots. His serious plays – those which begin unhappily and end happily, yet have in them no 'mirth' – he had also traced to Fletcher. But afterwards, as he would have us understand, he had a fresh insight. His serious plays he had in fact written under the influence of Davenant's *The Siege of Rhodes* and indirectly, through *The Siege,* under the influence of Renaissance romance; and he had done so quite unknowingly. He had no more realized, at least at the outset, that he was in fact working in a new genre than, when he was writing *The Siege,* Davenant had had any idea that he was actually developing an altogether new kind of play: a drama in which English tragi-comedy was mixed with Continental romance.

The illumination first occurred to him when he wrote the 'Preface to *Tyrannick Love*' (1670), the first of his plays to be called a heroic drama. Once he had the illumination he suddenly knew what task lay ahead, and it was not to take very long before he could fully realize his objective. Davenant's play is an epic drama, but it is so accidentally, and hence inadequately, incompletely, imperfectly. In 'Of Heroique Playes' he tells us that what in *The Siege of Rhodes* Davenant began, he (Dryden) has at last brought to perfection, or very close to it. He has so far developed two kinds of mixed drama: tragi-comedy and mixed comedy. With *The Conquest of Granada,* completed and performed during the winter of 1670–71, and published with 'Of Heroique Playes' in 1672, he has at last developed and perhaps perfected a third. And he has done so, he explains, by bringing into the new form what, because of his rigid classicism, Davenant had quite neglected: those elements of the wonderful, the admirable and the marvellous which until now had had their rightful place only in romance, never on the stage. To be precise, he has borrowed heavily – more so than in any of his earlier works – from the best of the Renaissance romances: Ariosto's *Orlando Furioso* (1532). Of course, he might have done so originally; but, as he tells us, he had to wait until he had freed himself sufficiently from all the strict demands of decorum and literary rules. In other words, he had to wait until he could fully exploit what he had publicly allowed himself in his 'Defence of *An Essay of Dramatick Poesie*': his private charter of freedom.

CHAPTER EIGHT

The heroic play
(concluded)

I

Dryden believed that Davenant's innovations in the English theatre – rhymed verse, heightened characters, realistic scenery, long recitatives – were prompted by nothing more noble than a desire to deceive. Davenant's experiment, moreover, was purely adventitious in nature; it was hesitant and groping rather than determined or well planned. *The Siege of Rhodes,* he informs us, was a *pièce d'occasion.* It was designed to escape the Puritan ban on plays, and Davenant's interest in his own work did not survive the Protectorate. As soon as the monarchy was restored, he abandoned his original design, 'review'd' his play and 'caused it to be acted as a just Drama'.[1]

But as Davenant's interest in the heroic play waned, Dryden's steadfastly increased. Indeed, as he explains in 'Of Heroique Playes', nothing in *The Siege of Rhodes* so much struck him and encouraged his further study and experiment as its accidental similarity – through its heightened metre and language, its exalted characters, its impressive spectacle – to those very heroic poems which Davenant had contemptuously dismissed in both his theory and his practice. To bring to perfection the form that Davenant (he believed) had unwittingly discovered, it was only necessary for him to create a drama based consciously and deliberately on the classical epic and the Renaissance epic or romance; and that realization, he tells us, came to him not when he was actually composing his later heroic plays but earlier, when after thinking further about Davenant's work, he chanced upon the *Furioso*:

> I observ'd then ... what was wanting to the perfection of his *Siege of Rhodes* ... And in the midst of this consideration, by meer accident, I open'd the next Book that lay by me, which was an *Ariosto* in *Italian;* and the very first two lines of that Poem gave me light to all I could desire.
>
>> Le Donne, I Cavalier, L'arme, gli amori
>> Le Cortesie, l'audaci imprese jo canto, &c.
>> [I sing of knights and ladies, of love and arms,
>> of courtly chivalry, of courageous deeds]
>
> for the very next reflection which I made was this, That an Heroick Play ought to be an imitation, in little of an Heroick Poem: and, consequently, that Love and Valour ought to be the Subject of it.[2]

Arthur C. Kirsch objects that this account is largely a fabrication, devised after the fact for plays that 'evolved for different reasons and perhaps with different intentions'. The claim that the heroic play was a heroic poem was an 'argumentative strategy' and not a 'substantive theory': it provided Dryden with little more than 'a ready-made and critically respectable justification for anything which his critics had found to castigate'. To understand his works we must turn not to Homer or Ariosto but to 'Fletcher's tragicomedies and to Jacobean and Caroline Court drama'. The elements of his theory and practice 'are far more traditional than his argument suggests'.[3]

There is an element of truth in what Kirsch says. As Dryden would have been the first to argue, there are some obvious similarities between his work and the previous half a century of English theatre. But there are also fundamental and significant differences between the two; and these, not the similarities, are what is most important. We may wish to dismiss the relation of an accidental encounter with Ariosto as mere fiction, but we do well to take seriously his explanation of heroic drama as 'an imitation, in little of an Heroick Poem'. For no other critical statement defines heroic drama so succinctly or so well.

Dryden's theory is that the heroic play is a cross between the Caroline drama and the epic – not the epic as explained by such critics as Hobbes and Davenant, but the epic as written, in the ancient world, by Homer, Virgil and Statius and, in Christian Europe, by Ariosto, Tasso and Spenser. To illustrate this theory, he cites his additions to the new drama – additions to what he has first borrowed from *The Siege of Rhodes* – and then traces them back in detail to the works of the most eminent writers of epic or romance. For example, he claims to have added imperfect heroes to his plays on the authority of Homer and Tasso:

> You see how little these great Authors did esteem the point of Honour, so much magnified by the *French*, and so ridiculously ap'd by us. They made their Hero's men of honour; but so, as not to divest them quite of humane passions, and frailties. They contented themselves to show you, what men of great spirits would certainly do, when they were provok'd, not what they were oblig'd to do by the strict rules of moral vertue. For my own part, I declare my self for *Homer* and *Tasso;* and am more in love with *Achilles* and *Rinaldo*, than with *Cyrus* and *Oroondates*.[4]

Similarly, he states that he had introduced the supernatural into the heroic play because it was the foundation of what was most beautiful in the works of '*Homer, Virgil, Statius, Ariosto*... [and] *English Spencer* ':

> For my part, I am of opinion, that neither *Homer, Virgil, Statius, Ariosto, Tasso,* nor our *English Spencer* could have form'd their Poems half so beautiful, without those Gods and Spirits, and those Enthusiastick parts of Poetry, which compose the most noble parts of all their writings. And I will ask any man who loves Heroick Poetry... if the Ghost of *Polydorus* in *Virgil,* the Enchanted wood in *Tasso,* and the Bower of bliss, in *Spencer*... could have been omitted without taking from their works some of the greatest beauties in them.[5]

A number of scholars have rejected Dryden's statements about the sources and analogues of the heroic play. They have no less rejected as inadequate his statements about the dominant and pervasive characteristics of the form. In 'Of Heroique Playes', according to Robert D. Hume, Dryden does little more than reveal a 'determination to take serious drama above the level of the ordinary' by means of rhyme and spectacular effects. According to James Anderson Winn, he does not so much construct a theory as 'shadow forth' a concern with 'fullness of plot, variety of characters, and beauty of style'.[6] To Cornell March Dowlin, 'Of Heroique Playes' is

> one of the sketchiest possible pieces of critical work: that rhyme was suitable, that a heroic poem should be the model (its love and valor, greatness and majesty), that the supernatural *might* be admitted, that battles *might* be represented, that the hero ought not be perfect; these are the elements of the recipe.[7]

These scholars have all failed to understand the manner in which Dryden develops his essay and discussion. The essay is profoundly elliptical: he expects his readers to know his relevant earlier essays by heart, particularly the *Essay of Dramatick Poesie* (1668) and the '[A]ccount' of *Annus Mirabilis* (1667). He speaks explicitly about his imperfect characters and his use of the supernatural – the better to refute Davenant's theory of the epic. But he would have us deduce from the earlier essays his distinctive theories about metre and style.[8] On the other hand, he apparently expects his reader to know the European epic tradition as well as he does and to have, in particular, a profound mastery of the *Orlando Furioso*. He may speak explicitly about his characters and subject matter and implicitly about his theory of language and versification. But the plays have innumerable other peculiarities and features; and these other characteristics, largely ignored by scholars, he suggests through a reference not to Homer or Virgil but to Ariosto. Ludovico Ariosto may not be Dryden's favourite poet; but the *Orlando Furioso*, he would have us understand, reverberates in almost every nook and cranny of his new mixed genre. Hence, we may not understand, or even surmise, Dryden's conception and treatment of the heroic play without our first referring to and understanding the uses to which he put Ariosto. His heroic plays are not classical epics from which the narrator has been removed. They are plays in which all the salient characteristics of the *Furioso* are everywhere present.

II

In our time, the *Furioso* is generally regarded as a romantic epic, a distinct literary form based upon elements drawn from two older genres, the classical epic and the medieval romance. Dryden, however, accepted that Renaissance school of thought which looked upon Ariosto's work in very different terms. Many Renaissance critics thought of the *Furioso* not as a hybrid poem but simply as a romance – a romance of exceptional complexity, but a romance none the less.[9] The question that engaged them was whether the romance was not itself a kind of epic. Could there not be, they asked themselves, two types of epic: the type written by the Ancients and the type written by the Moderns, one the ruling principle of which was unity and the other the ruling principle of which – in language, character, and plot – was variety? Critics who believed that the epic tradition embraced poems of both types thought of the *Furioso* as being both a romance and an epic. Or rather they called it an epic for the very reason that it was a romance.[10]

When read in this context, Dryden's reference to Ariosto acquires new meaning and takes on the force of a directive. In claiming inspiration from the *Furioso*, he attempts in effect to mould the expectations of his readers. He would not have us look in his heroic plays for the strict unity and sustained elevation that are found in the *Iliad* or the *Aeneid*: he would prepare us to meet a fluid and discontinuous world in which, as in the *Furioso*, the only constant is perpetual change.[11]

After discovering the value of Ariosto for his purpose, Dryden appears to have applied himself to a close study of the major romances of the sixteenth and seventeenth centuries. But however much he immersed himself in the whole tradition of Renaissance romance, his principal authority in writing heroic plays – so the plays themselves bear witness – was Ariosto. From Georges de Scudéry and La Calprenède he borrowed names for his characters and details for his plots. But from Ariosto he derived the dominant ethos of his work and his major techniques for handling structure, character, and language.[12] It is worth repeating that what he borrowed from Ariosto he never states explicitly. But when 'Of Heroique Playes' is read in the context of his criticism, both early and late, and of his heroic plays themselves, his theory and his practice become remarkably clear.

Dryden's interest in the *Furioso* and, through the *Furioso*, in the entire tradition of the romance, was inevitable. Having been derived from the romance, the Caroline drama could be made more heroic if only it were to approximate more closely its ultimate source. Dryden aimed therefore not at radically altering Caroline drama but at making additions in kind. Those aspects of romance which earlier playwrights had discarded, he would restore. Those aspects which were partially restored by Davenant, even though he did not borrow directly from any romance, Dryden would further heighten and develop.[13] Through his interest in romance and specifically the *Furioso*, which for him represented the epitome of the form, he hoped to bring to the English stage everything that the Caroline drama should have been and everything that through his own plays he hoped to realize.

In commenting upon the development of the heroic play, Dryden assumes the role of literary historian. He traces both origins and unifying themes and techniques, in short, to the classical epic, the sixteenth-century romance, especially the *Furioso*, and the Caroline drama, including *The Siege of Rhodes*. But a paradox remains. However much he emphasizes the importance of the *Furioso*, we are asked, in this one instance alone, to work out all the salient details for ourselves. For our doing so he sets the context by a discussion of the lively and the just. He insists, not unexpectedly, that his new drama contain in juxtaposition both qualities and that, while he is interested necessarily in the just, he is now interested primarily in a literature in which, as in the *Furioso*, the poet is 'indulg'd ... a farther liberty of Fancy'.[14] He gives us unfortunately no detailed examples of what he has in mind. But with his general critical statements at one elbow and his plays and Ariosto's poem at the other, we can provide ourselves with all the examples we may require.

III

As regards plot, Dryden argues that the heroic drama must contain a vast number of episodes. Whereas *The Siege of Rhodes* does not have even the fullness of plot required by the 'common Drama', the heroic play is to raise the customary English demand for copiousness of plot 'to a greater height'.[15] Now, if it is remembered that the 'common Drama' was expected to contain a vast multiplicity of events, and that these events were to include (to use Davenant's phrase) 'Turns and Counter turns, ... double walks, and interweavings of design', it must be concluded that he is asking for the kind of variety found only in the romance, a deduction which is confirmed by a comparison of any of his heroic plays with the *Furioso*.

The *Furioso* has always been famous for its bewildering profusion of episodes, its sudden jumps from one narrative line to another, its long digressions. 'The fertility of his [Ariosto's] fancy', writes C. S. Lewis,

> is 'beyond expectation, beyond hope'. His actors range from archangels to horses, his scene from Cathay to the Hebrides. In every stanza there is something new; battles in all their detail, strange lands with their laws, customs, history and geography, storm and sunshine, mountains, islands, rivers, monsters, anecdotes, conversations – there seems no end to it.[16]

Action succeeds action at such a rate that we soon must abandon any hope of keeping the unfolding pattern in our memory. We cannot remember where we have been; we have no idea of where we are going; we can only await the next turn of events.

Upon closer acquaintance, we do indeed find that Ariosto's plot is strengthened by a number of structural devices. Its proliferating episodes are contained within an easily apprehended narrative frame, the siege of Paris by the Saracens. We are brought to the siege in Canto II, and throughout the rest of the poem it is the one event to which we constantly return. Episodes, furthermore, are grouped around a few narrative threads (the madness of Orlando, the love of Ruggiero and Bradamant, the wanderings of Angelica), while from time to time the action is brought to a full stop and an interpolated tale or a rhetorical set-piece is inserted.[17] But as Graham Hough notes, these 'elements of recurrence and stability' are not easily remembered 'in the actual reading of the *Orlando Furioso;* what we chiefly experience is a multitude of local effects'.[18]

As Ariosto refuses to impose on his work the orderly structure of the traditional epic, so Dryden, as he imitates the *Furioso*, abandons the structural principles of conventional drama. For all its apparent waywardness, even English tragi-comedy has essentially a 'well-made' plot, with a clearly marked beginning, middle and end. The action may appear to lead nowhere; yet, as he points out in the dedication of *The Rival Ladies* (1664), it is never formless:

> [W]hen the whole Plot is laid open, the Spectators may rest satisfied, that every cause was powerfull enough to produce the effect it had; and that the whole Chain of them was with such due order Linck'd together, that

the first Accident would naturally beget the second, till they all render'd the Conclusion necessary.[19]

No such links bind together the parts of the heroic play. Like the *Orlando Furioso,* Dryden's heroic plays, and especially *The Conquest of Granada,* unfold with pomp and circumstance, with spectacle and grandiloquence and with intricacies that approach the labyrinthine. In addition to the major plot, which is centred on dynastic love and war, each play has generally a multiplicity of sub-plots, which are centred in petty lusts and intrigues, ignoble aspirations and defeats, and which therefore set the major action into bold and sometimes violent relief. The minor plots – though loosely – may perhaps obey the requirements of the classical theatre: they give at least the impression that here events unfold according to the three unities and the rules of decorum and verisimilitude. But in every instance, and never more so than in *The Conquest of Granada,* a drama in two parts, the major plot defies credibility: it verges all but completely on the disconnected and the anarchic and hence on what Aristotle would certainly have described as 'Things… impossible, or irrational,… or contradictory, or contrary to artistic correctness'.[20]

To complicate the fine art of story-telling, moreover, the several plots are not arranged in a coherent or logical juxtaposition with one another. They develop, all of them, as isolated episodes; the episodes each seem to be almost complete little dramas in themselves; and, like strands in some gigantic spider's web, they sporadically come together and fuse, and then separate and dissolve without immediate or clearly defined purpose, but adding always to the larger structure or 'design' the wonderful, the marvellous, the magnificent.[21]

Action follows action for any of a number of reasons: to unpack a theme, to explore a character, to allow for bravura display. However, although the heroic play is characterized by variety and profusion of incident, the range of its action, in comparison with the *Furioso,* is tightly compressed. Dryden tends to avoid, or to employ only on a modest scale, the technique of 'interlace', whereby (as in the *Furioso*) a number of different stories are kept going concurrently, the poet moving back and forth among them. Even when, as in *The Conquest of Granada,* he leaps back and forth among 'the plots of Almanzor, Almahide, and Boabdelin, of Lyndaraxa and her entourage…, and of Ozmyn and Benzayda', he nonetheless concentrates on his hero and achieves variety chiefly by ringing endless variations on a few basic situations. The adventures of Almanzor, in Part One, as summarized by Moody Prior, provides a good example of his method:

> On his first appearance, he [Almanzor] takes the part of the Abencerrages in a factional quarrel, because they appear to be the weaker side. He fights for Boabdelin, king of Granada, against the Spaniards because he is a guest of the city. He turns against Boabdelin because he was forbidden to free a noble Spanish prisoner in order to have the pleasure of capturing him again the next day, and he makes Abdalla king. He then sees Almahide, Boabdelin's mistress, and at once falls in love with her. Because Abdalla refuses to grant him Almahide over the claims of another supporter of the

revolt, he goes back to Boabdelin and dethrones the usurper whom he has just set on the throne. He then turns against Boabdelin, who will not give up Almahide.[22]

Of course, the heroic play is ultimately brought to an end: Granada is captured (*The Conquest of Granada*); the Mexicans are defeated (*The Indian Emperour*); Maximin is slain (*Tyrannick Love*). But in every play it appears that the ending is tacked on merely to bring the curtain down and is in no way required by the previous action. In every instance, we can imagine the conclusion as being postponed indefinitely. Like the *Furioso*, the heroic play aspires to be '*un libro perenne*'.[23]

The apparent lack of pattern and direction in Dryden's heroic plays has occasioned much confusion. Stabilizing elements are present, to be sure: individual episodes are immediately understandable and are governed by the unities of action, place and time; the minor actions which centre on lust and intrigue, though they may be kept going indefinitely, always move towards climax and resolution. But if demands for order are not ignored, the plays remain bewildering. They are centred in the episodic and the discordant, the improbable and the marvellous. Hence, it may be argued that Dryden's heroic drama is a total failure. So at least contemporary audiences frequently complained, and so too have scholars and critics complained for the past two or three hundred years. Dryden, however, does not leave us without his just defence. According to Tasso, every successful romance demonstrates the principle of 'discordant concord': it demonstrates that, beyond all the apparent discord in nature and in human life, there is a divinity who is in control of everything, resolves all tensions, and makes harmony ultimately prevail. '[T]he world', writes Tasso,

> that contains in its womb so many diverse things is one, its form and essence one, and one the bond that links its many parts and ties them together in discordant concord ... ; just so, I judge, the great poet (who is called divine for no other reason than that as he resembles the supreme Artificer in his workings he comes to participate in his divinity) can form a poem in which, as in a little world, one may read here of armies assembling, here of battles on land or sea, here of conquests of cities, skirmishes and duels, here of jousts, ... there the fortunes of love, now happy, now sad, now joyous, now pitiful.[24]

By asserting that he had 'modell'd [his] Heroique Playes, by the Rules of an Heroique Poem', Dryden claims no less for himself: for all the profusion of incident and detail, his heroic plays are unified or, as he says, 'well-form'd'.[25]

*

As it is 'varied with Accidents', so Dryden's heroic drama is also 'beautified with Characters'. The minor characters – saints and sinners, loyal aristocrats and factious power seekers – carry their dominant traits or qualities to an excess, so very much so that they all verge on becoming abstractions. The saints, 'patterns of exact vertue', subordinate themselves and their passions to public service and divine grace. For example, Acacis (in *The Indian Queen*) never acts impulsively, but always seeks to bend his will to the dictates of ethical law. Given the opportunity to escape his captors, he refuses in exalted terms:

> I as a Prisoner am by Honor ty'd.
> ...
> If such injustice shou'd my Honor stain,
> My aid wou'd prove my Nations loss, not gain.[26]

The sinners are also committed paradoxically to a life of reason, but a reason which has been corrupted by flagrant egoism and which flouts the laws of both man and God. Thus, Traxalla seeks as relentlessly to gratify his will as Acacis aspires to noble action:

> There's something shoots through my enliven'd frame,
> Like a new soul, but yet without a name:
> Nor can I tell what the bold guest will prove,
> It must be Envy, or it must be love;
> Let it be either, 'tis the greatest bliss
> For man to grant himself, all he dares wish;
> For he that to himself, himself denies,
> Proves meanly wretched, to be counted wise.[27]

All minor characters behave in a manner consistent with the laws of probability and verisimilitude: we recognize that such men and women do exist. And when the curtain comes down on the last scene of the last act, and they each receive their just rewards, we may be pleased, but we are not surprised: the cosmic order has prevailed; and things have worked out as we knew they would.

The major characters may also be either saints or sinners; but far more often they are men and women in conflict as much between good and bad impulses as between passion and reason, imagination and judgment. They are what Dryden calls 'character[s] of ... excentrique vertue'.[28] They do not so much carry their dominant qualities or traits to an excess as they oscillate, sometimes gratuitously, between violent extremes of every sort; and their behaviour so often violates the ordinary patterns of human life – normal or abnormal, saintly or vicious – that, when they are not monstrous, they appear altogether superhuman. In these characters judgment is completely subordinated to imagination, imagination to passion, and passion to every fleeting change in time and place and action.

Among the major characters none can be said to obey the laws of human probability or verisimilitude; and we know that they will never obey those laws: they are all very much larger than life. When the curtain comes down on the last scene of the last act, the saints and the sinners, like their counterparts in the minor plot, will receive their just rewards or punishments, in this world or the next, but with a difference: unlike their counterparts, the saints will rise higher in the empyrean and the sinners go further into the depths of hell. As for those of eccentric virtue, those who are in conflict with themselves and sometimes with nature and with nature's God, and who completely dominate the action, they will remain what they always have been: they will remain elemental forces. Henceforth, having seen the light, they will put their passions and their energies into service of both church and state, both man and God; but we also know that they will not have tamed those passions or energies one bit. Theirs will indeed be a life committed to moral truth; but it will remain a life centred perpetually in the wonders of the imagination alone.[29] While Dryden justifies his inconstant characters chiefly in Homeric terms, we are to understand that he has in mind Homer as redefined by Ariosto, who derives his own eccentric heroes from the strangely splintered characters of medieval romance.

In order to explore his chosen subject, the writer of a medieval romance ignored, as a rule, consistency in characterization and made his protagonists speak and behave as each successive event required. His characters, according to Eugène Vinaver, 'enact a line of argument that happens to interest him no matter what kind of characterization, real or unreal, may emerge as a result'.[30] Hence, Morgan le Fay may be, in the words of Roger Sherman Loomis, 'Arthur's tender nurse in the island valley of Avilion, or his treacherous foe. She may be a virgin or a Venus of lust'.[31] Her bewildering variety springs not from any inner dynamic of character but from the demands of the story. It was left for Ariosto, several centuries later, to make such discontinuities express what he took to be an essential fact in human nature. His characters do not change merely in accordance with the demands of the plot: they change because they lack a fixed inner self. A situation excites their passions, and their passions in turn alter the character which they each possessed before.[32]

To emphasize the instability of his heroes, Ariosto delights in subjecting them to a series of parallel tests, each with an unpredictable outcome. The adventures of the young knight Ruggiero are a case in point. Early in the poem, having been helped to escape the 'fraudulent' love of the enchantress Alcina, he learns to reverence 'virtuous behavior, perennial beauty, and infinite grace' and becomes steeled against the temptations of the flesh. Hence, when he comes upon the divinely fair Angelica, naked and chained to a rock, his first thoughts are of his beloved Bradamant:

> Ruggiero would have taken her for a statue fashioned in alabaster or some lambent marble, and tethered thus to the rock by some diligent sculptor's artifice, were it not that he distinctly saw tears coursing down her rose-fresh, lily-white cheeks and bedewing her unripe apple-breasts, and her golden tresses flowing in the wind.
>
> As he looked into her lovely eyes Ruggiero was reminded of his Bradamant; he was pricked with compassion and love, and could scarcely refrain from weeping.[33]

It is with considerable surprise therefore that we learn the outcome of a subsequent test. Alone with Angelica on a deserted beach, he clumsily tries to rape her.

Which of these actions truly exhibits the real Ruggiero? Is he the wayward young man, the virtuous knight, or the immoral satyr? It appears that Ariosto would have us believe that each of these roles is equally revealing of Ruggiero's nature, though each is in ironic conflict with the others. 'Consistently, programmatically', writes one critic, 'the *Furioso* refuses single vision and dissolves the fixities no less of narrative or rhetorical expectation than of scene and character and moral category'.[34] It is into this stream of ceaseless human change that Dryden also plunges his characters.

Dryden's protagonists, like Ariosto's, have no informing identity. All of them – Montezuma, Cortez and the rest – are collections of discordant qualities, with now one and now another of their attributes coming to the fore. What Acacis says to Montezuma, in *The Indian Queen,* may serve as the epigraph to all of his inconstant heroes:

> Like the vast Seas, your Mind no limits knows,
> Like them lies open to each Wind that blows.[35]

There is, however, one important difference between Ariosto's and Dryden's handling of character. In the *Furioso* the changes in character are instantaneous, violent and without transition. In the heroic drama, however, given Dryden's greater interest in human psychology, the very process of change is unfolded before us. Thus, Almanzor, once he has seen Almahide, provides us with a running gloss on his inner transformation from warrior to lover:

> I'me pleas'd and pain'd since first her eyes I saw,
> As I were stung with some *Tarantula:*
> Armes, and the dusty field I less admire;
> And soften strangely in some new desire.
> Honour burns in me, not so fiercely bright;
> But pale, as fires when master'd by the light.
> Ev'n while I speak and look, I change yet more;
> And now am nothing that I was before.
> I'm numm'd, and fix'd and scarce my eyeballs move;
> I fear it is the Lethargy of Love!
> 'Tis he; I feel him now in every part:
> Like a new Lord he vaunts about my Heart,
> Surveys in state each corner of my Brest,
> While poor fierce I, that was, am dispossest.[36]

Under Almahide's gentle guidance, Almanzor takes lessons in the virtuous life; and for a time we witness the 'remarkable spectacle of the eccentric super-hero being disciplined in the manners of a Caroline gentleman'.[37] But Almanzor's new self is short-lived; another self quickly emerges; and alone with Almahide, he behaves, if not as outrageously as Ruggiero on the beach, then as outrageously as the decorum of the stage allows:

> *Alman.* A happiness so nigh, I cannot bear:
> My loves too fierce; and you too killing fair.
> I grow enrag'd to see such Excellence:
> If words so much disorder'd, give offence,

My love's too full of zeal to think of sence.
Be you like me; dull reason hence remove;
And tedious formes; and give a loose to love.
Love eagerly; let us be gods to night;
And do not, with half-yielding, dash delight.
                    ...
Almah. If I could yield; (but think not that I will:)
You and my self, I in revenge, should kill.
For I should hate us both, when it were done:
And would not to the shame of life be wonn.

Alman. Live but to night; and trust to morrows mind:
'Ere that can come, there's a whole life behind.
Methinks already crown'd with joyes, I lie;
Speechless and breathless in an Extasie.
Not absent in one thought: I am all there:
Still closs; yet wishing still to be more near.[38]

By the end of the plays, Dryden's protagonists generally manage to achieve some kind of harmony or balance, and many critics believe that, in his celebration of this apparent stasis, we are to find the final vision of the plays. But it seems more likely that the order and harmony which he wishes us to admire have been present in the plays from their very beginning and exist not only in the characters themselves but above and around them. We are asked less to admire Montezuma and Almanzor than the artistic control of the poet who has created their values, guided their actions and contemplated their passions without giving way to passion himself.

*

Reflecting the diversity in plot and character, the plays have a rich diversity in language or style; and that diversity was also in large measure influenced by Dryden's pleasure in the *Furioso,* the language of which (according to Cinthio) is a constant mingling of the 'grave, sweet, sharp, troubled, and gay'.[39] The exquisite modulations of the poem have always been lost in translation; but Dryden of course read the poem in Italian. On the language of his minor characters, the influence of the *Furioso* was perhaps slight, even negligible. The language spoken by the minor characters, though occasionally enlivened with fantastic imagery, is surprisingly simple. Sentiments are transparently clear; and figures, such as those in Orazia's admonition of Montezuma, do not so much surprise as they illustrate or explain:

O *Montezuma,* cou'd thy love engage
Thy soul so little, or make banks so low
About thy heart, that thy revenge and rage,
Like suddain floods, so soon shou'd over-flow!
I thought you gentle as the gaulless Dove;
But you as humorsome as windes appear,
And subject to more passions then your Love.[40]

On the other hand, in the language spoken by the major characters, there is an interplay of two thoroughly opposed modes of discourse, between which the tensions never cease, although one is continually overwhelmed by the other: it is so thoroughly overwhelmed that at times it seems to disappear almost completely. In the language of the major characters there is a substratum of familiar diction, common imagery and conventional syntax. But superimposed on this language of statement, there is another language, which is as varied and various as anything in the *Furioso*. This second language is richly allusive, highly metaphorical, and self-consciously elaborate, even artificial. Like Ariosto's, it runs the gamut of many possibilities, extending from the ridiculous or the absurd, through lyric grace, to noble declamation:

> Let Fate be Fate; the Lover and the Brave
> Are rank'd, at least, above the vulgar Slave:
> Love makes me willing to my death to run;
> And courage scorns the death it cannot shun[41]

Like Ariosto, Dryden may set the ridiculous and the sublime into immediate proximity with each other and, by doing so, puncture every human pretension:

> What had the gods to do with me or mine?
> Did I molest your Heav'n? ——
> Why should you then make *Maximin* your Foe,
> Who paid you Tribute, which he need not do?
> Your Altars I with smoke of Gums did crown:
> For which you lean'd your hungry nostrils down,
> All daily gaping for my Incense there,
> More than your Sun could draw you in a year.
> And you for this these Plagues on me have sent;
> But by the Gods, (by *Maximin,* I meant)
> Henceforth I and my World
> Hostility with you and yours declare:
> Look to it, Gods; for you th' Aggressors are.
> Keep you your Rain and Sun-shine in your Skies,
> And I'le keep back my flame and Sacrifice.
> Your Trade of Heav'n shall soon be at a stand,
> And all your Goods lie dead upon your hand.[42]

Again like Ariosto, he constantly interplays the styles appropriate to many different genres. So in *The Conquest of Granada*, within the course of a little over twenty lines of dialogue, we encounter successively the language of domestic comedy, moral epistle and pastoral:

> [*K. Boab.*] Where, Marriage is thy cure, which Husbands boast,
> That, in possession, their desire is lost?
> Or why have I alone that wretched taste
> Which, gorg'd and glutted, does with hunger last?
> Custome and Duty, cannot set me free,

142

Ev'n Sin it self has not a Charm for me.
Of marry'd Lovers I am sure the first:
And nothing but a King could so be curst.

Q. Almah. What sadness sits upon your *Royal Heart?*
Have you a Grief, and must not I have part?
All Creatures else a time of love possess:
Man onely clogs with cares his happiness:
And, while he shou'd enjoy his part of Bliss,
With thoughts of what may be, destroys what is.

K. Boab. You guess'd aright; I am opprest with grief:
And 'tis from you that I must seek relief.
Leave us, to sorrow there's a rev'rence due: [*To the Company.*]
Sad Kings, like Suns Ecclip's, withdraw from view.

[*The Attendants goe off: and Chairs are set for the King and Queen.*]

Almah. So, two kind Turtles, when a storm is nigh,
Look up; and see it gath'ring in the Skie:
Each calls his Mate to shelter in the Groves,
Leaving, in murmures, their unfinish'd Loves.
Perch'd on some dropping Branch they sit alone,
And Cooe, and hearken to each others moan.[43]

Dryden, moreover, adopts a stylistic technique which is one of Ariosto's signature devices – a device which, before he came under Ariosto's influence, he had used on his own in *Annus Mirabilis*. In the *Furioso*, Ariosto may step back from his narrative, suspend the action and, in the most elaborate syntax and imagery, expatiate leisurely on his story, his protagonists, or even himself.[44] In the heroic plays, Dryden avails himself of the same practice; but since there is no narrator (or poet's voice) in the drama, he does so only after he makes a necessary adjustment to meet the requirements of the stage. In the middle of a scene a character may suddenly drop his persona, expatiate on himself or the action as if he were the omniscient author, and demonstrate far less concern with what is happening to him than with the pyrotechnics of syntax, metaphysical conceits, and complex witticisms. Here is Maximin commenting on a newly found experience of love:

This Love that never could my youth engage,
Peeps out his coward head to dare my age.
Where hast thou been thus long, thou sleeping form,
That wak'st like drowsie Sea-men in a storm?
A sullen hour thou chusest for thy birth:
My Love shoots up in tempests, as the Earth
Is stirr'd and loosen'd in a blust'ring wind,
Whose blasts to waiting flowers her womb unbind.[45]

At such moments, the character is suppressed to make way for the poet's voice; the character – whether man or woman – resembles no one so much as the Dryden we have come to know from the narrative poems and the satires.[46]

IV

In expounding his theory of the heroic play Dryden takes up a number of mis-cellaneous matters, among which the most important are his basic subject, theme and purpose, and the uses to which he puts music and dance, scenic design and the evocations of the supernatural. When he considers these several matters he is more explicit than when he writes about plot, character and style. Indeed, on a number of these issues he states his position twice: once in 'Of Heroique Playes' itself and once in the dedicatory address to the Duke of York, by which the essay is preceded. In our attempt to understand the theory we may therefore depend less on our own detailed comparisons of the heroic plays and the *Furioso* than on the parallels which he actually draws and the details which he cites.

As in the *Furioso*, so in the heroic plays (he tells us) his subject is 'Love and Valour'. His theme is the instability of human life as reflected in the actions of his inconstant heroes. His purpose is largely to please, yet as he pleases he does not neglect the moral life or the life of reason. In the dedication he consecrates his work to the education of a prince. The ends of his instruction are, however, far more broadly conceived. Through his ideal characters, he would inspire us, as he did Mrs Pepys, with 'patterns' of the virtuous life. And through his imperfect characters, we learn (again) from the dedication, he would provide us not with examples to follow but with a 'more exact Image' of ourselves. He would show us what in fact we do and not what we 'are oblig'd to do by the strict rules of moral vertue'. In the 'passions, and frailties' of his aberrant heroes, he would have us discover ourselves.[47]

Dryden informs us that his use of 'Drums and Trumpets' – and presumably of song, dance, and elaborate scenery – is designed to serve as a dramatic equivalent of one kind of set-piece, the long descriptive passage (the *ekphrasis* or *topographia*) found in every epic or romance. What Ariosto and other heroic poets 'relate' he will present directly before our senses. And he will do so not only because such devices 'perswade [the audience], for the time, that what they behold on the theater is really perform'd', but also because they heighten nature and 'raise the imagina-tion'.[48] As stage directions in each of the four plays suggest, the spectacle must indeed have been quite splendid:

The Scene opens, and discovers the Temple of the Sun all of Gold, and four Priests in habits of white and red Feathers attending by a bloody Altar, as ready for sacrifice.[49]

(The Indian Queen)

A pleasant Grotto discover'd: in it a Fountain spouting; round about it Vasquez, Pizarro, *and other* Spaniards *lying carelesly un-arm'd, and by them many* Indian Women, *one of which Sings the following Song.*[50]

(The Indian Emperour)

The Scene opens, and shews the Wheel.[51]

(Tyrannick Love)

After the Dance, a tumultuous noise of Drums and Trumpets.[52]

(The Conquest of Granada)

Finally, when he writes of the supernatural, he says nothing about how it is to be represented on stage. Nor is he concerned with what, when writing of the supernatural in poetry, Coleridge was to call the 'willing suspension of disbelief'. Dryden's only concern is that he not be accused of blasphemy: he is not bringing theology onto the stage. He would merely arouse wonder and awe. The supernatural is present to give the reader or viewer a pleasurable frisson and to provide the playwright with an opportunity to 'fly'. Like Ariosto, he embues his supernatural machinery with no special moral or metaphysical significance.[53]

V

For Dryden the heroic play was a troublesome subject. When he wrote about his work in other forms – tragedy, comedy, tragi-comedy, epic, satire, translation, opera – he understood what he was about at once or almost at once. Practice might precede theory; or theory, practice. But there was never a significant disjunction between the two. By the time he published one of his works, he could always explain its nature and purpose, its origins, and its dominant techniques. When it came to the heroic play, he developed a theory only very gradually. Although he knew the heroic tradition, ancient and modern, remarkably well when he composed *The Indian Queen* and *The Indian Emperor,* there is no evidence that he associated the new genre with either epic or romance before he published *Tyrannick Love* (1670). But the effects of this knowledge, once gained, were profound. If *The Conquest of Granada* (1672) shows a greater mastery of form than the first three plays, it does so because, during the interval between them, he had finally determined that the heroic play is 'of the same Nature with the Epick'. With this idea clearly before him, he attained an easy mastery of the conventions of the epic and the romance and, in the words of Arthur C. Kirsch, 'brought to fulfillment all the themes with which he had experimented in his earlier plays'.[54]

In the essay 'Of Heroique Playes', moreover, he at last provided his most comprehensive account and justification of the drama about which he had been thinking since 1664. The essay and play represented an enormous triumph; and with their joint publication Dryden could justly claim to have 'swept the stakes'.[55] But from our perspective, his boast is not without its ironies. Having mastered the theory and practice of the heroic play, and brought each to a kind of perfection, he would soon reject both. Having once rejected both, he would soon find ways of accommodating aspects of each within his later work as poet and especially as critic.

CHAPTER NINE

Sweeping of the stakes
(1672)

I

Dryden published the two parts of *The Conquest of Granada* in 1672. The original production, which had taken place the previous year, was an enormous success. But the epilogue to the second part, in which he appeared to insult his Elizabethan predecessors, caused considerable resentment. There he had declared, with a touch of disarming sarcasm, that barbarous ages produce barbarous literature and that, despite all their many excellences, the best writers of the preceding century could not (even in their best works) escape totally the failures of their time and place:

> They, who have best succeeded on the Stage,
> Have still conform'd their Genius to their Age.
> Thus Jonson did Mechanique humour show,
> When men were dull, and conversation low.
> Then, Comedy was faultless, but 'twas course:
> Cobbs Tankard was a jest, and Otter's horse.
> And as their Comedy, their love was mean:
> Except, by chance, in some one labour'd Scene,
> Which must attone for an ill-written Play:
> They rose; but at their height could seldome stay.
> Fame then was cheap, and the first commer sped;
> And they have kept it since, by being dead.[1]

As for the present age, which is the most civilized in English history, it has produced a most civilized literature, of which apparently Dryden's own accomplishments, including of course *The Conquest of Granada,* are a splendid and impressive example:

> If Love and Honour now are higher rais'd,
> 'Tis not the Poet, but the Age is prais'd.
> Wit's now arriv'd to a more high degree;
> Our native Language more refin'd and free.
> Our Ladies and our men now speak more wit
> In conversation, than those Poets writ.[2]

When he published the play, he included the epilogue and, despite the public outcry, defiantly kept it intact. He did, however, include in the volume, along with his preface, 'Of Heroique Playes', a kind of postscript, 'The Defence of the Epilogue', a remarkable attempt at self-justification.

The 'Defence' has never been well received. Dryden's contemporaries found it even more offensive than the epilogue; later generations have thought it shameful, carping and dull.[3] Even Hoyt Trowbridge, who analysed it with much brilliance, believed that '[t]he whole essay' was 'supererogatory' and concluded that Dryden did well to withdraw it from later editions of his work. The 'Defence', however, though somewhat narrow in its ostensible aims, is not 'of second-rate importance'.[4] It clarifies a key moment in Dryden's thinking, and its removal from the canon would interrupt the inner debate or dialogue which the essays hold among themselves.

*

Dryden's critical essays are commentaries on one another, as well as on the poems and plays to which they refer and on which they are always based. In the *Essay of Dramatick Poesie* (1668) he had hoped that in the new age new poets would create a literature that in every way would rival and even supersede the best works of the Elizabethans; in the 'Defence of the Epilogue' he boasts that, for the most part, his fondest hopes have at last been realized.

In 'Of Heroique Playes' (1672), while barely speaking about his commitment to the element of the just in literature – and hence to classical rules, both ancient and modern – he had explained at some length his commitment to elements of the lively and hence to flights of the imagination and 'the hand of Art'. In the 'Defence', while saying little about his preference for the imaginative in art, or about the extent to which it must supersede the requirements of sound judgment, he discusses the obverse side of the coin: the extent to which even the most imaginative poems must somehow be circumscribed by human judgment and hence by a sound (though minimal) classicism. Though appended to a heroic play, *The Conquest of Granada*, the essay says nothing about heroic drama, nothing at all. But the inference we are asked to draw, and to take seriously, is that, even at their most fantastic or outrageous, his heroic plays never once ignore or violate completely the principles of probability, decorum and good English usage.

II

The 'Defence', written obviously as an answer to hostile critics and pedants, is first and last an elaboration on the epilogue, the major arguments of which it supports with a fine sense of history, a keen mastery of the literature of the preceding hundred years and (once the premises are accepted) a logic of pristine directness and clarity. The entire discussion takes place in the context of what Dryden thinks of as the major English literary tradition. In the *Essay of Dramatick Poesie* he had explained that originally there had in fact been two traditions: one the Shakespearean, the other the Jonsonian. He had further argued that they were afterwards synthesized by Fletcher, though perhaps unknowingly; that he (Dryden) was the first actually to recognize the importance of the synthesis, to identify it as a new tradition and then to characterize it; and that through his poetry and his criticism he hoped one day to bring it to perfection. He had also explained that, if English poets and playwrights were to achieve excellence, that new tradition was the one in which they would henceforth have to write or otherwise hold their peace. He makes a number of the same pronouncements in the 'Defence', but with a significant difference. In the *Essay of Dramatick Poesie* he had spoken in fairly general terms; and his persona had been that of the courtier-poet. In the 'Defence' his pronouncements are often technical and remarkably detailed; and his persona is that of a chief legislator and unflinching judge.

Dryden's subject is the whole of literature, though (as one might expect) he emphasizes only the drama and in particular the three mixed forms – mixed comedy, tragi-comedy and, by implication, the heroic play – which at this moment in his life he so much favoured. These are the forms which, he remains convinced, give the most comprehensive view of human life and the moral law and which, he remains no less convinced, allow for the best arrangement or relation of the lively and the just, imagination and judgment, art and the classical rules. His specific concern, however, is not so much with the nature of literary genre as with the kind of 'Sence and Language' which the civilized poet of a civilized age must employ. He puts forth a theory not unlike that advanced in the nineteenth century by Sainte-Beuve and Matthew Arnold: style is the man. A language is a reflection of the 'way of living' or 'Spirit' of an entire society and culture. And contemporary English has been remarkably 'improv'd' through the influence of 'the Court', where 'conversation' both 'correct' and 'refin'd' has in turn been made possible by the most civilized of monarchs, Charles II. In his youth the King had spent his time profitably abroad, where he visited 'the most polish'd Courts of *Europe*' and 'receive[d] the impression of a gallant and generous education'. Upon his accession to the throne, 'he found a Nation lost as much in Barbarism as in Rebellion'; and 'as the excellency of his Nature forgave the one, so the excellency of his manners reform'd the other'.[5] Apparently, after his years of exile, Charles is at last the monarch of all he surveys, including the English language, for which he now sets and determines the highest possible standards.

As there must be a connection between the spirit or manners of an age and the language that educated men must speak, so 'it would be a wonder' if there were no link between the cultivated language of a society and the kind of literature it makes possible and, therefore, the very language that the best poets use.[6] Poetry may be a matter of a proper relationship between judgment and imagination; but that relationship centres ultimately on the manner in which the best poets use language. Poetry is not merely an imitation of nature or of a heightened nature: it is the transmutation of human nature and experience through the best possible language or, to put the matter in another way, through the best words, each in the right place.

Unfortunately, Dryden does not analyse or explain precisely what kind of best language he has in mind for poets and playwrights. He is concerned rather with the 'faults' or 'errors' that successful, and hence eminently civilized, poets must now avoid. They must expunge error and fault from their works in each of the four principal aspects or subdivisions of language: in diction (archaism, 'Solecism', neologism), in idiom (double negative or double comparative, 'Preposition in the end of the sentence', 'meanness of expression'), in grammar (faulty agreement of subject and verb, obsolete inflection, confusing shift in mood and tense, person and number), and in syntax ('ill placing of words [and phrases]', needless repetition, Latin or French construction).[7]

He condemns with severity all violations of good usage, but not with severity everyone who makes them. He is tolerant of those who occasionally misuse a word or phrase: 'all writers have their imperfections'. So too, he finds authors 'pardon-able' whose lapses, however frequent, reflect the ignorance of the times: their errors 'may more properly be call'd the Ages fault than theirs'.[8] But he is absolutely un-forgiving of those who, in their absurdity and pretension, would turn the English language into second-rate French:

> For I cannot approve of their way of refining, who corrupt our *English* Idiom by mixing it too much with *French:* that is a Sophistication of Language, not an improvement of it: a turning *English* into *French,* rather than a refining of *English* by *French.* We meet daily with those Fopps, who value themselves on their Travelling, and pretend they cannot express their meaning in *English,* because they would put off to us some *French* Phrase of the last Edition: without considering that, for ought they know, we have a better of our own ...[9]

The 'Defence', with its catalogue of 'errours', 'faults' and 'improprieties', has the appearance of a short primer of English usage. And its effectiveness as a pedagogic tool is not diminished in the least by its failure to provide us with models to follow. That omission does not matter and is not so relevant as we might at first assume. For the models are near at hand, and they are to be found, as Dryden more than once implies, in his own poetry and plays, and (along with his other works) in this essay in particular.

We are thus given the ruling that, at the very least, poets must be masters of propriety, correctness and simplicity. On the other hand, since we must not confuse excellence in poetry with cultivated speech, we are quickly reminded – in what appears to be a little handbook on rhetoric – that the language of poetry is not merely good conversation to which metre has been added. The language of poetry requires 'height'ning': like the characters of great theatre or the events in magni-ficent drama, language must give the illusion of a nature better than nature, of a mankind superior to the most noble of actual men and women. Such heightening, he then goes on to explain, is not made possible through what so frequently marred even the best work of the Elizabethans. It is not made possible through 'playing with ... words', 'absurd Raillery', dislocated syntax, 'bombast[ic]' declamation. It is made possible through 'Metaphors' and 'Wit'. Metaphor startles us into a new awareness of 'words ... [and their] Signification'; and it must be original, concrete, beautiful. Wit startles us into a new perception of 'Gentlemen ... [and their] follies'; and it must be moral, amusing and urbane.[10]

Of plot and character Dryden says surprisingly little; but he says enough to justify – at least for himself – the kind of theatre of which he approves and which reflects the kind of society and social order to which he feels committed. The men and women who are to be represented in the new plays of the new age are the most cultivated members of the aristocracy or those immediately below them.[11] They are to be defined entirely by the laws of church and state; and though there is never to be any preaching either in their behalf or in their condemnation, they must suffer always the consequences of moral truth and therefore of poetic justice. He says very little about the unities or dramatic structure; but in comments on the kind of drama which he clearly dislikes and condemns, he does suggest that there can be no drama in which the principle of verisimilitude, and hence the laws of nature, is violated absolutely. He does not condemn his heroic plays; and he does leave us with the impression that he would still subordinate the just to the lively, the rules of classicism to the imagination, and that in the overview he continues to relish a drama centred in the beautiful, the wonderful, and the pleasurable. But he would have us understand that, even in the most imaginative literature, 'Fancy' must be kept 'within ... bounds': the laws of probability can never be violated completely or completely ignored.[12]

Dryden's long discourse on what constitutes excellence in the drama and, by implication, in the whole of literature is not allowed to stand or fall solely on its own terms. He is no philosopher any more than he is a professional linguist; but as he has a theory of language, so he has a philosophy of history. He is committed to the idea of progress. In the seventeenth-century Quarrel of the Ancients and Moderns, he is obviously – almost militantly – on the side of the Moderns; and he supports his position with an unexpected and bold empiricism. '[O]ne Age learn[s] from another'; knowledge accumulates; civilizations advance; manners and customs necessarily improve.[13] Hence, the England of Charles II is markedly superior to that of 'the good Queen Bess'; and because there is a necessary connection between literature and the culture which produces it, as between men and their language, or between poets and the language which their contemporaries actually speak, so there is an immediate relationship between a literature and the society in which it flourishes.

When examined in this context, Dryden's observations on Elizabethan poetry demonstrate incontrovertibly the superiority of Restoration literature in most ways over anything produced by the Elizabethans, including the best of their playwrights. In the works of Shakespeare, Jonson and Fletcher one comes again and again on absurd plot, unseemly character, atrocious (and ungrammatical) English, as well as offensive metaphor, pun and wit. The plays of the past, it appears, had imagination without judgment, excesses of the lively without a modicum of the just, nature without art. And they had other faults as well, not the least of which was a narrow range of subject matter, which did not include the niceties of 'love' and 'honour':

> [T]he times were ignorant in which they liv'd. Poetry was then, if not in its infancy among us, at least not arriv'd to its vigor and maturity: witness the lameness of their Plots: many of which ... were made up of some ridiculous, incoherent story, which, in one Play many times took up the business of an Age ... If I would expatiate on this Subject, I could easily demonstrate that our admir'd *Fletcher* ... neither understood correct Plotting, nor that which they call *the Decorum of the Stage*. I would not search in his worst Plays for examples: he who will consider his *Philaster*,

his *Humourous Lieutenant,* his *Faithful Shepheardess;* and many others which I could name, will find them much below the applause which is now given them: he will see *Philaster* wounding his Mistriss, and afterwards his Boy, to save himself: Not to mention the Clown who enters immediately, and not only has the advantage of the Combat against the Heroe, but diverts you from your serious concernment, with his ridiculous and absurd Raillery.[14]

Dryden's condemnation of his forebears, with an appeal to his idea of progress, is of course not an absolute; and it is not comprehensive. He would not 'be wanting in [his] veneration of the past'; he would offer 'to dead Authors their just praises'. His verdict on Shakespeare is, in essence, the one he had published four years earlier. In the *Essay of Dramatick Poesie* he had described Shakespeare as a great but uneven genius:

> I cannot say he is every where alike; were he so, I should do him injury to compare him with the greatest of Mankind. He is many times flat, insipid; his Comick wit degenerating into clenches, his serious swelling into Bombast. But he is always great, when some great occasion is presented to him ...[15]

In the 'Defence' he reasserts the same position, though this time his tone is not affectionate but cold and irreverent:

> Never did any Author precipitate himself from such heights of thought to so low expressions, as he often does. He is the very *Janus* of Poets; he wears, almost every where two faces: and you have scarce begun to admire the one, e're you despise the other.[16]

Jonson and Fletcher are treated with even less favour: much of the early praise Dryden had lavished on the two men he now takes away and redirects elsewhere. He does find something to say of their achievements. To Jonson he ascribes 'the height and accuracy of Judgment' and to Fletcher, 'quickness and easiness'. But he cannot resist enumerating in great detail all the many faults of both men, and he positively gloats when he tells us that each, in the last few years, has lost preeminence in his chosen field: Jonson has been partially surpassed in humour; Fletcher has been completely surpassed in wit.[17]

If, according to his idea of progress, Restoration literature is superior to that of the preceding age, it follows that, according to the same idea, and all the principles which it governs (principles of tradition and genre, of plot and character, of language and subject matter), a total revaluation of the history of English drama is now in order; and Dryden is only too eager to make it, though of course good taste requires that he speak through indirection. Shakespeare is the only one of his predecessors whom, despite the failures, Dryden can still admire. Jonson and Fletcher are taken from their pedestals; and it would seem that, in their place, there now stands one man alone, the author of *The Conquest of Granada* and the 'Defence of the Epilogue': John Dryden himself.

151

Dryden's revaluation of his mighty predecessors did not go so far as his re-writing of literary history: before him, there had been little or no literary history which, after the fact, he could possibly rewrite. But he did allow himself the plea-sure and luxury of revising the *Essay of Dramatick Poesie,* which was republished with the now necessary changes in 1684. Many of his changes are merely verbal and show him removing from his early prose the errors in diction and syntax that he had castigated in the 'Defence'. But there is at least one substantive change which reflects his maturer views of the Elizabethans. In the first edition of the *Essay,* Dryden had written of Fletcher, and no less of Beaumont, in superlative terms: '[T]hey understood and imitated the conversation of gentlemen ... whose wilde debaucheries, and quickness of wit in reparties, no Poet can ever paint as they have done'.[18] But in the second edition he weakened the final clause to read 'whose wilde debaucheries, and quickness of wit in reparties, no Poet before them could paint as they have done'.[19] This revision was a necessary consequence of the role in English letters which he had assumed a dozen years before. Initially, he had pro-vided the English with only literary rules. In the 'Defence', he would have young playwrights and critics find models to imitate not in the past but in contemporary works, and especially his own, the poetry and prose alike. As far as comic wit was concerned, Fletcher was out; he was in.

The 'Defence' is, if only in passing, Dryden's history of the early English stage. As a history or account of that stage, it is obviously his revaluation of the great play-wrights who had come before him. As a revaluation of those playwrights, however, the essay has an ulterior purpose; and that purpose has two aspects, neither of which is immediately apparent, both of which sooner or later force themselves on our attention. Dryden would demonstrate at length, though implicitly, what in his essays on heroic drama he had barely touched upon. He would demonstrate that in his heroic plays, including *The Conquest of Granada,* despite his freedom or looseness in matters of characterization and plot structure and especially language, he had subscribed to all the requirements of sound judgment and hence decorum.[20] In much the same way, he would also demonstrate what in none of his criticism so far he had really considered. He would now demonstrate that he had succeeded and hence had justified himself in every dramatic form. Like the epilogue, to which it refers, the essay is a bold, almost shameless, elevation of himself, both as poet and critic, to a stature he had once hoped he might share with Jonson and Fletcher, if not with Shakespeare. He is the heir of Jonson and Fletcher; but the son has out-done his progenitors.

The 'Defence' sums up the whole of Dryden's first period as poet and critic, and brings that period to a close. At the same time, in the new emphasis that it gives to matters of stylistic correctness, it points forward to the criticism of the middle and later years.

III

At the beginning of his career, from the dedication of *The Rival Ladies* (1664) to the 'Defence of the Epilogue' (1672), Dryden attempted to define a native literary tradition. He would do so not only through the example of his own dramatic and non-dramatic poems but also, indeed primarily, through his literary criticism. And he had no doubt that he would succeed. He had confidence in himself and in his art; and he genuinely believed that, since history is governed by laws of progress, the new age must in literature, as in every other human endeavour, surpass the old.

Dryden's early criticism was based entirely on his own works, which in turn were explained and in large measure justified by the criticism. And both together – the poetry and the criticism – were to provide the models and the rules by which he would have his contemporaries, the new writers of the new age, instruct and guide themselves. The subject of the criticism, however, was not exclusively confined to his own writing. Throughout the early period, he presents us with richly suggestive remarks on the great European masters – from Homer and Virgil through Spenser and Corneille. More importantly, he is intent upon tracing the history of English drama from '*Queen* Gorboduc [*sic*]' (1561) down to his own time. Though not the first to insist upon the separate identity of English drama, he was the first to describe that drama sharply, to identify its native resources and to find within the fusion of its divergent strains the elusive formulae for its perfection. With this rich heritage behind him, he was pleased to discover in his own work a quintessential Englishness. As he repeatedly suggested, in the context of the seventeenth century, and specifically in the ontology of English drama, his plays were the culminating moment.

As Dryden was concerned with the nature and purpose of English drama, so too was he concerned with the nature and purpose of all literature: for example, with the notion that in imaginative writing, which must primarily give pleasure, moral instruction is better conveyed through an implicit moral vision than through overt and obtrusive didacticism. Only through moral vision is great literature, whether about the Town or the Court, this world or the next, truly redemptive. Similarly, he was concerned with the nature and purpose of criticism in general: the critical tradition that he would found was to be capable of general application. To this end he created for the English an entire critical vocabulary: he identified and defined not only such technical terms as 'humour', 'underplot' and 'repartie' but also such general concepts as 'kind' (literary genre), 'wit' and 'imagination'.[21] Moreover, he set forth the specific principles by which poets were to write and literary critics were to pass judgment: principles centred in such matters as imitation and literary models, the requirements of beauty and also of truth, whether natural or moral or both, and the precise nature of the major literary genres from farce and comedy to epic and tragedy.

As critic and literary historian, and both poet and playwright, Dryden early in his career felt challenged by three very different, though related, problems, which he never once doubted he would resolve; and in almost every instance he achieved what he set out to do. He had to define a native literary tradition: it was the only tradition in which he and his contemporaries must write and which they must then pass on to their literary heirs and descendants. He took the whole of literature as his proper domain; but he was committed in particular to the drama and to those mixed forms – tragi-comedy, mixed comedy, heroic play – which in his essays he would have to explain and justify and which in his plays he would have to develop and illustrate. He recognized that his own genius and preference lay with the drama; and he was convinced that through the mixed forms alone could playwrights in search of excellence imitate and gratify the fullest range of human nature and experience. He had also to decide how best to reconcile or combine what he liked to describe as the lively, or the imaginative in literature, and as the just, or the rules of classicism, both ancient and modern.

The three problems remained with him constantly; and they remained with him even as he from time to time shifted or modified his perspectives and points of view. At the outset he insisted that the imaginative in literature and the classical rules – the lively and the just – must be held in a strict balance with each other (dedication of *The Rival Ladies*, 1664). No sooner had he decided on symmetry and balance than he stated a preference not, as one might expect, for the classical or the just but for the imaginative or the lively (*An Essay of Dramatick Poesie*, published 1668, though written 1665–66). Once he had declared that preference, as we have seen, he immediately went on to defend a further imbalance of the lively over the just (the '[A]ccount' of *Annus Mirabilis*, 1667).[22] And he then argued for a complete subordination of the just to the lively ('Of Heroique Playes', 1672), though he was quick to add that even the noblest flights of imagination or fancy must be circumscribed by the rules of good English and the laws of probability and moral truth ('The Defence of the Epilogue', 1672). These several developments or shifts in perspective, however, demonstrate no inconsistency in his thought: they demonstrate rather its fundamental coherence and flexibility. They demonstrate, no less, his engagement always in the same first principles.

He was aware continually that, in his growing preoccupation with the pleasures of art rather than with the rules of composition, he was challenging the received opinion of the age. But he accepted nothing on authority. And he was certain that the reconciliation of opposites which he advocated, and which he subsumed under the rubric of '*A just and lively Image of Humane Nature*', could be successful only if the opposing elements – the simple style and the ornate, unity and multiplicity, verisimilitude and the wonderful – were defined through a gratifying and sound juxtaposition. They must support and heighten, rather than detract from, each other.

In his development of literary forms (sometimes old, more often new) and the attendant theories which explained and justified them, he occasionally met with difficulties; but these were merely the difficulties of an innovator and experimentalist. For all his incidental failings, his early criticism remains an impressive body of work. Out of the pettiness and vindictiveness of Restoration criticism, he rose to give an astonishingly perceptive account of his poetry. And from that point, spiralling ever outward, he proceeded to discuss the achievements of other English poets, the genres in which both he and they worked and the national literature of which they all inextricably formed a part. Because Dryden's early criticism extended beyond its immediate purpose of self-justification, it achieved far more than its immediate ends. It established the groundwork for the essays which he was to write in his second and third periods and, as if in tribute to his fondest hopes, has been a controlling presence in English criticism for more than three hundred years.

PART III
New directions

CHAPTER TEN

The classical moment
(1673–1679)

I

Of the three phases through which Dryden's criticism passed and developed, the second was the shortest; it was no more than an interregnum, but one which saw a number of changes, a few of them unexpected, even quite extraordinary. It lasted only six or seven years, from 1673 to 1679. During those years Dryden wrote very little criticism, theoretical or practical, and during the first three or four almost nothing at all. His mind seems to have been set on other things, not all of them noticeably pleasant.

After a steady run of essays in the 1660s and early 1670s, perhaps because of financial difficulties, loss of popularity and intellectual uncertainty, he abruptly gave up the writing of prefaces.[1] He waged a pamphlet war (1673–74) with a young dramatist, Elkanah Settle, whose meteoric rise challenged his pre-eminence in the theatre. And the challenge was made all the more galling since it was abetted by members of the nobility, including a number of his relatives, patrons and friends. Later (in 1679) he was severely beaten by hired thugs in Rose Alley, Covent Garden. 'An Essay on Satire' by one of his patrons, the Earl of Mulgrave, had been circulating in manuscript. It contained attacks on the Earl of Rochester and on two of the king's mistresses; and Dryden was suspected of being the author. Who actually ordered the beating has never been determined.[2]

On the positive side, he spent much of his time and almost all of his energy writing plays (on the average of about one a year) for a London audience: despite his grumbling, he was determined to remain the leading playwright of the age. But he did not altogether neglect his criticism. He never stopped writing prologues and epilogues to his plays. With 'The Authors Apology for Heroique Poetry; and Poetique Licence', which is a prose introduction to *The State of Innocence* (1677), an opera based on *Paradise Lost,* he returned to his prefatory habit. And at least one of the essays, 'The Grounds of Criticism in Tragedy' (1679), written at the close of the period, is one of his very best.

In the essays, as well as the prologues and epilogues, of the middle years Dryden commits himself to classical rules and ideals. He is convinced that poets and playwrights must obey the rules of composition and hence follow closely the principles of correctness and regularity. That conviction we find reflected in his own works. We find it reflected also in his determination to rewrite completely and so regularize two of Shakespeare's plays: *Anthony and Cleopatra* in 1678, *Troilus and Cressida* in 1679. He insists upon the rules, but he is no rules monger. He allows for reservations, qualifications, exceptions. He recognizes that there are authors who achieve excellence without their knowing anything at all about the rules. They transcend the rules; they obey them intuitively or, to use his term, 'luckily'. His classicism is severe, but it is the classicism of Graeco-Roman antiquity. It is never that of the diehards among the contemporary French or of the English who 'form their judgments by them': he is never adamantine. His manner of writing is severe, even at times argumentative; but it is never high-handed or, except in the tirades against Settle, merely aggressive.

Between the past and the present, continuities nevertheless remain. The break with the past, if there is a break, is never so radical or flagrant or comprehensive as literary historians and his biographers have sometimes argued. He takes up all the old subjects: the Quarrel of the Ancients and Moderns, the interplay between the lively and the just, as well as the importance of both rules and the imitation of great writers, both literary genre and literary tradition, both instruction and delight. When considering these subjects, he holds on to almost all of his old points of view. As a theoretical critic, he prefers narrative to other forms of verse, drama to epic, tragedy to comedy.[3] In narrative he is less concerned with plot than with character, less concerned with character than with language or style. Plots must contain the wonderful, but according to the requirements of probability and decorum. Characters are to be universal types; but the types must be realized physically, and they must be fully distinguished from one another. Language is to be concrete and emotionally charged, straightforward and metaphorical. Great literature must instruct without ever being didactic, and it must always give pleasure. As a practical critic, he returns to the playwrights of the preceding age, focusing his attention repeatedly on Shakespeare, whose faults he very much regrets, whose excellences he can never cease to admire.

II

Changes there of course are. They are made at a slow but deliberate pace; and they cannot be ignored. In the 'Prologue to *Aureng-Zebe*' (1676) Dryden declares the first of his many shifts in literary judgment. He confesses to having 'another taste of wit'. Despite past enthusiasm, he now prefers nature to artifice, blank verse to rhyme:

> Our Author by experience finds it true,
> 'Tis much more hard to please himself than you:
> And out of no feign'd modesty, this day,
> Damns his laborious Trifle of a Play:
> Not that its worse than what before he writ,
> But he has now another taste of Wit;
> And to confess a truth, (though out of time)
> Grows weary of his long-lov'd Mistris, Rhyme.
> Passion's too fierce to be in Fetters bound,
> And Nature flies him like Enchanted Ground.[4]

In the 'Epilogue to *Aureng-Zebe*' he regrets the errors to be found in his early plays, particularly in an old favourite, *The Conquest of Granada* (1672). He now demands that character and dialogue be integrated not only with each other but also with plot structure or design. The first principle of a good play is the harmony or coherence of its parts, each thoroughly in accord with the others. The principle is one on which he insists; and he will adhere to it however much the audience complains:

> A Pretty task! and so I told the Fool,
> Who needs would undertake to please by Rule:
> He thought that, if his Characters were good,
> The Scenes entire, and freed from noise and bloud;
> The Action great, yet circumscrib'd by Time,
> The Words not forc'd, but sliding into Rhime,
> The Passions rais'd and calm'd by just Degrees,
> As Tides are swell'd, and then retire to Seas;
> He thought, in hitting these, his bus'ness done,
> Though he, perhaps, has fail'd in ev'ry one:
> But, after all, a Poet must confess,
> His Art's like Physick, but a happy ghess.
> Your Pleasure on your Fancy must depend:
> The Lady's pleas'd, just as she likes her Friend.
> No Song! no Dance! no Show! he fears you'l say,
> You love all naked Beauties, but a Play.[5]

In 'The Authors Apology for Heroique Poetry; and Poetique Licence' (1677) Dryden writes in some detail about literary genre and in particular about the epic poem; but the subject that actually concerns him is very different. He identifies and, in broad outline, explains the kind of classicism which he newly accepts and which he would have others follow. His classicism is not entirely new; it is not his innovation. But such as it is, he defines it entirely on his own terms. He distinguishes between two kinds of classicism: that of which he approves; and that of which he does not approve – the classicism of '*Hypercritiques* of ... Poetry', whether the contemporary French or their English counterparts. Hence, he distinguishes between two kinds of literary rules: those of very recent origin; and those which, because they have received the 'approbation of all Ages', have a validity all their own. Among the rules which have withstood the test of time, he distinguishes further between those which are only 'little decencies', and which on occasion may be ignored, and those others which, centred as they are in principles of both common sense and decorum, are inviolable.[6]

In short, there are rules that, according to Dryden, must be obeyed. But no sooner has he said as much than, paradoxically, he falls into a seeming inconsistency or contradiction. When considering the rules, especially those which are inviolable, he allows for what he calls '*Poetique Licence*': 'the Liberty, which Poets have assum'd to themselves in all ages, of speaking things in Verse, which are beyond the severity of Prose'. He defends and justifies the use of fiction both in the language of poetry and in the subject matter: in language the 'use of the hardest

159

Metaphors, and of the strongest *Hyperboles*'; in subject matter the use of 'Hippocentaures', 'Chymæras', and 'Magick'. But the contradiction (or inconsistency) is neither so bold nor so far-reaching as it may at first appear to be. As there are rules that must be obeyed, so there is a limit beyond which poetic licence may not go. Even poetic licence must conform to rules that have withstood the test of time. It must conform to the dictates of probability; and it must conform to the use of an ancient and hence an established rhetoric. Dryden distinguishes between the necessary rules of classicism and those which he deems irrelevant or, at the very least, inessential. On the other hand, his defence of poetic licence is, in a final analysis, no defence at all. His classicism, though flexible, remains intact.[7]

In the 'Preface to *All for Love*' (1678), though granting once again that the English have a separate literary tradition, he now categorically denies that this tradition has much literary merit and, hence, that it can or should provide a basis for a theatre of the future. Like their counterparts in France, they must choose the Ancients as their 'Masters', and follow their masters where they lead.[8] In the 'Preface to *Oedipus*' (1679) he recognizes that to gratify the national custom and taste an English playwright must occasionally avail himself of parallel plots. But he adds that the ancient method, which sanctions only the single plot, is clearly to be preferred:

> Custom...has obtain'd, that we must form an under-plot of second Persons, which must be depending on the first...Perhaps after all, if we could think so, the ancient method, as 'tis the easiest, is also the most Natural, and the best. For variety, as 'tis manag'd, is too often subject to breed distraction: and while we would please too many ways, for want of art in the conduct, we please in none.[9]

In the dedication of his *Troilus and Cressida* (1679), 'To...Robert, Earl of Sunderland', he points to yet another change in his literary opinions. That change, he goes on to say, he explains in an accompanying essay, 'The Grounds of Criticism in Tragedy'. And he hopes that, in discovering what the change is, Lord Sunderland will not be too much dismayed. After all, there can be no fault in rejecting error for truth:

> In what I have...done, I doubt not but I have contradicted some of my former opinions, in my loose Essays of the like nature: but of this ['The Grounds of Criticism in Tragedy'], I dare affirm, that it is the fruit of my riper age and experience, and that self-love, or envy have no part in it.[10]

The changes that are to be found in the 'Grounds', the last essay of the middle period, are indeed remarkable. Qualities that he had originally thought peculiar to English literature he now realizes belong to a much older tradition, one extending back beyond Shakespeare and Fletcher to Graeco-Roman antiquity. Rules which he had originally accepted, and which he found incompatible with that older tradition, he now either modifies or, for the time being, rejects.

At the same time, throughout the criticism of the period he redefines completely the interconnections between feeling and thought and therefore between the wonderful and the probable, imagination and judgment, the lively and the just. Whenever he writes about or refers to mixed literary forms, whether heroic drama or tragi-comedy, he makes what is in fact an about-face: he rejects completely what he had once ardently championed. And he modifies (sometimes radically) his every conception and treatment of the rules governing not only, as one might expect, the three unities but also character types and inevitably the moral function of a good poem or play.

The first phase of Dryden's criticism and the second are of the same piece; but there are discontinuities. Dryden himself calls them to our attention; and he does so with candour, firmness, conviction. He shifts some of his perspectives, modifies a few of his opinions, reverses himself on three or four others. To explain or account for these changes is no easy matter, though it is always possible to speculate. As one goes through the criticism, one gets the impression that he has been stirred profoundly, for the moment, by the splendour of classicism and has decided to make it his own. One also gets the impression that he has been reading and re-reading Aristotle and Horace with new understanding and respect. On the other hand, as a matter of certainty, we do know that he has suddenly discovered Longinus, whose treatise *On the Sublime* has a stunning effect upon him.

III

The treatise *On the Sublime* is of uncertain authorship and date. For many centuries it was attributed to Cassius Longinus, a Greek rhetorician of the third century A.D.; but it no longer is.[11] By force of habit, however, the name 'Longinus' has been lent to the unknown author, whoever he was, whenever he may have lived. The oldest extant manuscript, a Greek text surviving from the tenth century, was first published in Basel in 1554 by Francesco Robortello. Despite numerous other editions, including a Latin translation (1636) by the elder Gerard Langbaine and one into English (1652) by John Hall, *On the Sublime* remained all but unknown in England until Boileau published his in 1674. And it is Boileau's translation which Dryden almost certainly read.[12]

Although he has in mind every sort of discourse, including public oratory, Longinus dwells mainly on two kinds of narrative verse – the epic poem and the drama – and he seems to prefer not the second but the first. His subject is literary excellence, which (he is convinced) can best be determined through the test of time:

> In general, consider those examples of sublimity to be fine and genuine which please all and always. For when men of different pursuits, lives, and ambitions, ages, languages, hold identical views on one and the same subject, then that verdict which results, so to speak, from a concert of discordant elements makes our faith in the object of admiration strong and unassailable.[13]

However it may or may not be determined, excellence in literature can best be achieved only through 'elevated language' or through the 'true sublime' as opposed to the 'false', which 'arise[s] in literature from a single cause', the 'pursuit of novelty in expression', and leads always to 'ugly and parasitical growths'. It leads to 'turbid ... expression' and 'confused ... imagery', 'high-flown' language and 'empty passion', and the mingling of what is 'ignoble' with what 'excites admiration'.[14]

To achieve excellence or the true sublime, a poet must have genius or, as Longinus says, qualities which are 'for the most part innate': a poet must have nobility of thought and nobility of feeling. If he has these two qualities, which are 'components of the sublime', he will then have 'the power of forming great conceptions' and further the power of 'vehement and inspired passion'.[15] But innate qualities are not enough. A poet must follow a number of first principles, these in turn based on the recognition that in art, as in life, harmony or coherence must necessarily prevail over multiplicity and discord:

> Among the chief causes of the sublime in speech, as in the structure of the human body, is the collocation of members, a single one which if severed from another possesses in itself nothing remarkable, but all united together make a full and perfect organism.[16]

A poet must therefore recognize, as a corollary, that in his art, as in his life, thought and passion are not to be regarded as separate and distinct: they must be understood and treated as inextricably related. A poet must not be a slave to convention: he must be original. But he must allow himself 'the imitation and emulation of previous great poets and writers':

> This writer [Plato] shows us ... that another way ... leads to the sublime ... It is the imitation and emulation of previous great poets and writers ... For many men are carried away by the spirit of others as if inspired, just as it is related of the Pythian priestess when she approaches the tripod, where there is a rift in the ground which (they say) exhales divine vapour. By heavenly power thus communicated she is impregnated and straightway delivers oracles in virtue of the afflatus. Similarly from the great natures of the men of old there are borne in upon the souls of those who emulate them (as from sacred caves) what we may describe as *effluences,* so that even those who seem little likely to be possessed are thereby inspired and succumb to the spell of others' greatness.[17]

As his genius is not violated when he submits to 'the imitation and emulation of great poets and writers', so a poet must realize that there can be no incompatibility between his genius and the 'rules of art':

> [W]e must raise the question whether there is such a thing as an art of the sublime or the lofty. Some hold that those are entirely in error who would bring such matters under the precept of art. A lofty tone, says one, is innate, and does not come by teaching; nature is the only art that can compass it. Works of nature are, they think, made worse and altogether

feebler when wizened by the rules of art. But I maintain that this will be found to be otherwise if it be observed that, while nature as a rule is free and independent in matters of passion and elevation, yet she is wont not to act at random and utterly without system. Further, nature is the original and vital underlying principle in all cases, but system can define limits and fitting seasons, and can also contribute the safest rules for use and practice. Moreover, the expression of the sublime is most exposed to danger when it goes its own way without the guidance of knowledge ...[18]

A poet or playwright must know and obey the rules of characterization and plot structure; but he has always to concentrate on the right language. He must know and employ 'noble diction', 'dignified or elevated composition' (or syntax), and '[t]he due formation of figures', especially those governing the 'elaboration of language' and the 'use of metaphors'.[19]

A poet has also to delight and to instruct; and he must understand that, in the greatest poetry, pleasure and instruction are one and the same. Poetry gives pleasure; and it pleases especially when, through elevated language or the sublime, we feel exhilaration or 'transport'. Poetry teaches, but not through obtrusive didacticism or through examples of poetic justice: it teaches best not by mere 'persuasion'. It teaches best when, in a moment of 'transport', 'the influences of the sublime bring power and irresistible might to bear [on the audience], and reign supreme...' Through a language which is elevated or sublime we experience simultaneously both pleasure and moral vision. At the very moment of our experiencing 'transport' as pleasure, we experience it as a means by which we get out of ourselves and so become more deeply moral, more deeply human: we 'resemble the Gods ... in benevolence and truth'.[20]

Dryden read *On the Sublime* with avidity. He found it a revelation: he found in it what for him seems to have bordered on a completely new way of looking at both nature and art. He modified or completely rejected theories and practices that he had until recently deemed sacrosanct and inviolable. He now became contemptuous of the interplay of the high and the low, the serious and the comic. He condemned the craze for novelty in action and expression. And he clearly distinguished the 'true sublime' from the false simulacra of extravagant language, hollow emotionalism, and self-conscious artifice. Hence, once he had read Longinus, he reached the inevitable conclusion. He saw his serious plays as examples of an art which had failed; and he forswore completely every commitment to his beloved mixed forms. What for years he had praised and even celebrated as the lively or the imaginative in serious plays, and especially in heroic drama – variety of episode in plot, fitfulness of passion in character, display of rhetoric in language – he now condemned outright as incoherence, contradiction and bombast. His two mixed forms illustrated, unfortunately, the 'false sublime'.

On the other hand, once he had read Longinus he looked with renewed favour on the Ancients. From his own point of view, he had now a better understanding of the relationship between genius and the rules, between originality and the emulation of great writers, and between pleasure and instruction. He redefined, for the time being, his several ways of handling thought and passion or, in his terms, the elements of the lively (or imagination and feeling) and the elements of the just (or thought and sound judgment). At the same time, he had now at his disposal what he held to be a fuller and better understanding of literary excellence and failure.[21]

*

It has often been said that, when in his middle period he turned to a strict classicism, or in any event to a classicism far more strict than he had so far espoused, Dryden did so because he had fallen under the influence of Thomas Rymer, a critic noted by contemporaries for his severity and rigour.[22] The argument is put forth most strongly by George Watson. According to Watson, once Dryden had become acquainted with *The Tragedies of the Last Age* (1678), Rymer's first important work, he began 'to defend neo-classical positions'; his 'critical doctrines' became 'less liberal and less "English" than in his early period'; and he even engaged in 'some disagreeable bootlicking of Rymer'.[23]

Dryden refers to Rymer in more than one essay of the middle period; but the evidence for his having been influenced by *The Tragedies of the Last Age* is apparently based on a single text, 'The Grounds of Criticism in Tragedy'. It is true that in the 'Grounds' Dryden considers the book, pays the man some tribute, and praises both his theories and their application. It is no less true that, even as he praises him, Dryden has powerful reservations: he qualifies what he praises. He explains that, in attacking the irregularities in Elizabethan drama, Rymer is essentially correct, but that, in rejecting English models for English playwrights, he is much too rigid and hence goes much too far.[24] It is equally true that what Dryden does not praise he rejects outright or condemns: Rymer's assertion that in the drama there can be no place for the improbable or the supernatural and that perfect characters must be allowed.

Things then are not what they seem. Dryden did find in Rymer much that, he felt, was to be admired. So far as one can determine, however, he accepted only that portion of Rymer's criticism which, in his opinion, had clearly and directly been shaped by Rymer's own studies either in Longinus or perhaps in the latter's French disciples and followers, especially Balzac, Racine, Rapin and of course Boileau.[25] Not only does Rymer mention Longinus by name and distinguish between the true sublime and the false. At the same time, like Longinus and like Dryden, whose 'Authors Apology' (1677) he occasionally seems to echo, he maintains that even the poet of genius must follow the rules, as well as the example of great predecessors, that in all good poetry 'thought' is 'portionable ... to ... passion', and that in the major genres 'profit' (or moral instruction) must always 'please'.[26]

In the literary criticism of Thomas Rymer Dryden found, if anything, justification for points of view that he had come upon elsewhere and for judgments to which he had already committed himself. After all, he had discovered Longinus in 1674. It was not until 1677, when he received a presentation copy of *The Tragedies of the Last Age,* that his studies in Rymer actually began.

IV

In 'The Grounds of Criticism in Tragedy', which is one of the most tightly argued of his essays and intellectually the most impressive, Dryden takes up the first principles of his middle period; and he does so with a confidence which is at times disarming. He centres the essay in the criticism that precedes it; nevertheless, he modifies principles to which he had until quite recently committed himself and he repudiates others. Throughout the essay he anticipates the criticism to come; but he will soon disavow or modify principles he now defends with enthusiasm, even vehemence.

The essay was originally written as an appendix to his short preface to *Troilus and Cressida*, his revision – or correction – of Shakespeare's original. The essay is artfully constructed; it is remarkable in its fundamental unity and coherence, emphasis and development, as well as in the subtlety and the fine logic of its argument. The introduction to the play thus consists of two parts (one on his literary practice, one on his critical theory), each linked inevitably and tightly to the other. In the first part, the preface, he explains, justifies and fully illustrates his reworking of Shakespeare's play. In the second and very much longer part, 'The Grounds of Criticism', he lays down the rules for the writing of a good tragedy, although he also has in mind very clearly 'the grounds and reasons' of literary excellence in general.

He re-enters the Quarrel of the Ancients and Moderns, once again – and only for the moment – reversing his customary position. He again sides with the Ancients against the Moderns: the Moderns are but the imperfect followers; the Ancients are the great originators. He considers two kinds of imitation: the imitation of nature, whether human nature or natural law; the imitation of authors by one another. And he argues rather cogently that, to the man of genius, the second is not less important than the first. In the preface he supports his position with a passage from Longinus:

> [']We ought not to regard a good imitation as a theft; but as a beautifull Idea of him who undertakes to imitate, by forming himself on the invention and the work of another man; for he enters into the lists like a new wrestler, to dispute the prize with the former Champion. This sort of emulation, says *Hesiod*, is honourable … when we combat for Victory with a Hero, and are not without glory even in our overthrow.[']27

In what follows in 'The Grounds of Criticism' he supports his position with a passage from Le Bossu:

> [']That all excellent Arts, and particularly that of Poetry, have been invented and brought to perfection by men of a transcendent Genius; and … therefore they who practice afterwards the same Arts, are oblig'd to tread in their footsteps, and to search in their Writings the foundation of them: for it is not just that the new Rules should destroy the authority of the old.[']28

Cressida pleading with Troilus for the life of Diomede. Illustration for *Troilus and Cressida*, in *The Dramatick Works of John Dryden Esq.* (1735)
(By permission of the William Andrews Clark Memorial Library, Los Angeles)

The Ancients imitated nature. Later poets and playwrights imitated the Ancients. It therefore follows that, if he would write a good tragedy, the modern playwright may choose among a number of competing alternatives. With the Ancients as his example and guide, he may try to imitate nature directly. Or he may try to imitate the Ancients themselves. Or if he is an Englishman and a Christian, he may imitate even English authors, and especially Shakespeare and Fletcher; but should he do so, as Dryden suggests he should, he must be judicious and selective:

> Here therefore the general answer may be given to the ... question, how far we ought to imitate *Shakespeare* and *Fletcher* ...; namely that we ought to follow them so far only, as they have Copy'd the excellencies of those who invented and brought to perfection Dramatic Poetry: those things only excepted which Religion, customs of Countries, Idioms of Language, &c. have alter'd in the Superstructures, but not in the foundation of the design.[29]

He names as two of his main authorities Aristotle and Horace: Aristotle because he argues that the concrete particulars of art are indistinguishable from the abstract universals which they evoke and because he demonstrates precisely in what way the excellence of a play or epic poem is determined by the consistency or harmony of its multiple parts; and Horace because he gives the best (that is, the simplest and the clearest) statement of classical rules for a good tragedy, rules governing specifically language, characterization and plot structure. With Aristotle and Horace as two of his authorities, and with Sophocles and Euripides as his ideal playwrights, he meanwhile discusses at length, occasionally with a wealth of technical detail, the uses and abuses of metaphor, the proper handling and development of character types and of course 'the mechanic beauties ... of the three Unities'.

Surprisingly, though he is no pedant, his classicism is quite rigid. On the basis of his new interests he rejects his tragi-comedies, and he does so without exception: 'He who treats of joy and grief together, is in a fair way of causing neither of those effects'.[30] Through his rejection of loosely ordered (or 'imperfect') plots, inconstant characters, 'variety of passions' and 'pointed Wit', he no less condemns his heroic plays.[31] And while comparing and contrasting Shakespeare and Fletcher – Shakespeare is 'a more Masculine' playwright, Fletcher is 'a more ... Womanish' playwright – he grants that, although he continues to admire both of them, he very much regrets as inexcusable their many blemishes: they ignored with abandon the rules of the classical theatre. He recognizes with Rapin, whom he quotes, that the classical rules are but 'Nature Methodiz'd':

> [']If the Rules be well consider'd, we shall find them to be made only to reduce Nature into Method, to trace her step by step, and not to suffer the least mark of her to escape us: 'tis only by these, that probability in Fiction is maintain'd, which is the Soul of Poetry...['][32]

He accepts the rules without question; but he is quick to grant that there are indeed excellences beyond their reach; and they too are imitations of nature, however faintly. He does not know why or how that can be; he is left in a quandary; and he fails to pursue the matter further.[33]

Ideally, a poet must obey the rules; and there are two ways of his doing so: he may do so 'luckily' (through intuition); he may do so 'laboriously' (through the study of critics like Horace or like Dryden himself).[34] In his new and pressing defence of the rules, Dryden is not as rigid as are, in his opinion, the contemporary French; and eventually he will allow the contemporary English far more leeway than he now does. But at the moment he clearly prefers, as his standard of excellence, the poet who, in imitating nature directly, follows the example of the best writers yet knows the rules exceedingly well and has mastered them. The one exception that he allows is Shakespeare, who has remained so far a major problem to him; but that problem is one he is now determined to resolve.

He again condemns Shakespeare for having violated the rules; and he is more severe than when, under the persona of Neander, he had condemned him in the *Essay of Dramatick Poesie* (1668). He also praises him, but no longer because of his flights of imagination and no longer because, in juxtaposing the just and the lively, he followed classical rules intuitively. He praises him in terms radically different from any he has so far employed, terms suggested by his reading in Longinus.

In his first period Dryden had argued that Shakespeare generally violated the rules; that he sometimes obeyed the rules, though intuitively, but only when they were set in opposition to the imaginative and the wonderful; and that he frequently gave pleasure in ways that had nothing to do with rules. In his second period Dryden argues that Shakespeare too frequently violated the rules but that in moments of inspiration he harnessed flights of the imagination to the requirements of probability and judgment.

At the centre of the essay, casting his direction and guidance out from that centre, there is Longinus. Dryden admits freely to the influence of Longinus on him.[35] Under that influence, however defined, he now holds and explains that the elements of the lively and the just must not, in a good play, be set in opposition to, or juxtaposition with, each other: they must be thought of and dealt with, instead, as each other's development or extension, as if they were in fact the two sides of a coin without thickness. Style is to contain in the same discourse a language of statement and a language of metaphor. Individual characters are to embody in themselves simultaneously the polarities of passion and reason, imagination and judgment; and they may even embody in themselves simultaneously the polarities of the natural and the supernatural, as does Shakespeare's Caliban:

> He [Shakespeare] seems... to have created a person which was not in Nature, a boldness which at first sight would appear intolerable: for he makes him a Species of himself, begotten by an Incubus on a Witch... Whether or no his Generation can be defended, I leave to Philosophy; but of this I am certain, that the Poet has most judiciously furnish'd him with a person, a Language, and a character, which will suit him, both by Fathers and Mothers side: he has all the discontents, and Malice of a Witch, and of

a Devil; besides a convenient proportion of the deadly sins ... His person is monstrous, as he is the product of unnatural Lust; and his language is as hobgoblin as his person ...[36]

Dryden's discussion of Caliban – indeed, his admiration for both the matter and manner of the entire characterization – carries with it implications that are in fact developed throughout the essay. He condemns Shakespeare wherever he violates the rules and violates them obtrusively. He praises him, but in terms radically different from those which, as Neander, he had expounded in the *Essay of Dramatick Poesie.*

He discusses Shakespeare's faults, but only in the most cursory terms. Particulars are given and illustrated in the short preface that immediately precedes the 'Grounds'; and they are taken all but entirely from the *Troilus,* which he has just revised, corrected, rewritten. He focuses his attention on a single play and its inexcusable failings; but he draws inferences about the plays in general and he suggests that we follow his example.

The language of the *Troilus* is at times 'scarce intelligible'. Of the words and phrases which can be understood, 'some are ungrammatical, others course; and his whole stile is so pester'd with Figurative expressions, that it is as affected as it is obscure'.[37] The characters in the play are not clearly defined. When they are introduced, 'Hector, Troilus, Pandarus, and Thersites' are 'promising enough'; but then, as if he 'grew weary of his task', Shakespeare leaves them 'unfinish'd' and 'lets 'em fall'. Worse still, the whole of the action is not carefully or properly developed. Unity of place is flagrantly ignored; there is a lack of coherence between the major and the minor plots; scene follows scene without regard to 'Order and Connection'. Indeed, 'the latter part of the Tragedy is nothing but a confusion of Drums and Trumpets, Excursions and Alarms'.[38]

His subject matter is that of the believing Christian; and he is not unaware of Divine Providence. But at the end of the play we experience no exhilaration, no transport. We are left with no sense that, with or without poetic justice, the true, the beautiful and the good are one and the same. Folly has the victory over wisdom; vice is not itself destroyed: 'Cressida is false, and is not punish'd'.[39]

In the 'Grounds' Dryden only touches upon Shakespeare's many failings. His concern is to explain and demonstrate, with reference to all the plays, the various means by which, in following the classical rules 'luckily' (or intuitively), Shakespeare achieves excellence or 'true sublimity'. His language has the power to move us profoundly through 'nobleness of expression in its proper place'. At such moments the writing displays a fine restraint. Similes and metaphors are used, but not 'at every word'. They are always apt; and they are always subordinated to a language of statement. Hence, he avoids those vices of style which elsewhere beset his work. He gives us not a mere 'sound of words' but 'sence', not 'madness' but 'vehemence', not 'an extravagant thought' but 'a sublime one'.[40]

His characters, as a rule, are not only distinguished and distinguishable from one another, they are vividly described with a rich abundance of concrete detail;

and through a powerful interplay of opposing faculties they come vividly to life. Character is true to type; and type predetermines in every instance appropriate action and dialogue. As the embodiment of two very human types (the concerned father, the concerned king), Henry IV thus alternates, according to circumstance, between two very different patterns of behaviour and two very different modes of discourse. Varied and various as he is, he always behaves as the occasion warrants. In this respect, the manner of his portrayal is far closer to the best classical models than is Racine's handling of Bajazet:

> Sophocles gives to *Oedipus* the true qualities of a King, in both those Plays which bear his Name: but in the latter which is the *Oedipus Colonæus,* he lets fall on purpose his Tragic Stile, his Hero speaks not in the Arbitrary tone; but remembers in the softness of his complaints, that he is an unfortunate blind old man, that he is banish'd from his Country, and persecuted by his next Relations. The present *French Poets* are generally accus'd, that wheresoever they lay the Scene, or in whatsoever Age, the manners of their Heroes are wholly *French: Racine's Bajazet* is bred at *Constantinople;* but his civilities are convey'd to him by some secret passage, from *Versailles* into the *Seraglio.* But our *Shakespear,* having ascrib'd to *Henry the Fourth* the character of a King, and of a Father, gives him the perfect manners of each Relation, when either he transacts with his Son, or with his Subjects.[41]

Of the plots, when taken individually, nothing positive can be said: here, according to Dryden, Shakespeare nods. Nevertheless, as if each were a play entire unto itself, individual scenes are models of dramatic construction. Shakespeare does not commit the mistake for which Longinus 'animadverts severely upon *Æschylus*': the mistake of writing 'nothing in cold bloud', but of always being 'in a rapture, and in fury with his Audience'. Shakespeare knows how to build a scene, how to raise the passions 'by the just degrees of Nature', and how 'to observe the crisis and turns of them, in their cooling and decay'. Thus, many scenes are not only 'lively' and 'moving': they are also 'extreamly natural' and deserve the praise of 'judicious men'.[42]

In the plays at their very best, Shakespeare ('that Divine Poet') makes the 'wonderfull' seem 'probable' and the 'probable' seem 'wonderfull': 'that which is not wonderfull, is not great, and that which is not probable, will not delight a reasonable audience'.[43] His purpose is to teach and to give pleasure, but not in different parts or segments of the same work and not in appeals directly to the contemplative life. He does so in works the segments or parts of which are entirely appropriate to one another and hence are properly linked together. He does so, at the same time, by helping us to get out of ourselves. He pleases through instruction; he instructs delightfully; and through the sublimity of his works he enables us, in a moment of transport, to create as our own his every conception and flight.[44] He succeeds in realizing his purpose because he himself had that elevated spirit which he would encourage in his audience and which he would have them experience fully. Nobility of statement, Longinus reminds us, can reflect only nobility of character: 'It is not possible that those who throughout their lives have feeble and servile thoughts and aims should strike out anything that is remarkable, anything that is worthy of an immortality'.[45] And Dryden of course agrees: a 'Poet...[must not be] bound Prentice to a Wheel-wright...[or follow] a Ragman'.[46]

According to Sir Walter Scott, 'The Grounds of Criticism in Tragedy' reveals a far greater understanding of Shakespeare than anything Dryden had so far written, including the *Essay of Dramatick Poesie*.[47] The point was well made; and it is still valid. Dryden had the additional dozen or more years in which to reread the plays and to study them. But the argument is not immediately relevant. With but one exception, his damning of mixed forms, he does not anywhere in the 'Grounds' violate or contradict any of his first judgments. He has studied and mastered Aristotle and Horace; and for the moment he has fallen under the spell, more or less, of a strict classicism. He has discovered Longinus, for whom all great literature – and especially every successful epic or drama – must demonstrate not only a thoroughly unified or coherent plot but also a complete harmony or fusion of the wonderful and the probable, as well as of metaphor and statement, passion and reason, pleasure and instruction. Shakespeare remains, nevertheless, what he has always been: a very great English playwright, although even in the best of his works he is unfortunately imperfect. With the one exception, the mingling of the high and the low, whether in single plots or in the interplay of parallel plots, the failures and the achievements are exactly what he had initially declared them to be. They are now merely defined and illustrated in a new context.

It is ironic that, upon completing 'Of Heroique Playes', Dryden went on to repudiate the very drama he had so well defined. There is now a further irony, of which at the time he might not have been aware. No sooner had he completed 'The Grounds of Criticism in Tragedy' than he began to amend it. He reversed himself (once again) in the Quarrel of the Ancients and Moderns. And though he remained committed to Longinus, he gradually permitted himself a flexibility which a strict classicism would never allow.

CHAPTER ELEVEN

The great tradition
(1680–1700)

I

Shortly after the death of Charles II in 1685, Dryden became a Catholic. The new king, James II, also a Catholic, renewed his patents of office. But at the accession of the Protestant William III in 1688, Dryden and the government were suddenly at odds with each other; he was ousted as Poet Laureate and Historiographer Royal; and one source of his income was thereby denied. For these several reasons, although there may well have been others, he returned in 1689 with a tragedy, *Don Sebastian,* to the public theatre, for which he had last written in 1682, also a tragedy, *The Duke of Guise.* He also committed himself increasingly to verse translation, which he had at first undertaken more or less sporadically, beginning in 1680 with translations of Ovid's *Epistles* (the *Epistulae Heroidum*). For his last translation, *The Works of Virgil* (1697), he may have received as much as fourteen hundred pounds, an enormous sum at the time.[1]

Despite attacks against him as both man and poet (against his conversion, his political satires, his various translations, his critical theories) he was generally regarded as the major literary figure of the age; and his output – poems, plays, translations, critical essays, operas, a masque, prologues and epilogues to his own works and those of his friends – only increased. Indeed, he wrote more criticism in these years than he had written during the entire first half of his career. The fact never ceases to astound when one realizes the extent and excellence of the criticism itself. Fashions in literature, as in everything else, come and go; but the criticism remains a major achievement in English literary history.

In his third and last period as a literary critic, Dryden 'something to perfection brought'. The period began in about 1680; it ended with his death twenty years later. During this period, his longest and clearly the most prolific, he extended the range and scope of his criticism. He touched on a variety of subjects that he had so far neglected. He established interconnections between theories old and new. He set his theories, both old and new, in ever larger contexts, literary, critical, historical.

He was not a systematic philosopher; he certainly was no metaphysician. The passing of the years nevertheless brought what Wordsworth might have called 'the philosophic mind'. Despite the vicissitudes of daily life, both personal and professional, or perhaps because of them, it brought a new self-confidence; and that confidence brought new and original shifts in perspective. He could and would demonstrate that, as in every great work of art unity underlay diversity, so in his criticism, when taken as a whole, diversity underlay a fundamental unity: despite development and change, it remained, with a few exceptions, thoroughly consistent. With the few exceptions – his statements about mixed forms, rhyme in the drama, literary progress – he demonstrated in essay after essay that the criticism which he had put forth at the start of his career was consistent with what he had been expounding ever since.

At the same time, with shifts in perspective, he recognized that in all of the arts, there were complexities which could never be reduced to any formula. The rules of literature must be obeyed; but a man of genius may on occasion transcend them. Poets and playwrights must subscribe to that great tradition which began in antiquity and which, ever since, has pleased many and pleased them long; but for his very survival an English author has no choice but to meet, from time to time, the demands and requirements of his immediate audience and public. The elements of the lively and the just should be treated as if they are in fact one and the same; but in any given poem or play there may be a circumstance or passage in which they may be set in opposition to, or in juxtaposition with, each other.

*

Despite his enthusiasm at the time, Dryden had never committed himself irrevocably to a strict classicism; and it was therefore inevitable that, as he thought the matter over, and perhaps even brooded about it, he would superimpose on the classicism of his middle years several important qualifications: that he would assert, under pressing circumstances, the priority (once again) of the lively over the just, the imaginative over the dictates of probability and natural law. He could not help himself: temperamentally he could not do otherwise. He continued to find pleasure in Homer, Chaucer and Shakespeare, not one of whom, according to the rules of a strict classicism, had consistently written either correctly or well.

Moreover, from the leading classicists across the Channel, many of whom he had earlier regarded as mere pedants (as '*Hypercritiques* of ... Poetry'), he gradually received word that, in every great work of literature, there are indeed excellences which no rules can either explain or justify. French literature was no longer, and it may never have been, so monolithic as he had once assumed: the French were divided not only against one another but also against themselves. From what must at first have seemed the most unlikely of sources, he received unexpected encouragement against a restrictive classicism of any sort. French critics were, in any event, undergoing a significant change: they were becoming more flexible than they had ever been. They were urging on poet and critic alike a greater freedom than they themselves had once found acceptable or would allow. And to that urging – though the fact has never been sufficiently recognized – Dryden (after some wavering) did respond: his literary preferences, and hence his intuitions, were no less reliable than what he had already borrowed from Aristotle and Horace, Longinus and Quintilian.

All the major French critics of the seventeenth century were committed to a thoroughgoing classicism. In art, they argued, there are rules, and the rules must be obeyed. They justified themselves, as we might expect, by appeals to Aristotle,

Horace and (towards the end of the century) Longinus, as well as to the most famous of their immediate predecessors, especially the Italians: Vida, Castelvetro and Julius Caesar Scaliger.[2] They also justified themselves by defining their position as that of Frenchmen who were, simultaneously, monarchists, Cartesians and practising Catholics.

The poets to whom the critics addressed themselves agreed in principle with them; yet there were mutterings of discontent. Too strict an adherence to literary rules, it was frequently said, could stifle the creative act and simplify, even distort, human nature. And in the drama, according to Corneille, too strict an adherence to the three unities, which were generally assumed to enhance the illusion of verisimilitude, could violate every law of probability:

> The rule of the unity of time is founded on this statement of Aristotle 'that the tragedy ought to enclose the duration of its action in one journey of the sun or try not to go much beyond it'. These words gave rise to a famous dispute as to whether they ought to be understood as meaning a natural day of twenty-four hours or an artificial day of twelve;... and, for myself, I find that there are subjects so difficult to limit to such a short time that not only should I grant the twenty-four full hours but I ... should should push the total without scruple as far as thirty. There is a legal maxim which says that we should broaden the mercies and narrow the rigors of the law ...; and I find that an author is hampered enough by this constraint which forced some of the ancients to the very edge of the impossible. Euripides, in *The Suppliants,* makes Theseus leave Athens with an army, fight a battle beneath the walls of Thebes, which was ten or twelve leagues away, and return victorious in the following act; and between his departure and the arrival of the messenger who comes to tell the story of his victory, the chorus has only thirty-six lines to speak. That makes good use of such a short time.[3]

According to Corneille, 'It is easy for critics to be severe'. He urged that the critics themselves 'give ... plays to the public'. They would then 'slacken the rules': they would recognize 'what constraint their precision brings about and how many beautiful things it banishes from [the] stage'.[4]

The poets made their complaints. The critics listened; and by the 1670s they were more or less convinced. The rules were still thought to be valid and valuable. But French critics were now willing to grant that, when inspired by his genius or by the presence of the Holy Spirit, a poet might transcend the rules. In every great work of literature, there may truly be excellences which cannot be defined. And in the presence of these *'grâces secrètes'* and *'beautés cachées'*, the baffled critic had to admit to *'un je ne sais quoi'*.[5] For as La Bruyère noted in his *Characters* (1688–94), there are mysteries in art which cannot be reduced to rules and which cannot therefore be legislated:

> There are some Artificers or Intelligent Men, whose Genius is as vast as the Art or Science they profess: They pay with Interest, by their Skill and

Invention, what they borrowed from its Principles. They frequently break through the Rules of Art to enoble it, and deviate from the common Roads, if they do not lead to what is great and extraordinary; they go alone, they leave all company a long way behind whilst they are Climbing the Eminences, and penetrating into the Abysses of their Profession, animated by the Advantages of their Irregularity. Whilst the Timorous and Sedate, as they can never reach them, so they never admire them; they cannot so much as comprehend, and much less imitate them; they live peaceably within the Compass of their own narrow Sphere...[6]

Similar concessions were made by Bouhours, Fénelon and Rapin.

Concessions were made by even Boileau, the leading classicist of the age:

> Chuse a sure Judge to Censure what you Write,
> Whose Reason leads, & Knowledge gives you light,
> Whose steady hand will prove your Faithful Guide,
> And touch the darling follies you would hide:
> He, in your doubts, will carefully advise,
> And clear the Mist before your feeble eyes.
> 'Tis he will tell you, to what noble height
> A generous Muse may sometimes take her flight;
> When, too much fetter'd with the Rules of Art,
> May from her stricter Bounds and Limits part...[7]

In 'Sleep and Poetry', written when he was about twenty-one, John Keats attacks those poets – 'Ill-fated, impious race!' – who 'were closely wed / To musty laws lined out with wretched rule / And compass vile'. In particular, he attacks those poets who held 'a poor, decrepid standard out / Mark'd with most flimsy mottos, and in large / The name of one Boileau!' It is not likely that, before he wrote the poem, he could have looked at *The Art of Poetry* very carefully. If he had looked at it, even in translation, he could not have done so with much effort or understanding. He could not have studied it with either sympathy or detachment: with (in one of his own phrases) 'negative capability'.

Dryden had always read widely in French literature; and the habit was to continue through the last decades of his life. But there was one respect in which his verdict on that literature was to undergo a radical change. With one or two exceptions, he continued to hold a low opinion of French poetry:

> The *French* have set up Purity for the Standard of their Language; and a Masculine Vigour is that of ours. Like their Tongue is the Genius of their Poets, light and trifling in comparison of the *English;* more proper for Sonnets, Madrigals, and Elegies, than Heroick Poetry.[8]

French criticism was another matter altogether. From his present point of view, French critics were (or they had recently become) far more flexible than he had ever thought possible; and in passing comments on them he made what can only be called a recantation.

Like Matthew Arnold almost two hundred years later, he declares that in literary criticism the French are in every way superior to the English: 'For, impartially speaking, the *French* are as much better Criticks than the *English,* as they are worse Poets'.[9] Dryden's tribute to the French we shall have to take at face value, but not the inference which we are all but forced to make. In the light of his own practice as critic, we must conclude that in French theory he has found a new direction for himself and for the English critics who will come after him: with the help of the French he has at last come to the realization that a respect for the rules of literature is compatible with a violation of them. The inference, however, is one that we shall have to take with a grain of salt.

Dryden might well cite the French for the sole purpose of bolstering his position. Along with other thinkers of the age, especially men of letters, English or French, he liked making an appeal to authority. He liked making that appeal even when he would urge that authority itself might sometimes be disregarded. It was generally thought good form to do so. In the larger perspective, it must nevertheless be said that he celebrated in his French authorities essentially what, in any event, he had always been inclined to accept and defend: the importance of originality in all great literature. And here he went perhaps further than the most flexible of French critics, La Bruyère, would ever allow. Indeed, from that preoccupation and emphasis it is for the modern reader no very bold leap to one of the first principles in Coleridge's *Biographia Literaria:* that a poet need obey no rules except those sanctioned by his imagination.

II

Throughout the late criticism Dryden continues to assume the same two roles he has always played: that of the poet who writes literary criticism, that of the critic who is both poet and playwright. He no more calls our attention to the two roles than he has in the past; but in several of the late essays – the 'Preface to *Ovid's Epistles*', the 'Preface to *Sylvæ*' (1685), 'A Parallel of Poetry and Painting' (1695), 'To John, Lord Marquess of Normanby' (the dedication of the *Æneis,* 1697) – he pauses, defines and illustrates his terms, and encourages inference. Explanation is forced upon us, albeit implicitly.

As a literary critic, he explains the nature and function of poetry no less than its purpose. As a poet, he explains the nature, function and purpose of criticism itself. Poetry is a heightened imitation of nature; it must be written in metre, never in prose; and it must demonstrate originality or 'invention', but only so far as human nature allows:

> [A] Poet is a Maker, as the word signifies: And who cannot make, that is,
> invent, has his name for nothing ... But ... if Invention is to be taken in so
> strict a sense, that the Matter of a Poem must be wholly new, and that in
> all its Parts; then ... the History of *Troy* was no more the Invention of
> *Homer,* than of *Virgil.* There was not an Old Woman, or almost a Child,
> but had it in their Mouths, before the *Greek* Poet or his Friends digested
> it into this admirable order in which we read it. At this rate, as *Solomon* has

told us, there is nothing new beneath the Sun: Who then can pass for an Inventor, if *Homer,* as well as *Virgil* must be depriv'd of that Glory?... The Poet, who borrows nothing from others, is yet to be Born.[10]

Poetry must originate in the poet's imagination and judgment; it must appeal to the imagination and judgment of the reader. It must give pleasure; without ever being didactic, it must give moral instruction. Literary criticism analyses, evaluates, judges and must always carry out its manifold tasks in the spirit of generosity and moderation:

> True judgment in Poetry ... takes a view of the whole together, whether it be good or not; and where the beauties are more than the Faults, concludes for the Poet against the little Judge; 'tis a sign that malice is hard driven, when 'tis forc'd to lay hold on a Word or Syllable; to arraign a Man is one thing, and to cavil at him is another.[11]

Both poet and critic must further centre their vision and their work in that one literary tradition which can be traced all the way back to Homer and Aristotle and to Horace and Virgil and which culminates, apparently, in Dryden himself.

*

Throughout the late essays Dryden writes with self-assurance and certainty. But he is never solemn or merely argumentative. The essays are 'loose' or discursive. They are, in general, lightly touched with humour. And they are written in a language which, in the preface to *The Hind and the Panther* (1687), he declares appropriate for 'Domestick Conversation': they are written in a 'free and familiar' style.[12] In many respects they suggest the essays of Montaigne, which in his last piece of criticism, the 'Preface to *Fables Ancient and Modern*' (1700), he cites as a model: '[T]he nature of a preface is rambling, neither wholly out of the way, nor in it. This I have learned from the practice of honest Montaigne...'[13] Dryden may or may not be the first poet-critic to write informal literary essays; but he gives the essay in criticism its most significant definition. And that definition has influenced literary critics from Joseph Addison, Oliver Goldsmith and Samuel Johnson, through William Hazlitt and Matthew Arnold, T. S. Eliot and Lionel Trilling, to the present.

*

In one essay after another – in 'To ... Lord Radcliffe' (the dedication of *Examen Poeticum,* 1693), 'A Discourse concerning ... Satire' (1693), the 'Preface to *Fables*' – as he sums up his final view on the matter, Dryden reasserts his old belief in the idea of literary and social progress:

> If I am the Man, as I have Reason to believe, who am seemingly Courted, and secretly Undermin'd: I think I shall be able to defend my self, when I am openly Attacqu'd: And to shew besides, that the *Greek* Writers only gave us the Rudiments of a Stage, which they never finish'd; that many of the Tragedies in the former Age amongst us, were without Comparison beyond those of *Sophocles* and *Euripides.*[14]

We can only say that [Chaucer] lived in the infancy of our poetry, and that nothing is brought to perfection at the first. We must be children before we grow men. There was an Ennius, and in process of time a Lucilius, and a Lucretius, before Virgil and Horace; even after Chaucer there was a Spenser, a Harington, a Fairfax, before Waller and Denham were in being; and our numbers were in their nonage till these last appeared.[15]

But he allows easily enough for three qualifications. He recognizes that not every age can produce '[a]nother *Homer*, ... another *Virgil*'.[16] He understands that, in every art, rules which have withstood the test of time are permanently true: they never change. He points out, though not without a touch of irony, almost sadness, that an age of refinement, like his own, may suffer in both life and art a momentary loss of energy and power:

> Well then; the promis'd hour is come at last;
> The present Age of Wit obscures the past:
> Strong were our Syres; and as they Fought they Writ,
> Conqu'ring with force of Arms, and dint of Wit;
> Theirs was the Gyant Race, before the Flood;
> And thus, when *Charles* Return'd, our Empire stood.
> Like *Janus* he the stubborn Soil manur'd,
> With Rules of Husbandry the rankness cur'd:
> Tam'd us to manners, when the Stage was rude;
> And boistrous *English* Wit, with Art indu'd.
> Our Age was cultivated thus at length;
> But what we gain'd in skill we lost in strength.
> Our Builders were, with want of Genius, curst;
> The second Temple was not like the first...[17]

III

Dryden approaches literature entirely through its variety of genres. Having realized that he will never be another Shakespeare, he writes fewer plays. He comes to regard the epic, and not tragedy, as the most exalted of literary forms:

> To raise, and afterwards to calm the Passions, to purge the Soul from Pride, by the Examples of Humane Miseries, which befall the greatest; in few words, to expel Arrogance, and introduce Compassion, are the great effects of Tragedy: Great, I must confess, if they were altogether as true as they are pompous. But are Habits to be introduc'd at three Hours warning? Are radical Diseases so suddenly remov'd?... It is one Reason of *Aristotle's* to prove, that Tragedy is the more Noble, because it turns in a shorter Compass; the whole Action being circumscrib'd within the space of Four-and-Twenty Hours. He might prove as well that a Mushroom is to be preferr'd before a Peach, because it shoots up in the compass of a Night.[18]

Except when discussing its subordinate status, he says little about tragedy, apart from an occasional remark on what provokes pity and terror, and almost nothing about comedy, high or low. He does write a few tragi-comedies, a form he had earlier attacked and then given up. But in his statements about the form – in the 'Preface to *The Spanish Friar*' (1680), the 'Preface to *Cleomenes*' (1692) and especially 'A Parallel of Poetry and Painting' – his attitude is strangely ambivalent:

> The *Gothique* manner, and the barbarous Ornaments, which are to be avoided in a Picture, are just the same with those in an ill order'd Play. For example, our *English* Tragicomedy must be confess'd to be wholly *Gothique*, notwithstanding the Success which it has found upon our Theatre, and in the *Pastor Fido* of *Guarini*... Neither can I defend my *Spanish Fryar*, as fond as otherwise I am of it, from this Imputation: for though the comical parts are diverting, and the serious moving, yet they are of an unnatural mingle. For Mirth and Gravity destroy each other, and are no more to be allow'd for decent, than a gay Widow laughing in a mourning Habit.[19]

Tragi-comedy is, he believes, inferior to both high and low comedy alike. But it appeals to and expresses 'the Genius of the Nation';[20] the form is one which, in any event, London audiences demand.

*

Having decided that he will never be another Shakespeare, Dryden turns to the epic, only to realize that he will never write an *Iliad* or an *Aeneid* or a *Divine Comedy*. He does, however, make the attempt; and when he fails – his plans for an Arthuriad come to nothing – he translates the epics of others. The epic now dominates his thought; and repeatedly in essay or dedication he explains what is distinctive in the genre, sometimes in technical and elaborate detail. But he seldom goes beyond what he had undoubtedly borrowed from Aristotle and Horace, or from such learned authorities as Segrais and Le Bossu. He compares the epic and the drama, emphasizing not so much the similarities as the differences. He explains the epic poet's narrative point of view and his handling of historical detail. He comments on the characteristics of the epic hero. He discusses at some length exactly how the epic poet is to handle the unities of time, place and action and the difficult problem of what Aristotle calls 'the probable impossibility'.

On the other hand, when he draws upon his experiences as Poet Laureate and explains how even the greatest literature may be shaped by the forces of literary patronage, Dryden is not only brilliant but perhaps original. The subject of patronage had of course been touched upon many times long before Dryden took it up; but it had seldom, if ever, been treated with the daring and insight which, in the 'Discourse concerning... Satire', he brings to his analysis of how public obligation, interacting with private circumstance, undermined Horace's entire moral vision:

> *Horace*, as he was a Courtier, comply'd with the Interest of his Master [Augustus], and avoiding the Lashing of greater Crimes, confin'd himself

to the ridiculing of Petty Vices, and common Follies: Excepting only some reserv'd Cases, in his *Odes* and *Epodes,* of his own particular Quarrels; which either with permission of the Magistrate or without it, every Man will Revenge, tho' I say not that he shou'd; for *prior læsit,* is a good excuse in the Civil Law, if Christianity had not taught us to forgive. However he was not the proper Man to arraign great Vices, at least if the Stories which we hear of him are true, that he Practis'd some, which I will not here mention, out of honour to him. It was not for a *Clodius* to accuse Adulterers, especially when *Augustus* was of that number: So that though his Age was not exempted from the worst of Villanies, there was no freedom left to reprehend them ... And our Poet was not fit to represent them in an odious Character, because himself was dipt in the same Actions.[21]

*

Having decided that he will be neither another Shakespeare nor another Homer, Dryden tries his hand at a variety of minor literary forms, the so-called lesser genres, on which the force of tradition was less pervasive, less intense. He takes up and discusses satire ('Discourse concerning ... Satire') and panegyric ('To the Earl of Abingdon', the dedication of *Eleonora,* 1692), as well as pastoral ('To ... Lord Clifford', the dedication of the *Pastorals,* 1697) and the Pindaric ode ('Preface to *Sylvæ*'), and among others opera ('Preface to *Albion and Albanius*', 1685) and dialogue ('Life of Lucian', 1711).[22] The essays are perhaps uneven in quality, but in several of them, as one might expect, he has important things to say. He provides the English with their definition of opera, one to which in his *Dictionary* Samuel Johnson will later defer:

> An *Opera* is a poetical Tale or Fiction, represented by Vocal and Instrumental Musick, adorn'd with Scenes, Machines and Dancing. The suppos'd Persons of this musical Drama, are generally supernatural, as Gods and Goddesses, and *Heroes*, which at least are descended from them, and are in due time, to be adopted into their Number. The Subject therefore being extended beyond the Limits of Humane Nature, admits of that sort of marvellous and surprizing conduct, which is rejected in other Plays.[23]

He reminds us, though with tactful indirectness, that panegyric celebrates not the individual but the ideal:

> Doctor *Donn* the greatest Wit, though not the best Poet of our Nation, acknowledges, that he had never seen Mrs. *Drury,* whom he has made immortal in his admirable *Anniversaries;* I have had the same fortune; though I have not succeeded to the same Genius. However, I have follow'd his footsteps in the Design of his Panegyrick, which was to raise an Emulation in the living, to Copy out the Example of the dead. And therefore it was, that I once intended to have call'd this Poem, the Pattern: And though on a second consideration, I chang'd the Title into the Name of that Illustrious Person, yet the Design continues, and *Eleonora* is still the

Pattern of Charity, Devotion, and Humility; of the best Wife, the best Mother, and the best of Friends.[24]

Unlike earlier writers in the century, he has a keen sense of the discipline and craftsmanship required for the Pindaric ode:

Since *Pindar* was the Prince of Lyrick Poets; let me have leave to say, that in imitating him, our numbers shou'd for the most part be Lyrical: For variety, or rather where the Majesty of the thought requires it, they may be stretch'd to the *English* Heroick of five Feet, and to the *French* Alexandrine of Six. But the ear must preside, and direct the Judgment to the choice of numbers: Without the nicety of this, the Harmony of Pindarick Verse can never be compleat; the cadency of one line must be a rule to that of the next; and the sound of the former must slide gently into that which follows; without leaping from one extream into another. It must be done like the shadowings of a Picture, which fall by degrees into a darker colour.[25]

And in his discussion of verse satire in the 'Discourse' he has no equal in his own century or the next.[26]

Among the lesser forms Dryden appears to have no very great preference, excepting perhaps satire. Generalizations about his over-riding conception of literary genre, moreover, are extremely difficult to make. But there are inferences that, on the whole, seem reasonable. He prefers narration to description, description to mere exposition. He dislikes the autobiographical lyric. He disapproves of any poem which never rises above historical fact, 'dry Philosophy' or a 'crude preparation of Morals'.[27]

*

Whether writing about the epic or the drama or about the lesser forms, Dryden has always in mind the rules which must, appropriately, govern each in turn, although his concern is, in general, the requirements demanded of any and every poet, whatever the genre in which he writes. A poet requires both genius and rules, the one circumscribing the other. He must be original and inventive; but he must rely on other poets as well as on that tradition in which all great poets have been writing since Homer. As he insists in the 'Preface to *Albion and Albanius*',

the first Inventors of any Art or Science, provided they have brought it to perfection, are, in reason, to give Laws to it; and according to their Model all after Undertakers are to build. Thus in Epique Poetry, no Man ought to dispute the Authority of *Homer*…Thus *Pindar,* the Author of those Odes, (which are so admirably restor'd by Mr. *Cowley* in our Language,) ought for ever to be the Standard of them; and we are bound according to the practice of *Horace* and Mr. *Cowley,* to Copy him.[28]

The poet must obey the rules of composition; but he must also distinguish between the rules which are 'Nature Methodiz'd' and those other rules, the contrivance of English and French extremists, rules which are best ignored. He must next realize that, once he has obeyed the rules, his work has only just begun. Something more is required of him, yet what that something is 'no master can teach'. Dryden refers to it with such words as 'grace', 'spirit' and 'charm'. Its precise quality, however, eludes his every attempt at formulation; and in its mysterious presence, though he is the most gifted of critics, even he is reduced to exclaiming, '*nequeo dicere & sentio tantùm* [I cannot express and only feel]'.[29] The poet must also integrate his imagination with his judgment; but he has to understand that his imagination may sometimes take a noble flight, in which case he may achieve an excellence otherwise impossible. Dryden tells us that he has experienced such moments himself. One came upon him as he sat writing *Eleonora*, a poem dedicated to 'the Memory of the Late Countess of Abingdon'. That the work violates literary rules he is the first to admit, but he has more than ample justification – and authority – on his side. Some critics will no doubt point to many 'faults'; he does not care. He is certain of his achievement:

> We, who are Priests of *Apollo*, have not the Inspiration when we please; but must wait till the God comes rushing on us, and invades us with a fury, which we are not able to resist ... Let me not seem to boast ...; for I have really felt it on this Occasion; and prophecy'd beyond my natural power ... The Reader will easily observe, that I was transported, by the multitude and variety of my Similitudes; which are generally the product of a luxuriant Fancy; and the wantonness of Wit. Had I call'd in my Judgment to my assistance, I had certainly retrench'd many of them. But I defend them not; let them pass for beautiful faults amongst the better sort of Critiques: For the whole Poem, though written in that which they call Heroique Verse, is of the Pindarique nature, as well in the Thought as the Expression; and as such, requires the same grains of allowance for it.[30]

*

Once again, for all his emphasis on classical ideals and practice, or on the interconnections between the lively and the just, Dryden is no pedant. He is more flexible than he has ever been; and once again he never forgets that there are literary rules to be obeyed or, at the very least, to be used as signposts or guides. He thus explains and illustrates the rules governing metre and language, characterization and plot (or 'design'), as well as both subject matter and theme. He prefers 'English Heroique' verse to any other metre. He urges that metaphors be apt and that language be concrete, familiar, correct. He explains that characters, in whatever genre the poet writes, must be universal types, but types which can be visually conceived by reader and poet alike. He explains that every poem, whatever the genre, must be coherently organized and tightly developed. He insists that both subject and theme reflect a society that is hierarchical and stable, civilized and Christian.

*

Increasingly, as a practical critic, Dryden writes about other authors. He writes essays, as well as prologues and epilogues, in which he praises his friends and attacks his enemies. In general, however, the poets and playwrights about whom he writes – major figures from antiquity to the present – fall neatly into two categories. He has a double standard in his criticism. There are those authors who have achieved excellence by following the rules of a strict classicism; there are all those others who have violated the rules, but have somehow achieved excellence by transcending them.

In commenting on and judging those who belong to the first category he uses as his paradigm Virgil, whose 'refinement' and 'correctness' he has earlier noted in the '[A]ccount' of *Annus Mirabilis* (1667), and a translation of whose complete works he finally publishes, each with a dedicatory essay, in 1697. In commenting on and judging poets and playwrights who belong to the second category, he uses as his paradigm his analysis and evaluation of Shakespeare in the *Essay of Dramatick Poesie* (1668). He approves of and celebrates the authors in both categories, though he admires only those in the first, and he avowedly prefers those in the second. In which of the two categories Dryden places himself we are never told; but in light of all that he now says and argues, it must obviously be the first. That there may perhaps be an inconsistency in his having a double standard of literary excellence seems never to trouble him. If it does, he is (again) conveniently silent.

IV

Having admitted to himself that he will never write the great play or epic which, as a young man, he may have hoped he could and would write, and having consequently committed himself to translation, Dryden translates from ancient Greek and Latin, from medieval English and medieval Italian. Why, as a translator, he chooses the epic and not the drama it is impossible to say. One can only guess that, given his theory and his purpose, he finds the epic both more of a challenge and less of a difficulty.[31] The translations – notably those included in *Ovid's Epistles, Sylvæ, Satires of … Juvenal [and] … Persius* (1693), *Examen Poeticum*, *The Works of Virgil* (1697), *Fables Ancient and Modern* – are all introduced by essays. And in each essay in turn he elucidates and passes judgment on the poem before him, his opinions often grounded in his recent studies in the academic scholarship of the age. Once he had scorned the learned; now he finds them indispensable. At the same time, he sets the poem in the context of his own theories and of that great tradition which it helps to define; and he expatiates at length on the kind of translation which he has attempted and of which he approves, often merely repeating himself, as if to emphasize and justify his every effort. He does not translate as if he were living in some other, far-off time and place. He writes (and translates) as if he were the dead poet's alter-ego or reincarnated other self. His kinship with the dead, he explains in the 'Preface to *Sylvæ*', gives him leave to exceed his 'Commission' and to blur the distinction between translated and original verse:

I must acknowledge, that I have many times exceeded my Commission; for I have both added and omitted, and even sometimes very boldly made such expositions of my Authors, as no *Dutch* Commentator will forgive me. Perhaps, in such particular passages, I have thought that I discover'd some beauty yet undiscover'd by those Pedants, which none but a Poet cou'd have found. Where I have taken away some of their Expressions, and cut them shorter, it may possibly be on this consideration, that what was beautiful in the *Greek* or *Latin,* wou'd not appear so shining in the *English:* And where I have enlarg'd them, I desire the false Criticks wou'd not always think that those thoughts are wholly mine, but that either they are secretly in the Poet, or may be fairly deduc'd from him: or at least, if both those considerations should fail, that my own is of a piece with his, and that if he were living, and an *Englishman,* they are such, as he wou'd probably have written.[32]

He edits where, he is convinced, some careless printer has obviously made a mistake. He deletes as and where he likes. He adds as and where he likes. He includes any paraphrase that will make the ancient poem a thoroughly modern one.

V

During his last period as a critic, and especially during his last ten years or so, whether he writes about his own works or about those by other poets and playwrights, Dryden increasingly turns his attention in upon himself. The essays become increasingly autobiographical. The flood of personal reflection reaches a head in the postscript to his translation of Virgil, in which he writes about his getting on in years and about his health, about his political and religious opinions, about those who attack him in his distress and those who generously support him:

What *Virgil* wrote in the vigour of his Age, in Plenty and at Ease, I have undertaken to Translate in my Declining Years: strugling with Wants, oppress'd with Sickness, curb'd in my Genius, lyable to be misconstrued in all I write; and my Judges, if they are not very equitable, already prejudic'd against me, by the Lying Character which has been given them of my Morals. Yet steady to my Principles, and not dispirited with my Afflictions, I have, by the Blessing of God on my Endeavours, overcome all difficulties; and, in some measure, acquitted my self of the Debt which I ow'd the Publick, when I undertook this Work ...

'Tis enough for me, if the Government will let me pass unquestion'd. In the mean time, I am oblig'd in gratitude, to return my Thanks to many of them, who have not only distinguish'd me from others of the same Party, by a particular exception of Grace, but without considering the Man, have been Bountiful to the Poet: Have encourag'd *Virgil* to speak such *English,* as I could teach him, and rewarded his Interpreter, for the pains he has taken in bringing him over into *Britain,* by defraying the Charges of his Voyage. Even *Cerberus,* when he had receiv'd the Sop, permitted *Æneas* to pass freely to *Elysium.* Had it been offer'd me, and I had refus'd it, yet still some gratitude is due to such who were willing to oblige me: But how much more to those from whom I have receiv'd the Favours which they have offer'd to one of a different Perswasion ...[33]

The Earl of Peterborough, who did him 'Favours'; Sir William Boyer, who 'Invited ... [him] to *Denham-Court*'; Dr. Guibbons and Dr. Hobbs, who both attended him without fee – all are then mentioned and thanked.

Nothing in his last essays – indeed, nothing in the whole of his criticism – impresses so much, however, as the detachment with which, as a self-critic, he passes judgment upon a whole lifetime of literary output; and even as he does so, he identifies his proper place and role not only in English literary history but in all the rest of Western literature as well. Though not a Sophocles or a Shakespeare, he has written a few very good plays. Though not a Homer or Virgil or Dante, he has written a number of first-rate poems. As for his translations, they have so far not been equalled in England; and his criticism is without exception everything that at the beginning of his career he had once hoped it would be. In passing these judgments on himself, he surely could not have been more detached; he could not have been more accurate.

CHAPTER TWELVE

The Battle of the Books
(1680–1700)

I

With the 'Preface to *Ovid's Epistles*' (1680), which appeared a few months after 'The Grounds of Criticism in Tragedy', Dryden assumes a new persona. He is now the independent man of letters; and the role is one which, in the years ahead, he will play with increasing authority and ease. He assumes the position of the foremost, though self-appointed, translator of the age. He now begins to reconcile the major principles of his first period with those recently set forth in the second: the great or successful poem is one in which there is a proper balance of the lively and the just; at the same time, it is one in which, for the most part, judgment and imagination are transformed into extensions or aspects of each other.

Dryden is the dedicated and conscientious practical critic. He explains and illustrates what is generally distinctive in an author's work, along with its achievements and failures. What is distinctive in the work he traces to what is generally distinctive in the author's imagination and judgment. He traces both to what earlier, in the *Essay of Dramatick Poesie* (1668), Eugenius had called the 'Character of [an] Authour'.[1] But in his treatment of an author's literary (as opposed to his moral) character he now dwells on what is truly idiosyncratic. He projects the whole of his discussion into the larger context – political and social and literary – of the age in which the author lived and wrote. And out of this broad discussion of an author's literary character he introduces into our literature an entirely new genre: the literary biography.

The preface was conceived as an introduction to his translations from Ovid, but it is not until the second half of the essay that Dryden takes up his position as the official translator of the age. He begins with the famous translators who have preceded him – Jonson, Denham, Cowley – and carefully and methodically he repudiates them all. Jonson disfigures his author; Sir John Denham and Abraham Cowley all but ignore theirs. He distinguishes among three very different kinds of translation, while keeping always in mind his own preference and justification: metaphrase, or literal translation; paraphrase, 'where the Authour is kept in view... but his words are not so strictly follow'd as his sense'; and imitation, 'where the Translator ... assumes the liberty not only to vary from the words and sence, but to forsake them both as he sees occasion'.[2]

Dryden dislikes literal translation: given the differences between languages, '['t]is almost impossible to Translate verbally, and well, at the same time...' He also dislikes imitation: though something 'Excellent may be invented', the results ought, properly speaking, to be considered a 'new', or original work, and not a translation. His own preference lies entirely with paraphrase, a kind he has been the first to 'propos[e]', since it allows the translator to achieve both 'perspicuity [and] gracefulness'.[3]

In expounding a middle way between 'crabbed ... "faithfulness" and inaccurate ... licence',[4] Dryden goes on to explain that only those translations which meet his present criteria does he regard as desirable and worthwhile. The translator must not lose the 'sence' of the original: '[t]he sence of an Authour, generally speaking, is to be Sacred and inviolable'.[5] Nor dare the translator forget that he and his author may not be contemporaries. The work he is translating must not become something which he himself, living in another time and place, might have written. He must capture and, where he can, re-create what is peculiar to, and hence idiosyncratic in, the work before him. The flavour and texture of the original must not be lost:

> If the Fancy of *Ovid* be luxuriant, 'tis his Character to be so, and if
> I retrench it, he is no longer *Ovid*. It will be replyed that he receives
> advantage by this lopping of his superfluous branches, but I rejoyn that
> a Translator has no such Right ...[6]

Dryden will eventually qualify his insistence on fidelity to meaning; his insistence on fidelity to manner he will later reverse completely.[7]

He is confident of the correctness of his opinions; but he also asks that, if he has erred, he be excused:

> [I]f after what I have urg'd, it be thought by better Judges that the praise
> of a Translation Consists in adding new Beauties to the piece, thereby to
> recompence the loss which it sustains by change of Language, I shall be
> willing to be taught better, and to recant.[8]

In the whole of the rest of the preface, he centres his interest on Ovid, obviously one of his favourite poets. He begins with the argument that, the life of Ovid having already been written by George Sandys, he cannot 'add any thing to Mr. *Sandys* his undertaking'. He will simply remind the reader

> that he [Ovid] flourish'd in the reign of *Augustus Cæsar,* that he was
> Extracted from an Antient family of *Roman* Knights; that he was born to
> the Inheritance of a Splendid Fortune, that he was design'd to the Study
> of the Law; and had made considerable progress in it, before he quitted
> that Profession, for this of *Poetry,* to which he was more naturally form'd.[9]

What does concern Dryden is '[t]he Cause of his [Ovid's] Banishment', which he goes on to discuss for several pages. He reviews all the charges made and all of the possible crimes of which the poet may have been guilty; but nothing said or known leaves him satisfied. He gives up every 'ghess of the *Grammarians*' and arrives at the only conclusion which, so far as he is concerned, makes any sense: 'the cause was notoriously known at *Rome,* though it be left ... obscure to after Ages'.[10] Lest he be accused of 'speak[ing] too partially in his behalf', Dryden is willing to admit that Ovid did have his moral lapses. As the rich son of wealthy parents, he was no doubt extremely self-indulgent; and there can be no question that, while at the imperial court, he ignored 'severity of Manners'. Such weaknesses as he had, however, Dryden attributes to the exuberance of a pampered 'Youth', and he goes on to remind us that his 'Lasciviousness' was a matter of 'words' and not of 'Deeds'. Dryden denies the charge of 'Incontinency', and in a final verdict accepts Ovid's own explanation of the banishment and exile: 'his offence was that of Errour only, not of wickedness'.[11]

Any and almost every speculation about Ovid the man, Dryden decides, must be ultimately left up in the air. He will therefore 'leave Conjectures on a Subject so incertain'. He turns instead 'to write somewhat more Authentick of this Poet'. He begins by placing him in the only context which, at the moment, seems to matter: 'That he frequented the Court of *Augustus,* and was well receiv'd in it, is most undoubted: all his Poems bear the Character of a Court, and appear to be written as the *French* call it *Cavalierement...*'[12]

Lest once again he be accused of 'speak[ing] too partially', Dryden grants that, like the man, the poetry also has its failings. Ovid is often a very imitative poet. He is not as 'polish'd' as Tibullus; he is without the 'Learning' of Propertius. He is needlessly repetitious: 'he sometimes cloys his Readers instead of satisfying them'. He has little sense of history: 'he has Romaniz'd his *Grecian* Dames too much, and made them speak sometimes as if they had been born in the City of *Rome,* and under the Empire of *Augustus*'. Worse still, the 'Copiousness of his Wit' is such that he frequently 'leav[es] the Imitation of Nature, and the cooler dictates of his Judgment, for the false applause of Fancy': what he says and how he says it then have little or no connection with each other. The men and women of whom he writes, caught up in a false rhetoric, 'speak more Eloquently than the violence of their Passion would admit'.[13]

As he redeems the man, so Dryden is the first to redeem the poet. Though he is undoubtedly imitative of others, Ovid is not 'to [be] defraud[ed] ... of the Glory of his Invention'. In his 'most perfect' work his style 'is tenderly passionate and Courtly'.[14] Though he does at times lose control of himself,

> this very Fault is not without it's [*sic*] Beauties: for the most severe Censor cannot but be pleas'd with the prodigality of his Wit... Every thing which he does, becomes him, and if sometimes he appear too gay, yet there is a secret gracefulness of youth, which accompanies his Writings...[15]

In the structure of his elegies – in 'the most material part, which is the Conduct' – it is 'certain that he seldom has miscarried': '[O]ur Poet has always the Goal in his Eye, which directs him in his Race; some Beautiful design, which he first establishes, and then contrives the means, which will naturally conduct it to his end'.[16] This most wayward of poets is in some things the most correct.

In his tribute Dryden pays attention in particular to the men and women, the dramatic characters, whom Ovid creates and to the vividness and truth with which they spring to our attention and become part of our experience:

> If the Imitation of Nature be the business of a Poet, I know no Authour who can justly be compar'd with ours, especially in the Description of the Passions … Now I will appeal to any man who has read this Poet, whether he find not the natural Emotion of the same Passion in himself, which the Poet describes in his feign'd Persons? His thoughts which are the Pictures and results of those Passions, are generally such as naturally arise from those disorderly Motions of our Spirits.[17]

This may not be the first time that Dryden has spoken of Ovid in such terms: the same observations are made in the '[A]ccount' of *Annus Mirabilis* (1667).[18] The tribute nevertheless remains striking. It is the same kind of tribute which he has continually paid to Shakespeare, which he has sometimes paid to himself and which in the next decade he will pay to Chaucer.

Dryden dwells on his overall impression of the poems, but he also examines them individually. He centres most of his attention on the one work, the *Heroides* (or the *Epistles*), which he has translated, but he also comments on the *Elegies,* the *Art of Love,* and the *Metamorphoses.* He takes up all these works more or less chronologically; and, as he points to Ovid's development from 'Imperfection' to 'his riper age', he analyses, evaluates, and passes judgment. He is again the judicial critic, and again and again the most tolerant of men. Ovid is obviously one of the poets in whom Dryden takes delight: throughout his judicial discussion of the works he inevitably finds more to praise than to blame. He grants that there are rules of decorum which Ovid too frequently violates. But even as he names the faults, Dryden is never severe: he is unexpectedly rather gentle. A number of the rules which we might expect him to take into account – the rule, for instance, that an air of plausibility be imparted to the supernatural – and which Ovid at times clearly, at times obtrusively, ignores, he never once considers. He recognizes instead that, in his interplay of 'some Beautiful design' and 'Copiousness of … Wit', Ovid may sometimes achieve a happy balance of the lively and the just and that, while violating the accepted rules of composition, he may achieve a 'secret gracefulness' beyond the reach of art.

The discussion of Ovid is based upon two very different conceptions of poetry – one looking back to Dryden's middle period and centred on the observance of the rules, the other looking forward to his readings in La Bruyère and Dominique Bouhours and centred on ideals that are not susceptible to precise formulation. Inevitably, the first conception or approach sounds the dominant note. The second is heard faintly and only in passing. It is in fact quite muted. The essay, we shall have to remember, is the first to be written in his final period. It is the harbinger of things to come. Some years are still to pass before, as a theoretical critic, he will admit to bafflement and wonder and allow for an irreducible mystery in art.

Yet Dryden does more than pay Ovid his due. According to standards set forth by Longinus, the very same standards which in 'The Grounds of Criticism in Tragedy' he had recently applied to Shakespeare's plays, Ovid at his very best (we are told) identifies and so unites the demands of the imagination with those of sound judgment: concrete particulars with abstract universals, intensity of experience with simplicity of language, and always moral instruction with the primary aim of every great poet, that of giving pleasure to the reader. It is worth pointing out that, in his final tribute to Ovid, Dryden looks forward to what in the *Biographia Literaria* Coleridge held to be the proper definition of the ideal poet:

> The poet, described in *ideal* perfection, brings the whole soul of man into activity... He diffuses a tone and spirit of unity... by that synthetic... power, to which we have exclusively appropriated the name of imagination. This power ... reveals itself in the balance or reconciliation of opposite or discordant qualities: of sameness, with difference; of the general, with the concrete; the idea, with the image; the individual, with the representative; the sense of novelty and freshness, with old and familiar objects; a more than usual state of emotion, with more than usual order; judgement ever awake ..., with enthusiasm and feeling profound or vehement ...[19]

Whether or not when he wrote the *Biographia* Coleridge had Dryden specifically in mind we cannot know. By the time he wrote the *Biographia,* Dryden's voice and opinions, though soundly rejected by all the Romantics, were still very much in the air. Without perhaps realizing all that he had contributed to English literary criticism, none of them could hardly, if at all, escape his influence.

In the essays of the last years Dryden will frequently make excursions into autobiography, even at times allowing himself the privilege of private confession in public, but not now and not here. Nevertheless, as in the whole of the rest of his criticism, so in the preface one may discern, from his pronouncements on matters literary, his pronouncements on matters both moral and political. As a Tory, although he dislikes Augustus, whom he thinks of as vindictive, he accepts unequivocally the foundations of imperial government and royal authority. In doing so, he is obviously paying oblique tribute, as Poet Laureate, to his own monarch, Charles II. As a Christian moralist, he speaks out against the 'Lasciviousness' which the behaviour of Augustus encouraged and which may have had an unwholesome effect on even the best of Ovid's early verse. Dryden concludes further that, in his final rejection of Ovid, Augustus behaved very badly: he sent him for no justifiable reason into exile. It can be no wonder that, in chiding Augustus for his mistreatment of Ovid, as well as for much that may be morally objectionable in the verse, Dryden takes sides not with the emperor, but with the poet. What is surprising is that, in chiding Augustus for immorality, he is not afraid of offending his king. Charles had many virtues; but sexual propriety was never one of them. We can only assume that, as an independent man of letters and as the leading poet and critic of the age, Dryden has enough courage at last to speak his mind. Besides, Charles did have a sense of humour, and he was without a trace of the emperor's vindictiveness and hypocrisy.[20]

Even as he writes of Ovid, Dryden places him among the most important of his predecessors and contemporaries. However great his own concern with the social and political contexts of poetry, it always remains subordinate to his interest in literary tradition. In the years ahead he will chart the lineage of poets in fascinating detail. But even now he passes beyond his early, elliptical studies of forms and conventions to provide a circumstantial account of literary culture in first-century Rome. We are given a charming portrait of Ovid at work amidst 'the famous Poets of his Age': '*Macer, Horace, Tibullus, Propertius,* and many others'. They read his poems, imitated his work and 'communicated their Writings to him', almost certainly for amendment. Austere and unapproachable, there was Virgil, whom Ovid once saw at a distance but did not know personally. And absent in body, but always present to mind, there were the '*Greeks,* whom (as the Masters of their Learning,) the *Romans* usually did imitate'.[21]

Dryden is profoundly aware of Ovid's contribution to the advancement of Roman letters. He notes that Ovid, perhaps having learned from Horace the major failing of Propertius and Tibullus – 'that those Poets seldom design'd before they writ' – gave the elegy a new unity of design and simplicity of language. Ovid also created a new literary genre. He joined the epistle to the elegy, and took as his subject in the new hybrid form not his own very private experience in love but the often sung complaints of famous lovers.[22] Dryden acknowledges the power of Ovid's invention. But he is concerned not only with one poet's originality. He is concerned no less with the collective nature of literary progress in which poets, living and dead, and even critics play their part. According to Dryden, Ovid's genius lay in combining existing elements in Graeco-Roman literature. His achievement is a testament both to his own powers and to the vitality of the tradition in which he worked.

Where he himself stands in relation to this tradition, Dryden never says. For some years, ever since the 'Preface to *All for Love*' (1678), he has been proclaiming the importance of following the Ancients. And the sudden cessation of those pronouncements suggests that he now lives with the past on familiar terms. More than any explicit statement he might have made, his easy commerce with classical authors and their modern imitators declares that he writes from within the tradition and has made it his own. And because he is part of that tradition and subscribes to its rules, he can judge Ovid with an authority that equals or exceeds that of the ancient critics whom he cites. For he knows the tradition from its beginnings up through its most recent developments, and he can bring to bear upon it the latest scholarship and commentary.

The preface is not the first of the essays to contain a carefully delineated character sketch. By the time he wrote the preface he had already published sketches of Shakespeare and Jonson and of Beaumont and Fletcher. In those early studies he had used an author's works mainly to illustrate obedience to or violations of the classical rules; and he had often been content with the most general of observations.[23] In the preface every assertion of the rules Dryden subordinates to an emphasis on Ovid and his works; and the delineation is centred not so much on generalization as on the idiosyncratic and the unique: on those qualities which 'distinguish, and as it were individuate him from all other writers'.[24] It is not easy to account for this shift in emphasis and perspective; we can only guess that he is still writing under the immediate authority of Longinus. Whatever his pre-occupation with the rules of composition, or with broad generalizations about an author's works, Longinus never ceases to identify, in all kinds of ways, what distinguishes one poet from the many others with whom he may or may not have much in common.

Statements about, even long expositions of, a poet's literary character were not uncommon among rhetoricians and critics in the ancient world and throughout the Renaissance. Examples may be found in the works of Cicero, Dionysius of Halicarnassus, the Elder Seneca, Julius Caesar Scaliger, Isaac Casaubon, and Ben Jonson. Without much effort, Dryden may have found in many of those writers, long before he ever read Longinus, models for his own excursions in character writing and consequently for much of his method.[25] His ventures into literary biography are another issue. The biography of Ovid is divided, more or less, into three clearly defined units: his life and times, with a statement about his person-ality; his literary character; and his individual works, discussed and evaluated, in their Roman setting, more or less chronologically. In what he was doing or trying to do, Dryden was perhaps helped along by his reading in the learned commenta-tors who, like Scaliger and Casaubon, went beyond textual problems and discussed Roman poets frequently in the context of their age and of biographical detail. In any event, one must grant that the preface has not the clarity of outline or the complexity and sweep of his later efforts in the same form – the 'Life of Plutarch' (1683), for example, or even the discussion of Chaucer in the 'Preface to *Fables*' (1700). Nevertheless, in establishing an essential connection between Ovid's life and his works and in discussing both in terms of the customs, both literary and political, of imperial Rome, the finished product is entirely Dryden's own. It is one more of his important contributions to literary history.

The preface determines and, with a few exceptions, becomes the paradigm for the whole of the criticism to come. And that paradigm is to have a tremendous effect on almost every major critic into our own time.[26] It may be found as an influ-ence on Johnson in the eighteenth century, on Coleridge and Hazlitt and both Arnold and Saintsbury in the nineteenth, and in the twentieth century on critics and scholars as different as Joseph Wood Krutch and Lionel Trilling, Richard Ellmann and Leon Edel, Edgar Johnson and Michael Holroyd. Only in the second half of the twentieth century have we been informed, at times rather loudly, that all biographical approaches to literature are grossly in error: that, in the under-standing or interpretation of a piece of great literature, nothing matters but the reader himself – not the author or his other works or the age in which he lived and wrote. Nevertheless, Dryden's standards of excellence and the paradigm he estab-lished for the study and enjoyment of great literature must inevitably prevail. When we read any work of literature we can no more completely ignore the author and his place in history than, when we enter society, we can ignore completely (except at our peril) the men and women with whom we converse, their customs and the language which they speak.

II

The Quarrel of the Ancients and Moderns lasted about four hundred years. It began early in the fourteenth century when Dante and his circle celebrated the great philosophers and poets of antiquity but argued that, because they had not been baptized into the True Church, even the wisest and most virtuous of the ancients could not be saved: they could not enter into the Christian heaven.[27] It continued until the Enlightenment, at which time major thinkers in the West – Hume, Bentham, Godwin in England, Voltaire, Rousseau, Condorcet in France – explained that, when guided by pure reason, mankind could escape from the burden of the past, enjoy a new code of moral and philosophical truth, and so perhaps enter into a golden age. The Quarrel thus began and ended with the victory of the Moderns over the Ancients. Attempts have since been made by classical poets and scholars – by Matthew Arnold in the nineteenth century, by T. E. Hulme and Irving Babbitt in the twentieth – to start the controversy all over again. But their attempts to breathe new life into the Ancients have been without success. Ever since the Enlightenment the West has increasingly been committed to the notion that, only by ignoring the past, can mankind avoid repeating its past mistakes.

Participants in the debate were, on the whole, men of letters: they were poets, playwrights and literary critics. Others included statesmen and political theorists, theologians and philosophers, historians and economists, as well as rhetoricians, philologists and grammarians. The issue at stake was whether the West had fallen into decline since antiquity or whether, because of the law of universal progress, it had very much improved: whether or not, because of a new dispensation in faith and morals and because of advances made in empirical science, Western culture had become very much more civilized and hence refined. Adversaries on both sides of the question clearly agreed on the achievements of the Ancients; but the problems that confronted both sides were perplexing in the extreme. Despite the new dispensation and despite all the most extraordinary advances in the physical sciences, Christendom had not so far produced another Homer and Virgil, another Aristotle or Horace or Longinus.

Dryden was inevitably drawn into the debate. He was very much a man of the century in which he lived; and there were few if any intellectual currents to which he did not respond in one way or another. More striking is that, however much he admired the Ancients, he remained fairly consistently a Modern. Except for three or four years in his middle period, he always believed in the idea of progress. The Ancients, he argues, are no doubt the great originators; but insofar as the Moderns stand on their shoulders, the Moderns have the greater perspective and wisdom. So he tells us in the *Essay of Dramatick Poesie* and again in the dedication of *Examen Poeticum* (1693). It is true that he finally came to accept the idea that civilizations have their ups and downs: that progress is not linear but cyclical. But this refinement of his point of view is consistent with the earliest statement of his position. With the Ovid essay, at any rate, Dryden became committed to the disciplines of classical scholarship and learning; and that commitment was to grow by leaps and bounds until, in the following decade, he was caught up in the last drawn-out engagement between the Ancients and Moderns: the Battle of the Books.

*

The entire controversy over the Ancients and Moderns had at times its political and theological currents, but it centred almost completely in matters scientific and literary. On the other hand, it took, in the final decade of the seventeenth century, a rather unusual turn. Leading figures in the controversy in England now debated with one another about the comparative merits of ancient and modern learning and, more specifically, about the role of recent scholarship in elucidating the civilizations of the past. This controversy began when Sir William Temple, to confute extravagant claims put forth in behalf of the Moderns by Thomas Burnet and Charles Perrault, published *An Essay upon the Ancient and Modern Learning* (1690). Here Temple argued that, despite modern boasting, the greatest advances in philosophy and science had been made, long before recorded history, by the sages of China, India and Chaldea. Of far greater moment, he further asserted that in literature 'the oldest Books we have are still in their kind the best'. And in proof of this second claim he cited the works of Aesop and Phalaris:

> The two most ancient [books] that I Know of in Prose, among those we call prophane Authors, are *Æsop's* Fables and *Phalaris's* Epistles, both living near the same time, which was that of *Cyrus* and *Pythagoras*. As the first has been agreed by all Ages since for the greatest Master in his kind, ... so I think the Epistles of *Phalaris* to have more Race, more Spirit, more Force of Wit and Genius, than any others I have ever seen, either ancient or modern.[28]

Temple was aware that the authenticity of the *Epistles* had been questioned by the fifteenth-century humanist Angelo Poliziano, 'who attributed them to *Lucian*'. But Temple was assured that only Phalaris himself was 'Capable of Writing ... what *Phalaris* did'. And he brushed aside Poliziano's attribution as an example of the pedantry which had done so much to undermine learning.[29]

The first important response of the Moderns did not appear until 1694, when William Wotton published his *Reflections upon Ancient and Modern Learning*. Wotton, in general, took a moderate view. He claimed philosophy and science for the Moderns, but conceded literature to the Ancients, though he did allow for the possibility that, here too, the Moderns might one day be supreme. There was, however, one point on which he was anything but conciliatory. In a separate chapter in his book, he insisted that, in the preceding two hundred years, there had been startling advances in '*Philological Learning*', a phrase which for him encompassed work in such disciplines as textual criticism, chronology, and ecclesiastical history. And he boldly declared that these advances enabled the Moderns to see the ancient world with a clarity denied to any of the Ancients:

> [T]he Question is not whether any Modern Critick has understood *Plato* or *Aristotle, Homer* or *Pindar,* as well as they did themselves, for that were ridiculous; but whether Modern Industry may not have been able to dis-

cover a great many Mistakes in the Assertions of the Ancients about Matters not done in their own Times, but several Ages before they were born. For the Ancients did not live all in one Age ...; and so as liable to Mistakes when they talk of Matters not transacted in their own Times ... Wherefore if one reflects upon the Alteration which Printing has introduced into the State of Learning, when every Book once printed becomes out of Danger of being lost, or hurt by Copiers ..., it will not seem ridiculous to say, That *Joseph Scaliger, Isaac Casaubon, Salmasius, Henricus Valesius, Selden, Usher, Bochart,* and other Philologers of their Stamp, may have had a very comprehensive View of Antiquity, such a one as Strangers to those Matters, can have no idea of; nay a much greater than, taken together, any one of the Ancients themselves ever had, or indeed, could have.[30]

His position received some important confirmation when, in 1697, he appended to the second edition of his book Richard Bentley's *Dissertation upon The Epistles of Phalaris, and ... the Fables of Æsop,* in which the *Fables* and the *Letters,* regarded in the ancient world as indeed works by Aesop and Phalaris, were shown to be late and clumsy forgeries.[31]

Wotton and Bentley's replies to Temple's graceful essay deeply offended the statesman's friends, the so-called Christ Church Wits.[32] There then began a paper scuffle in which the value of modern scholarship was categorically either affirmed or denied. The debate lasted until the middle of the eighteenth century, and throughout the controversy the fundamental issue remained the same. How are the classics to be studied? Are they to be pursued through the traditional arts of rhetoric practised by men of taste and culture, or are they to be approached through learned disciplines, which can only be the province of the scholar? This and not the question of the relative merits of ancient and modern literature formed the real basis of the dispute.

III

Dryden's involvement in the Battle of the Books has always been denied.[33] He wrote no work which can be fitted easily into the strokes and counterstrokes of the debate; he never mentions the specific problems around which controversy swirled: the existence of a very ancient (or prehistoric) wisdom, the authenticity of the *Epistles of Phalaris.* Nor in his published works did he ever refer by name to the leading disputants – among the Ancients Sir William Temple and the Christ Church Wits, among the Moderns William Wotton and Richard Bentley.[34] That Dryden was involved, however, though sporadically and at a distance, we have more than ample evidence. We have his reflections on the role of the scholar in literary study. We have also the many observations of the most distinguished of his adversaries, a distant relative: the young Jonathan Swift. Swift was on the side of the Ancients. In Dryden, whose point of view and first principles he frequently misconstrued, Swift found all that he despised among the Moderns and hence an inviting object of attack in both *A Tale of a Tub* and *The Battle of the Books.*

In 1696, when in the employ of Sir William Temple, Swift began *A Tale of a Tub,* a 'diverting' tale, albeit one with a serious purpose. He put it aside for about a year, during which he wrote the whole of *The Battle of the Books,* the very title of which has enjoyed some historical importance. It was once used to define all the literary squabbles of the age; in our time, generally speaking, it has been used to define only those centred on the uses and abuses of encyclopaedic learning. Swift returned to the *Tale* in 1698; and finally he published the two works together in the same volume in 1704.[35]

In *A Tale of a Tub* Swift concerns himself mainly with those non-believers and wits who would (in his opinion) undermine the whole of the Christian religion. During the course of the narrative, a rather sardonic allegory about the mis-adventures of three brothers, each representing one of the three main branches of Christianity (Catholicism, Puritanism and of course Anglicanism), he introduces a number of digressions, including one on madness and even one on digressions. The many subjects which in his digressions he touches upon and frequently returns to are those involving the literary quarrels in which his friends and enemies have long been engaged. Modern poets and critics, he argues, are in every way inferior to their ancient counterparts; but in particular he takes aim at those classical scholars who in their encyclopaedic commentaries on ancient literature display nothing less than a total lack of common sense and a rather morbid pride in their false or useless learning. And among those he singles out for particular blame, he points to Dryden.

The attack in *A Tale of a Tub* against the misuse of learning is made in digressions. In *The Battle of the Books,* though he does take up the dispute over the *Epistles of Phalaris,* the subject is paradoxically all but ignored. As he unfolds his allegorical battle and satire (books ancient and modern fight over which of them will occupy the higher reaches of Parnassus), Swift is concerned not so much with the misuse of learning as with the superiority of ancient writers like Aristotle and Virgil over moderns like Descartes, Milton and Dryden. If we would understand his judgments on the new learning and specifically on Dryden's scholarship, as well as Dryden's pronouncements on the very same subjects, we shall have then to consider the one work, *A Tale of a Tub,* into which the controversy over learning seems to have made its way as a late addition.[36]

Swift grants that the Moderns – the historians and the commentators – can at least rescue forgotten texts, make necessary emendations and unravel obfuscated syntax. However, historical criticism as an end in itself he considers either useless or dangerous. When it is harmless, scholarly investigation of attribution, dates of composition and genealogy of forms does little more than increase the boredom in the world. When destructive, it weakens the power of the Greek and Roman classics to mould character by diverting attention from the ethical lessons of these works to peripheral and essentially trivial issues.[37] For those of his antagonists engaged in the Battle of the Books Swift has only contempt. Their entire edifice is based on a commitment to ideas of progress; but wherever he looks – among the scientists, the religious sceptics, the classical scholars – he finds only moral and intellectual decay. And at the forefront of the battle, along with Wotton and Bentley, Swift places Dryden.

Throughout the *Tale,* whenever the occasion presents itself, Swift ridicules Dryden for unseemly practices and execrable taste. Edward Rosenheim has summed up Swift's position in no uncertain terms. Dryden is singled out, he tells us, for embodying 'all the literary vices which Swift plainly finds offensive in other contemporary authors': 'public lamentation, self-pity, and self-advertisement'.[38] That Swift does in fact castigate Dryden as a typical hack is readily apparent; but his assault has another aspect, which so far has received little attention. Dryden is assailed not just for his literary failings but also for his arid pedantry: for sharing the aims, principles and methods of Wotton and Bentley.

Swift's twofold attack on Dryden – as popular writer and as modern scholar – appears proleptically, in the 'Introduction' to the *Tale,* in the catalogue of the 'prime Productions' of 'the Grub-Street brotherhood'. The list intermingles both popular and learned works. And in each category Dryden is given much prominence. Swift accuses him of being the supposed author of a piece of vulgar fiction, *Tommy Potts,* which Dryden could not possibly have written; and Swift obviously knows as much: he is merely doing his best to be nasty.[39] More significantly, he takes up arms against Dryden as a scholar. Of the two learned works mentioned, one is a treatise of 'immense Erudition'; the other is a handy work of reference. Predictably, the first is Wotton's encyclopaedic *Reflections.* The second comes as something of a shock. Elsewhere Swift identifies aids to learning with Bentley, the inveterate lover of 'large *Indexes,* and little *Compendiums*'.[40] But here for his supreme example of the type he turns to Dryden, and not to a prose work but unexpectedly a poem: 'THE *Hind and the Panther.* This is the Master-piece of a famous Writer now living, intended for a compleat Abstract of sixteen thousand Scholmen from *Scotus* to *Bellarmin*'.[41] Of course, *The Hind and the Panther* serves no such purpose. Though based on wide reading, it is an eloquent plea for Catholic toleration; and at least one Anglican, Edward Gibbon, converted after reading its effective defence of Catholic dogma, particularly that of papal authority and that of transubstantiation. Swift's judgment is wildly reductive, yet it serves to point out how closely he links Dryden to the world of pedantry and learning.

That Dryden has cast his lot with the scholars is made more evident when Swift turns to the critical prose. He tells us that the prefaces of Dryden were once admirable. They served as a 'Bill of Fare to the Book' and even instructed the reader in the rudiments of criticism. But of late they have become much changed. They have swollen vastly in size and become so crammed with learning that 'yawning Readers ... do now a-days twirl over forty or fifty Pages of *Preface* and *Dedication* ... as if it were so much *Latin*'.[42] Later in the *Tale,* in 'A Digression concerning Criticks', Swift shows us at some length the kind of the matter which has so horribly distended the body of Dryden's criticism.

The 'Digression' is an attack on modern scholarship and, more particularly, on Dryden's 'Discourse concerning ... Satire', the very work which Swift has principally in mind when he ridicules Dryden's later prefaces. In the 'Discourse' Dryden provides a detailed history of satire and traces its origins back through the ancient Roman practice to the recriminations of Adam and Eve after the Fall. Swift believes such genealogies are entirely spurious. And to show what he thinks of them he constructs a genealogy of his own:

> Every *True Critick* is a Hero born, descending in a direct Line from a Celestial Stem, by *Momus* and *Hybris,* who begat *Zoilus,* who begat *Tigellius,* who begat *Etcaetera* the Elder, who begat *B-tly,* and *Rym-r,* and *W-tton,* and *Perrault,* and *Dennis,* who begat *Etcaetera* the Younger.[43]

The rest of the 'Digression' continues the parody. There is the same immersion in the literary 'Antiquities' of Rome; the same care in distinguishing the main lines in the development of a subject from distinct, collateral branches; the same insistence on clear and precise definitions; and the same leap from literary history to the formulation of prescriptive rules. In the 'Discourse', '[h]aving ... brought down the History of Satire from its Original, to the times of *Horace*', Dryden frames the standards by which a modern satire should be written.[44] In the 'Digression', '*HAVING* thus amply proved the Antiquity of Criticism, and described the Primitive State of it', Swift sets forth rules or 'Maxims', all of them deliberately outrageous, for distinguishing a 'True Modern Critick' from a mere 'Pretender':

> THE first is, That *Criticism,* contrary to all other Faculties of the Intellect, is ever held the truest and best, when it is the very *first* Result of the *Critick's* Mind...
> SECONDLY; The *True Criticks* are known by their Talent of swarming about the Noblest Writers, to which they are carried meerely by Instinct, as a Rat to the best Cheese...
> LASTLY; A *True Critick,* in the Perusal of a Book, is like a Dog at a Feast, whose Thoughts and Stomach are wholly set upon what the Guests *fling away,* and consequently, is apt to *Snarl* most, when there are the fewest *Bones.*[45]

The 'Discourse' and the 'Digression', come together most closely in Swift's parody of the learned style. This parody occurs when he attempts to prove that the type of the '*True Critick*' was known by the Ancients, who (out of caution) represented him allegorically through the figure of an ass:

> IT well deserves considering, that these *Antient Writers* in treating Enigmatically upon the Subject, have generally fixed upon the very *same Hieroglyph,* varying only the Story according to their Affections or their Wit. For first: *Pausanias* is of Opinion, that the Perfection of Writing correct was entirely owing to the Institution of *Criticks;* and, that he can possibly mean no other than the *True Critick,* is, I think, manifest enough from the following Description. He says, *They were a Race of Men, who delighted to nibble at the Superfluities, and Excresencies of Books; which the Learned at length observing, took Warning of their own Accord, to lop the Luxuriant, the Rotten, the Dead, the Sapless, and the Overgrown Branches*

from their Works. But now, all this he cunningly shades under the following Allegory; that the Nauplians *in* Argia, *learned the Art of pruning their Vines, by observing, that when an* ASS *had browsed upon one of them, it thrived the better, and bore fairer Fruit.*[46]

Miriam Starkman believes that the passage 'is an obvious parody on Bentley'. 'A glance', she writes, 'at almost any page of Bentley's *Epistles of Phalaris* will indicate with what success Swift has caught Bentley's manner to the life: his collation of abstruse sources, his digressive interpolations, ... his detailed and accomplished erudition'.[47] But Bentley's manner is not uncommon. It is typically a manner of the seventeenth-century scholar. And as a comparison of Bentley with Dryden makes clear, it is the very manner of Dryden when he dons the scholar's robes. Here are the two men on Greek and Roman satire. First Bentley:

> The Greek *Satyrica,* was only a jocose sort of tragedy, consisting of a chorus of Satyrs (from which it had its name), that talked lasciviously, befitting their character; but they never gave *reproofs to the vicious men of the times;* their whole discourse being directed to the action and story of the play, which was Bacchus, or some ancient hero turned a little to ridicule. There's an entire play of this kind yet extant, the *Cyclops* of Euripides ... As for the abusive poem or *satire* of the Romans, it was an invention of their own; *Satira tota nostra est,* says Quintilian, *satire is entirely ours:* and if the Greeks had any thing like it, 'twas not the satyrical plays of the tragic poets, but the old comedy, and the *silli* made by Xenophanes, Timon, and others. *Satire,* says Diomedes, *among the* ROMANS IS NOW *an abusive poem, made to reprove the vices of men.* Here we see 'twas a poem of the Romans, not of the Greeks; and 'twas *now,* that is, after Lucilius's time, that it became abusive ...[48]

Now Dryden:

> *Thespis,* or whosoever he were that Invented Tragedy, (for Authors differ) mingl'd with them a Chorus and Dances of *Satyres,* which had before been us'd, in the Celebration of their Festivals; and there they were ever afterwards retain'd. The Character of them was also kept, which was Mirth and Wantonness ... Amongst the Plays of *Euripides,* which are yet remaining, there is one of these Satyriques, which is call'd the *Cyclops* ...
>
> The *Grecians,* besides these Satyrique Tragedies, had another kind of Poem, which they call'd *Silli;* which were more of kin to the *Roman* satire: Those *Silli* were indeed Invective Poems, but of a different Species from the *Roman* Poems of Ennius, Pacuvius, Lucilius, Horace, and the rest ...

> *Quintilian* says, in plain words, *Satira quidem tota, nostra est* [Satire, on the other hand, is all our own]: And *Horace* had said the same thing before him ...[49]

In his parody Swift never mentions either man by name. But given the larger contexts in which he has only Dryden in mind, it is not unlikely that, among those he ridicules, Dryden must be included.

Whether or not in his satire Swift is especially hostile to Dryden has over the centuries been much discussed. It must be allowed that Swift is opposed to all the Moderns, including Dryden, for their self-satisfied optimism. By disposition he generally believes that the world around him is in a state of moral decline. He believes too that all the Moderns, including Dryden, have in a variety of ways publicly humiliated Sir William Temple, his employer and benefactor.[50] The many disagreements between the two men, however, have additional causes. The two are related to each other, though distantly. Swift is a member of the Church of England, in which in 1694 he is ordained. And Swift apparently resents what he deems a relative's defection from the true faith. In 1685, upon the death of Charles II, the latter's brother James, another convert to Rome, had become the reigning monarch. But three years later James was forced into exile. With the fall of the House of Stuart, to which Dryden remained unswerving in his loyalty, James was succeeded by William III and the House of Orange; and to the House of Orange Swift has given avowedly his complete allegiance. Swift and Dryden are thus opposed to each other in matters philosophical, theological and political, as well as literary. More to the point, Swift does argue that all too frequently in his later criticism, whatever his other errors, Dryden covertly defends not only the Catholic Church but also the Jacobite cause. For all the professions of morality and conscience which are to be found in his prose, Dryden has spent the last decades of his life in 'Faction, and Apostacies, and all manner of Vice'.[51]

At any rate, the two men do agree on the many lapses in the new learning; but Swift would throw out the baby with the bath. In many of his attacks on Wotton and Bentley, Swift is on the side of the angels, but not in his onslaught against Dryden. He fails to recognize that Dryden is far less involved in the controversy than he insists. He fails to recognize that, as practising poet and playwright, and as a dedicated literary critic, Dryden is far more hostile to the misuses of scholarship than even he is. He also fails to recognize that, in all the best of the late criticism, and sometimes in the lesser works, Dryden would always emphasize not his erudition but rather the necessity that we read great poetry with understanding and pleasure.

CHAPTER THIRTEEN

A critic and scholar
(1680–1700)

I

In the 'Preface to *Ovid's Epistles*' (1680) Dryden as a professional man of letters is, at the same time, both literary critic and classical scholar. His interest in, his very commitment to, studies in ancient literature is obviously no late development. Initially at Westminster School and later at Trinity College, Cambridge, he received an excellent classical education. And beginning with his earliest essays Greek and Roman authors provide him with many of his touchstones of wisdom and eloquence. At first his approach to ancient literature is much like that of Sir William Temple. He believes that canonical texts are immediately accessible to educated readers and require no specialized knowledge for their study and enjoyment. In the *Essay of Dramatick Poesie* (1668), shortly after Crites points out that we do not understand the language and customs of Rome sufficiently to appreciate the wit of Terence and Plautus, Crites is answered by Eugenius, who contends – in what is undoubtedly an echo of Dryden's opinion – that what little escapes us in Roman wit is hardly a matter for concern.[1] Indeed, throughout the early and middle essays, those who labour hard to acquire the encyclopaedic learning which Crites thinks desirable are always treated as objects of ridicule.

The publication of the 'Preface to *Ovid's Epistles*' marks a turning point in the criticism, and announces a new tone and direction in Dryden's approach to classical literature. It is clear that he has read the historians, the commentators, the grammarians – all neatly collected in Borchard Cnipping's variorum edition of 1670 – and the knowledge he has acquired enables him to explore the literary circles in which Ovid moved, the impact of court morals upon his wit, as well as the interplay of fact and fiction and of tradition and innovation in the poems. A dispute about the wording of a text, the elucidation of a contemporary reference – these are matters which are important to him for the first time.

In future years, his scholarly judgments will grow in range and independence, but his methods will remain unchanged. He will do no original research, but follow a practice which, in 'The Character Polybius and His Writings' (1693), he ascribes to Polybius, who 'weigh'd the Authors from whom he was forc'd to borrow ... and oftentimes corrected them ... by comparing them each with other'.[2] Dryden thus quickly finds his place among the scholars. The one problem which remains for him is how best to integrate learned commentary with critical statement: how to make it serve, rather than to detract from, the experience of great literature.

II

Whatever its possible limitations, 'The Life of Plutarch' (1683) illustrates the kind of classical study – and ultimately the kind of learned criticism – to which Dryden will henceforth commit himself. The essay is one of his longest works on a single author, and the most sympathetic. It is the first to establish with firmness his persona not only as a man of letters and literary biographer but also, in a variety of important ways, as a dedicated modern scholar, albeit one who would make his erudition 'pleasant and agreeable to all sorts of Readers'.[3]

Dryden must have felt that the essay justified itself. He appears also to have found some justification in Plutarch, another of his favourite authors. Plutarch was quite popular in the Middle Ages. His vogue during the Renaissance and the seventeenth century, in both England and France, was even greater. In France it begins with Jacques Amyot's translation of *Plutarch's Lives* in 1559; in England, with Sir Thomas North's version of Amyot's work in 1579. In the *Lives* Plutarch writes not about poets and philosophers but about men of action. Poets and philosophers, historians and statesmen nevertheless turned to the work not solely because of their interest in the ancient world. They turned to it also for Plutarch's handling of detail, his vivid and graceful narrative and the brilliance of his prose, which alternates between calm reflection and moving declamation.

Dryden's biography was designed to introduce a translation of Plutarch's *Lives,* undertaken, under the sponsorship of Jacob Tonson, by forty separate contributors. Using as their text not a French source but the original Greek, the translators aimed to surpass North in accuracy and faithfulness. For his part Dryden sought to make his 'Life' similarly accurate and faithful by basing his work on 'the best Authors'.[4] Though he sometimes moves beyond ancient historian or modern scholar to pass a judgment of his own, he conceives of his task mainly as one of synthesis. With skilful economy, he weaves together fact and opinion scattered here and there throughout many learned works and transforms his sprawling sources into an engaging account.[5] To dismiss what he has accomplished as a 'rapidly executed hack-work' is to ignore his considerable achievement.[6]

In the 'Life of Plutarch', with its well-defined structure and impressive detail, Dryden takes up such matters as Plutarch's life and times, his major works and their distinguishing characteristics, and his heavy reliance on the famous and not so famous biographers and historians, antiquarians and poets who preceded him. As a literary critic and classical scholar, Dryden attempts a marriage of eloquence and learning. Through the clarity and grace of his language, as well as the sheer gusto of his narrative, he brings Plutarch vividly to life before us as a good, even saintly man. Through the citation of his many authorities, and chiefly the massive edition of Plutarch by John Rualt ('Rualdus'), he would urge that all his facts, whether biographical or historical, are truly relevant and sound. And his approach to biography, he clearly believes, is very much the same as that employed by Plutarch himself.

The high point in the essay is his discussion of the *Lives*. On the one hand, he treats Plutarch as a literary man and the individual biographies as if they were each a narrative of engrossing power. He touches on the astonishing range of the style, the individualizing of character, the psychological insights, as well as the fondness for anecdote and digression. He ignores the common Renaissance view that each life is a short epic in prose and instead regards each as a kind of tragedy. Plutarch spirits the reader from the public sphere of pomp and glory to 'the private Lodgings of the Heroe: you see him in his undress, and are made Familiar with his most private actions and conversations'. In the *Lives* you may behold

> a *Scipio* and a *Lelius* gathering Cockle-shells on the shore, *Augustus* playing at bounding stones with Boyes; and *Agesilaus* riding on a Hobby-horse among his Children. The Pageantry of Life is taken away; you see the poor reasonable Animal, as naked as ever nature made him; are made acquainted with his passions and his follies; and find the *Demy-God* a *Man*.[7]

On the other hand, Dryden treats Plutarch as a latter-day Renaissance scholar and the individual lives as if they had each been written for inclusion in a very modern biographical dictionary. Though a stranger to archives himself, Dryden notes with approval, even admiration, the thoroughness and completeness of a method of research which leaves 'nothing unswept behind'. He lists, one after another, Plutarch's many sources and praises his accuracy and discrimination in their use. The facts that Plutarch marshals are never allowed to become a repellent mass, but always serve to reveal clearly the men about whom he writes, and no less clearly the growth, development and decay of the societies in which they lived:

> [H]e applied himself, with extream diligence, to collect not only all books which were excellent in their kind, and already publish'd, but also all sayings and discourses of wise Men ..., as likewise the Records and publick Instruments, preserv'd in Cities, which he had visited in his Travels ...: To which purpose he took a particular Journy to *Sparta*, to search the Archives of that famous Commonwealth, to understand thoroughly the model of their ancient Government, their Legislators, their Kings, and their *Ephori*, digesting all their memorable deeds and sayings, with so much care, that he has not omitted those even of their Women, or their private Souldiers ... The same methods he also took in divers other Commonwealths ... Without these helps it had been impossible for him to leave in writing so many particular observations of Men and manners, and as impossible to have gatherd them, without conversation and commerce with the learned Antiquaries of his time. To these he added a curious Collection of Ancient Statues, Medals, Inscriptions, and Paintings, as also of proverbial sayings, Epigrams, Epitaphs, Apothegmes, and other Ornaments of History ...[8]

Dryden finds Plutarch's immense erudition all the more impressive by its being the possession of a man who is humble, courteous and detached, as eager to learn as desirous to teach. Always essentially a moralist, Plutarch 'allures us to virtue'. And as Dryden suggests, the appeal proceeds ultimately from the profound humanity of the writer himself.

Dryden first read Plutarch when he was an undergraduate at Trinity College. We cannot determine with any degree of certainty, however, whether the *Lives* had any direct influence on his earliest excursions into literary biography and classical scholarship. But from his celebration of Plutarch, whose very practice and judgment he carefully follows, we may deduce that in the *Lives* he discovered justification for the kind of criticism he had already begun to write. Plutarch assured him that he was headed in the right direction.

III

Dryden was very much a part of what was to be called the Battle of the Books long before the Battle ever started. Once it started he was already prepared to take up his arms against extremists of every sort, though he did so more often by example than by polemic. But he did on one occasion write a barely concealed polemic of a most impressive sort. The 'Discourse concerning the Original and Progress of Satire' (1693) contains a sharp but good-natured attack on the learned, one which is made all the more effective by its wholehearted acceptance of scholarly principles and methods. Dryden will have none of the fashionable contempt for learning. As soon as he begins to relate the history of satire, he declares his allegiance to philology and makes it clear that his discussion will proceed 'according to those Informations' which he has 'receiv'd from the Learned *Casaubon, Heinsius, Rigaltius, Dacier,* and the *Dauphin's Juvenal*'.[9] The implied distinction is significant. He has faith in the 'Informations' of the philologists but rather little faith in the philologists themselves. The learned may provide the basic or essential facts out of which sound opinions may be formed, but they are frequently incapable of forming such opinions themselves.

For one thing, commentators generally make very poor critics. Years of concentrating on a single figure gradually destroy their detachment; and they come to believe that the best author must, of necessity, be the one on whom they have spent years of labour. Love of learning gives way to love of self. Scholarship, it seems, encourages spiritual pride. Against its corruptive tendencies, even the Roman satirists cannot prevail:

> Every Commentator, as he has taken pains with any of them [Horace, Juvenal, Persius], thinks himself oblig'd to prefer his Author to the other two: To find out their Failings, and decry them, that he may make room for his own Darling... As Authors generally think themselves the best Poets, because they cannot go out of themselves, to judge sincerely of their Betters: So it is with Critiques, who, having first taken a liking to one of these Poets, proceed to Comment on him, and to Illustrate him; after which they fall in love with their own Labours, to that degree of blind

fondness, that at length they defend and exalt their Author, not so much for his sake as for their own.[10]

In pressing the claims of Persius, 'Casaubon', Dryden tells us, 'comes back always to himself'.[11] His is a failing which most of the commentators share.

It is not as critics that the commentators deserve attention, but as literary historians. To them we properly turn when we wish to understand the nature and development of literary forms or the political and social references in individual works. But even in these matters – the very heart of their expertise – the commentators are frequently wanting. Their learning is extraordinary, but often inadequate for the problems addressed. Scholars may lack the facts they need; or, if they have them, they may still misconstrue a historical detail or a textual crux. Through their efforts, knowledge does indeed advance, but slowly, intermittently, and not without some false steps and temporary accretion of error. These considerations do not impel Dryden to deprecate learning. They do, however, induce in him a healthy degree of scepticism. Again and again, he urges us to approach the learned with the utmost 'Diffidence and Caution'.[12] Of all the positions taken in the Battle of the Books, his is the most sensible and convincing.

*

One of the pleasures of the 'Discourse' is to find Dryden, as he examines the history of satire, taking his own good advice. He provides us with both general counsel and with an example of how to proceed. As a literary critic, he is only too willing to dismiss the judgments of the scholars. The case they mount for this or that satirist is compromised by partisanship and hence is of not much use. And after a brief struggle with their special pleading, he finds it easier and more productive to waive them aside and to proceed on his own. But with their glosses of doubtful passages and their histories of satire, he is far less dismissive. On these subjects, he says, the commentators must be attended to, though never slavishly followed. Since their judgments are sometimes right and sometimes wrong, the careful reader must proceed through their arguments with the utmost circumspection. He must be prepared to turn from one authority to another or to withhold his assent from each and every authority in order to suggest answers of his own. For the educated reader does have it in his power to make an advance in knowledge, even though he may lack one or more marks of professional competence which the learned possess.

In the 'Discourse' Dryden considers the value of commentary itself. He believes that the cumulative efforts of many generations have succeeded in making intelligible much in the Roman satirists that was 'dark' and confusing before. He acknowledges his debts; he points to his disagreement with many prevailing interpretations; and he sees the need, since a good deal of obscurity remains, for much new work. But these matters, though important in his view, do not detain him very long. They are considered only briefly in the essay and only occasionally in his annotations, where for the most part he confines himself to glossing, for the benefit of the unlettered reader, famous names in myth and legend: he identifies Romulus, for instance, and Orestes. The scholarly issue that engages him in the 'Discourse' is the history of satire. He takes up all of the many forms which satire assumed in the ancient world. However, perhaps to simplify his task, he centres his attention on one type alone: the satire set forth in expository verse.

Dryden's account interweaves two kinds of history: one the history of a literary form, the other a history of the important scholarship on the subject. We learn simultaneously of the stages by which Roman satire came into being and of the succession of scholars who brought that development to light. And it is hard to tell which of the two interests him the more. Both accounts contain a wealth of detail. They are not easy reading. But they are impressive, and the more so since, at the same time, he makes it abundantly clear just where he agrees or disagrees with the men and the learning that he sets before us.

Dryden summarizes the theories of four classical scholars: Julius Caesar Scaliger, Daniel Heinsius, Isaac Casaubon and André Dacier. Scaliger and Heinsius, we learn, strike the first blow in 'the War' over the origins of 'Satire as a Species of Poetry'. They 'will have it descend ... to Rome' from the Greek satyr play, an early form of tragedy. And they support their position by 'deriv[ing]' the Latin word for satire ('*satira*') from the Latin word for satyr ('*satyrus*', from the Greek '*saturos*'), 'that mixt kind of Animal ... made up betwixt a Man and a Goat'.[13] Scaliger published his views in 1561; Heinsius restated them more than fifty years later. Meanwhile, a new and more fruitful approach to the history of satire was developed by the great French humanist Isaac Casaubon.

In his seminal study *De Satyrica Grecorum Poesi et Romanorum Satira* (1605), Casaubon attacks the twin parts of the argument – the generic and the etymological – for the Greek origin of Roman satire. Dryden has obviously been impressed by the work; and he takes up the major details in it scrupulously. First, we are told, Casaubon points out that, despite the assertions of many scholars, no direct connection can be established between Roman satire and the literature of Greece. In their early history Greek and Roman forms of satire are separate but analogous: they 'had the same beginning ...; Both were invented at Festivals of Thanksgiving ...; And both were prosecuted with Mirth and Raillery, and Rudiments of Verses...'[14] In their later history the two forms are separate and distinct. Nowhere can one discern a trace of influence between them, and certainly not between the Greek satyr play and what the Romans eventually came to identify as satire: that is, the formal verse satires of '*Ennius, Pacuvius, Lucilius,* and *Horace*'. Dryden here finds Casaubon's scholarship irrefutable; and he restates it with considerable force:

> [Greek] Satyrique Tragedy, and the *Roman* Satire have little Resemblance in any of their Features. The very Kinds are different ... The Character and Raillery of the *Satyres* [or Roman satires] is the only thing that cou'd pretend to a likeness, were *Scaliger* and *Heinsius* alive to maintain their Opinion. And the first Farces of the *Romans,* which were the Rudiments of their Poetry, were written before they had any Communication with the *Greeks;* or, indeed, any Knowledge of that People.[15]

Casaubon next considers the part of the argument based on etymology. Scaliger and Heinsius assume that, because the Latin word '*satira*' derives from the Latin word '*satyrus*', itself from the Greek '*saturos*', Roman satire must have a Greek origin. 'But', as Dryden goes on to explain, 'Casaubon ..., with Reason, condemn[s] this derivation; and prove[s] that from Satyrus [or '*Saturos*'], the word Satira, as it signifies a Poem, cannot possibly descend'. He shows that the Latin '*satira*' has another history altogether:

> Casaubon judg[es] ... that ['*satira*'] was deriv'd from Satura, a *Roman* word, which signifies Full, and Abundant; and full also of Variety ... According to this Derivation, from Satur comes Satura, or Satira according to the new spelling; as *optumus* and *maxumus* are now spell'd *optimus* and *maximus*. Satura ... is an Adjective, and relates to the word *Lanx*, which is understood. And this *Lanx*, in *English* a Charger, or large Platter, was yearly fill'd with all sorts of Fruits, which were offer'd to the Gods at their Festivals ...[16]

The paraphrase then continues:

> This word Satura has been afterward apply'd to many other sorts of Mixtures; as ... a kind of *Olla*, or hotch-potch, made of several sorts of Meats. Laws were also call'd *Leges Saturæ;* when they were of several Heads and Titles; like our tak'd Bills of Parliament.[17]

On this evidence Casaubon 'conjectur[es]' that it was from common Latin usage that the 'Satyres [satires] of *Ennius, Lucilius,* and *Horace* ... took their Name; because they are full of various Matters, and are also Written on various Subjects ...' This, Dryden believes, is a 'probabl[e]' inference, and one not unsupported by ancient authority.[18] Nonetheless, he recognizes that it was called into question three-quarters of a century later in a brief but important essay by André Dacier. To that essay, '*Préface sur les satires d'Horace*' (1687), he next turns; and again he is scrupulous in his details.

Dacier is convinced that neither Ennius nor Lucilius nor Horace originated the use of the word 'satire' as a literary term: Casaubon not withstanding, the innovation had come down to them already predetermined. In Dacier's view, the early Romans 'Acted ... a kind of civil cleanly Farce' which 'appear'd under the name of Satire, because of its variety'. That kind of satire (or farce), at one time immensely popular, went into eclipse when, in the third century B.C., Livius Andronicus introduced comedies and tragedies to the Roman stage. But it was soon revived, at the end of every comedy, as 'a separate Entertainment'.[19] It enjoyed a new success; and the vogue was, in particular, not lost upon Ennius, who discovered in farce (at least those parts not essentially dramatic) a possibility never seen before:

> *Ennius* ..., haveing seriously consider'd the Genius of the People, and how eagerly they follow'd the first Satires [or farces], thought it wou'd be worth his Pains, to refine upon the Project [that of reviving the form], and

> to write Satires [or farces] not to be Acted on the Theater, but Read. He preserv'd the Ground-work of their Pleasantry, their Venom, and their Raillery ... : And by this means, avoiding the danger of any ill Success, in a Publick Representation, he hop'd to be as well receiv'd in the Cabinet, as *Andronicus* had been upon the Stage.[20]

Dryden accepts Casaubon's correction of Scaliger and Heinsius; he is equally convinced by Dacier's correction of Casaubon. But the fact that knowledge advances over time leads him to believe that Dacier's account of satire may itself require correction:

> I am now almost gotten into my depth; at least by the help of *Dacier,* I am swimming towards it. Not that I will promise always to follow him, any more than he follows *Casaubon;* but to keep him in my Eye, as my best and truest Guide; and where I think he may possibly mislead me, there to have recourse to my own lights, as I expect that others should do by me.[21]

He does indeed discover an error in Dacier and offers to rectify it with a 'Proposition' of his own to which he has given much thought.[22]

According to Dryden, Dacier's mistake is to undervalue the role of Livius Andronicus in the whole development of early verse satire. Dacier believes that Ennius, the first Roman satirist, borrowed nothing from Andronicus, the first Roman playwright: Ennius, Dacier argues, based his work not on the 'Regular' comedies of Andronicus, but on Roman farce. With that theory, Dryden disagrees. He holds that Andronicus, 'a *Grecian* born', and 'instructed ... in the Manners and Decencies of the *Athenian* Theater', would certainly have modelled his plays on the 'old Comedy of *Aristophanes,* and the rest of the *Grecian* Poets'.[23] And he cannot imagine that Ennius would have preferred the crude jests of the Romans to 'the fine Railleries of the Greeks'. The question, Dryden admits, cannot be resolved either way: the plays of Andronicus and the Roman farces have both been lost. Still, he is confident that, given the available evidence, his is the 'more probable Opinion':

> [W]e have *Dacier* making out that *Ennius* was the first ... in that way of Writing, which was of his Invention; that is, Satire abstracted from the Stage, and new modell'd into Papers of Verses, on several Subjects. But he will have *Ennius* take the Ground-work of Satire from the first Farces of the *Romans;* rather than from the form'd Plays of *Livius Andronicus,* which were Copy'd from the *Grecian* Comedies. It may possibly be so; but *Dacier* knows no more of it than I do. And it seems to me ... that he rather imitated the fine Railleries of the *Greeks,* which he saw in the pieces of *Andronicus,* than the Coursness of his old Countrymen, in their Clownish Extempory way of jeering.[24]

This speculation serves Dryden in a number of important ways. After Casaubon had completely dissociated Roman satire from the literature of Greece, Dryden finds a means by which to relate them again, and he thereby reasserts, albeit with a new twist, the unbroken continuity of the Graeco-Roman tradition. It also enables him to contribute to the study of satire historical judgments of his own, although he is quick to remind us that his judgments are but opinions, that he advances them with a measure of healthy scepticism, and that at some time in the future they too may be corrected or modified, or perhaps completely superseded.

IV

Jonathan Swift notwithstanding, Dryden in his late criticism does wear his learning lightly. There are nevertheless occasions when his work is immersed in abstruse problems, as in the history of satire and, again, in the volume on Virgil. In essay after essay, from the beginning of his career to the end, Dryden refers to Virgil; and he does so always with reverence, even awe. Despite some wavering, chiefly in the years following his first encounter with Longinus, he remains convinced that modern poets are, or will eventually be, superior to their ancient counterparts, but never to Virgil. Virgil inevitably sets the standard by which all poets (past, present and future) will have to be judged. Dryden had hoped that he might one day write an English *Aeneid;* and he did make a number of attempts, but none of them, he realized, very successful. He had therefore to compromise. Starting in 1693 he undertook one of the major enterprises of his life. He began his translation of the *Aeneid* (or the '*Æneis*'), as well as of the *Eclogues* (or the '*Pastorals*') and the *Georgics*. As he carried out this difficult and arduous task, he consulted several dozen earlier translations. He also consulted the most authoritative editions and commentaries, probably including those by Jean Regnauld de Segrais, J. Van Emenes and Pancratius Maaswyck, and Charles de la Rue ('Ruæus').[25] And from his working methods, as reconstructed by J. McG. Bottkol, we can see that the scholars enjoyed quite as much of his attention as the translators:

> [H]e sat with a favorite edition open before him ..., read the original carefully, often the Latin prose *Interpretatio* [paraphrase], and invariably studied the accompanying annotations. When he came to a difficult or disputed passage, he repeatedly turned to other editors, studied and compared their varying opinions, and then chose to follow one authority or another or even to make a new interpretation for himself. Also he had open before him on the table one or more earlier English translations ...[26]

Dryden's extensive reading and study not only allowed him to produce a translation which is generally accurate according to the textual scholarship of the age, it also allowed him to produce something of a scholarly edition of his own. In what seems to have been his original plan, he intended to write both dedications and 'learned' prefaces to each of Virgil's poems, as well as an extensive body of notes. Later he had a change of mind. The notes were considerably cut back; and two of the prefaces were farmed out: Knightly Chetwood was assigned the one to the *Eclogues,* and Joseph Addison the one to the *Georgics*. The preface to the *Æneis,* however, was written by Dryden himself, and it was combined with an address to

John Sheffield, the Marquess of Normanby, so as to produce what he called a 'Prefatory Dedication'.[27] It is a major essay of the final period; and unlike his brief dedications of the *Eclogues* and the *Georgics*, it contains an important exploration of the value of scholarship to criticism.

In the essay Dryden carefully avoids the moral lapses – those of most commentators – which he had condemned in the 'Discourse'. Though he has very decided views on the greatness of Virgil, he does not seek to elevate him by blackening the reputations of other poets. Though he has a high opinion of his own merits as editor and translator, he is utterly free from the delusion that Virgil exists for him and not he for Virgil. He is also free from another failing, which he now considers for the first time. In order to seem more original than they are, commentators often neglect to credit their sources. They ransack other authors for 'Objections and Solutions', and then present the borrowed learning as their own. Dryden, for his part, is disgusted by the practice. He has no ambition to be thought 'more Learned' than he is. For the age, he is remarkably scrupulous in 'nam[ing] the Authors' from whom he borrows, and no less scrupulous in the modest claims he advances for his own originality.[28] Unfortunately, what are some of the undoubted strengths of the work – its celebration of good scholarship and its insistence on proper ethics in its use – have done nothing to enhance its reputation. Indeed, that Dryden has often drawn upon the scholarship of others has led to the charge that the dedication is largely derivative and therefore second-rate.[29]

The essay, one of literary appreciation and judgment, offers both a recantation and a refutation. Dryden abandons opinions he previously held but now finds mistaken. He also defends the *Aeneid* against 'a whole Confederacy' who object to the conduct of the hero, the time-scheme of the action and the moral of the poem.[30] In each of these tasks the argument is founded upon – indeed, it has been made possible by – his recently acquired knowledge of Virgilian scholarship.

Dryden benefited enormously from reading learned prefaces and commentaries. He could now mount a defence of Virgil which, only five years before, was beyond his power. In an essay published in an English version as 'Reflections upon the French Translators' (1692), Saint-Évremond considers editions of the Roman classics in his native tongue. As he is passing judgment on Segrais's *Eneide* (1668), he digresses from his subject to attack the behaviour of Virgil's hero. He finds that the quality of 'Piety' renders Aeneas too unwarlike, too weak and tender-hearted, to be placed in an epic poem:

> [T]he good *Æneas*... hardly concerns himself in important, and glorious Designs. It suffices him not to be wanting in the Offices of a pious, tender, and compassionate Soul. He carries his Father on his Shoulders, he conjugally laments his dear *Creusa*; he causes his Nurse to be Enterred, and makes a Funeral Pile for his Pilot, in shedding a thousand Tears.
>
> This was a poor Heroe in *Paganism*, that might be a great Saint amongst the *Christians*, very proper to afford us Miracles, and a more worthy Founder of an Order, than a State.[31]

What led Virgil into giving his poem this unlikely hero? The answer, the French critic believes, is to be found in the temper of the poet. Aeneas reveals the 'secret Inclination' of his maker. He is a self-portrait of the artist as a 'compassionate' man.[32]

Saint-Évremond is aware that for his translation Segrais wrote a preface in which the character of Aeneas is warmly defended. But he remains convinced that the insipid hero is past redemption and that the arguments of the learned translator are misconceived. '[W]ho', he asks, 'is not tired with the good *Æneas* and his dear *Achates*?'[33]

Dryden undertook to answer these remarks twice, first in 'A Character of Saint-Evremond' (1692) and later in the dedication of the *Æneis*. In his first response he seems puzzled and at a loss at what to say. As 'a Religious Admirer of *Virgil*', he wishes that Saint-Évremond 'had not discover'd our Father's Nakedness'. Nevertheless, he thinks the case against Aeneas is so well proved as to allow for no defence: '[W]e must confess that Æneas was none of the greatest Hero's, and that *Virgil* was sensible of it *himself*'. He would, however, account for the defect in the hero in terms that he finds more plausible than Saint-Évremond's. He begins by pointing out that Virgil was 'bound … to follow the Footsteps of *Homer*', who presents the Trojan as unsuccessful in war. The authority of Homer, he believes, ultimately accounts for Aeneas's lack of prowess. But to make clear why the poet made his hero into a kind of saint, he thinks another explanation is required, one that takes into account the outward circumstances of the poet's life. He reminds us that, as a courtier, Virgil was obliged to please; and knowing that Augustus, who was an indifferent soldier, 'lov'd to be flatter'd for being Pious', he gave 'him who was to represent his Emperour' piety as his chief virtue.[34]

The next time he took up the issue of Aeneas's character, Dryden did so when strengthened with a surer command of the poem. In the years between the publication of 'A Character of Saint-Evremond' and the writing of the dedication, he had read and absorbed Segrais's 'admirable Preface' – the same preface which Saint-Évremond had dismissed out of hand. What Segrais taught him was that, when Virgil describes Aeneas as *pious*, he chooses a word with a meaning very different from that of its modern cognates. Latin *pietas*, whatever Saint-Évremond may have thought, denotes not saintly conduct alone, but 'the whole Duty of Man towards the Gods; towards his Country, and towards his Relations'.[35] It is a far more appropriate virtue with which to endow a hero than valour alone:

> In reality, they who believe that the Praises which arise from Valour, are superior to those, which proceed from any other Virtues, have not consider'd … that Valour, destitute of other Virtues, cannot render a Man worthy of any true esteem … But the same cannot be said of Piety; which excludes all ill Qualities, and comprehends even Valour it self, with all other Qualities which are good.[36]

Moreover, once no longer under the spell of Saint-Évremond's essay, Dryden immediately realizes that Aeneas does possess the intrepid courage Saint-Évremond demands of a hero: '[M]ore could not be expected from an *Amadis,* a Sir *Lancelot,* or the whole *Round Table*...'[37]

Dryden's readings in Segrais also allow him to answer a long-standing question about the poem. For more than a century critics had debated whether '*Virgil's* Action were within the Year, or took up some Months beyond it'. Dryden recognizes that the matter is insignificant in itself and of no conceivable interest to the majority of his readers: '[T]he whole Dispute is of no more concernment to the common Reader, than it is to a Ploughman, whether *February* this Year had 28 or 29 Days in it'.[38] Nevertheless, he is fascinated by Segrais's answer to the problem since it neatly illustrates how specialized knowledge can resolve disputed critical points. And he explains it at some length, even though the explanation makes occasionally for very strenuous reading.

Following Segrais, who is both participant in and historian of the quarrel, Dryden informs us that the dispute hinges on a single point: the dating of the opening scene, the storm at sea which Aeneas encounters as he sails from Sicily. If the storm occurs in 'the latter end of Winter, or beginning of the Spring', then the subsequent actions of the poem, all the disputants are agreed, must take up to sixteen months. On the other hand, if the storm occurs in the late summer, the action is correspondingly shortened. From Segrais Dryden also learns that Ronsard and his followers, who argue for an early departure, 'suppose that when *Æneas* had buried his Father, he set sail immediately for *Italy*'. For, they ask, 'having no more to do in Sicily... after that Office was perform'd, what remain'd for him, but, without delay, to pursue his first Adventure?' But Segrais himself, who proposes a later date, reasons that 'the Obsequies of his Father ... would detain him for many days', as would 'the refitting of his Ships' and the 'refreshing [of] his Weather-beaten Souldiers'. For his part, Dryden inclines to the second interpretation since it appears to be 'better grounded' in the descriptive details of the poem. But what chiefly impels him to accept it is that Segrais moves beyond 'what are but Suppositions' and supports his reading with an ingenious scientific argument.

Segrais demonstrates that, as Dryden says, Virgil is 'an exact Astronomer'. Segrais first 'observ[es]' that Ilioneus, a companion of Aeneas, attributes the storm to the constellation Orion ('*nimbosus Orion*'). Now Orion rises twice, once at the beginning of day in summer (it is then 'Heliacal') and once at the end of day in winter (it is then 'Achronical'). When it rises helically, Orion 'causes ... or presages Tempests on the Seas'; when it rises achronically, it 'causes ... or presages' rain. A summer dating would thus seem to be demanded by Virgil's choice of epithet, '*nimbosus*' (tempestuous). That the dating is in fact accurate, according to Dryden, is confirmed when Segrais underscores a second reference to Orion, now with the epithet '*aquosus*' (rainy), and this time the season, '*hyems*' (winter), is never in doubt:

> *Segrais* has observ'd farther, that when *Anna* [Dido's sister] counsels *Dido* to stay *Æneas* during the Winter; she speaks also of *Orion;*
>
> *Dum pelago desævit hyems, & aquosus* Orion [While winter and watery Orion spend their rage on the sea].

> If therefore *Ilioneus,* according to our Supposition, understand the
> *Heliachal* rising of *Orion: Anna* must mean the *Achronical,* which the
> different Epithetes given to that Constellation, seem to manifest. *Ilioneus*
> calls him *nimbosus, Anna aquosus.* He is tempestuous in the Summer
> when he rises *Heliacally,* and Rainy in the Winter when he rises
> *Achronically.*[39]

Dryden never tires of celebrating the learning and perceptiveness of Segrais. Still,
he thinks that he has something of his own to add, and he is eager to bring it to
our attention.

In considering Virgil's aims in the *Aeneid,* critics and scholars had generally
conceived of the poem as an uncritical celebration of the Roman Empire.[40] In 'A
Character of Saint-Evremond', Dryden had accepted this view, though for him the
poem was shaped not so much by political allegiance as by a desire to flatter a
patron.[41] Through his studies, however, he had come to find his original position
crude and unsatisfying; and in the dedication he offers us a more subtle explanation.
Virgil, he now believes, did have political loyalties, though not to the monarchy
of Augustus, but to the old Republic: he was 'of Republican principles in his Heart'.
At the same time, he knew that the 'Commonwealth was lost without ressource:
The Heads of it destroy'd; the Senate new moulded, grown degenerate...' Though
reluctantly, he therefore threw his support to Augustus, since he alone offered the
prospect of security and peace:

> [H]aving maturely weigh'd the Condition of the Times in which he liv'd:
> that an entire Liberty was not to be retriev'd: that the present Settlement
> had the prospect of a long continuance in the same Family, or those
> adopted into it: that he held his Paternal Estate from the Bounty of the
> Conqueror ...: that this Conquerour, though of a bad kind, was the very
> best of it....: These things, I say, being consider'd by the Poet, he
> concluded it to be the Interest of his Country to be so govern'd: To infuse
> an awful Respect into the People, towards such a Prince: By that respect to
> confirm their Obedience to him; and by that Obedience to make them
> Happy.[42]

Several modern critics believe that, in the discussion of Virgil's politics, Rome
represents England after the Glorious Revolution of 1688, and Augustus the new
monarch by another name. But they disagree on whether through the implied
analogy Dryden expresses his own reluctant acceptance of William III's government
or his continued disapproval.[43] What is certain is that Dryden's account tells us
much, from his point of view, about a Roman poet's conception of his emperor;
what it tells us of an English poet's conception of his king must remain in doubt.
Here is criticism, in any event, that at least finds in Virgil an element of political
sophistication. If Dryden's Virgil still seems too confident and cheerful, we are at
least spared the portrait of the naive eulogist drawn by Segrais, Le Bossu and other
seventeenth-century commentators.

Knowledge and study are not the only tools by which Dryden has penetrated
into the meaning of the poem. He also enjoys another means of access: a sympa-

thetic understanding of Virgil based on shared temperament and interests. As a poet who has also written about public events, he is aware that Virgil has sometimes woven into his poem matters of private concern. Poets are an irascible brood, and they have long memories. Even as they sing of the rise and fall of empires, they remember to reward their friends and to punish their enemies:

> Neither were the great *Roman* Families which flourish'd in his time, less oblig'd by him [Virgil] than the Emperour ... I could not but take notice, when I Translated it [Book V], of some Favorite Families to which he gives the Victory, and awards the Prizes, in the Person of his Heroe, at the Funeral Games which were Celebrated in Honour of *Anchises* ... I likewise either found or form'd an Image to my self of the contrary kind; that those who lost the Prizes, were such as had disoblig'd the Poet, or were in disgrace with *Augustus,* or enemies to *Mæcenas:* And this was the Poetical Revenge he took. For *genus irritabile Vatum* [the irritable race of bards], as *Horace* says. When a Poet is thoroughly provok'd, he will do himself Justice, however dear it cost him ... I think these are not bare Imaginations of my own, though I find no trace of them in the Commentatours: But one Poet may judge of another by himself. The Vengeance we defer is not forgotten.[44]

The final sentence is to be understood not as a threat of future retaliation on Dryden's part, but as an allusion to acts of revenge he has already taken. At first unsure whether Virgil used the funeral games to settle old scores ('I likewise either found or form'd an Image to my self'), he advances to certainty ('I think these are not bare Imaginations of my own') as he suddenly remembers (or so he suggests) his own attacks on contemporaries which he has inserted into the translation ('But one Poet may judge of another by himself').

Guided by these promptings in the dedication, scholars have discovered many passages where Dryden clearly obtrudes his views into the very translation itself.[45] One striking instance occurs in Dryden's account of Aeneas's journey to Hades, when the hero encounters the souls of those who committed unpardonable acts. Virgil's emphasis is on the ubiquity of evil; but in his catalogue of the violent and deceitful, he dwells mainly on those who, in general, have violated family ties:

> Hic quibus invisi fratres, dum vita manebat,
> Pulsatusve parens, & fraus innexa clienti;
> Aut quis divitiis soli incubuêre repertis,
> Nec partem posuêre suis, quæ maxima turba est ...

> (Here were they who in lifetime hated their brethren, or smote a sire, and entangled a client in wrong; or who brooded in solitude over wealth they had won, nor set aside a portion for their kin – the largest number this ...)[46]

In his translation Dryden follows Virgil rather closely, but with an important difference. He particularizes the crimes he names, especially those that take place within royal families:

> Then they, who Brothers better Claim disown,
> Expel their Parents, and usurp the Throne;
> Defraud their Clients, and to Lucre sold,
> Sit brooding on unprofitable Gold:
> Who dare not Give, and ev'n refuse to lend
> To their poor Kindred, or a wanting Friend:
> Vast is the Throng of these ...[47]

Dryden here speaks of many royal culprits, but he seems to have in mind only one: Mary Stuart. Mary died in 1694, some six years after she had replaced her father, James II, on the throne and denied the succession to her brother. And Dryden intimates she is now in Hell for the crimes she committed against both her family and the state.[48]

Jacobite politics also enters into the translation of the famous invocation of the poem, in which Dryden shifts the subject back and forth between the eponymous hero and the hounded King James:

> Arms, and the Man I sing, who, forc'd by Fate,
> And haughty *Juno's* unrelenting Hate,
> Expell'd and exil'd, left the *Trojan* Shoar:
> Long Labours, both by Sea and Land he bore,
> And in the doubtful War, before he won
> The *Latian* Realm, and built the destin'd Town:
> His banish'd Gods restor'd to Rites Divine,
> And setl'd sure Succession in his Line:
> From whence the Race of *Alban* Fathers come,
> And the long Glories of Majestick *Rome*.[49]

Several of the words here ('banish'd', 'restor'd', 'Rites'), and even one entire verse ('And setl'd sure Succession in his Line'), have no counterpart in the Latin, and suggest interests far more English and Catholic than Roman and pagan.[50] They suggest moments when Dryden's scholarship does not fail him: he chooses simply to ignore it. They suggest the holiday moments that he describes in the dedication, when poets ignore the business at hand to indulge in their own preoccupations.

*

Dryden's interest in scholarship is evident not only in the dedication of the *Æneis* but also in the body of notes that he wrote for all three of Virgil's poems. He had originally planned to devote at least 'half a yeares time' to this part of the edition, in the belief that an additional display of learning would enhance his reputation. But finding that the publisher would 'not allow any thing towards' the project, he resolved to write only 'Marginall' glosses for the 'unlearned, who understand not the poetical Fables'. In the end, however, he returned to his original plan, executed it on a modest scale, and left the unlearned to shift for themselves.[51]

In the six dozen or so notes he appended to the text, almost all of which are devoted to the *Aeneid*, there are no identifications of well-known 'Persons, Places or Fables'. Dryden assumes in his readers some knowledge of the ancient world and concerns himself with investigating recondite matters. His 'Observations', as he tells us, are 'scattering', or unsystematic.[52] Nevertheless, he manages to take up the customary tasks of the scholarly editor: the elucidation of obscure references and customs; the tracing of sources and analogues; the establishment of the text, along with, of course, the interpretation of disputed passages.

One subject to which Dryden often returns is the way Virgil may organize the incidents and details of his epic, though cryptically, around the celebration of patrons. Thus, in the careful attention devoted to the funeral games in Book V, Dryden discovers a hidden compliment to Augustus:

> *Virgil* seems to me, to have excell'd *Homer* in all those Sports, and to have labour'd them the more, in Honour of *Octavius*, his Patron; who instituted the like Games for perpetuating the Memory of his Uncle *Julius:* Piety, as *Virgil* calls it, or dutifulness to Parents, being a most popular Vertue among the *Romans*.[53]

Drawing upon his sure grasp of the period, he also finds, hidden in the narrative of Book VIII, a helpful service to Maecenas. Virgil sends Aeneas to seek aid in Etruria because, as Dryden says, Etruria is 'the Country of *Mæcenas*', and Virgil hoped 'to indear his Protector to his Emperour' by suggesting 'there had been a former Friendship betwixt their Lines'.[54]

In addition to revealing Virgil's hidden references to contemporaries in the *Aeneid*, Dryden devotes considerable attention to the poet's debts throughout his works to earlier writers. In his commentary on the dedication, L. Proudfoot unfairly rebukes Dryden for failing to grasp '[t]he extraordinary conservatism with which Virgil went about his task, taking and adapting from Homer, Ennius, Apollonius Rhodius, and many others'.[55] But Virgil's traditionalism – or, as Dryden says, his having 'borrow'd so many things from Homer, Apollonius Rhodius, and others who preceded him' – is actually one of the principal subjects of the essay.[56] While his interests in the dedication centre more on the traditional element in all great art than on Virgil's debts, Dryden does have much to say in the notes on the poet's specific borrowings. His general method is first to name a source and then comment upon how Virgil both appropriated and transformed it. After noting that the funeral games in the *Aeneid* are modelled on those in Apollonius Rhodius's *Argonautica*, he draws our attention to the deletion of the equestrian events and attributes their absence to Virgil's sense of artistic economy:

> [T]he Reader may observe the great Judgment and distinction of our Authour in what he borrows from the Ancients, by comparing them. I conceive the reason why he omits the Horse-race in the Funeral Games, was because he shows *Ascanius* afterwards on Horseback, with his Troops of Boys, and would not wear that Subject thread-bare...[57]

With the literary sources of the other two poems, Dryden appears not to have been very much concerned. Of all the source studies, however, the most perceptive is the one which he appended not to the *Aeneid* but to *Eclogue IX:* 'In the

Ninth Pastoral, *Virgil* has made a Collection of many scattering Passages, which he had Translated from *Theocritus*: And here he has bound them into a Nosegay'.[58] Classical scholarship has made possible the most subtle of exegeses. Our pleasure in the poem is enhanced by a recognition of how much of it Virgil skilfully culled from Theocritus. We cannot enjoy the eclogue fully unless we perceive that it is a miniature florilegium of works by another poet.

Dryden's learning is best displayed in the notes in which he addresses textual problems and attendant difficulties in translation. His attempts to resolve a crux involve him in collating texts, canvassing authorities, searching for literary parallels, and citing relevant folkways and customs. He may sometimes make careless mistakes, but he has an excellent sense of the principles and methods which the scholarly editor brings to his work. One of the small but persistent issues in Virgilian scholarship has concerned the correct reading of the four concluding lines of *Eclogue IV*. In the poem, after recounting the future life of a newborn child who will grow up to restore the golden age, Virgil considers the first moments of the infant with his parents:

> Incipe parve puer risu cognoscere matrem:
> Matri longa decem tulerunt fastidia menses.
> Incipe parve puer, cui non risere parentes,
> Nec Deus hunc mensa, dea nec dignata cubili est.[59]

The much debated question concerns the act of smiling ('risere') mentioned in the third line. Does the infant smile at the mother, do the parents smile at the infant, or do the infant and parents smile at each other? As translator, Dryden accepts the first possibility:

> Begin, auspicious Boy, to cast about
> Thy Infant Eyes, and with a smile, thy Mother single out;
> Thy Mother well deserves that short delight,
> The nauseous Qualms of ten long Months and Travel to requite.
> Then smile; the frowning Infant's Doom is read,
> No God shall crown the Board, nor Goddess bless the Bed.[60]

In the note to the passage he states the rationale for his decision.

In defence of his choice Dryden mentions that he has the support of many authorities, including '*Erythræus, Bembus,* and *Joseph Scaliger*'. He also quotes a parallel passage in Catullus, in which an infant similarly rewards his mother with a smile. But the case, he admits, is extremely weak. He 'may be mistaken'. The entire phrase, 'cui non risere parentes', suggests that it may be the parents who smile.[61] And to complicate the matter even further, there may even be a third possibility: 'What if I shou'd steer betwixt the two Extreams, and conclude, that the Infant, who was to be happy, must not only smile on his Parents, but also they on him?'[62] This interpretation is well supported by traditional beliefs:

The crowning of Virgil. Frontispiece to *The Works of Virgil* (1697).
Engraving by Michiel Van Der Gucht after an engraving by Claude Mellan
(from a design by Nicholas Poussin)
(By permission of the William Andrews Clark Memorial Library, Los Angeles)

> For *Scaliger* notes that the Infants who smil'd not at their Birth, were observ'd to be ... sullen ... during all their Life: And *Servius,* and almost all the modern Commentators affirm, that no child was thought Fortunate on whom his Parents smil'd not, at his Birth.[63]

Dryden has the good sense not to speak more positively about the subject than the evidence will allow. He leaves the question, finally, where we sometimes find it in modern commentaries on the *Eclogues,* completely unresolved.[64]

Throughout his notes, of whatever kind, Dryden enters into friendly competition with the scholars. He may be dependent on their original research, but he thinks he has the knowledge and sense to correct their judgments. The claim is not new to his work. What makes it of interest is the accompanying awareness that, in what he is doing, he is not alone. He sees around him many men who, though they have no reputations as scholars, hold no university posts and do not devote all their time to classical studies, have nonetheless made contributions to learning. He singles out, among others, the Earl of Roscommon, who has published excellent notes on *Pastoral VI,* and Sir Robert Howard, who 'has given us the most Learned, and the most Judicious Observations' on Aeneas's journey to Hades.[65] Dryden, however, is principally concerned not with rescuing neglected books, but with commemorating his 'Friends' that have been content to disseminate their knowledge through conversation. There is the 'Ingenious ... *Anthony Henley*', who informed him of an interesting analogue to the infant's smile in *Eclogue IV.* There is also Sir *William Bowyer,* an old college friend, and now a gentleman farmer, who understood what those with only bookish knowledge failed to perceive: that the *Georgics* is not an agricultural treatise but a poem.[66] These 'Friends', diverse in their backgrounds and pursuits, testify to the presence of a rich literary culture in England. They also testify to the foolishness of turning the classics over to the experts and discouraging intelligent readers from judging the Ancients by their own lights.

*

Dryden had none of Swift's contempt for the minute investigations of the scholar. Nor did he share the contempt of Pope, who mercilessly pilloried Bentley in *The Dunciad:*

> Avaunt —— is Aristarchus yet unknown?
> Thy mighty Scholiast, whose unweary'd pains,
> Made Horace dull, and humbled Milton's strains.
> Turn what they will to Verse, their toil is vain,
> Critics like me shall make it Prose again.[67]

Had Dryden chosen to lampoon Bentley, he would have attacked the moral failures of the man and not the nature of the work. For however much more extensive they may have been, Dryden's interests included those of Bentley. A scholar might not be a critic, but a critic of ancient poetry had, in his view, perforce to be a scholar. He cannot begin to understand the poets of another age without the aid of learning.

V

Throughout the sixteenth and seventeenth centuries, modern scholarly methods were used to interpret not only classical civilization but early English civilization as well. Antiquarian research into the Anglo-Saxon and medieval periods evoked, predictably, the contempt of such Ancients as Temple and Swift, but it enjoyed the enthusiastic support of many Moderns, among them William Wotton and Dryden himself.[68] In 1663, in a commendatory poem published with Walter Charleton's *Chorea Gigantum*, Dryden praised Charleton's archaeological investigation into the nature of Stonehenge. He appears, however, not to have made any extensive use of antiquarian scholarship until he undertook the translations of medieval authors in the 1690s.

In the 'Preface to *Fables Ancient and Modern*' (1700), while still very much involved in the Battle of the Books, Dryden is both classical scholar and medievalist. He remains as much interested in Homer, Virgil and Ovid as he has ever been. But he now turns his attention, as scholar and critic, to the Middle Ages, to the works of Dante and Boccaccio, though he centres it mainly on Chaucer. In his comments on Chaucer, as well as indirectly through his suggested emendations of *The Canterbury Tales,* a number of which have been accepted by Chaucerians since the eighteenth century, he studies both the man and his works in the context of the age during which he wrote.[69] Dryden's accomplishments as a Chaucerian have been equated unfairly with what, in the light of later research, we know to be his few errors, particularly his coming down on the wrong side of the debate over Chaucer's versification. Much of Dryden's discussion is well informed: the remarks on Chaucer's learning, on his use of French and Italian models, and on his means of 'adorn[ing]' his native tongue. Although in his grasp of the period Dryden cannot compete with the most distinguished medievalists of the seventeenth century, in his approach to Chaucer, as William L. Alderson notes, his 'instincts are not unscholarly'.[70]

In his studies of Ovid, Plutarch, Virgil and the Roman satirists, whether he is accepting learned arguments or rejecting them, Dryden makes a point of mentioning the scholars who have preceded him. In the preface, though he refers vaguely to the texts he has consulted ('all the editions', 'the last edition'), he mentions no Chaucerians by name. As a consequence, the sources of the essay have remained something of a mystery. We can point to a few books that provided him with assistance, especially the 1598 and 1602 editions of Chaucer's works by Thomas Speght, with their lives, notes and glossaries of difficult terms. But further investigation is required to reveal the full extent of his research. It is possible that he received from Pepys, who suggested he put into modern English the portrait of the 'Good Parson',[71] a copy of Caxton's second edition of *The Canterbury Tales.* It is also possible that he consulted some of the specialized works that were published in the seventeenth century on the medieval period – for instance, Henry Spelman's *Glossarium Archaiologicum* (1664) or Stephen Skinner's *Etymologicon Linguae Anglicanae* (1669) – or that he received assistance from any of a number of distinguished medievalists who were concurrently conducting research at Oxford or Cambridge.[72] If his work on the Latin authors ever served him as a guide, his preparation for his translation of Chaucer is then likely to have been thorough and conscientious.[73]

In many respects, the preface is like all the other essays in which, throughout the 1680s and 1690s, Dryden is both critic and learned scholar. But even as he makes perfectly clear what in his judgment sound learning must be, he allows his excursions into scholarship to take suddenly and unexpectedly a new direction. He has been approaching literature for some twenty years through historical methods, and all at once he has the sense that he has been terribly misled. After arranging the history of literature into a coherent pattern, he becomes aware that the pattern of development is anything but neat. It is characterized by strange leaps, odd disappearances and abrupt returns. A poet like Spenser has more in common with a poet dead for two centuries than he has with the writers of his immediate past. The reputation of a poet like Chaucer becomes almost completely eclipsed and is then unaccountably renewed. The path of literature, far from following a linear direction, is wayward and confused, perhaps better explained through occult theories of death and rebirth than through laws of historical causation.[74] Of course, had Dryden realized how frequently Chaucer's works were published in the sixteenth century and how widely they were known, he would never have been led to such speculations. But the error was fruitful. Dryden's imperfect knowledge of the Renaissance Chaucer led him to grasp the importance of discontinuity in literary history: the fact that poets often take their inspiration not from their immediate predecessors but from poets long dead and all but forgotten, as Eliot was inspired by Donne and the other metaphysical poets more than two centuries after they had ceased to be read. Where the new insight might have led Dryden we cannot tell, and Dryden is no guide. We can only assume that, had he continued to write, his criticism would have developed, as it had in the past, in a new and surprising direction.

At any rate, with but one exception, the 'Discourse', the preface is the most important of the late essays in which, in his twofold role, that of critic, that of scholar, Dryden makes little or no distinction between the requirements of sound learning and those of literary taste and judgment. With but the same exception, it is the most impressive of the late essays in which classical rules and a sense of history circumscribe and inform each other.

CHAPTER FOURTEEN

The modern temper
(1693–1700)

I

Dryden had always been interested in history and biography. Towards the end of his life, as he turned increasingly to the fine art of translation, that interest was given renewed emphasis and direction. It helped to determine the structure of his essays, which may now unfold, either in whole or in part, according to the rule of a strict chronology. It also helped to define the groundwork of his first principles, as well as the manner in which, in all practical criticism, he would have great works of literature analysed, evaluated and judged. These last developments culminated in two works: the 'Discourse concerning the Original and Progress of Satire' (1693) and the 'Preface to *Fables Ancient and Modern*' (1700). The two essays may seem at first glance to have nothing in common; but centred as they both are in the same perspectives and perceptions, the first looks forward clearly to the second.

II

The 'Discourse' was originally published as an introduction to translations from the works of Persius and Juvenal, the Persius translated all but entirely by Dryden, the Juvenal by Dryden and others selected by him, including his sons Charles and John. The longest of his essays ('this vast Preface'), the 'Discourse' is also the most learned and encyclopaedic. It gives a sweeping history of satire, from its origin in crude 'Scoffs and Revilings', through its first flowering in ancient Rome, to its later development and hybridization in the Renaissance and the late seventeenth century.[1] He says all but nothing about the major satirists of the Middle Ages, including one of his favourites, Chaucer, although he is to take care of that lacuna seven years later in the 'Preface to *Fables*'. His purpose, which we are never allowed to forget, is to defend satire from the charge that it is the mere vapouring of diseased or anti-social minds. He also defends himself; and he defends himself not only as satirist but as man of letters and loyal Englishman.

The essay is divided into five sections. In the first, Dryden addresses Charles Sackville, now Earl of Dorset, to whom the essay is dedicated and to whom he had earlier dedicated the *Essay of Dramatick Poesie* (1668).[2] He recognizes that, in matters political, he and Dorset have little in common. Dorset, who is a Whig, favoured the deposing of James II and accepts, apparently without qualification, the new monarchy; Dryden, who is a Tory, continues to think of James as the rightful king and cannot help regarding William III as a mere usurper. Yet he can also recognize that, beyond political agreements or disagreements, there are transcendent values, which are to be found in great works of art; and on these noble

222

values the two can and do agree.[3] Hence, although they are separated in the world of affairs, they may govern jointly the world of letters. Dryden's role as 'Councellour' is to define the laws, and Dorset's role as 'Prince' is to put them into execution. For his part, Dorset is perfectly fitted to the task. He is a distinguished poet and, though a satirist, of a loving and forgiving disposition.[4]

The tribute which Dryden extends to Dorset is counterbalanced with what he apparently considers a necessary tribute to himself. And while the one is made in the spirit of the courtier-poet or of a mock humility, so the other is made with a matter-of-fact directness: with a full and sober understanding of genuine accomplishment. Dryden recognizes that, as playwright and poet, as critic and literary historian, he holds an important place in English letters and that, as a consequence, he has made a truly significant contribution to the national culture. He nevertheless has to admit that he has not done all that he had wanted to do and that, in his judgment, he could have done. In short, he has not written the one poem – a great national epic – about which he has been thinking since the mid-1660s. In the past he never received the kind of encouragement or patronage which might have made it possible for him to do so; and now he is too old and too poor.[5]

For that failure in his career he has no misgivings; and he makes no apologies. The shame is not his own but the nation's. And as proof of what he might have accomplished under a more generous government, he now sets down the rules according to which the great English epic may yet be written, perhaps in the immediate future. The English have a genius for the epic, as (he insists) the French do not; but (quite apart from the lack of patronage) the English do not know the most important rules by which the poet who would write a heroic poem must guide himself.

Dryden's directives are almost entirely traditional. He identifies the epic with the practice of Virgil and censures the epic poets of the last two hundred years for their experimentation in subject, in language and in form.[6] The modern poet is not to reinvent the epic: he is only to adapt it to the religion and customs of his time. In particular, he is to substitute for the warring gods of the heathens the supernatural machinery provided and sanctioned by the Christian religion: in place of Juno and Neptune, the 'Guardian Angels appointed by God Almighty, as his Vicegerents, for the Protection and Government of Cities, Provinces, Kingdoms'. When made, Dryden believes, the substitution will make possible the creation of 'a Nobler, a more Beautiful and more Perfect Poem, than any yet extant since the Ancients', though one which can never excel the works of Homer and Virgil. Had he been encouraged with more than 'fair Words, by King *Charles* II', he might have written that kind of epic himself. And he is not above suggesting that, with such a poem to commend it, the 'Imperial Line' might not have been overthrown.[7]

*

In the second part of the essay, which is almost as long as the first, Dryden gives a history of satire, together with a long commentary on the major classical scholars – Scaliger, Heinsius, Casaubon, Dacier – who have written about the form, with whom he occasionally agrees, but in whose works he finds, on the whole, errors in both fact and judgment.[8] We are thus left with the impression that, from his point of view, the critic who is also a poet must have the last say on the writing of literary history. He explains that satire developed in ancient Rome out of the imitation ultimately of Old Comedy; and that the English word 'satire' ought not to be confused with 'satyr'. He distinguishes between two kinds of satire – the formal or expository (or so-called Horatian) and the narrative (or Varronian) – and suggests that, the academic scholars notwithstanding, the one is not to be preferred to the other.[9]

These many observations Dryden sets within the framework of a theory of history. Like poets who write in other genres, satirists establish among themselves a tradition, in which they subscribe to many of the same rules and, on the whole, to the same moral absolutes. On the other hand, in the Quarrel of the Ancients and Moderns, he sides (once again) with the Moderns. Like the rest of modern literature, including the drama, though so far not the epic, satire is now superior to its ancient counterpart. It now unites all the known graces of which the form is capable; and, as best exemplified in Dorset's poems, it is committed to forgiveness and love and therefore the Christian Dispensation.[10]

*

In the third part of the essay Dryden takes up the satires of Persius and Juvenal, to whose works the 'Discourse' is an introduction, although he also includes in his discussion the satires of Horace, one of his favourites, whose satires, oddly enough, he never translated, except for occasional lines and phrases. He compares and contrasts the three satirists, dwelling mainly on their characteristics, failures and achievements, but returning inevitably to what, it seems, interests him the most: the influence of history and biography on great works of literature.

He rejects the argument of Casaubon that Persius's obscurity and confusion were a deliberate tactic designed to protect the satirist from the wrath of Nero. Perhaps with his own early endeavours in mind, he attributes these faults instead to the poet's 'Youth and Inexperience'.[11] He notes with approval the 'common observation' that Juvenal and Horace each adopted their satiric techniques to the times in which they wrote: Juvenal, living in a desperate age, wrote vitriolic satire; Horace, living in a virtuous age, wrote gentle satire. On the other hand, he is quick to point out that artistic choices, in the final analysis, transcend both time and place. Once again, style is the man. With his 'Commonwealth Genius', Juvenal would have been contemptuous of any government under which he lived. And Horace, 'a well Manner'd Court Slave', would have been gentle and accommodating whatever the provocations or wickedness around him.[12]

In analysing and passing judgment on the three satirists Dryden is guided in every instance by his own first principles but never once loses his splendid detachment. Hence, he dismisses those scholars or critics who, governed by personal interest, are perverse in their taste and so engage in pointless praise and blame:

> It had been much fairer, if the Modern Critiques, who have imbark'd in the Quarrels of their favourite Authors, had rather given to each his proper due; without taking from another's heap, to raise their own ... But to come to particulars: *Heinsius* and *Dacier*, are the most principal of those, who raise *Horace* above *Juvenal* and *Persius. Scaliger* the Father, *Rigaltius,* and many others, debase *Horace*, that they may set up *Juvenal:* And *Casaubon*, who is almost single, throws Dirt on *Juvenal* and *Horace*, that he may exalt *Persius* ...[13]

He 'treat[s] in a new Method, the Comparison betwixt *Horace, Juvenal,* and *Persius*'. That method consists in nothing more than in giving each 'his proper due', in judging each without 'partiality, or prejudice'.[14]

He begins by considering the extent to which the three poets fulfil the demands of all good literature. In 'Versification, and Numbers', 'the greatest Pleasures of Poetry', the 'hobbling' steps of Persius cannot equal the steady 'Amble' of Horace; and in turn Horace's easy 'Amble' cannot keep pace with Juvenal's stately 'Gallop'. Dryden also judges them by the rules which refer specifically to satire. Since satire is 'of the nature of Moral Philosophy', Persius, who is consistent in his teaching, is superior to Horace, who shifts continually from one moral point of view to another; and both are superior to Juvenal, who does not teach but declaims.[15]

What really concerns Dryden, however, is not the ranking of poets by the rules, but the way in which, by breaking long-established rules, poets ('free Spirits') make possible new and better works. Some poets assist in the development of satire by perceiving latent or hidden potentialities within the form itself. Thus, Horace rejected the savageness of his predecessor Lucilius in order to realign satire more closely with Old Comedy, out of which it had originally sprung. But other poets engage in innovation of a far more radical kind. They do not merely develop one or another aspect of satire: they transform it profoundly through an infusion of other literary forms. In expository verse satire a great revolution was effected by Persius and Juvenal, both of whom abandoned the comic muse for the lofty style of epic. In narrative satire transmutations of the genre have been continuous. As Dryden's catalogue of works suggests ('the *Golden Ass* of *Apuleius*', 'the *Encomium Moriæ* of *Erasmus*', '*Mother Hubbard's Tale* in *Spencer*', as well as his own '*Absalom,* and *Mac Fleckno*'), the major practitioners, though sharing certain general principles, have each attempted to make the form anew.[16]

*

The rest of the essay, which is relatively short, is taken up by the fourth and fifth parts. In the fourth, which is a manifesto, addressed as much to his contemporaries as to his literary descendants and heirs, Dryden lays down the rules according to which, in his opinion, all good satire must be written.[17] Satire, he tells us, is a repudiation of vice and, at the same time, a celebration of virtue. It may have originated (among the ancient Romans) in Old Comedy; and it may be either expository or narrative; but it has much in common with what he now considers the noblest of all the genres: the epic. Like the epic, it asserts not only a moral order in nature but also that Divine Providence in which the moral order begins and ends. Hence, although the immediate purpose is entertainment or pleasure, all good satire serves ultimately a moral purpose, a purpose best realized through irony or bold indirectness. Through hyperbole (or the mock heroic) it demonstrates the worst pretensions of vice; through belittlement (or a 'fine Raillery') it demonstrates the utter absurdity. In either case, he would have us understand that, in the moral order, vice can never have any significance and therefore can never be successful. Or, as Yeats says in 'The Four Ages of Man', 'At stroke of midnight God shall win'.

The specific rules which Dryden takes up, and which help set the context of the essay as a whole, reflect an entire lifetime of critical theory and practice. He prefers gentle raillery to vituperation. He prefers satire to lampoon: an attack against a vice to an attack against an individual. He urges a language which is in verse, not prose, and which exhibits smoothness, vigour, clarity and ease. Generalizations about moral good and evil he would have illustrated, and therefore given immediacy, through concrete particulars and contemporary reference. He allows for as much discursiveness as the occasion may dictate, but not so much as may violate the rules governing unity and coherence: every well-constructed satire sets in opposition a single vice and single virtue.[18] He urges, and even insists upon, originality, or at least as much as the poet's genius is capable of; but he also argues that flights of imagination (or excursions into the lively) must be subordinated carefully to the rules of probability, verisimilitude and decorum.

As for his own satires, especially *Absalom and Achitophel* (1681) and *Mac Flecknoe* (1682), which, obviously, his rules are intended both to explain and justify, he is confident that, although he does occasionally nod, his achievements far outweigh his possible failures. True, he may not have written the great epic that he had once hoped to write, but he is certain that, as a satirist, he holds an important place not only in English letters but in the history of Continental literature as well. As he had once suggested that in the drama he had imitated the excellences of his three mighty predecessors, Shakespeare, Fletcher and Jonson,[19] so he now suggests that he has borrowed and combined whatever is best in the works of the great Roman satirists: Horace's banter, Juvenal's elevation and Persius's design. In doing so, he has among the famous satirists of the seventeenth century, either living or dead, only two peers: in England, Dorset; in France, Boileau.[20] Of the many others, especially his countrymen Donne, Cowley and Butler, he has a rather low opinion.

It may perhaps be argued that, because the 'Discourse' is centred on the kind of satire, formal exposition, which he did not write, Dryden's brief account of his own poems, which are Varronian, is a confession that, if he has succeeded, he has done so (to his regret) in an inferior mode: he has failed to write a formal or 'true Satire'. But to argue as much is to pay scant justice to his integrity and to his remarkable powers of discrimination. In one of his satires Juvenal declares the work itself a failure; but, according to Dryden in his headnote to the poem, the statement is not to be taken seriously. No poet, especially a good satirist, creates a body of work which, in published poem or essay, he would flagrantly damn, except of course with tongue in cheek.[21] The 'Discourse' may give a history of the kind of satire that Dryden did not write; but it is also a celebration of the kind, the mock epic, which fired his imagination, which more closely than expository or formal satire approximated the national epic he never wrote, and which (as he knew) he helped to perfect. That in these matters his remarks were sound we have, as our evidence, the enormous influence he was to have on almost every major satirist – Swift, Young, Pope, Fielding, Burns, Lord Byron, Wilde, Shaw, T. S. Eliot – since his death.

The essay concludes with an explanation and justification of Dryden's theory of translation (his reliance on free paraphrase), a theory that was first advanced in the 'Preface to *Ovid's Epistles*' (1680) and was afterwards to be taken up in great detail in the 'Preface to *Fables*'. Only through free paraphrase, he explains, can the modern poet and translator make ancient and foreign works 'intelligible' and 'pleasant' to his contemporaries. In thus declaring his intention and purpose, however, Dryden would have us understand the extent to which his translations in the present volume are original English poems and, in a sense, entirely his own.[22] He may have spent his entire career as satirist writing mock epics. In the present volume he gives to his countrymen a form used very well in antiquity, a form now improved by him and, no less than the mock epic, brought to near perfection.

*

Like the rest of his criticism, the 'Discourse' is a restatement of literary principles and rules which Dryden had deduced from his own works, including not only his satires but also his miscellaneous other poems and his plays. It has, however, a further dimension. Very much more than anything he has so far written, though perhaps not so much as the 'Preface to *Fables*', which he will write and publish several years later, it is (to an extraordinary extent) an *apologia pro vita sua,* a defence of his moral character, albeit one written in the very best of spirits. And it is also an *apologia* in another sense: it defends not so much the man as the poet, and not so much the poet as the work. Roman satirists traditionally began a collection of their poems with a verse commentary on their qualifications for writing satire, together with reflections on satire itself – its nature, its form and purpose, its history and development, as well as its relationship to tragedy and epic. Horace wrote such a poem (*Satires* II.i); Persius wrote one (*Satires* I); so too did Juvenal (*Satires* I).[23] And in the 'Discourse', to show that he follows the Roman example and does very much the same kind of thing, Dryden refers to these works no less than six times.

The *Essay of Dramatick Poesie,* which is about the drama, is a near parody of the contemporary French theatre. The 'Discourse', which is about satire, is itself a kind of satire. It is, in many respects, a formal satire in prose. It confines itself to topics common in Roman satire and it brings them very much up to date. At the same time, it illustrates most of the rules or principles which Dryden would have all modern satirists obey. Despite his excursions into autobiography, biography and encyclopaedic learning, along with encapsulated histories of Western literature, political systems and religion, the language of the essay is never bookish, preten-

John Dryden
Portrait by Sir Godfrey Kneller (*c.* 1698)
(By permission of Trinity College Library, Cambridge)

tious or abstruse. It is the language of a well-bred, well-informed gentleman and man of letters; and despite the seriousness of his purpose, or his exercises in declamation and the grand style, it is, on the whole, light in tone, even conversational and quite relaxed.

The essay gives at times every impression that it is merely discursive and that it follows the idle ruminations of a needlessly self-indulgent temperament. The five-part division is in fact carefully organized and developed. The several parts of the essay fit together remarkably well. They form among themselves a brilliant mosaic, every fragment of which sheds light on, and is informed by, each of the others. The essay touches on an incredible number of very different and seemingly unrelated subjects. But Dryden not only connects them absolutely to one another, he subordinates them all to his principal subject and theme: the nature and function of a specific literary genre.

Throughout the essay, as he asserts Eternal Providence, Dryden holds up to ridicule all those who through ignorance or spiritual pride have fallen into error. They include poets and literary critics, philosophers and statesmen, and secular moralists. He would no doubt forgive them all; and religious man that he is, he grants that he should: '[W]e know, that, in Christian Charity, all Offences are to be forgiven; as we expect the like Pardon for those which we daily commit against Almighty God'.[24] But the flesh is weak, and he cannot easily forget the misguided errors that he feels impelled to correct.

Occasionally, like Juvenal, he may then write with mockery, bitterness and contempt:

> But, good God, how remote they [the 'Lampooners'] are in common Justice, from the choice of such Persons as are the proper Subject of Satire! And how little Wit they bring, for the support of their injustice! The weaker Sex is their most ordinary Theme: And the best and fairest are sure to be the most severely handled. Amongst Men, those who are prosperously unjust, are Intitled to a Panegyrick. But afflicted Virtue is insolently stabb'd with all manner of Reproaches.[25]

More often, like Horace, whose manner he admires, he prefers gentle raillery:

> I answer'd not the *Rehearsall*, because I knew the Author [Buckingham] sate to himself when he drew the Picture, and was the very *Bays* of his own farce...[26]

> True it is, that some bad Poems, though not all, carry their Owners Marks about 'em. There is some peculiar aukardness, false Grammar, imperfect Sense, or at least Obscurity; some Brand or other on this Buttock, or that Ear, that 'tis notorious who are the Owners of the Cattel, though they shou'd not Sign it with their Names.[27]

> If rendring the exact Sense of these Authors ... had been our business, *Barten Holiday* had done it already to our hands: And, by the help of his Learned Notes and Illustrations, not only *Juvenal,* and *Persius,* but what yet is more obscure, his own Verses might be understood.[28]

As the self-appointed vessel of Divine Truth, moreover, Dryden sets forth his many examples of error in the broadest possible context. The context is that of man's fallen nature:

> After God had curs'd *Adam* and *Eve* in Paradise, the Husband and Wife excus'd themselves, by laying the blame on one another; and gave a beginning to those Conjugal Dialogues in Prose; which the Poets have perfected in Verse ...
>
> This Original, I confess, is not much to the Honour of Satire; but here it was Nature, and that deprav'd: When it became an Art, it bore better Fruit.[29]

Dryden had always demonstrated, even in his earliest criticism, a keen sense of humour. During the last twenty years of his life he relied increasingly on a language or rhetoric which was simple, finely polished and direct. With the 'Discourse' these tendencies in his character and manner were very much enhanced, yet never so much as when, in his very last essay, he wrote about and celebrated the one English poet and satirist, Chaucer, whose heir he declared himself to be.

III

In 'Preface to *Fables*' (1700) Dryden again explains his first principles (all of them), again sets them in a broad history of Western literature and again illustrates what he explains. The essay holds to his last period the same relationship that 'Of Heroique Playes' (1672) holds to the first period and 'The Grounds of Criticism' (1679) holds to his second. It is one of the three or four longest of his essays and certainly the most impressive – in some respects one of the most imaginative and one of the most important. It is his last essay: he died shortly after having completed it. It may thus be counted as his last will and literary testament. Although it is a summary of his current opinions, it is also a kaleidoscopic view of almost forty years of literary inquiry, aspiration and achievement. And it is as much a tribute to himself as a tribute and bequest to the new century.

*

In its very conception and execution, as he suggests, the essay reflects surprisingly what elsewhere in the late criticism he either qualifies or condemns: his past interest in both tragi-comedy and heroic play. In the very act of writing the essay, he comments on it, calling our attention directly and indirectly to how (as in his tragi-comedies) he alternates between subjects of high seriousness and those of high and low comedy, and to how (as in his heroic plays) he leaps from one subject to another, returns to subjects taken up momentarily and dropped, weaving together artfully and purposefully the most disparate subjects and seemingly the most unrelated.

From one point of view, the essay is discursive, a quality he finds commendable, even necessary in works of this kind: '[T]he nature of a preface is rambling, never wholly out of the way, nor in it'.[30] From another point of view, it is not. Among the most deliberate of writers, especially in his digressions, he lets us know early on that his apparent maze is not without a plan: '[T]houghts, according to Mr. Hobbes, have always some connection'.[31] He might admit to some exuberance in the development of his themes. But he insists that he has not been as reckless as 'a certain nobleman, who, beginning with a dog-kennel, never lived to finish the palace he had contrived'.[32] And understanding what should come first and what last, he has not begun his work 'where he should have ended it'.[33] Dryden is skilled in his craft. For all its suggestion of waywardness, the essay is beautifully planned.[34]

*

He assumes his two roles, that of literary theorist, that of practising critic; and we can scarcely tell where the one role ends and the other begins. In the opening pages, and intermittently thereafter, he justifies the art and science of translation. It is 'made ... [for those] who understand sense and poetry ... when that poetry and sense is put into words which they understand'. Hence, it is the only means by which 'the greater part' of his 'countrymen' may have 'the same advantage' as enjoyed by the most learned, an advantage otherwise lost to them or unfortunately neglected.[35] He justifies himself as translator. To the dedicated poet a good translation is no less original than perhaps a work of his own invention, although in this matter he may well be wrong: '[L]et the reader judge, and I submit to his decision'.[36] He justifies his mode of translation. He translates as if the dead poet were still very much alive and writing for the present age:

> I have not tied myself to a literal translation; but have often omitted what I judged unnecessary, or not of dignity enough to appear in the company of better thoughts. I have presumed farther in some places, and added somewhat of my own where I thought my author was deficient, and had not given his thoughts their true lustre, for want of words in the beginning of our language.[37]

And he is the more 'emboldened' to change where he will since he recognizes that his foot, too, is in the wheel: 'Another poet, in another age, may take the same liberty with my writing...'[38]

The rest of the preface is an introduction to and commentary on four poets, Homer and Ovid, Boccaccio and Chaucer, all of whom are old favourites and translations from whose works, after arduous labour and much delay, he has at last completed and commits to publication. But that part of the preface is not so much a commentary on four poets as it is a history of Western literature; and as literary history, it verges on being a synoptic guide to poets and playwrights, critics and even philosophers from antiquity through the Middle Ages and the Renaissance to the very year of its composition. Although he is concerned with all kinds of literary excellence, he confines himself to a single genre, that of the poets he discusses: he writes mainly about the epic poem and its many approximations in verse and prose in ancient, medieval and modern allegory and fable, novella and romance.

231

He mounts the battlements. Once more he engages himself in the Quarrel of the Ancients and Moderns, and he takes his customary place. He sides with the Moderns against the Ancients: as history unfolds, mankind becomes more civilized. Truth remains constant, but manners and morals improve; rules remain constant, but literary style and genre are perfected. In his own behalf he nevertheless allows for two exceptions, each apparently based on private judgment and taste. He prefers Homer to Virgil, though the latter wrote after Homer and is obviously the more correct of the two and the more refined:

> [T]his I dare assure the world beforehand, that I have found, by trial, Homer a more pleasing task than Virgil ... For the Grecian is more according to my genius than the Latin poet ... The chief talent of Virgil was propriety of thoughts, and ornament of words: Homer was rapid in his thoughts, and took all the liberties, both of numbers and of expressions, which his language, and the age in which he lived, allowed him.[39]

Ovid wrote 'in the golden age of the Roman tongue'. Boccaccio wrote after 'Dante had begun to file [the Italian] language', and he 'likewise received no little help from his master Petrarch'. Chaucer wrote 'in the dawning of our language': he is 'a rough diamond, and must first be polished ere he shines'.[40] However, Dryden prefers Chaucer to them both. Ovid is 'full' of 'conceits and jingles' and 'glittering trifles', all of which 'in a serious poem ... are nauseous, because they are unnatural'. But 'Chaucer writ with more simplicity, and followed Nature more closely than to use them'.[41] Boccaccio's tales 'were not generally of his own making, but taken from authors of former ages, and by him only modelled'; and Chaucer 'borrowed many tales from the Italian'. But 'the advantage is wholly on Chaucer's side': Chaucer 'has refined on Boccace and has mended the stories which he has borrowed in his way of telling'.[42]

He points out (once again) that there are two kinds of imitation. Poets imitate nature, both human nature and natural law, and they imitate one another. Perhaps because he would further justify himself as translator, he dwells on the second, the kind of imitation by which (he explains) great poets share among themselves a vast network of influences (or cross-references) independent of both time and place. Homer influenced Ovid and Virgil; Virgil influenced Dante, who influenced Petrarch, who influenced Boccaccio, all four of whom in turn influenced Chaucer; and Chaucer influenced Spenser, who influenced Milton, all three of whom (presumably) influenced Dryden himself.

Great poets (himself no doubt included) share among themselves a major literary tradition, in which they are one another's contemporaries, as he is Homer's. The poets within that tradition may even be said to form a 'famil[y]', in which the living and the dead are closely linked, as his soul is linked to Chaucer's soul, just as Spenser's was before him: 'Spenser more than once insinuates that the soul of Chaucer was transfused into his body; and that he was begotten by him two hundred years after his decease'.[43] Because great poets constitute one tradition or family, they may be compared, as he compares Homer with Virgil, Chaucer with

Ovid and Boccaccio, and by implication himself with any and all of the clan. For the same reason, they may be judged – they may be praised and blamed – by the same criteria and by the same rules.

He does not cite Aristotle at all; he mentions Horace and Longinus but only in passing. He no longer requires the support of their great names. In at least matters literary he is in every respect their equal. Or so we are led to infer. He explains that a poem must represent general truth through concrete detail; that in the imitation of nature, whether human nature or natural law, it must imitate what is harmonious and probable; and that it must be based on sound rules of propriety or decorum: it must be based on rules that govern the propriety not only of metre and style but also, in narrative verse, of both characterization and plot (or 'design'). He recognizes that the enjoyment of poetry originates inevitably in beautiful language, although he is quick to add that beautiful language is never enough:

> Words, indeed, like glaring colours, are the first beauties that arise and strike the sight; but if the draught be false or lame, the figures ill disposed, the manners obscure or inconsistent, or the thoughts unnatural, then the finest colours are but daubing, and the piece is a beautiful monster at the best.[44]

Poetry, he grants, must give pleasure; but he is far more concerned with 'some instructive moral' than, perhaps, he has ever been.

With the whole of Western literature as his context, he considers with painstaking care the application of the rules and their violation.[45] In matters literary, notwithstanding an occasional disclaimer, he is both judge and jury. But his classicism is anything but rigid. The rules of classicism may well be 'Nature Methodiz'd', and they must be obeyed. But the great poet achieves excellence beyond any of the rules; and that this should be so no longer surprises him or leaves him in a quandary. He accepts the principle as a fact, inexplicable but given.

He returns again and again to the elements of the 'lively' and the just (or 'judgment') and to their interplay. Once again, as in the *Essay of Dramatick Poesie*, he allows for their separation. But as in 'The Grounds of Criticism in Tragedy', he clearly prefers that they be treated as extensions or aspects of each other. In the best poetry the probable is always made to seem wonderful, the wonderful always made to seem probable; characters embody, though each in his own way, opposing faculties in human nature, as well as opposing 'humours'. Language is simultaneously both simple and 'metaphorical'; pleasure is by necessity morally instructive. In the best poetry, moreover, poets realize their twofold purpose – pleasure through instruction, instruction through pleasure – by means of words and 'fables' (or examples) that reflect ideally values both aristocratic and Christian and, at the same time, their own capacity for noble thought and feeling.

*

The essay is divided into six parts: an introduction, in which Dryden explains his 'present undertaking'; a conclusion, in which he defends what he has at last completed; and four long middle sections, which he arranges and develops more or less chronologically, in each of which he concentrates on the work he has rendered 'into modern English' and includes in the present volume. For each author that he considers he gives biographical detail. For each work that he considers he gives something of its historical context. He also analyses and interprets the work, evaluates and judges it, quoting or paraphrasing it where necessary, commenting on its possible sources and analogues, illustrating in what way it is or is not an improvement on a likely original.

Cosmopolitan though he may be in his outlook, European though he no doubt is in his vision and the breadth of his learning, Dryden is first and foremost a loyal and devoted Englishman. He is 'studious to promote the honour of [his] native country'; he would save from neglect where he can 'the fame and memory' of the first major English poet.[46] Hence, both literally and symbolically he places Chaucer, along with *The Canterbury Tales,* at the very centre of the preface, and he there allows him more space – more than half the essay – than he allows anyone else.

Chaucer is, according to Dryden, 'the father of English poetry'; and 'from [him] the purity of the English tongue began'. He gives the salient facts in Chaucer's life, and emphasizes those facts which suggest parallels with his own. He thus dwells mainly on Chaucer's service to church and state, his immediate contacts with the monarchy and the royal court, and his 'little bias towards the opinions of Wickliff'.[47] He writes with affection about Chaucer's personality and character, even with admiration:

> He is a perpetual fountain of good sense ...[48]

> He must have been a man of a most wonderful comprehensive nature ...[49]

> I found I had a soul congenial to his ...[50]

> [No] man ever had, or can have, a greater veneration for Chaucer than myself.[51]

He explains and illustrates the relationship between Chaucer's life and his works, between his works and the age in which he lived, insisting that Chaucer's failures as a poet were due to the barbarism of the age, his achievements the result solely of his personality, imagination, and genius.

Where Chaucer violates the rules, or at least those he deems essential to good writing, Dryden is rather severe. He lists the faults, one at a time; and in no uncertain terms he disapproves of them all. Chaucer's verse is 'not harmonious' (Dryden fails to recognize that in Chaucer's pentameters a final 'e' is an unstressed syllable):

> I cannot go so far as he who published the last edition of him; for he would make us believe the fault is in our ears, and that there were really ten syllables in a verse where we find but nine ... It were an easy matter to produce some thousands of his verses which are lame for want of half a foot, and sometimes a whole one, and which no pronunciation can make otherwise.[52]

His language suffers from 'redundancy'; his vocabulary is not, in every instance, adequate for his purpose: '[I]n some places ... my author was deficient, and had not given his thoughts their true lustre, for want of words in the beginning of our language'.[53] Some of his pilgrims are 'vicious'; some are 'licentious', even 'obscene'. His stories are not always well constructed:

> I deny not ... that, living in our early days of poetry, he writes not always of a piece; but sometimes mingles trivial things with those of greater moment. Sometimes also, though not often, he runs riot, like Ovid, and knows not when he has said enough.[54]

Still, Dryden comes not to blame Chaucer, but to praise him. Where Chaucer violates rules that are not especially important, Dryden passes over the entire issue quickly, or he remains tactfully and completely silent. Where Chaucer violates the most important rules, and where the violations are perhaps flagrant, Dryden finds mitigating circumstances; he counterbalances failure with achievement; and he suggests that disapproval be tempered with charity and forgiveness. Where Chaucer has been unjustly condemned 'for inveighing ... against the vices of clergy', Dryden rushes to the defence: an attack against a corrupt clergyman is an attack against the man, not 'the dignity of his order'. Besides, 'A satirical poet is the check of the laymen on bad priests'.[55]

Though Chaucer could not possibly have known about or have read the *Poetics* or the *Art of Poetry* or *On the Sublime*, and though he obviously could not have foreseen the 'Preface to *Fables*', Dryden claims not only that he knew the rules intuitively but also that, on the whole, he used them both wisely and well. Many of his verses 'consist of ten syllables'; and all the rest have 'the ... sweetness of a Scotch tune ...', which is natural and pleasing'.[56] His language has a 'wonderful facility and clearness'. His pilgrims – their 'manners' and 'passions', 'their humours, their features, and their very dress' – are fully realized: 'I see ... before me ... all the Pilgrims in the *Canterbury Tales* ... as distinctly as if I had supped with them at the Tabard in Southwark'.[57] Most of his stories are remarkably well constructed: they have unity and coherence, development and emphasis. In his handling of decorum, he is in many things above reproach:

> All his pilgrims are severally distinguished from each other ... The matter and manner of their tales, and of their telling, are so suited to their different educations, humours, and callings, that each of them would be improper in any other mouth. Even the grave and serious characters are distinguished by their several sorts of gravity: their discourses are such as belong to their age, their calling, and their breeding; such as are becoming of them, and of them only.[58]

Chaucer never ceases to delight and give pleasure. His moral instruction is precisely and admirably what it should be, and it is never obtrusive. In short, at his very best, as in 'The Knight's Tale', Chaucer is almost the equal of not only Virgil but Homer as well:

> I prefer in our countryman, far above all his other stories, the noble poem
> of *Palamon and Arcite*, which is of the epic kind, and perhaps not much
> inferior to the *Ilias* or the *Æneis:* the story is more pleasing than either of
> them, the manners as perfect, the diction as poetical, the learning as deep
> and various, and the disposition full as artful ... [59]

Chaucer sets opposing elements of the lively and the just in a proper balance
or reconciliation with each other. As if he had in fact read Longinus, he treats them
as if they were also aspects of each other and each other's extension. In the same
work he subordinates metaphor to 'simplicity' of statement; and his metaphors are
always apt. He centres in the same character emotion and reason, vice and virtue,
the general and the particular. As in 'The Wife of Bath's Tale', he makes the
wonderful probable, the probable wonderful. And in the fusion of pleasure and
instruction he compels us to recognize in ourselves the vices we laugh at in others,
to recognize in others and to emulate the virtues to which we ourselves aspire.

Though he borrowed much from his contemporaries and predecessors, Chaucer
is one of the most 'original' of poets and one of the most 'inventive'. 'As he knew
what to say, so he knows also when to leave off...' He 'followed Nature everywhere; but was never so bold to go beyond her...'[60] Though he occasionally
violates the rules, including those of a strict decorum, he frequently transcends
them. And he does so never more successfully, never more 'wonderful[ly]', than
when in his 'General Prologue' he represents general human nature through the
concrete particulars of individual men and women. '[H]ere', declares Dryden, 'is
God's plenty':

> [T]here is such a variety of game springing up before me that I am dis-
> tracted in my choice, and know not which to follow ... We have our fore-
> fathers and great-grand-dames all before us, as they were in Chaucer's
> days: their general characters are still remaining in mankind, and even in
> England, though they are called by other names than those of Monks, and
> Friars, and Canons, and Lady Abbesses, and Nuns ...[61]

*

Throughout the preface, as he discusses other poets, Dryden turns to a discussion
of himself. He writes about his own life and works; and he employs the same critical
method. He takes up 'this my present work'. He thinks it is 'equal' to his other
works. But of his own endeavours 'an author is the most improper judge'; and he
will 'therefore ... leave [it] wholly to the mercy of the reader'.[62] For whatever faults
the 'present work' does have he will 'ask no grains of allowance ... but those which
are given of course to human frailty'.[63] Authors 'who think too well of their own
performances' write prefaces in which first and last they excuse what they have failed
to accomplish: 'They ... are apt to boast ... how little time their own works have cost
them, and what other business of more importance interfered ...'[64] He finds the
practice unseemly, even 'despicable'; and he will have none of it.

As a critic, he may now and again hold an opinion which others do not share;
but he would impose it on no one: '[T]he readers are the jury, and their privilege

remains entire to decide according to the merits of the cause: or, if they please, to bring it to another hearing before some other court'.[65] As a translator, he 'must grant that something must be lost in all transfusion, that is, in all translations; but the sense will remain, which would otherwise be lost, or at the least be ... scarce intelligible, and that but to a few'.[66] If in his translations of Chaucer he has 'altered him anywhere for the better', he 'must at the same time acknowledge' that he 'could have done nothing without him: *facile est inventis addere* [it is easy to add to what is already invented] is no great commendation; and I am not so vain to think I have deserved a greater'.[67] He is also convinced that a good translation 'is not the talent of every poet'; and he 'may say, without vanity' that, as a translator of Virgil and Ovid, he has not so far been surpassed.[68] As a playwright, he is at the very least as good as Fletcher; as a poet, he has inherited the 'laurel' from Chaucer.[69]

In his present collection he has done his best to write 'nothing which savours of immorality or profaneness' or anything 'which shocks religion or good manners'. If he has not always succeeded, he has failed only through 'inadvertency'.[70] In the past, he admits, some of his 'thoughts and expressions' have not been what they should be: they 'can be truly argued of obscenity, profaneness, or immorality'. But he has made his amends: 'I have pleaded guilty ... and retract them'.[71] Unfortunately, he has enemies: 'such men ... have written scurrilously against me without any provocation'.[72] They have attacked him whenever and wherever they could: '[M]y enemies ... are so far from granting me to be a good poet that they will not allow me so much as to be a Christian, or a moral man ...'[73] His enemies have gone out of their way to accuse him 'wrongfully': '[They have] perverted my meanings by [their] glosses, and interpreted my words into blasphemy and bawdry of which [the words] were not guilty'.[74]

He names his friends and admirers, and he praises them. He names his enemies and detractors, and he strikes back, but in a manner which defies retaliation and disarms it. In 'A Discourse concerning ... Satire' he had argued that the most effective satirist relies not on the bludgeon but the pinprick, not on invective but on raillery:

> How easie it is to call Rogue and Villain, and that wittily! But how hard to make a Man appear a Fool, a Blockhead, or a Knave, without using any of those opprobrious terms! ... Neither is it true, that this fineness of Raillery is offensive. A witty man is tickl'd while he is hurt in this manner; and a Fool feels it not. The occasion of an Offence may possibly be given, but he cannot take it. If it be granted that in effect this way does more Mischief; that a Man is secretly wounded, and though he be not sensible himself, yet the malicious World will find it for him: Yet there is still a vast difference betwixt the slovenly Butchering of a Man, and the fineness of a stroke that separates the Head from the Body, and leaves it standing in its place.[75]

Towards the end of the preface, as he actually lists his enemies, he takes his own best advice:

> His ... [Luke Milbourne's] translations of Virgil have answered his criti-
> cisms on mine ... I am satisfied ... that, while he and I live together, I shall
> not be thought the worst poet of the age.[76]

> I will deal the more civilly with his [Sir Richard Blackmore's] two poems,
> because nothing ill is to be spoken of the dead: and therefore peace be
> to the Manes of his *Arthurs*.[77]

> [H]e [Jeremy Collier] is too much given to horse-play ... and comes to
> battle like a dictator from the plow. I will not say, *The zeal of God's house
> has eaten him up;* but I am sure it has devoured some part of his good
> manners and civility.[78]

Here, in the last paragraphs of his last essay, written shortly before his death,
Dryden laughs at his enemies, reduces them to absurdity absolute, and has a
glorious time of it.

Early in the preface, he contemplates the present moment. He is an old man;
and his health has not been good. But he still has his wits about him. In a passage
that recalls his first essay, he surveys his mental powers. He finds they are what they
have always been, and with one possible exception even better:

> I think myself as vigorous as ever in the faculties of my soul, excepting
> only my memory, which is not impaired to any great degree; and if I lose
> not more of it, I have no great reason to complain. What judgment I had,
> increases rather than diminishes; and thoughts, such as they are, come
> crowding in so fast upon me that my only difficulty is to choose or to
> reject, to run them into verse or to give them the other harmony of
> prose ...[79]

Immediately thereafter, he celebrates the kind of criticism and translation to which,
through much of his life, he has committed himself, samplings of which he includes
in this his latest work. At the same time, he celebrates the kind of poetry and plays
to which, through most of his life, he has also committed himself, samplings of
which ('some original papers of my own') he includes with his translations from
Homer, Ovid, Boccaccio and Chaucer.

More significantly, as a statement of first principles, the preface as a whole bears
the whole stamp of his personality and genius. It is easygoing but self-confident,
good-humoured and firm, learned but graceful, stunning in its flexibility, exhila-
rating in its intelligence and good sense. It is the kind of essay or criticism which,
in the present age, our structuralists, deconstructionists, post-structuralists,
hermeneuticists, and semioticians would do well to read and study and take to
heart.

PART IV
A summing up

CHAPTER FIFTEEN

Evaluations

I

In passing judgment on his own poetry, or on the poetry of other authors both past and present, Dryden is remarkably sound: history has proved as much. He is no less sound when towards the end of his career he at last evaluates his criticism. In a dedication addressed to the Earl of Dorset, which he published in 1693, seven years before his death, Dryden looks back on a lifetime of achievement; and he concludes that, among English authors before him, there were no critics of any merit and there was no clearly defined body of criticism. So far as criticism in England is concerned, he is the 'Draw[er] ... of ... [the] Art'.[1] But he is not only the inventor of English criticism: he is the one who has clearly defined, for critics and poets alike, the very tradition, as well as the governing principles and rules, of literary excellence.

In reflecting on his achievement, he gives us no details; but he does not have to. He tells us that the 'Out-Lines' of his criticism are set forth quite fully in the *Essay of Dramatick Poesie* (1668); and we know at once what he has in mind. Whatever help they may derive from the ancient Greeks and Romans or from the modern French, as he explains throughout the *Essay* and frequently demonstrates, English poets and critics must now accept as theirs a literary tradition that combines the opposing native tendencies, the Shakespearean and the Jonsonian. They must maintain a proper distinction among literary genres, though preferring always the higher genres – epic poem and serious drama – to any of the others. They must never forget what excellence in literature is and 'ought to be'; it is '*A just and lively Image of Humane Nature ... for the Delight and Instruction of Mankind*'. And whatever importance they may perhaps give to the 'rules of the Ancients', 'those rules which the French observe', and 'the old Rule[s] of Logick', or even to 'the punishment of Vice, and the reward of Virtue', 'the nearest imitation of Nature', and 'verisimility' or 'the liklihood of truth', they must give priority to 'the hand of Art'. As for 'the hand of Art', it begins and ends with 'the soul of man' and 'the Soul of Poesie'. It begins and ends with 'variety and copiousness', with 'sweetness' and 'the chiefest graces', with 'the greatest beauty ... [and] magnificence' and 'the greatest pleasure of the Audience', and always of course with 'a ... pleasant way of writing', albeit through a 'Language ... arriv'd to its highest perfection', a 'Language ... noble, full, and significant'.

Dryden's late evaluation of himself as critic is worth quoting at some length. It is written in the best of his late manner. It is written with ease and intelligence and with what he himself might have called 'elegancy', 'majesty' and 'grace'. 'When', he explains to the Earl of Dorset,

I was my self, in the Rudiments of my Poetry, without Name, or Reputation in the World, having rather the Ambition of a Writer, than the skill; when I was Drawing the Out-Lines of an Art without any Living Master to Instruct me in it; an Art which had been better Practis'd than Study'd here in *England,* wherein *Shakespear* who Created the Stage among us, had rather Written happily, than knowingly and justly; and *Johnson,* who by studying *Horace,* had been acquainted with the Rules, yet seem'd to envy to Posterity that Knowledge, and like an Inventer of some useful Art, to make a Monopoly of his Learning: When thus, as I may say, before the use of the Loadstone, or knowledge of the Compass, I was sailing in a vast Ocean, without other help, than the Pole-Star of the Ancients, and the Rules of the French Stage amongst the Moderns, which are extreamly different from ours, by reason of their opposite taste; yet even then, I had the presumption to Dedicate to your Lordship: A very unfinish'd Piece, I must Confess, and which only can be excus'd, by the little Experience of the Author, and the Modesty of the Title, *An Essay.*[2]

*

In passing a late judgment on himself as critic, Dryden considered only his contribution to literary theory. If we examine his criticism more broadly, however, we can discern that it is composed of two aspects or layers. On the one hand, he attempted to establish an objective aesthetic standard, consisting of a system of rules, a history of forms and analyses of traditions. On the other hand, he attempted also to evaluate specific texts – those written by other poets, but chiefly those written by himself.[3] If we would determine how successful he was in performing each of these related tasks – the theoretical and the practical – , we can do no better than to consult the 'Life of Dryden' (1779) by Samuel Johnson, the next great critic in England. Despite certain qualifications, and despite his repudiation of the self-criticism, Johnson nonetheless agreed with Dryden's own estimate of himself as poet, translator and critic.

II

'Johnson was', according to James and Helen Kinsley, 'the first ... to write of Dryden's work on a level comparable with that of Dryden himself'. The statements about the criticism occupy only a modest portion of the 'Life'. But, as the Kinsleys observe, they are 'the first substantial and objective account of Dryden's essays'.[4] And they have had, in fact, a tremendous influence. For more than two centuries they have given verdicts on the criticism not only their shape but their direction as well. Much in the criticism, however, Johnson frankly and avowedly dislikes; and whole portions of it he ignores. He says little about Dryden's interest in extending the frontiers of poetry, or of his attempt to reconcile opposing traditions, or of the total interconnections between the poetry and the criticism and between the practical criticism and the critical theory. His observations remain nevertheless penetrating, comprehensive and essentially sympathetic.

When he takes up the practical criticism, Johnson not infrequently condemns it in terms that are essentially those of the Christian moralist. He sees much to disapprove of whether Dryden is discussing his own work or the work of others. In the self-criticism he finds a moral failing in almost every statement of praise or defence. It is true that his repugnance disappears when, as he reminds us, he is thrown under enchantment by the very prose in which these faults appear. Moral judgment then seems less urgent: 'Every thing is excused by the play of images and the spriteliness of expression'.[5] But his indignation returns whenever he contemplates the lapses in and of themselves. He then points to what he takes to be only egotism; and he is appalled:

> He is always angry at some past, or afraid of some future censure; but he lessens the smart of his wounds by the balm of his own approbation, and endeavours to repel the shafts of criticism by opposing a shield of adamantine confidence.[6]

He likes no better the judgments which, as practical critic, Dryden passes on his contemporaries and rivals. Here again Johnson finds egoism; and he is again the Christian moralist. In assaulting other critics Dryden behaves no better than a common hack:

> To his cricticks he is sometimes contemptuous, sometimes resentful, and sometimes submissive. The writer who thinks his works formed for duration mistakes his interest when he mentions his enemies ... From this principle Dryden did not oft depart; his complaints are for the greater part general; he seldom pollutes his page with an adverse name. He condescended indeed to a controversy with Settle, in which he perhaps may be considered rather as assaulting than repelling; and since Settle is sunk into oblivion, his libel remains injurious only to himself.[7]

In Dryden's comments on poets long dead – on those who are not rivals of the moment – Johnson finds nothing with which he can possibly disagree. Dryden is entirely detached; and Johnson has only praise. Thus, in commenting on the *Essay of Dramatick Poesie,* he singles out the portrait of Shakespeare as an example of the critical sublime:

> The account of Shakespeare may stand as a perpetual model of encomiastick criticism ... The praise lavished by Longinus, on the attestation of the heroes of Marathon by Demosthenes, fades away before it. In a few lines is exhibited a character, so extensive in its comprehension and so curious in its limitations, that nothing can be added, diminished, or reformed; nor can the editors and admirers of Shakespeare, in all their emulation of reverence, boast of much more than of having diffused and paraphrased this epitome of excellence ...[8]

As he distinguishes between the two kinds of practical criticism, the good and the bad, so Johnson distinguishes between the two very different kinds of literary theory. There is the theory that Dryden concocted merely to explain away or to justify his own worst failings:

When he has any objection to obviate, or any license to defend, he is not very scrupulous about what he asserts, nor very cautious, if the present purpose be served, not to entangle himself in his own sophistries.[9]

But there is a portion of the critical theory which, according to Johnson, is completely independent of personal requirement or need; and for this theoretical criticism his esteem is unbounded. He holds its 'general precepts' to be beyond reproach, since they have their foundation in 'the nature of things and the structure of the human mind'.[10] Moreover, he thinks that, as a body of work, it is endowed with the mark of all great theory. It overwhelms the reader with its energy, brilliance, learning and range.[11]

Johnson's 'Life' too has its enchantments. And for the student of Dryden nothing fascinates more than the extent to which Johnson echoes the criticism, both the first principles which he may fail to identify or name and the literary judgments which he sometimes accepts but more often condemns.[12] Johnson may say nothing about Dryden's continual preoccupation with fancy and judgment and hence with the lively and the just. But no sooner does he celebrate what he most admires in the essays than he explains that, to a language of statement, which is always correct, graceful and clear, Dryden adds nobility and imaginative sweep:

They have not the formality of a settled style, in which the first half of the sentence betrays the other. The clauses are never balanced, nor the periods modelled; every word seems to drop by chance, though it falls into its proper place. Nothing is cold or languid; the whole is airy, animated, and vigorous: what is little is gay; what is great is splendid.[13]

Johnson is clearly disturbed by Dryden's self-criticism, but not inevitably and not consistently. He may indeed disapprove of Dryden's insistence upon his many achievements as poet, translator and critic. In almost every instance, as he continually reminds us, he finds an example of moral failure: again and again he accuses Dryden of egoism and spiritual pride. Yet that disapproval, however vehement, is centred inevitably in a twofold paradox; and in both of its aspects the paradox disarms judgment. On the one hand, Johnson's own achievements as both critic and poet have their obvious parallels, even no doubt their origins, in Dryden's practice and first principles; and it has long been recognized that, throughout the 'Life', Johnson's language often recapitulates that of Dryden's criticism at its most characteristic and its very best. On the other hand, when he praises Dryden, though the fact has so far been either neglected or ignored, Johnson employs the same terms, often the very same forms of expression, as those which in their original context he outright condemns. He actually summarizes or paraphrases Dryden, and, on occasion, he even echoes the criticism word for word. He moreover does these things without any suggestion that, in spite of himself, he must accept as completely valid Dryden's glowing estimate of himself and of his importance in the history and development of English literature.[14]

How or why Johnson does what he does we cannot determine with certainty. We cannot believe that, without acknowledgement, he would knowingly set down as his own another writer's illuminating comments: elsewhere he is scrupulous in tagging what he borrows. Nor would he expect the fact of paraphrase or summary to be readily apparent. Edmond Malone first projected his edition of Dryden's prose in 1791. On the difficulty of acquiring Dryden's essays in the late eighteenth century he is instructive:

> In making, therefore, this Collection of his [Dryden's] Critical and Miscellaneous Essays, which are found dispersed in a great variety of books, many of them now not easily to be procured, I trust that, while I have done an acceptable service to good letters and to the publick, I have at the same time in some degree contributed to the fame of the author; a considerable portion of whose valuable writings will thus become accessible and familiar to a more numerous class of readers than the votaries of the Muses ...[15]

Before Malone's edition of 1800 the essays of Dryden were not easily available; and Johnson would not therefore assume in his readers an easy recognition of Dryden's prose.

At the same time, the parallels are too numerous, extended and exact to be the product of Johnson's independent judgment or to be derived by him from eighteenth-century literary commonplace. We have no choice but to infer that, quite simply, he relies on what he has forgotten having read: he relies on what we now call unconscious memory.[16] We are left with the further surmise that, independently of what he may praise or blame, he has been influenced by Dryden's criticism far more than even he can know.

In the 'Preface to *Fables Ancient and Modern*' (1700), as we have seen, Dryden again draws a self-portrait, this one his last; and like the many others, brief though it is, it too may be called a literary character. At one point, among other things, he reviews in arresting detail the whole of his imaginative life, especially when he is engaged in the act of creation: '[T]houghts, such as they are, come crowding in so fast upon me that my only difficulty is to choose or to reject ...'[17] Johnson gladly accepts the observation and gladly makes it his own. He applauds Dryden for his insight; and he repeats the passage twice, once in almost a direct quotation: 'He [Dryden] certainly wanted neither sentiments nor language; his intellectual treasures were great ... "His thoughts", when he wrote, "flowed in upon him so fast, that his only care was which to use, and which to reject".'[18] Many pages later, he repeats Dryden's statement, though now in what amounts to a very close paraphrase: 'When once he had engaged himself in disputation, thoughts flowed in on either side: he was now no longer at a loss; he had always objections and solutions at command ...'[19]

Johnson here accepts Dryden's statement about himself, no doubt, for a number of reasons. It is a truth with which, in all candour, he is in total agreement; it is made in the most general and impersonal manner; it carries with it no undercurrents of self-centredness or artful boast. More striking, however, is the fact that, when actually paraphrasing Dryden, Johnson does seem quite unaware that he is doing so. We may therefore hazard a guess. Dryden's criticism has so thoroughly become a part of him that, through unconscious memory, he continually feels impelled to paraphrase it or, at any rate, to think in terms of it. Johnson may, as a result, accept what upon deliberation he prefers to condemn. He may repeat even Dryden's praise of himself; and he may repeat that praise without the intervention of a moral censor.

Johnson echoes the self-criticism when he speaks of individual poems and plays. He echoes it again when he explains Dryden's role in the development of English poetry. This is Dryden, commenting on his translation of Virgil, then on the rest of his work:

> For, what I have done [the *Virgil*], Imperfect as it is, for want of Health and leisure to Correct it, will be judg'd in after Ages, and possibly in the present, to be no dishonour to my Native Country; whose Language and Poetry wou'd be more esteem'd abroad, if they were better understood. Somewhat (give me leave to say) I have added to both of them in the choice of Words, and Harmony of Numbers which were wanting, especially the last, in all our Poets, even in those who being endu'd with Genius, yet have not Cultivated their Mother-Tongue with sufficient Care; or relying on the Beauty of their Thoughts, have judg'd the Ornament of Words, and sweetness of Sound unnecessary.[20]

This is Johnson:

> [T]he veneration with which his name is pronounced by every cultivator of English literature is paid to him as he refined the language, improved the sentiments, and tuned the numbers of English Poetry.[21]

In discussing the verse, Dryden and Johnson differ chiefly on how many achievements they allow. Dryden takes up three subjects ('Words', 'Numbers', 'Thoughts') and makes claims for himself in just two. Albeit with a slight change in vocabulary ('language' for 'Words', 'sentiments' for 'Thoughts'), Johnson takes up the same subjects and advances claims for Dryden in all three.

Johnson could not be more laudatory than he is; but not unexpectedly he adds, a qualification in his next paragraph. Dryden boasts of a solitary effort: he brought about a revolution in prosody entirely on his own. With a surer grasp of literary history, Johnson knows better. He points out that the 'new versification, as it was then called', had first appeared some decades before Dryden even began to write:

> After about half a century of forced thoughts and rugged metre some advances towards nature and harmony had been already made by Waller and Denham; they had shewn that long discourses in rhyme grew more pleasing when they were broken into couplets, and that verse consisted not only in the number but the arrangement of syllables.[22]

Whatever his originality as a poet, in other words, Dryden could not escape the direct influence of his immediate predecessors; and in pointing specifically to Waller and Denham Johnson is merely repeating what, by the middle of the eighteenth century, had become a widely accepted commonplace. That commonplace, however, as far as can be determined, had its very origin in an observation first made by Dryden himself:

> [T]he Excellence and Dignity of ... [rhyme], were never fully known till Mr. *Waller* taught it; He first made Writing easily an Art: First shew'd us to conclude the Sense, most commonly, in Distichs; which in the Verse of those before him, runs on for so many Lines together, that the Reader is out of Breath to overtake it. This sweetness of Mr. *Wallers* Lyrick Poesie was afterwards follow'd in the Epick by Sir *John Denham* ...[23]

Dryden mentions his debt to other poets in the dedication of *The Rival Ladies*, published in 1664; his contributions to English poetry in the 'Postscript to the Reader', published with the *Virgil* thirty-two years later. Johnson of course knew both works remarkably well. Whether by conscious design or unconscious recall, he sets Dryden's two statements in wonderful juxtaposition with each other. Whether knowingly or not, he allows the younger Dryden to amend tacitly a lapse made by his older and much more confident self.

From the poetry Johnson turns to the translations, though not so much to the practice as to the theory on which the practice is based. He begins with the argument which Dryden expounds in the 'Preface to *Ovid's Epistles*' (1680). Johnson makes it perfectly clear that without qualification he accepts the theory, the whole of it, and that he cannot but admire Dryden for both his learning and his common sense. He paraphrases the theory very closely, following Dryden's argument concept for concept, detail for detail. And he fully acknowledges what he borrows. He frankly admits his debt. This is Dryden:

> No man is capable of Translating Poetry, who besides a Genius to that Art, is not a Master both of his Authours Language, and of his own: Nor must we understand the Language only of the Poet, but his particular turn of Thoughts, and of Expression, which are the Characters that distinguish, and as it were individuate him from all other writers ... The like Care must be taken of the more outward Ornaments, the Words: when they appear (which is but seldom) litterally graceful, it were an injury to the Authour that they should be chang'd: But since every Language is so full of its own proprieties, that what is Beautiful in one, is often Barbarous, nay sometimes Nonsence in another, it would be unreasonable to limit a Translator to the narrow compass of his Authours words: 'tis enough if he choose out some Expression which does not vitiate the Sense ... The sence of an Authour, generally speaking, is to be Sacred and inviolable. If the Fancy of *Ovid* be luxuriant, 'tis his Character to be so, and if I retrench it, he is no longer *Ovid*. It will be replyed that he receives advantage by this lopping of his superfluous branches, but I rejoyn that a Translator has no such Right ... [24]

Here is Johnson:

> When languages are formed upon different principles, it is impossible that the same modes of expression should always be elegant in both. While

247

they run on together the closest translation may be considered as the best; but when they divaricate each must take its natural course. Where correspondence cannot be obtained it is necessary to be content with something equivalent. 'Translation therefore', says Dryden, 'is not so loose as paraphrase, nor so close as metaphrase'.

All polished languages have different styles: the concise, the diffuse, the lofty, and the humble. In the proper choice of style consists the resemblance which Dryden principally exacts from the translator. He is to exhibit his author's thoughts in such a dress of diction as the author would have given them, had his language been English: rugged magnificence is not to be softened; hyperbolical ostentation is not to be repressed, nor sententious affectation to have its points blunted. A translator is to be like his author: it is not his business to excel him.[25]

Johnson's divergence from the passage which he otherwise follows very closely is slight, though not irrelevant. It demonstrates the extent to which he is wholly immersed in his subject. His remark on 'paraphrase ... [and] metaphrase', which we are to take as a quotation, is based not upon the 'Preface to *Ovid's Epistles*', but on a memorable sentence from the dedication of the *Æneis* (1697): 'The way I have taken, is not so strait as Metaphrase, nor so loose as Paraphrase'.[26] His remark on 'a dress of diction' is based on another sentence from the same work: 'I have endeavour'd to make *Virgil* speak such *English,* as he wou'd himself have spoken, if he had been born in *England* ...'[27] It is worth noting that, by including in a paraphrase of the Ovid essay statements from the *Æneis* essay, published seventeen years later, Johnson ignores significant differences between the two works. In the *Æneis* essay Dryden locates his own translation, which modernizes the ancient text, in the middle ground between a literal translation and a paraphrase. In the Ovid essay he insists that a good translation, which retains an author's idiosyncrasies, must occupy the middle ground between a literal translation and a free imitation. Johnson departs from one essay only to paraphrase another.

In his treatment of Dryden as translator nothing is more striking than that, in praising Dryden, Johnson uses the same language, including the same turns of phrase and even the same literary and historical references as those which Dryden uses (again in the 'Preface to *Ovid's Epistles*') when unabashedly he praises his own theory. But now there is no acknowledgment of a borrowing or of a debt; and none seems to be implied. Here is Dryden:

All Translation I suppose may be reduced to ... three heads:
First, that of Metaphrase, or turning an Authour word by word, and Line by Line, from one Language into another ... [T]he Verbal Copyer is incumber'd with so many difficulties at once, that he can never disentangle himself from all ... We see *Ben. Johnson* could not avoid obscurity in his literal translation of *Horace* ...
The consideration of these difficulties, in a servile, literal Translation, not long since made two of our famous Wits, *Sir John Denham,* and *Mr. Cowley* to contrive another way of turning Authours into our Tongue, call'd by the latter of them, *Imitation* ... Imitation and verbal Version are

in my Opinion the two Extreams, which ought to be avoided: and therefore ... I have propos'd the mean betwixt them ... [28]

Here is Johnson:

> Ben Jonson thought it necessary to copy Horace almost word by word;
> Feltham, his contemporary and adversary, considers it as indispensably
> requisite in a translation to give line for line. It is said that Sandys, whom
> Dryden called the best versifier of the last age, has struggled hard to
> comprise every book of his English *Metamorphoses* in the same number of
> verses with the original. Holyday had nothing in view but to shew that he
> understood his author, with so little regard to the grandeur of his diction,
> or the volubility of his numbers, that his metres can hardly be called verses;
> they cannot be read without reluctance, nor will the labour always be
> rewarded by understanding them. Cowley saw that such 'copyers' were a
> 'servile race'; he asserted his liberty, and spread his wings so boldly that he
> left his authors. It was reserved for Dryden to fix the limits of poetical lib-
> erty, and give us just rules and examples of translation.[29]

Close though his summary of the preface may be, Johnson once more diverges
from the text he is recasting. And he demonstrates further his complete immersion
in his subject. His reference to Owen Felltham (or 'Feltham') may be his own; but
his remarks on Barten Holyday and George Sandys have their counterparts elsewhere in Dryden. In all likelihood, the reference to Holyday's obscurity and to his
failure in 'diction ... [and] numbers' he borrows through unconscious memory from
another work, the 'Discourse concerning ... Satire' (1693):

> But *Holiday,* without considering that he Writ with the disadvantage of
> Four Syllables less in every Verse, endeavours to make one of his Lines, to
> comprehend the Sense of one of *Juvenal's*[.] According to the falsity of
> the Proposition, was the Success. He was forc'd to crowd his Verse with ill
> sounding Monosyllables ...: And by that means he arriv'd at his Pedantick
> end, which was to make a literal Translation: His Verses have nothing of
> Verse in them, but only the worst part of it, the Rhyme: And that, into the
> bargain, is far from good. But which is more Intollerable,... the very Sense
> which he endeavours to explain, is become more obscure, than that of his
> Author. So that *Holiday* himself cannot be understood ...[30]

The reference to Sandys has a more complex origin. It is a composite of three
separate observations: two from Dryden, one favourable, the other unfavourable;
and one, unfavourable, from Abraham Cowley. The statement that, according to
Dryden, Sandys is 'the best versifier of the last age' Johnson takes directly from the
'Preface to *Fables*' (1700), though with a change in a single word: 'He who has
arrived nearest to it [a good translation of Ovid], is the ingenious and learned
Sandys[,] the best versifier of the former [not the 'last'] age ...'[31] He would, however, refute Dryden. And in support of his position he cites as his authority Cowley,
for whom, along with Holyday, Sandys was a member of a 'servile race'.[32] Admit-
tedly, Johnson and Dryden are, at this point, as far apart as they can possibly be.

But it is worth mentioning that Johnson's position is one which Dryden had originally accepted, though it was later rejected, and which he had stated rather fully in the dedication of *Examen poeticum* (1693):

> [I]f it [paraphrase] be a Fault, 'tis much more pardonable, than that of those, who run into the other extream, of a litteral, and close Translation, where the Poet is confin'd so streightly to his Author's Words, that he wants elbow-room, to express his Elegancies. He leaves him obscure; he leaves him Prose, where he found him Verse. And no better than thus has *Ovid* been serv'd by the so much admir'd *Sandys*.[33]

Johnson must have read the dedication. That when he wrote on Sandys he did not consciously have it in mind must be allowed. Because of the striking similarity between Johnson's views on Sandys and Dryden's early attack, it must also be allowed that, hovering in the background of the quotation from Cowley, and perhaps reinforcing it, is the whole of the Dryden passage. Yet Dryden did change his opinion; and Johnson's commentary on the three poets – Sandys, Cowley and Dryden – serves an unexpected and incidental purpose. It is worth keeping in mind. With Johnson as our intermediary, we are in fact reminded how, years after the event, Dryden can reverse gracefully and silently what he deems a past blunder or mistake.

Finally, Johnson takes up Dryden's place and standing as a literary critic. He is convinced that, despite his many reservations, what is best in the criticism has been unfairly neglected, and is therefore the more in need of careful assessment. Perhaps through unconscious memory, he repeats with unexpected involvement, even solicitude, Dryden's own estimate of the criticism. He traces the whole of eighteenth-century literary theory back to Dryden; but once he has done so, he shifts his perspective. As if he had prophetic vision, he looks forward to Dryden from the vantage point of the sixteenth century. His discussion of 'the state of English criticism before ... [the] *Essay of Dramatic Poesy*' is not, as Catherine N. Parke believes, an exercise in 'the biographical imagination': it is not the 'bring[ing] into view [of] aspects of [a] writer's work ... that sometimes border on invisibility'.[34] The discussion is rather a paraphrase of and a meditation on what Johnson had read in the opening pages of the 'Discourse concerning ... Satire'.

Indeed, unlike his comments on the literary character, the poetry and the translations, the paraphrase is so exceedingly close that Dryden appears to be speaking to us directly, though in the idiom and rhetoric of the eighteenth century. We do not so much have Johnson echoing Dryden, unconsciously once again, as Dryden translated by Johnson. Dryden speaks such English as he would no doubt have spoken had he been born in England a full century later. The evidence is unmistakable. It also demonstrates the extent to which the same touch of nature made the two men very much akin. The passage which inspired Johnson has already been quoted.[35] Let us now turn to Johnson himself:

> Dryden may be properly considered as the father of English criticism, as the writer who first taught us to determine upon principles the merit of

composition. Of our former poets the greatest dramatist wrote without rules, conducted through life and nature by a genius that rarely misled, and rarely deserted him. Of the rest, those who knew the laws of propriety had neglected to teach them.

Two *Arts of English Poetry* were written in the days of Elizabeth by Webb and Puttenham, from which something might be learned, and a few hints had been given by Jonson and Cowley; but Dryden's *Essay on Dramatick Poetry* was the first regular and valuable treatise on the art of writing.

He who, having formed his opinions in the present age of English literature, turns back to peruse this dialogue, will not perhaps find much increase of knowledge or much novelty of instruction; but he is to remember that critical principles were then in the hands of a few, who had gathered them partly from the Ancients, and partly from the Italians and French. The structure of dramatick poems was not then generally understood. Audiences applauded by instinct, and poets perhaps often pleased by chance ...

To judge rightly of an author we must transport ourselves to his time, and examine what were the wants of his contemporaries, and what were his means of supplying them. That which is easy at one time was difficult at another. Dryden at least imported his science, and gave his country what it wanted before; or rather, he imported only the materials, and manufactured them by his own skill.[36]

The paraphrase is Johnson's; the argument is Dryden's. Differences between the two points of view are not, in a last analysis, quite relevant.

Whatever his reservations, Johnson is generally sympathetic toward Dryden's literary criticism, whether theoretical or practical. However, once he turns in particular to the self-criticism, the sympathy all but completely disappears. On the whole, he not only dislikes the self-criticism; he also disapproves of it. On occasion, he may even regard it with a measure of contempt. When passing his final verdict, he declares that it adds little or nothing to our appreciation of Dryden, the man or the work. He is largely unaware of its influence on him. But that he has read it and knows it, understands and echoes it makes his study of Dryden that much the richer.

III

Since the publication of the 'Life', verdicts on Dryden's criticism have tended to be cast in the Johnson mould. Critics from the early nineteenth century through the 1960s – Scott and Saintsbury, George Watson and Arthur C. Kirsch – commonly distinguish between the critical theory which is a kind of self-aggrandizement and the critical theory that, at its very best, is its own excuse for being. They often pay tribute to the practical criticism when Dryden writes about poets long dead; but they are quick to add that, when he writes about rivals or himself, the criticism is either misleading and worthless or completely inaccurate and downright bad.[37] Later critics – Robert D. Hume, Edward Pechter, James Engell

– carry this approach toward its furthest extreme. They ignore Dryden's practical criticism all but completely and define his greatness in terms of some limited aspects of his general theory: his eclecticism, his sense of history, the tone and quality of his mind.[38] Both groups fail to recognize the fundamental integrity of the criticism, whether theoretical or practical or both; the complete harmony between the self-criticism and the critical theory, as well as between the critical theory in general and the poetry which it explains and justifies; and the extent to which, even as they condemn the self-criticism, they echo again and again Dryden's own best estimates of himself and his rightful place in the history of English literature.

Among the major critics, however, there has been one, T. S. Eliot, who did in large measure escape the Johnson influence. Eliot had little, if anything, to say about Dryden's interest in literary tradition. Whether he recognized the fact or not, that interest and concern had a profound influence on him. He made it his own, although he used a slightly different terminology; and he did turn portions of it inside out. According to Dryden, we must remember, there had been two traditions in early seventeenth-century English literature, the Shakespearean and the Jonsonian; and towards the end of his life, he was convinced he had in his best works achieved their reconciliation. According to Eliot, however, there had been in the native literature a single tradition; and that tradition, which he associated with John Donne and the Metaphysicals, was one in which thought and feeling (he said) were closely interfused. Poets thought with their feelings; 'their mode of feeling was directly and freshly altered by their reading and thought'. Then, later in the century, he went on to explain, 'something ... happened to the mind of England'. A 'dissociation of sensibility set in'. Thought and feeling were sundered; and 'while language became more refined, the feeling became more crude'.[39]

As poet and playwright, moreover, John Dryden was one of the main culprits; and ever since, Eliot argues, there have been two traditions, each opposed to the other. For these traditions Eliot unfortunately has no name. He merely associates one with Dryden and the later formalists, the other with eighteenth-century Miltonists and their Romantic descendants, poets who (like Shelley and William Morris) lived in what he calls 'a dream-world'.[40] That Eliot's two traditions are the two identified by Dryden, though under another rubric, is rather obvious.[41] That his two traditions should have to be reconciled is one subject to which in his critical prose he returned frequently. That in his own poetry he had fully achieved that end he never said. He was not so outspoken about his accomplishments as Dryden had been about his; but we are left to assume that, at least in *The Four Quartets,* he pointed in the right direction.

In evaluating Dryden as poet, Eliot found much that was wrong. Dryden had 'a commonplace mind'. He 'lacked insight, he lacked profoundity'. His poems contain 'an exaggeration of particular qualities to the exclusion of others'. And he is useful to the modern world precisely because he did some things 'magnificently well' and others not at all.[42] But if in the poems Eliot perceived 'the splitting up of personality',[43] he discovered in the critical essays a completely unified sensibility. Thus, he judged the prose style admirable in its equipoise, balance and proportion. Here there was no disjunction between thought and feeling, idea and image. And the wit, with all its levity, had sufficient seriousness to keep from becoming mere fun:

> He has all the virtues you would expect. He neither descends too low, nor attempts to fly too high; he is perfectly clear as to what he has to say; and he says it always with the right control and changes of intensity of feeling. His wit exceeds that of all his contemporaries; it contributes elegance and liveliness of figure, without ever overreaching itself into facetiousness.[44]

Eliot's celebration of the criticism went beyond its prose. He commended the literary theory for the way it 'justly' keeps in place 'the part of inspiration (or free association)' in the creative act and 'the part of conscious labour'.[45] And he found harmony of another kind exactly where we might expect him to miss it: in the 'almost ideal balance between the critic and the ... poet'.[46] Eliot seems to have thought that, as he shifted from the first role to the second, Dryden recapitulated within himself the history of the seventeenth-century mind. To Eliot his sensibility appeared now whole and now divided. However, when he judged the criticism in direct relationship to the poetry, Eliot momentarily abandoned this view. He now, quite accurately, saw both bodies of work as the joint effort of a single intelligence. What the critic proposed the poet executed; what the poet executed the critic approved:

> [W]hat Dryden accomplished [in his poetry] was no by-product and no accident. Never was there a worker more conscious of what he was attempting ... The theory of Coleridge is partly, certainly, as was that of Wordsworth, a defence of his conscious precepts of workmanship; but with Wordsworth, and still more with Coleridge, we can say that their theory does not wholly account for the best of their poetry. In this way, Dryden was a far more *conscious* poet than either; perhaps more conscious than any poet of great eminence since. His essays are his conscious thoughts about the kinds of work he was doing ... I can think of no man in literature whose aims are so exactly fulfilled by his performance ...[47]

And he recognized that, after all is said and done, Dryden remains his own best critic. The lesson is one which has yet to be fully heeded.

IV

Despite tributes from Johnson and Eliot, Dryden's critical works have not been given the recognition which they rightly deserve. He is the father of English criticism; and his influence has indeed been pervasive. It has even been pervasive when it has been ignored, misunderstood, condemned. It has even been pervasive in ways which escaped, somehow, Johnson and Eliot alike. Dryden established, to a remarkable extent, a distinctly English style of criticism: a mode of judging literature which is urbane and cheerful, well informed but never pedantic, digressive rather than monumental.[48] In addition, in a less discernible way, he has continued to leave his mark on literary theory. In moments of despondency, when English critics begin to feel that all is not well in the republic of letters, they have always instinctively turned back to Dryden and his fundamental principle. They have hearkened to his insistence that English literature, as an expression of national character and genius, fulfills itself by combining somehow the just with the lively. The tendency can be seen when, during the eighteenth century, critics like Addison, Burke and Johnson himself found Augustanism wanting and turned, for compensation, to the pleasures of the imagination or to amplitude and the sublime or to novelty and splendour.[49] Since the eighteenth century it can be seen, for example, in Hazlitt's premise that a poet's feelings or emotions must interact with objective representations of human nature and the external world;[50] in Arnold's requirement that a poetry of statement be lightly graced with charm, natural magic and joy;[51] in Eliot's own belief that in the modern world the English poet should infuse into his world of 'day-dreamy feeling' an urbane formalism.

Dryden tried to check the excesses of the just or the rules of classicism, both ancient and modern, through an emphasis on the imaginative in literature, or the lively. So his early successors, critics like Addison, Burke and Johnson, followed his precise example: they would find in touchstones of the lively or the imaginative a counterbalance to the excesses of Augustanism or the just, though they had far more restraint than he had and far less daring. So too Dryden's later heirs and descendants, critics like Hazlitt, Arnold and Eliot, would prune the excesses of Romanticism, or what he would have called the lively, through a recourse to classical rules and ideals, or what he called the just.

V

Dryden's criticism is the criticism of a poet; and like the poetry, it instructs through pleasing. It is possible to read the criticism for the sake of the prose alone. But as the poems offer more than the delights of a great style, so too does the criticism. Indeed, both the plays and the criticism please for the same reason and in the same way.

Like the plays, the criticism tells a good story: the account of a writer's life. The plot is orderly in its outlines; but as in any tragi-comedy, it is full of complications. It starts in happiness, plunges to a kind of despair and ends on a note of intellectual and artistic self-knowledge. Its middle follows naturally from its beginning; and the end is what it could not otherwise have been. It is a moral tale, for the protagonist takes responsibility for all of his actions.

Like his own *dramatis personae*, Dryden displays frailty and weakness. He thinks his merits disregarded; he laments his fortune; he is perhaps over-solicitous of his health. But this domestic comedy is only the underplot to the intellectual and serious action of the main plot. In the criticism as in his plays, the favorite exercise of his mind is ratiocination. And lest his discussion be too quickly ended, he piles argument upon argument in seemingly endless profusion. To read the scholastic debates in the heroic plays with interest and pleasure, the best preparation is first to read Dryden on rhyme.

But the critic has an altogether finer mind than any of his boastful heroes. For that matter, he is a more amusing fellow than any of his 'Character[s] of Wit'. Critics have often asserted that Dryden lacked the gifts to compose high comedy. '[H]is most polished figures of comedy', as Eliot observes, 'are, compared to the finest Restoration comedy, almost bumpkins; that delightful lady of *Marriage à la Mode*, Melantha, is still too "humourous" in her French affectations; and the fun of *Mr. Limberham* is not altogether well-bred'.[52] But there is, as Eliot himself realized, at least one great wit to be found in Dryden's canon: the Dryden of the critical prose. His mockery of French punctilio – and in particular of Racine's treatment of Hippolytus – must have impressed even Congreve:

> Yet, in this nicety of manners does the excellency of *French* Poetry consist: their Heroes are the most civil people breathing; but their good breeding seldom extends to a word of sense ... Thus their *Hippolitus* is so scrupulous in point of decency, that he will rather expose himself to death, than accuse his Stepmother to his Father ... This was good manners with a vengeance; and the Audience is like to be much concern'd at the misfortunes of this admirable Heroe: but take *Hippolitus* out of his Poetique Fit, and I suppose he would think it a wiser part, to set the Saddle on the right Horse, and chuse rather to live with the reputation of a plain-spoken honest man, than to die with the infamy of an incestuous Villain. In the mean time we may take notice, that where the Poet ought to have preserv'd the character as it was deliver'd to us by Antiquity, when he should have given us the picture of a rough young man, of the *Amazonian* strain, a jolly Huntsman, and both by his profession and his early rising a Mortal Enemy to love, he has chosen to give him the turn of Gallantry, sent him to travel from *Athens* to *Paris,* taught him to make love, and transform'd the *Hippolitus* of *Euripides* into Monsieur *Hippolite*.[53]

In reading Dryden for pleasure, we ought also profit from what we read. Not all of his ideas will transform our conception of literature: he gives us much counsel which we do not wish to hear. After Hazlitt, it is difficult to believe in the idea of artistic progress, even in the limited sense in which Dryden eventually came to define it. Discussions of unity of time and place, however conceived, may leave us cold. But Dryden does not always dig in those exhausted mines. His central critical principles are of enduring importance. No other English critic so well demonstrates that broadly classical values in literature promote and do not detract from grandeur. No other demonstrates so well the interconnections between sound criticism and great literature; and the demonstration by him is all the more impressive since he was simultaneously both poet and critic. And no other critic demonstrates so well that – in literature as in criticism, in criticism as in life – the need is always to combine somehow the restraints of judgment and the flights of imagination. Dryden has set standards for English literature which it would be a mistake to ignore.

Notes

References when first cited are given in full; thereafter they are given in a shortened form. The editor of a volume (or part of a volume) in the California Dryden is named in the Notes when either he or his commentary is discussed in a note or in the text, otherwise not. An essay in a collection of essays is cited after the name of the author both in the Notes and in the Bibliography. Two or more essays in a collection, each by a different author, are cited in the Notes after the author's name, but in the Bibliography after the name of the editor.

INTRODUCTION

1 James Anderson Winn (*John Dryden and His World* (New Haven, Yale University Press, 1987)) is interested in the criticism primarily for what it tells us about Dryden the man. A reading of the criticism as 'a set of polemical gestures' is contained in Steven N. Zwicker's *Politics and Language in Dryden's Poetry: The Arts of Disguise* (Princeton, Princeton University Press, 1984). In *Dryden: The Public Writer, 1660–1685* (Princeton, Princeton University Press, 1978), which he calls 'a supplement to Charles E. Ward's indispensable biography', George McFadden considers the relationship of the criticism to Restoration political and social issues. See also the works by McKeon and Reverend listed in the Bibliography.

The first important study of the intellectual backgrounds of the criticism was Louis I. Bredvold's *The Intellectual Milieu of John Dryden: Studies in Some Aspects of Seventeenth-Century Thought*, University of Michigan Publications, Language and Literature, no. 12 (Ann Arbor, University of Michigan Press, 1934). Other approaches to Dryden's thought may be found in Thomas Hanzo's *Latitude and Restoration Criticism*, Anglistica, no. 12 (Copenhagen, Rosenkilde and Bagger, 1961) and Edward Pechter's *Dryden's Classical Theory of Literature* (London, Cambridge University Press, 1975). Also, see the following: Phillip Harth, *Contexts of Dryden's Thought* (Chicago, University of Chicago Press, 1968), pp. 1–55; Richard Foster Jones, 'Science and Criticism in the Neo-Classical Age of Literature', *Journal of the History of Ideas*, 1 (1940), 381–412. Ruth Salvaggio, *Dryden's Dualities*, English Language Studies Monograph Series, no. 29 (Victoria, University of Victoria Press, 1983).

Most of Dryden's technical interests have been studied in detail. Much work has been done on his theory of literary genres: for example, his theory of comedy (Frank Harper Moore, *The Nobler Pleasure: Dryden's Comedy in Theory and Practice* (Chapel Hill, University of North Carolina Press, 1962)) and his theory of satire (William Frost, 'Dryden's Theory and Practice of Satire', in *Dryden's Mind and Art*, ed. Bruce King (Edinburgh, Oliver and Boyd, 1969), pp. 189–205). George McFadden has written about his statements on metre ('Dryden and the Numbers of His Native Tongue', in *Essays and Studies in Language and Literature*, ed. Herbert H. Petit, Duquesne Studies, Philological Series, no. 5 (Pittsburgh, Duquesne University Press, 1964), 87–109); and Morris Freedman, about his statements on rhyme ('Milton and Dryden on Rhyme', *Huntington Library Quarterly*, 24 (1961), 337–44). For his ideas on poetic structure, see Paul Ramsay, *The Art of John Dryden* (Lexington, Kentucky, University of Kentucky Press, 1969), pp. 5–15. For an important discussion of Dryden's theory of translation, see William Frost, *John Dryden: Dramatist, Satirist, Translator* (New York, AMS Press, 1988), pp. 99–216. For Dryden's importance to modern critical theory, see James Engell, *Forming the Critical Mind: Dryden to Coleridge* (Cambridge, Mass., Harvard University Press, 1989), pp. 15–43. See also Paul H. Fry, *The Reach of Criticism: Method and Perception in Literary Theory* (New Haven, Yale University Press, 1983), pp. 87–124.

Studies of Dryden's sources are legion. Among the more important are John M. Aden, 'Dryden and Boileau: The Question of Critical Influence', *Studies in Philology*, 50 (1953), 491–509; Paul Hammond, 'Figures of Horace in Dryden's Literary Criticism', in *Horace Made New: Horatian Influences on British Writing from the Renaissance to the Twentieth Century*, ed. Charles Martindale and David Hopkins (Cambridge, Cambridge University Press, 1993), pp. 127–47; John Sherwood, 'Dryden and the Critical Theories of Tasso', *Comparative Literature*, 28 (1966), 351–9.

2 For modern discussion, both occasional and incomplete, of the just and the lively in Dryden's criticism, see Ralph Cohen, 'John Dryden's Literary Criticism', in *New Homage to John Dryden* (Los Angeles, William Andrews Clark Memorial Library, 1983), p. 74; Frank Livingston Huntley, 'The Unity of John Dryden's Dramatic Criticism', Ph.D. diss. University of Chicago, 1941; Pechter, *Dryden's Classical Theory*, pp. 11–13, 25–6; Paul Ramsay, *The Lively and the Just: An Argument for Propriety*, University of Alabama Studies, no. 15 (Tuscaloosa, Alabama, University of Alabama Press, 1962), 139–41. For modern discussion, both occasional and incomplete, of judgment and imagination (or fancy) in Dryden's criticism, see John M. Aden, 'Dryden and the Imagination: The First Phase', *PMLA*, 74 (1959), 28–40; Robert D. Hume, 'Dryden on Creation: "Imagination" in the Later Criticism', *Review of English Studies*, n.s., 21 (1970), 295–314; Clarence DeWitt Thorpe, 'The Psychological Approach in Dryden', in *The Aesthetic Theory of Thomas Hobbes*, University of Michigan Publications in Language and Literature, no. 18 (Ann Arbor, University of Michigan Press, 1940), 189–220.

Thomas Hanzo, Robert D. Hume and Frank Livingston Huntley write of the just and the lively chiefly or exclusively with regard to the *Essay of Dramatick Poesie*: Hanzo, *Latitude and Restoration Criticism*, pp. 87–98; Hume, *Dryden's Criticism* (Ithaca, Cornell University Press, 1970), pp. 190–203; Huntley, *On Dryden's 'Essay of Dramatic Poesy'*, University of Michigan Contributions in Modern Philology, no. 16 (Ann Arbor, University of Michigan Press, 1951). Donald F. Bond, John Bullitt and Walter Jackson Bate, and Edward Pechter write of judgment and imagination with regard to only two or three essays: Bond, 'Distrust of the Imagination in English Neo-Classicism', *Philological Quarterly*, 14 (1935), 54–69; Bullitt and Bate, 'Distinctions Between Fancy and Imagination in Eighteenth-Century English Criticism', *Modern Language Notes*, 60 (1945), 9–10; Pechter, *Dryden's Classical Theory*, pp. 24–7, 124–6.

Definitions of all four terms, quite brief and very much simplified, are given in H. James Jensen's *A Glossary of John Dryden's Critical Terms* (Minneapolis, University of Minnesota Press, 1969). They are given, moreover, without regard to contexts, development and importance.

For other references, all of them equally brief and incomplete, see (for the just and the lively) the following: James T. Boulton (ed.), *Of Dramatick Poesie* (London, Oxford University Press, 1967), pp. 16–17; David Daitches, *Critical Approaches to Literature* (London, Longmans Green, 1956), pp. 73–8; H. James Jensen, 'A Note on Restoration Aesthetics', *Studies in English Literature*, 14 (1974), 317–26; Earl Miner, 'Renaissance Contexts of Dryden's Criticism', *Michigan Quarterly Review*, 12 (1973), 114–15; Mary Thale, 'Dryden's Critical Vocabulary: The Imitation of Nature', *Papers on Language and*

Literature, 2 (1966), 323–4; William K. Wimsatt, Jr. and Cleanth Brooks, *Literary Criticism: A Short History* (New York, Alfred A. Knopf, 1957), pp. 185–8. And (for judgment and imagination) see: Scott Elledge, 'Cowley's Ode *Of Wit* and Longinus on the Sublime: A Study of One Definition of the Word *Wit*', *Modern Language Quarterly*, 9 (1948), 185–98; R[aman] Selden, 'Hobbes, Dryden, and the Ranging Spaniel', *Notes and Queries*, n.s., 20 (1973), 388–90; F. W. Bateson, 'Contributions to a Dictionary of Critical Terms. I. Comedy of Manners', *Essays in Criticism*, I (1951), 89–93.

In what is now the standard biography, James Anderson Winn's *John Dryden and His World*, little or no attention is paid either to the four terms or to the patterns of critical theory and practice which Dryden intended them to signify. See, for example, *John Dryden*, pp. 160–5.

Among all those who have written about Dryden's criticism, there are finally those who would avoid his terminology, but who touch upon the subjects to which his terminology refers. See, for example, the review of scholarship in Huntley, 'The Unity of John Dryden's Dramatic Criticism', pp. 1–49 *passim*, as well as the following: Walter Jackson Bate, *Criticism: The Major Texts* (New York, Harcourt Brace, 1952), pp. 127–8; John C. Sherwood, 'Dryden and the Rules: The Preface to *Troilus and Cressida*', *Comparative Literature*, 2 (1950), 73–83 *passim*.

3 *A Dissertation Concerning the Perfection of the English Language* ..., in *Epistles, Odes, &c. Written on Several Subjects*... (London, 1724), p. xl.

4 On the lack of permanent value in Dryden's criticism, see David Hopkins, *John Dryden* (Cambridge, Cambridge University Press, 1986), pp. 46–8. Cf. Hume, *Dryden's Criticism*, pp. ix–x.

5 On the dichotomy between the criticism and the works it introduces, see George Watson (ed.), *'Of Dramatic Poesy' and Other Critical Essays* (London, J. M. Dent, 1962), I, p. v. Also, see Arthur C. Kirsch, *Dryden's Heroic Drama* (Princeton, Princeton University Press, 1965), pp. 3–4; David Bruce Kramer, *The Imperial Dryden: The Poetics of Appropriation in Seventeenth-Century England* (Athens, Georgia, University of Georgia Press, 1994), pp. 16–62.

6 On the lack of consistency in the criticism, see the following: Engell, *Forming the Critical Mind*, p. 17ff; Morris Freedman, 'Milton and Dryden on Tragedy', in *English Writers of the Eighteenth Century*, ed. John H. Middendorf (New York, Columbia University Press, 1963), pp. 158–9; Fry, *Reach of Criticism*, pp. 88–98, 218; George Watson, *The Literary Critics: A Study of English Descriptive Criticism* (Baltimore, Penguin, 1962), p. 41; James Anderson Winn, *'When Beauty Fires the Blood': Love and the Arts in the Age of Dryden* (Ann Arbor, University of Michigan Press, 1992), p. x.

7 On the lack of development or change in the criticism, see the following: Hume, 'Dryden on Creation', pp. 295–314; Huntley, *Dryden's 'Essay'*, p. 70; Huntley, 'Dryden's Dramatic Criticism', pp. 219–22; Christopher MacLachlan, 'Dryden, Truth, and Nature', *British Journal of Aesthetics*, 20 (1980), 153–9; Pechter, *Dryden's Classical Theory*, pp. 151–4.

8 On 'An account of the ensuing Poem', the preface to *Annus Mirabilis*, see Zwicker, *Politics and Language*, pp. 39–41.

9 On the *Essay of Dramatick Poesie*, see Winn, *John Dryden*, p. 164. See also Hume, *Dryden's Criticism*, p. 204.

10 On the 'Preface to *The Tempest*', see Hume, 'Dryden on Creation', p. 297. For an interpretation of the Preface as 'an extraordinary encomium', see Maximillian E. Novak (ed.), *The Works of John Dryden*, X (Berkeley, University of California Press, 1970), pp. 321–2,

326–7. Also, see Mary Edmond, *Rare Sir William Davenant* (New York, St. Martin's Press, 1987), pp. 198–9. Edmond, incidentally, uses a part of Dryden's tribute as the epigraph to her book.

11 On the 'Preface to *An Evening's Love*', see Wimsatt, *Literary Criticism*, p. 204. Cf. Moore, *The Nobler Pleasure*, pp. 94–8.
12 On 'Of Heroique Playes', see the following: Kirsch, *Dryden's Heroic Drama*, pp. 8–15; John Harrington Smith (ed.), *Works*, VIII, pp. 284–9; Winn, *John Dryden*, pp. 145–8.
13 Hume, *Dryden's Criticism*, p. 213; Pechter, *Dryden's Classical Theory*, p. 60; Watson, *The Literary Critics*, p. 54.
14 Fry, *Reach of Criticism*, pp. 94–8.

CHAPTER ONE
The ends of criticism

1 F. N. Lees, 'John Dryden', in *From Dryden to Johnson*, ed. Boris Ford (Baltimore, Penguin, 1965), p. 111. For a similar judgment, though stated with far more severity, see Hopkins, *John Dryden*, p. 46.
2 *Criticism: The Major Texts*, p. 123.
3 *The Idiom of Poetry*, rev. edn (Bloomington, Indiana University Press, 1963), p. 48. In its entirety, Atkins's catalogue is much longer.
4 *English Literary Criticism: 17th and 18th Centuries* (London, Methuen, 1951), p. 143.
5 *Dryden's Classical Theory*, pp. 11–13.
6 *Dryden's Criticism*, pp. 187–230; 'Dryden on Creation', pp. 295–314. The instability which Hume notes in his book on Dryden he explains away in his article, published in the same year.
7 'Life of Dryden', in *Lives of the English Poets*, ed. George Birkbeck Hill (1905; rpt. New York, Octagon Books, 1967), I, p. 418. Most editors of Johnson, deferring to Hill, trace the quotation back to Pope's *Dunciad* (III.40). But James A. Winn, who has examined the issue anew, shows that Johnson actually took the phrase from that part of Ovid's *Metamorphoses* which he translated as 'Of the Pythagorean Philosophy' (l. 581). See Winn, 'Introduction', *Critical Essays on John Dryden*, ed. James A. Winn (New York, G. K. Hall, 1997), p. 1.
8 Baxter Hathaway, *Marvels and Commonplaces: Renaissance Literary Criticism* (New York, Random House, 1968), p. viii.
9 *Discourses on the Heroic Poem*, trans. Mariella Cavalchini and Irene Samuel (Oxford, Clarendon Press, 1973), p. 37.
10 For a brief discussion of the importance of the problem in Restoration criticism, see Wallace Jackson, *The Probable and the Marvelous: Blake, Wordsworth, and the Eighteenth-Century Critical Tradition* (Athens, Georgia, University of Georgia Press, 1978), pp. 6, 11–14.
11 For discussion of the spirit of the age, especially as regards the issue of compromise in church and state, see Hanzo, *Latitude and Restoration Criticism*, pp. 15–52.
12 The importance of the terms in Dryden's criticism was first noticed by Frank Livingston Huntley. For a listing of Huntley's work and later discussions of the subject, see below, pp. 258–9.
13 In the treatment of his two polarities, the lively and the just, Dryden increasingly associates the lively and flights of the imagination (or fancy) not only with medieval and Renaissance romance but also with elements of the supernatural (or the wonderful) in

pagan myth and the Christian religion and, further, with political radicalism and mere Whiggery. The just and the dictates of sound judgment (or right reason) he associates increasingly not only with ancient and Renaissance classicism but also with empirical science and hence with the laws of nature (the laws, for example, of probability, cause and effect, and universal harmony) and, further, with the well-ordered state and Tory politics. Neither of his two polarities – the lively alone, the just alone – is possible without the other or even desirable. As he explains their possible balance or reconciliation, he also explains their multiple aspects, in each instance, as necessary equations. And the most important of the equations are clear enough: that of an imaginative literature (or the art of the wonderful) with the romance and with what later generations will call 'Romanticism'; the classical rules (or an art centred in the life or reason) with both empirical science (that is, the laws of nature) and with a stabile government, specifically the Stuart establishment. Dryden's political opinions are discussed in Winn's *John Dryden* and Zwicker's *Politics and Language*; his religious beliefs in Harth's *Contexts of Dryden's Thought* and G. Douglas Atkins's *The Faith of John Dryden: Change and Continuity* (Lexington, Kentucky, University of Kentucky Press, 1980); his reactions to seventeenth-century science in Bredvold, *Intellectual Milieu*, pp. 47–72; Helen Burke, 'Annus Mirabilis and the Ideology of the New Science', *ELH*, 57 (1990), 307–34.

14 The speakers in the *Essay of Dramatick Poesie*, though they use the phrase as part of their definition of the drama, stress that it is relevant to all literature and, by implication, to all criticism. See *An Essay of Dramatick Poesie*, in *Works*, XVII, p. 15.

15 ''Tis true, those beauties of the *French*-poesie are such as will raise perfection higher where it is, but are not sufficient to give it where it is not: they are indeed the Beauties of a Statue, but not of a Man, because not animated with the Soul of Poesie ...' (*Dramatick Poesie*, in *Works*, XVII, p. 44).

16 For an example of each, see 'Prologue to *The Tempest*', in *Works*, X, p. 6; *Dramatick Poesie*, in *Works*, XVII, p. 15.

17 *John Dryden: A Study of His Poetry*, rev. edn (Bloomington, Indiana University Press, 1960), p. 53.

18 'Discourse concerning the Original and Progress of Satire' [1693], in *Works*, IV, p. 4.

19 *The Life of Dryden* (1834; rpt. Lincoln, Nebraska, University of Nebraska Press, 1963), p. 451. Cf. Hume, 'Dryden on Creation', pp. 298, 313–14. The *Life*, though part of Scott's *Works of John Dryden*, was also published separately in 1808 and 1826. In 1834, an annotated version was published by John Gibson Lockhart as part of a collection of Scott's miscellaneous prose. All quotations from the *Life* are taken from a reprint of the Lockhart edition.

20 Watson (ed.), '*Of Dramatic Poesy*', I, p. v.

21 *The Literary Critics*, pp. 59–60. Cf. Hopkins, *John Dryden*, p. 46.

22 See, for example, Scott, *The Life of Dryden*, pp. 49–53, 102, 109; Watson (ed.), '*Of Dramatic Poesy*', I, p. xvi–xvii.

23 Earl Miner, 'The Poetics of the Critical Act: Dryden's Dealings with Rivals and Predecessors', in *Evidence in Literary Scholarship: Essays in Memory of James Marshall Osborn*, ed. René Wellek and Alvaro Ribiero (Oxford, Clarendon Press, 1979), pp. 45–62. For a classic statement of the popular view, see William E. Bohn, 'The Development of John Dryden's Literary Criticism', *PMLA*, 22 (1907), 67–75.

24 *Dramatick Poesie*, in *Works*, XVII, p. 55.

25 'Life of Dryden', in *Lives*, I, p. 412; for a modern appraisal, see Hopkins, *John Dryden*, pp. 51–3.

26 *The Imperial Dryden*, pp. 17–62.

27 For fuller discussion of these objections, see the following: Bonamy Dobrée, *Restoration Comedy: 1660–1720* (Oxford, Oxford University Press, 1924), pp. 39–57; Alfred Harbage, *Cavalier Drama: An Historical and Critical Supplement to the Study of the Elizabethan and the Restoration Stage* (1936; rpt. New York, Russell and Russell, 1964), pp. 48–69; John Loftis, *The Spanish Plays of Neoclassical England* (New Haven, Yale University Press, 1973); Nancy Klein Maguire, *Regicide and Restoration: English Tragicomedy, 1660–1671* (New York, Cambridge University Press, 1992), pp. 54–9; Pechter, *Dryden's Classical Theory*, pp. 91–112; Paul Spencer Wood, 'Native Elements in English Neo-Classicism', in *Essential Articles for the Study of English Augustan Backgrounds*, ed. Bernard N. Schilling (Hamden, Connecticut, Archon Books, 1961), pp. 392–401. (First published in *Modern Philology*, 24 (1926), 201–8.)

28 On the occasion of these quarrels, see Winn, *John Dryden*, pp. 255–61, 307–9.

29 On the dating of *Mac Flecknoe*, see David M. Vieth, 'The Discovery of the Date of *Mac Flecknoe*', in *Evidence in Literary Scholarship*, ed. Wellek and Ribiero, pp. 63–87. The relationship of the poem to previous literary quarrels is discussed in Paul Hammond, 'Flecknoe and *Mac Flecknoe*', *Essays in Criticism*, 35 (1985), 315–29; Richard Oden (ed.), *Dryden and Shadwell* (Delmar, New York: Scholars' Facsimiles and Reprints, 1977), pp. vi–xxii.

30 For a discussion of these essays, see below, pp. 81–90, 103–17, 147–54.

31 On Dryden's absorption in Longinus, see below, pp. 163–71.

32 *Mac Flecknoe*, in *Works*, II, p. 56.

33 *Seventeenth-Century English Literature* (London, Oxford University Press, 1950), p. 129.

34 'Discourse concerning... Satire', in *Works*, IV, p. 59.

35 As Alastair Fowler notes,

> Sir Robert Howard, Dryden's brother-in-law, although at first his patron, secretly worked against him; the Earl of Rochester, a patron and friend in 1671, was doubted by 1673 and could be suspected – unjustly – of having Dryden beaten up in 1679. There were enemy patrons ... inimical to Dryden's patrons ... There were enmities, or at least rivalries, between sibling clients of the same patron ('That Great Neglected Poet: The "Silent Graces" and Moral Authority of Dryden's Verse', rev. of *The Poems of John Dryden*, ed. Paul Hammond, *Times Literary Supplement*, 7 July 1995, p. 3).

36 Watson (ed.), '*Of Dramatic Poesy*', I, p. vii. The forces which impelled Dryden and, later, other Restoration authors to defend themselves are discussed by Deborah C. Payne in her forthcoming study *Patronage, Professionalism, and the Marketplace of Restoration Theatre: 1660–1685*; Kevin Dunn, *Pretexts of Authority: The Rhetoric of Authorship in the Renaissance Preface* (Stanford, Stanford University Press, 1994), pp. 58–81, 102–38.

37 For some of the English precedents, see Clara Gerbert (ed.), *An Anthology of Elizabethan Dedications and Prefaces* (1933; rpt. New York, Russell and Russell, 1966).

CHAPTER TWO
From theory to practice (1664)

1 'Prologue to *Marriage à-la-Mode*', in *Works*, X, p. 226. For a more detailed analysis of this common formula, see Wilson, *The Court Wits of the Restoration: An Introduction* (Princeton, Princeton University Press, 1948), p. 4.

2 'Prologue to *Cynthias Reuells*', in *Ben Jonson*, ed. C. H. Herford and Percy and Evelyn

Simpson (Oxford, Clarendon Press, 1932), IV, p. 43.

3 'Prologue to *The Rival Ladies*', in *Works*, VIII, p. 103.

4 'Life of Dryden', in *Lives*, I, p. 367. In the 'Preface to *Tamerlane the Great*' (1681), Charles Saunders attributes 'no small part of [the] success' of his play to 'Mr Dryden himself, who ... was pleas'd to Grace it with an Epilogue'. See 'Preface to *Tamerlane the Great*', quoted in Autrey Nell Wiley (ed.), *Rare Prologues and Epilogues: 1642–1700* (1940; rpt. Port Washington, New York, Kennikat Press, 1970), p. xxx.

5 For my remarks on the pieces to Oldham and Congreve, see below, p. 178 and p. 299 n. 11. On poems addressed to other writers, poems in which he sets forth critical judgments, both theoretical and practical, see Miner, 'The Poetics of the Critical Act', *Evidence in Literary Scholarship*, ed. Wellek and Ribiero, pp. 45–62.

6 'The Defence of the Epilogue', in *Works*, XI, pp. 216–17.

7 *Notes and Observations on 'The Empress of Morocco'*, in *Works*, XVII, p. 84. On the problem of attribution, see Winn, *John Dryden*, pp. 582–3.

8 'Defence of the Epilogue', in *Works*, XI, p. 216.

9 Eugenio Garin, *L'Educazione in Europe 1400–1600*, quoted and trans. in Daniel Javitch, *Poetry and Courtliness in Renaissance England* (Princeton, Princeton University Press, 1978), pp. 10–11.

10 *Poetry and Courtliness*, p. 107.

11 Vivian De Sola Pinto, *Restoration Carnival: Five Courtier Poets* (London, Folio Society, 1954), p. 9. On Charles's interest in restoring the Court, see also the following: Michael Foss, *The Age of Patronage: The Arts in Society, 1660–1750* (Ithaca, Cornell University Press, 1971), p. 20; William Gaunt, *Court Painting in England from Tudor to Victorian Times* (London, Constable, 1980), pp. 136–7; Patrick Morrah, *Restoration England* (London, Constable, 1979), pp. 40–2. For a contemporary account, see Anthony Hamilton, *Count Gramont at the Court of Charles II*, trans. Nicholas Deakin (London, Barrie and Rockliff, 1965), pp. 3–5.

12 Wilson goes on to explain the situation in some detail:

> During the greater part of the reign of Charles II, there were only two theatrical companies; from 1682 to 1695, there was only one. The managers of the theatres – two courtiers – were the King's officers; the actors and actresses were the King's servants. Plays could be presented only with the approval of the Master of the Revels, and appeals from his authority were carried to Charles himself. The presence of His Majesty at a play usually meant a large audience and a good profit, while command performances at Whitehall brought round sums from the Privy Purse (*The Court Wits*, p. 142).

See also James Sutherland, 'The Impact of Charles II on Restoration Literature', in *Restoration and Eighteenth-Century Literature: Essays in Honor of Alan Dugald McKillop*, ed. Carroll Camden (Chicago, University of Chicago Press, 1963), pp. 251–63. Cf. Robert D. Hume, *The Development of English Drama in the Late Seventeenth Century* (Oxford, Clarendon Press, 1976), pp. 487–8.

13 On Dryden's family background and early career, see Winn, *John Dryden*, p. 2ff.

14 Dryden had known Howard since 1657; and in 1663 he was to marry Howard's sister. Through Howard and the Howard family, he probably was made known to Edward Hyde, Earl of Clarendon, who appears to have secured the royal bounty which gave Elizabeth Howard her dowry. On these matters, see Winn, *John Dryden*, pp. 95–103, 119–28. On Dryden's orchestration of his bid for patronage, see Foss, *Age of Patronage*, pp. 25–6.

15 'For I confess my chief endeavours are to delight the Age in which I live. If the humour of this, be for low Comedy, small Accidents, and Raillery, I will force my Genius to obey it, though with more reputation I could write in Verse' ('A Defence of *An Essay of Dramatick Poesie*', in *Works*, IX, pp. 7–8).

16 'Preface to *Secret Love*', in *Works*, IX, p. 115; 'To the Right Honourable Charles Lord Buckhurst', in *Works*, XVII, p. 4.

17 On literary divisions in the Court, see McFadden, *Dryden: The Public Writer*, p. 110. On the largely corresponding political divisions, see J. R. Jones, *Country and Court: England, 1658–1714* (Cambridge, Mass., Harvard University Press, 1978), pp. 161–3. On the need for caution and tact in addressing Court figures, see Winn, *John Dryden*, pp. 163, 325–6. Also, see Donald Davie, 'Dramatic Poetry: Dryden's Conversation Piece', *Cambridge Journal*, 5 (1952), 556.

18 Although he could write like a courtier, Dryden could not act like one. See Winn, *John Dryden*, pp. 249–50. For a contemporary's judgment, see George Etherege, Letter to John Dryden, 20 March 1687, in *Letters of Sir George Etherege*, ed. Frederick Bracher (Berkeley, University of California Press, 1974), p. 103. On the extent of Dryden's actual relationship with the Court, see McFadden, *Dryden: The Public Writer*, pp. 121–2.

19 'Preface to *The Tempest*', in *Works*, X, p. 3.

20 In a letter (1691) to Dryden, written in answer to one which Dryden had sent him, William Walsh mentions Castiglione by name; and in his discussion of Castiglione on love he clearly suggests that Dryden not only was familiar with *The Courtier* but had for a long time been very much impressed by it. According to James M. Osborn, 'Walsh's comments indicate that Dryden had recommended that he look into Castiglione ...' (*John Dryden: Some Biographical Facts and Problems*, rev. edn (Gainesville, University of Florida Press, 1965), p. 232).

21 On *The Courtier* and its influence on Elizabethan and Jacobean writers, see the following: M. H. Curtis, *Oxford and Cambridge in Transition: 1558–1642* (Oxford, Clarendon Press, 1959), pp. 128, 134, 136; Harris Francis Fletcher, *The Intellectual Development of John Milton* (Urbana, University of Illinois Press, 1961), II, 335, 579; Javitch, *Poetry and Courtliness*; Ruth Kelso, *The Doctrine of the English Gentleman in the Sixteenth Century*, University of Illinois Studies in Language and Literature, no. 14 (Urbana, University of Illinois Press, 1929); Wayne A. Rebhorn, *Courtly Performances: Masking and Festivity in Castiglione's 'Book of the Courtier'* (Detroit, Wayne State University Press, 1978); Marion White Singleton, *God's Courtier: Configuring a Different Grace in George Herbert's 'Temple'* (Cambridge, Cambridge University Press, 1987).

22 At no point during the Restoration, as modern scholarship has now more than amply demonstrated, was *The Book of the Courtier* completely unknown or entirely neglected. Much of its influence appears to have come from indirect sources: the popularity of Sidney and Shakespeare, Jonson and Herbert, on all four of whom Castiglione had left his mark; and the tremendous effect that he must have had on the English Court while it was in France, where the cult of the poet-courtier and the courtier-poet had been kept very much alive by Louis XIV and his circle. Nonetheless, copies of the book have been traced to a large number of private libraries, including those of the Earl of Halifax, John Locke, and Daniel Defoe. Of the three men whom Dryden debates with in the *Essay of Dramatick Poesie* (1668), two almost certainly had some knowledge of *The Courtier*. Sir Charles Sedley owned a copy of the work; and Lord Buckhurst must have been aware that his distinguished ancestor Thomas Sackville, whom Dryden mentions in the dedication of *The Rival Ladies* (1664), wrote commendatory pieces for two translations of *The*

Courtier, one in English (1561), the other in Latin (1571). The extent to which the book was widely read, and actually studied or imitated, is another matter and is not immediately relevant. What is relevant is that Dryden was not concerned with following an uncommon vogue or with reviving a dead tradition. He would redefine and so re-establish a literary and social ideal to which for the moment he felt personally drawn, an ideal which, as he well knew, appealed to many of his acquaintances who were court figures, including the Earl of Clarendon; and Clarendon must have read *The Courtier*: he grew up when, early in the century, the book was still moderately fashionable; and he does appear in middle age to have cherished many of its values and ideals. On the later influence of *The Courtier* in England and France, see the following: René Bray, 'Honnête homme', in *Dictionnaire des Lettres Françaises: Le Dix-Septième Siècle*, ed. Cardinal Georges Grente (Paris, Arthème Fayard, 1954); Peter Burke, *The Fortunes of the Courtier: The European Reception of Castiglione's 'Cortegiano'* (Cambridge, Polity Press, 1995); V[ivian] De Sola Pinto, *Sir Charles Sedley, 1639–1701: A Study in the Life and Literature of the Restoration* (New York, Boni and Liveright, 1927), pp. 37, 285.

23 'Preface to *The Rival Ladies*', in *Works*, VIII, p. 95; 'To ... Charles Lord Buckhurst', in *Works*, XVII, p. 6.
24 'To ... Charles Lord Buckhurst', in *Works*, XVII, pp. 5–6.
25 'Preface to *Secret Love*', in *Works*, IX, p. 117.
26 'Preface to *Tyrannick Love*', in *Works*, X, p. 109.
27 'Epilogue to *Tyrannick Love*', in *Works*, X, p. 192.
28 'When he [Dryden] has any objection to obviate, or any license to defend, he is not very scrupulous about what he asserts, nor very cautious, if the present purpose be served, not to entangle himself in his own sophistries' ('Life of Dryden', in *Lives*, I, p. 415).
29 See, for example, the following: Fry, *Reach of Criticism*, pp. 88–98, 218; Pechter, *Dryden's Classical Theory*, pp. 59–61; James Sutherland, *English Literature of the Late Seventeenth Century* (Oxford, Clarendon Press, 1969), p. 412; George Williamson, 'Dryden as Critic', *University of California Chronicle*, 32 (1930), 71–6.
30 In the playfulness of the early criticism Dryden was no doubt influenced, at least in part, by the Court Wits, two of whom – Sedley and Buckhurst – he had actually met, with all of whom he would curry favour. They were widely known, and occasionally celebrated, for the playfulness in their conversation, as well as in their poems and plays. On the Court Wits, see Wilson, *The Court Wits*; on Dryden's relation with the Wits, see Winn, *John Dryden*, pp. 162–4.
   When he wrote no longer for the aristocracy alone, but for a very much larger audience, one which included primarily the middle class, Dryden gave up the role of courtier-poet and with it the early playfulness; he would now write with the seriousness of a committed author.
31 'To ... Roger Earl of Orrery', in *Works*, VIII, p. 97.
32 *Ibid.*
33 'Life of Dryden', in *Lives*, I, p. 412.
34 'Preface to *An Evening's Love*', in *Works*, X, p. 204.
35 *Ibid.*, pp. 210–11.
36 Throughout the Restoration, book sales increased dramatically; and authors were no longer solely dependent, as Frank A. Mumby writes, on 'the leisured and cultured classes' (*Publishers and Booksellers*, rev. 5th edn (London, Jonathan Cape, 1974), p. 14).
37 'Preface to *All for Love*', in *Works*, XIII, p. 13.
38 Dryden's new conception of the role of the poet was, in part, the result of personal

disappointment with the Court. See McFadden, *Dryden: The Public Writer*, p. 120ff. Dryden's changing relations with his patrons is discussed in Dustin Griffin, *Literary Patronage in England, 1650–1800* (Cambridge, Cambridge University Press, 1996), pp. 70–98.

39 'Discourse concerning ... Satire', in *Works*, IV, pp. 59–60.

40 'Life of Plutarch', in *Works*, XVII, p. 277.

41 'Preface to *Sylvæ*', in *Works*, III, p. 3; 'Preface to *Don Sebastian*', in *Works*, XV, p. 71.

42 'Preface to *Examen Poeticum*', in *Works*, IV, p. 373.

43 As a critic Dryden assumed a different persona in each of the three stages of his career; but throughout the criticism, as in many of his other works, especially his satires, comedies and translations, he consistently relied on and developed a rhetoric which had its roots in the native tradition of the plain style. That style can be traced back to Chaucer; and in the sixteenth and seventeenth centuries it had (before Dryden) its most fervent advocates in classical scholars like Roger Ascham and Sir Thomas Elyot, humanists like Richard Hooker and Francis Bacon, and poet-critics like Sir Philip Sidney and Ben Jonson.

At the same time, it corresponded to, and so for many English rhetoricians found justification in, the plain style of classical antiquity. The classical plain style was the subject of the ancient controversy between the philosophers who (like Plato and Aristotle) would subordinate the manner of expression to the matter and the rhetoricians who (like Isocrates) would subordinate the matter of expression to the manner. It was also conceived of as being one of the three easily distinguishable kinds of rhetoric: the high, the middle, the low. The aim of the high style was to persuade or to move; that of the middle to please; and that of the low (or the plain) to teach. So at least Cicero argued in *De Oratore*. The debate between philosophers and rhetoricians eventually became a controversy between those who (like the Asiatics) preferred a rhetoric or style essentially florid and metaphorical and those who (like the Atticists) urged (in the name of truth) a style essentially plain (that is, simple, clear, denotative, urbane, and perspicacious).

The debate was revived in the sixteenth century not only in England but also in Italy, Spain and France. Dryden's own part in the debate appears to have been negligible. But his preference for the plain style (in both verse and prose) he clearly demonstrated in even his very early publications. And it is that style which, throughout his career, he never ceased to develop, which he established as his criterion for literary excellence in most genres, and which he handed over to posterity as the best medium for expository prose. On the place of the plain style in rhetorical theory, see Wesley Trimpi, *Ben Johnson's Poems: A Study of the Plain Style* (Stanford, Stanford University Press, 1962), pp. 3–91. The history of the plain style in seventeenth-century England is discussed in Robert Adolph, *The Rise of the Modern Prose Style* (Cambridge, Mass., M. I. T. Press, 1968); George Williamson, *The Senecan Amble: A Study in Prose Form from Bacon to Collier* (Chicago, University of Chicago Press, 1951).

Dryden's use of the plain style has sometimes been taken to mean that his works lack imaginative reach. For studies that avoid this blunder, see K. G. Hamilton, *John Dryden and the Poetry of Statement* (East Lansing, Michigan State University Press, 1969); K. G. Hamilton, 'Dryden and Seventeenth-Century Prose Style', in *John Dryden*, ed. Earl Miner (1972; rpt. Athens, Ohio, Ohio University Press, 1975), pp. 297–324.

44 *The Rival Ladies*, though the first of Dryden's plays to be published, was not the first to be performed. It was preceded by *The Wild Gallant*, staged in February 1663, and *The Indian Queen*, staged (it is believed) in January 1664. *The Wild Gallant*, however,

was a total failure; and *The Indian Queen*, though a moderate success, was associated during the Restoration not with Dryden but with his collaborator, Sir Robert Howard. A further point. It has been suggested by Robert Hume and Judith Milhous that *The Rival Ladies* may have been produced as early as the autumn of 1663. See 'Dating Play Premières from Publication Data, 1660–1700', *Harvard Library Bulletin*, 22 (1974), 380.

45 Dryden wrote a prologue and epilogue to *The Wild Gallant* and to *The Indian Queen*, and in each of these verse essays he touches on literary theory, but in a cursory and superficial manner. *The Rival Ladies* has no epilogue. *The Wild Gallant* has no dedication, but it has a brief preface, published in 1669; and in it he merely expresses disappointment with the play. *The Indian Queen* has neither preface nor dedication. It is with the 'Prologue to *The Rival Ladies*' that we have the first fully developed example of the form.

46 'Prologue to *The Rival Ladies*', in *Works*, VIII, p. 103. Dryden does not censure these devices in themselves, but their uncoordinated and unskillful use. They are all found - even, it seems, the practice of variable lighting ('They blow out Candles') – in *The Rival Ladies*.

47 'Prologue to *The Rival Ladies*', pp. 103–4.

48 The connection between Dryden's prologue and Tuke's work was first noted by Allison Gaw, 'Tuke's *Adventures of Five Hours*, in Relation to the "Spanish Plot" and to John Dryden', in *Studies in English Drama*, ed. Allison Gaw, Publications of the University of Pennsylvania, Series in Philology, no. 14 (Philadelphia, University of Pennsylvania, 1917), 17–18. The relationship was further elaborated by Ned Bliss Allen, *The Sources of John Dryden's Comedies* (1935; rpt. New York, Gordian Press, 1967), pp. 55–65. The findings of Gaw and Allen have largely been ignored in commentaries on the prologue, including those by Kinsley, Monk, and Watson.

49 8 January 1663, in *The Diary of Samuel Pepys*, ed. Robert Latham and William Matthews (Berkeley, University of California Press, 1971), IV, p. 8.

50 *Dramatick Poesie*, in *Works*, XVII, pp. 45, 58.

51 'A New Play', in *The Adventures of Five Hours*, ed. A. E. Swaen (Amsterdam, Swets and Zeitlinger, 1927), p. 51.

52 *Ibid.*

53 'Epilogue to *The Adventures of Five Hours*', in *Adventures*, p. 127.

54 Dryden had already provided an answer to Tuke in the 'Epilogue to *The Wild Gallant*, as it was first Acted', and the answer helps clarify his later remarks:

> There is not any Person here so mean,
> But he may freely judge each Act and Scene:
> But if you bid him choose his Judges then,
> He boldly names true English Gentlemen:
> For he ne'r thought a handsome Garb or Dress,
> So great a Crime to make their Judgement less:
> And with these Gallants he these Ladies joyns,
> To judge that Language their Converse refines (*Works*, VIII, p. 89).

Since the play is a comedy and hence a portrait of common life, anyone may judge the action ('each Act and Scene'). But as courtier-poet Dryden allows that, of the members of his audience, only 'Ladies' and 'Gentlemen' are equipped to judge his 'Language'.

55 'To ... Henry Howard ...', in *Adventures*, pp. [55–6].

56 The sources of Dryden's psychology of artistic creation are traced in Monk (ed.), *Works*, VIII, pp. 272–3; the sources of his theory of the drama, in Kirsch, *Dryden's Heroic*

Drama, pp. 15–18. Although he provides a sound account of the subject, Kirsch fails to distinguish adequately between Dryden's theory of tragi-comedy and his theory of the heroic play.

57 *A History of Restoration Drama: 1660–1700*, 4th edn, vol. I of *A History of English Drama: 1660–1900* (Cambridge, Cambridge University Press, 1952), p. 219. Tuke does not mention that his work is a loose translation of a contemporary Spanish play, Antonio Coello's *Los empeños de seis horas* (1657). In a preface to a later edition (1671) he admits a Spanish source, which he does not name and which he mistakenly attributes to Calderòn. Literary research has since supplied the missing information and corrected the error. See Gaw, 'Tuke's *Adventures*', p. 23.

58 According to John Loftis, Dryden models his play not on Spanish sources but on 'Spanish studies of Jacobean and Caroline times', a fact which helps explain the 'approximation' of his work to 'Fletcherian tragi-comedy'. See *Spanish Plays*, p. 104.

59 'To … Roger Earl of Orrery', in *Works*, VIII, p. 98.

60 *Ibid.*, p. 95. In his prologue, Tuke celebrates the 'close Contrivance' of his plot; and in his epilogue he returns to the subject, while he also commends himself for his handling of time and place:

> Here's a fine Play indeed, to lay the Scene
> In three Houses of the same Town, O mean!
> Why we have several Plays, where I defie
> Th'Devil to tell where the Scene does lie:
> Sometimes in Greece, and then they make a step
> To Transilvania, thence at one Leap
> (To) Greece again: this shows a ranging Brain,
> Which scorns to be confin'd t' a Town in Spain.
>   Then for the Plot;
> The possible *Adventures of Five Hours*;
> A copious Design, why'in some of ours
> Many of th'Adventures are impossible …
> ('Epilogue to *The Adventures of Five Hours*', in *Adventures*, pp. 127–8).

In the dedication, Dryden's point is that, without probability and decorum, the unifying devices which Tuke names are entirely worthless.

61 'To … Roger Earl of Orrery', in *Works*, VIII, p. 97.

62 *Ibid.*

63 *Ibid.*

64 *The Rival Ladies* contains three pairs of young lovers, who constantly interact. In later tragi-comedies Dryden will separate his paired lovers, and place one or more pairs in a world of dynastic intrigue and one or more pairs in a world of domestic comedy.

65 'To … Roger Earl of Orrery', in *Works*, VIII, pp. 95, 98.

66 *Ibid.*, p. 97.

67 *Ibid.*, p. 101.

68 *Ibid.*, pp. 96–7.

69 *Ibid.*, p. 95.

70 *Ibid.*, p. 100.

71 *Ibid.*, p. 99. *Angli suos* etc. (John Barclay, *Icon animorum* (1614), pp. 74–5; trans. Watson). Dryden's quotation is inexact and, as Monk notes (*Works*, VIII, p. 278), the second clause ('*caeteras … habent*') is Dryden's addition.

CHAPTER THREE
A French play (1665–1668)

1 In his dedication of the work, Dryden takes pains to let us know that the *Essay* represents an earlier stage of his thought. He dates it from the period of his country stay. Most critics believe that it was drafted in the late summer or early autumn of 1665 (that is, soon after the historical event to which it refers). Although the date on the title page is 1668, the official date of publication, the *Essay* had actually been registered in the preceding August, five months earlier; and it may have gone on sale towards the end of the year. See Monk *et al.* (eds), *Works*, XVII, p. 331.

2 'To ... Charles Lord Buckhurst', in *Works*, XVII, pp. 3, 5. In the present study I use the text of the California Dryden, which prints the 1668 edition with emendations from the second edition, most of which are stylistic. For my discussion of a significant change in the second edition, see below, p. 152.

3 The dialogue is supposed to take place on 3 June 1665 ('that memorable day' of the opening sentence), when a naval battle between the English and Dutch was actually being fought in the English Channel. For the historical event to which the *Essay* refers, see David Ogg, *England in the Reign of Charles II*, 2nd edn (Oxford, Oxford University Press, 1956), I, pp. 286–8. Dryden was caught up in the Quarrel of the Ancients and Moderns, in one way or another, during much of his life. For a discussion of his continued involvement, see below, pp. 44–52 (early period), pp. 160, 165–7 (middle period) and pp. 177–8 (final period).

4 On the traditional identification of the speakers, see Stanley Archer, 'The Persons in *An Essay of Dramatic Poesy*', *Papers on Language and Literature*, 2 (1966), 305–14. For a dissenting view, see David B. Haley, *Dryden and the Problem of Freedom: The Republican Aftermath, 1649–1680* (New Haven, Yale University Press, 1997), pp. 163–5, 270.

5 For reasons that are not clear, however, Dryden attributes to Sir Robert Howard (Crites) an enthusiasm for classical drama which Howard did not in fact share. For Howard's actual views, see, 'Preface to *Four New Plays*', in *Critical Essays of the Seventeenth Century*, ed. J. E. Spingarn (1908; rpt. Bloomington, Indiana University Press, 1957), II, pp. 98–100.

6 See above, pp. 25–8.

7 According to Nicol Smith,

> Dryden states contradictory views, and very fairly, as they are all tenable. If we suspect how his preferences lay, we note his freedom from the didactic manner which was common in earlier criticism, and indeed few of our critics at any time have habitually tried to preserve so open a mind. He has a problem, the drama itself has a problem, and it must be examined sceptically (*John Dryden* (London, Cambridge University Press, 1950), pp. 13–14).

For a later statement of this view, see Pechter, *Dryden's Classical Theory*, pp. 36–51.

8 For an interesting statement of Dryden's partiality to Neander, but one which differs radically from my own, see Harth, *Dryden's Thought*, pp. 33–4. Harth's argument has been more fully developed in Howard Weinbrot, *Britannia's Issue: The Rise of British Literature from Dryden to Ossian* (Cambridge, Cambridge University Press, 1993), pp. 150–92. See also Richard V. LeClercq, 'The Academic Nature of the Whole Discourse of *An Essay of Dramatic Poesy*', *Papers on Language and Literature*, 8 (1972), 27–38.

9 'To Charles ... Lord Buckhurst', in *Works*, XVII, p. 6.

10 *Ibid.*, p. 5. Zwicker believes that Dryden's antics are designed to deceive, and not to

amuse, the reader (*Politics and Language*, pp. 43–5, 50).

11 *The Art of Poetry*, in *Satires, Epistles, and Ars Poetica*, trans. H. Rushton Fairclough (Loeb Classical Library, 1929), pp. 404–5.
12 'To the Reader', in *Works*, XVII, p. 7.
13 *Dramatick Poesie*, in *Works*, XVII, p. 11.
14 *Ibid.*, p. 15.
15 On 'judicious[ness]' and 'fire', see Lawrence B. Wallis, *Fletcher, Beaumont, and Company: Entertainers to the Jacobean Gentry* (New York, King's Crown Press, 1947), pp. 18–22. The significance of the definition would have been particularly clear to those readers who knew the background of the *Essay*. In 1661 Samuel Sorbière published his *Relation d'un voyage en Angleterre*, in which he ridiculed the English stage for its violations of the rules. Dryden's work was, in part, an answer to Sorbière; but it was preceded by another English response, Thomas Sprat's *Observations on Mons. Sorbièr's Voyage into England* (1665). There Sprat argues that English drama is indeed civilized and possesses both 'regular[ity]' and 'livli[ness]'. A contemporary familiar with Sprat's work – or English dramatic criticism – would recognize that Dryden's definition is essentially a description of English plays. See George Williamson, 'The Occasion of *An Essay of Dramatic Poesy*', in *Seventeenth-Century Contexts* (Chicago, University of Chicago Press, 1970), pp. 272–88. (First published in *Modern Philology*, 44 (1946), 1–9.) See also Arthur C. Kirsch (ed.), *Literary Criticism of Dryden* (Lincoln, Nebraska, University of Nebraska Press, 1966), p. x.
16 *Dramatick Poesie*, in *Works*, XVII, pp. 16–17.
17 *Ibid.*, p. 15.
18 *Ibid.*
19 *Ibid.*, pp. 21–2.
20 *Ibid.*, p. 26.
21 *Ibid.*, p. 23.
22 *Ibid.*, p. 31.
23 *Ibid.*, p. 33. Indeed, they are virtually identical. Dryden allows Neander's position to be stated twice, once by Eugenius and once by Neander himself.
24 *Ibid.*, p. 37.
25 *Ibid.*, p. 34.
26 *Ibid.*, pp. 51–2.
27 *Ibid.*, pp. 25, 44, 53.
28 *Ibid.*, p. 46.
29 *Ibid.*, p. 47.
30 *Ibid.*, p. 54.
31 *Ibid.*, pp. 55, 57–8, 60. The *examen* was the formal method used by the Académie Française to ascertain whether or not literary works observed the accepted rules of composition. It was best known to English readers, however, through the criticism of Corneille, where it was used not to enforce the rules but to question their severity. On the nature and history of the *examen*, see Kramer, *The Imperial Dryden*, pp. 36–8.
   Kramer chides Dryden for failing to acknowledge that the *examen* form, and much else in the *Essay*, is taken from Corneille (*The Imperial Dryden*, pp. 18–19, 30–46). The complaint is unjustified. Dryden actually names the principal text of Corneille from which he borrows, '*Corneille's* ... Discourse of the three Unities' (in *Works*, XVII, p. 51), quotes from it more than once and employs its terminology – which he leaves untranslated – in the work. In the 'Defence of *An Essay of Dramatick Poesie*' (1668), after stating with

some modesty that most of the *Essay* 'is borrowed from the observations of others', he names Corneille, along with Aristotle, Horace and Jonson, as one of his authorities (in *Works*, IX, p. 13). Modern scholars may offer exhaustive accounts of the debt to Corneille, but it seems odd to expect from Dryden that he do the same: critics do not usually write commentaries on themselves. Moreover, the best of the scholars' accounts do establish the independence of Dryden's thought, a point which even Kramer seems to concede when he complains of Dryden's 'trick' of 'subsum[ing] the Franco-Cornelian aesthetic in a more varied and comprehensive system' (*The Imperial Dryden*, p. 34).

32 Cf. Mary Thale, 'Dryden's Critical Vocabulary', p. 324.

33 *Dramatick Poesie*, in *Works*, XVII, pp. 55–7.

34 Caroline writers also recognized Fletcher as a synthesizer. See Wallis, *Fletcher, Beaumont, and Company*, p. 17.

35 *Dramatick Poesie*, in *Works*, XVII, pp. 63–4.

36 See, for example, Bate (ed.), *Criticism: The Major Texts*, p. 124. Cf. Haley, *Dryden and the Problem of Freedom*, pp. 164, 167–8.

37 *Dramatick Poesie*, in *Works*, XVII, p. 43.

38 *Ibid.*, pp. 53–4.

39 *Ibid.*, pp. 64–5.

40 *Ibid.*, pp. 68, 74. Cf. 'Preface to *Secret Love*', in *Works*, IX, p. 116. Robert Hume does not recognize this shift in subject and argues that the entire *Essay* is centred on heroic drama. 'The dramatic practice implicitly recommended in *Of Dramatic Poesy*', writes Hume, 'is that which Dryden was to explore during the next few years in his rimed "heroic" plays' (*Dryden's Criticism*, p. 204).

41 For a further discussion of this subject, see below, pp. 120–3.

42 *Dramatick Poesie*, in *Works*, XVII, pp. 65–6.

43 *Ibid.*, p. 67.

44 *Ibid.*, p. 74.

45 *Ibid.*

46 See, for example, Monk *et al.* (eds), in *Works*, XVII, p. 357.

47 *Ibid.*, pp. 348–52.

48 *Dramatick Poesie*, in *Works*, XVII, p. 33.

49 *Ibid.*, p. 37.

50 *Ibid.*, pp. 47–8.

51 'Defence of *An Essay*', in *Works*, IX, p. 4.

52 *Observations on Monsieur Sorbière's Voyage into England*, quoted in Williamson, 'The Occasion of *An Essay of Dramatic Poesy*', in *Seventeenth-Century Contexts*, p. 277. A few years earlier the same point had been made by Davenant in *The Play-house to be Lett* (1662; 1673):

> The *French* convey their arguments too much
> In Dialogue: their speeches are too long.
>
> ...
>
> Such length of speeches seem not so unpleasing
> As the contracted walks of their designs
> (in *The Works of Sir William Davenant* (1673; rpt. New York,
> Benjamin Blom, 1968), II, p. 75).

Over the course of his life, Dryden alternately referred to his work as '*An Essay*', a 'Discourse' and a 'Dialogue'.

53 *Dramatick Poesie*, in *Works*, XVII, p. 38.

54 *Ibid.*, p. 80.
55 Of John Dryden as author we get a glimpse, though fleetlingly, in the very brief address 'To the Reader', published along with the dedication and the *Essay*. The role of the courtier-poet is dropped; the language is simple, almost bare; and the purpose of the *Essay* is stated in no uncertain terms: 'The drift of the ensuing Discourse was chiefly to vindicate the honour of our *English Writers* from the censure of those who unjustly prefer the *French* before them' (*Dramatick Poesie*, in *Works*, XVII, p. 7).
56 *Ibid.*, p. 80. Neander's moment of absent-mindedness and self-absorption is probably modelled on an incident in *The Book of the Courtier*, in which Cardinal Bembo becomes lost in his thoughts. See Baldassare Castiglione, *The Book of the Courtier*, trans. Charles S. Singleton (New York, Anchor-Doubleday, 1959), p. 357.
57 'Life of Dryden', in *Lives*, I, p. 412.

CHAPTER FOUR
The new imbalance (1667–1668)

1 *Dramatick Poesie*, in *Works*, XVII, p. 75.
2 *Poetics*, in *Aristotle's Theory of Poetry and Fine Art*, trans. and ed. S. H. Butcher, corrected 4th edn (1911; rpt. New York, Dover Books, 1951), pp. 83, 87, 93–7. On the influence of this aspect of Aristotelian theory on Renaissance criticism, see Danilo Aguzzi-Barbagli, '*Ingegno*, *Acutezza*, and *Meraviglia* in the Sixteenth-Century Great Commentaries to Aristotle's *Poetics*', in *Petrarch to Pirandello: Studies in Italian Literature in Honour of Beatrice Corrigan*, ed. Julius A. Molinaro (Toronto, University of Toronto Press, 1973), pp. 73–93.
3 Dryden's own criticism was first used against him in R. F., 'A Letter to the Honourable Ed. Howard Esq' [1668], in *Drydeniana* (New York, Garland Publishing, 1975), I, pp. 1–12. R. F., however, may well have been imitating a practice already established in the coffee houses. Dryden briefly answered the attack in 'Preface to *Tyrannick Love*', in *Works*, X, p. 113.
4 'Preface to *Albion and Albanius*' [1685], in *Works*, XV, p. 9.
5 'Preface to *Secret Love*', in *Works*, IX, pp. 116–17.
6 Another prologue and epilogue to the play were first printed, though without attribution, in the *Covent Garden Drollery* (1672). Neither of them is important as criticism. See 'Prologue to *Secret Love*', in *Works*, IX, pp. 121–2; 'Epilogue to *Secret Love*', in *Works*, IX, pp. 202–3.
7 'An account' in *Works*, I, 56.
8 L. A. Beaurline and Fredson Bowers (eds), *John Dryden: Four Comedies* (Chicago, University of Chicago Press, 1967), p. 29.
9 'Preface to *Secret Love*', in *Works*, IX, p. 115.
10 For the best account of the entire subject, see Michael McKeon, *Politics and Poetry in Restoration England: The Case of Dryden's 'Annus Mirabilis'* (Cambridge, Mass., Harvard University Press, 1975), pp. 79ff.
11 *Ibid.*, p. 268.
12 Pepys, 3 February 1664, *Diary*, V, p. 37.
13 Because of real hostility between the King and the City of London, the dedication may seem to be an exercise in irony. In my view, however, there is nothing in the dedication to suggest irony; and there is sound evidence that, because of his behaviour during the fire, the King had begun to win favour and that, in his role of courtier-poet, Dryden now

hoped to build on that favour. For an opposing point of view, see Zwicker, *Politics and Language*, pp. 38–9. See also Annabel M. Patterson, *Marvell and the Civic Crown* (Princeton, Princeton University Press, 1978), pp. 144–5.

14 'To the Metropolis of Great Britain', in *Works*, I, p. 48.

15 On Dryden's views on the social function of poetry, see Cedric D. Reverend II, 'Dryden's "Essay of Dramatic Poesie": The Poet and the World of Affairs', *Studies in English Literature*, 22 (1982), 375–93.

16 'An account', in *Works*, I, p. 52. *Omnia sponte* etc. (Source unknown; trans. by ed.). George R. Noyes observes (*The Poetical Works of Dryden*, rev. edn (Boston, Houghton Mifflin, 1950), p. 946) that 'the line seems like one from a schoolboy's exercise ...'

17 *The Advancement of Learning* [1605], ed. G. W. Kitchin (London, J. M. Dent, 1915), pp. 82–3. For a fine analysis of Bacon's views on poetry and rhetoric, see James Stephens, *Francis Bacon and the Style of Science* (Chicago, University of Chicago Press, 1975).

18 *History of the Royal Society* [1667], ed. Jackson I. Cope and Harold Whitmore Jones (St. Louis, Washington University Press, 1958), pp. 111–12. For other examples of attacks on *'fine speaking'* during the Restoration, see Richard Foster Jones, 'Science and English Prose Style in the Third Quarter of the Seventeenth Century', *PMLA*, 45 (1930), 997–1009. Jones's thesis, however, must be approached with care. Its shortcomings are explained in Brian Vickers, 'The Royal Society and English Prose Style: A Reassessment', in *Rhetoric and the Pursuit of Truth: Language and Change in the Seventeenth and Eighteenth Centuries* (Los Angeles, William Andrews Clark Memorial Library, 1985), pp. 1–76.

19 'The Author's Apology for his Book', in *The Miscellaneous Works of John Bunyan*, ed. Graham Midgley (Oxford, Clarendon Press, 1980), VI, pp. 138–9.

20 On the Puritan aesthetic, see the following: Roger Pooley, 'Language and Loyalty: Plain Style at the Restoration', *Literature and History*, 6 (1980), 2–18; Roger Pooley, 'Plain and Simple: Bunyan and Style', in *John Bunyan, Conventicle and Parnassus: Tercentenary Essays*, ed. N. H. Keeble (Oxford, Clarendon Press, 1988), pp. 91–111; Lawrence A. Sasek, *The Literary Temper of the English Puritans* (1961; rpt. New York, Greenwood Press, 1969).

21 *Intellectual Milieu*, p. 8.

22 *Notes and Observations*, in *Works*, XVII, p. 182.

23 'An account', in *Works*, I, p. 50.

24 See, for example, James Heath, *A Brief Chronicle of the Late Intestine VVar in the Three Kingdoms of England, Scotland and Ireland, With the Intervening Affairs of Treaties, and other Occurrences relating thereunto. As also the several Usurpations, Foreign Wars, Differences and Interests depending upon it, to the happy Restitution of our Sacred Soveraign King Charles the Second, With all memorable Affairs since His Time...*, 2nd impression (London, 1663). For a discussion of other parallels with historical writing, see Zwicker, *Politics and Language*, pp. 40–2.

25 Sprat, *History*, pp. 111–13. The demands made on the scientist differed only in degree from those made on writers in other fields. According to Sprat, for example, the best histories are ones which are 'masculinely,... chastly, and ... unaffectedly done' (p. 40). For 'purity and shortness ... are the chief beauties of Historical Writings' (sig. B4^v). For a different interpretation of Sprat's theory of style, see Margery Purver, *The Royal Society: Concept and Creation* (Cambridge, Mass., M. I. T. Press, 1967), pp. 99–100; Vickers, 'The Royal Society and English Prose Style', pp. 10–15.

26 'An account', in *Works*, I, pp. 51–2.

27 'Preface to *Gondibert* [1650]', in *Critical Essays*, ed. Spingarn, II, pp. 3, 11.

28 'Answer to Davenant's "Preface to *Gondibert*"', in *Critical Essays*, ed. Spingarn, II, p. 56.

29 'An account', in *Works*, I, p. 50.

30 *Ibid.*, p. 53.

31 *Ibid.*

32 According to James Engell, Dryden is concerned not with 'a particular kind of text, but a particular kind of effect'. On the contrary, Dryden associates particular effects with particular genres. He is concerned not with the pleasure of literature in general but with the specific pleasure to be derived from the epic or historical poem. For Engell's interpretation, see *Forming the Critical Mind*, pp. 36–7.

33 'An account', in *Works*, I, p. 54.

34 *Ibid.*, pp. 54–5. *Materiam superabat* etc. (*Metamorphoses* II.5; trans. by ed.).

35 Bernard Weinberg, *A History of Literary Criticism in the Italian Renaissance* (Chicago, University of Chicago Press, 1961), II, pp. 341–2.

36 *The Prelude: 1799, 1805, 1850*, ed. Jonathan Wordsworth *et al.* (New York, W. W. Norton, 1979), p. 185.

37 'An account', in *Works*, I, p. 55.

38 Once one has read Dryden on Virgil one reads modern appreciations, such as the following by C. M. Bowra, with the shock of recognition:

> Homer sweeps us away by the irresistible movement of lines through a whole passage to a splendid climax ... But in Virgil, great though the paragraphs are, compelling though the climax is when it is reached, we are more concerned with the details, with each small effect and each deftly placed word, than with the whole. We linger over the richness of single phrases, over the 'pathetic half-lines', over the precision or potency with which a word illuminates a sentence or a happy sequence of sounds imparts an inexplicable charm to something that might otherwise have been trivial (*From Virgil to Milton* (London, Macmillan, 1945), p. 5).

39 *Virgil: A Study in Civilized Poetry* (Oxford, Clarendon Press, 1963), pp. 41–96.

40 'Aspects of Dryden's Imagery', in *Dryden's Mind and Art*, ed. King, p. 25.

41 The faults in the poem, and the predilection which is their cause, Samuel Johnson identified at once and, as we might expect, explained with his usual acumen, precision and brevity:

> This poem is written with great diligence, yet does not fully answer the expectation raised by such subjects and such a writer ... [H]e has sometimes his vein of parenthesis and incidental disquisition, and stops his narrative for a wise remark. The general fault is that he affords more sentiment than description, and does not so much impress scenes upon the fancy as deduce consequences and make comparisons ...
>
> Of the king collecting his navy, he says:
>
>> It seems as every ship their sovereign knows,
>> His awful summons they so soon obey;
>> So hear the scaly herds when Proteus blows,
>> And so to pasture follow through the sea.
>
> It would not be hard to believe that Dryden had written the first two lines seriously, and that some wag had added the two latter in burlesque ('Life of Dryden', in *Lives*, I, pp. 430–1).

42 For examples of misreadings over the last three centuries, see the following: *The Friendly Vindication* [1673], in *Drydeniana*, V, p. 10; W. P. Ker (ed.), *Essays of John Dryden* (Oxford, Clarendon Press, 1900), I, p. xlix; Watson (ed.), '*Of Dramatic Poesy*', I, p. 104; Moore, *The Nobler Pleasure*, pp. 42–5; Kramer, *The Imperial Dryden*, p. 29.

43 Ker (ed.), *Essays of John Dryden*, I, p. xlix.

44 'Prologue to *Secret Love*', in *Works*, IX, p. 119.

45 *Ibid.*

46 'Second Prologue to *Secret Love*', in *Works*, IX, p. 120.

47 *Ibid.*

48 'Preface to *Secret Love*', in *Works*, IX, pp. 115–17.

49 *Ibid.*

50 *Ibid.*, pp. 115–16.

51 *Ibid.*, p. 117.

52 *Ibid.*, p. 116.

CHAPTER FIVE

A charter of freedom (1668–1670)

1 *The Duke of Lerma* is an adaptation of a now lost Elizabethan play. For a discussion of the relationship between Howard's work and its source, see H. J. Oliver, *Sir Robert Howard (1628–1698): A Critical Biography* (Durham, North Carolina, Duke University Press, 1963), pp. 97–107.

2 Relevant documents on the history of this quarrel can be found in D. D. Arundell (ed.), *Dryden and Howard: 1664–1668* (Cambridge, Cambridge University Press, 1929).

3 On the political and social dimensions of the quarrel, see McFadden, *Dryden: The Public Writer*, pp. 72–83. Cf. Winn, *John Dryden*, pp. 195–8.

4 'To the Reader', in *Dryden and Howard*, ed. Arundell, p. 97.

5 *Ibid.*, p. 94.

6 *Ibid.*, p. 97.

7 *Ibid.*

8 *Ibid.*, pp. 93, 95.

9 *Ibid.*, p. 95.

10 *Ibid.*

11 *Ibid.*, p. 97.

12 *The School of Women Criticized*, in *The Works of Mr. de Molière*, trans. John Ozell (1714; rpt. New York, Benjamin Blom, 1967), I, pp. 74–5.

13 'A Defence of *An Essay*', in *Works*, IX, p. 9.

14 *Ibid.*, pp. 11–2.

15 *Ibid.*, p. 14.

16 Hoyt Trowbridge, 'The Place of Rules in Dryden's Criticism', in *From Dryden to Jane Austen: Essays on English Critics and Writers, 1660–1818* (Albuquerque, University of New Mexico Press, 1977), pp. 16–28. (First published in *Modern Philology*, 44 (1946), 84–96.)

17 'Defence of *An Essay*', in *Works*, IX, p. 14.

18 *Ibid.*, p. 15.

19 *Ibid.*, pp. 13–14.

20 *Ibid.*, p. 11.

21 *Ibid.*, pp. 5–7.

22 *Ibid.*, pp. 5–6.

23 *Ibid.*, p. 6.

24 'An account', in *Works*, I, p. 55.

25 'Defence of *An Essay*', in *Works*, IX, p. 12.

26 *Ibid.*, p. 11.

27 *Ibid.*, pp. 6–7.

28 *Ibid.*, p. 19.

29 *Ibid.*, p. 12. James Engell, I believe, mistakes Dryden's position:

> Making a distinction as valuable as it is subtle, Dryden says that 'poesy must resemble natural truth, but it must *be* ethical'. That is, poesy or art cannot copy or give us exact reference to life, to our ideas, to things or to experience. It simply *re-sembles* these to our minds and feelings … And Dryden would contend that this process could be 'free' from ethics only if the imitation in no way resembled 'natural truth' or experience (*Forming the Critical Mind*, p. 42).

Earlier in his essay, Dryden establishes, though in terms somewhat different from Engell's, that poetry is not a copy of life. In the passage to which Engell refers, his concern is to establish limits to the poet's invention. He more than asserts that poetry cannot be '"free" from ethics'. He insists that poetry must be moral.

30 'Defence of *An Essay*', in *Works*, XI, p. 18.

31 *Ibid.*, p. 20.

32 *Ibid.*, pp. 16–19.

33 *Ibid.*, p. 12.

34 *Ibid.*

35 According to Robert D. Hume, Dryden's criticism exhibits no 'definite shift of direction' until 1670, at which point the change is sudden and 'dramatic'. See 'Dryden on Creation', p. 297.

36 *Dramatick Poesie*, in *Works*, XVII, p. 52.

37 'Preface to *Tyrannick Love*', in *Works*, X, p. 111.

38 *Dramatick Poesie*, in *Works*, XVII, pp. 76–7.

39 'Defence of *An Essay*', in *Works*, IX, p. 6.

40 'An account', in *Works*, I, pp. 54–5.

41 *Dramatick Poesie*, in *Works*, XVII, pp. 55–7.

42 'Prologue to *The Tempest*', in *Works*, X, p. 6.

43 *Ibid.*

44 *Ibid.*

45 *Ibid.*, pp. 6–7.

46 'Preface to *The Tempest*', in *Works*, X, p. 3.

47 *Ibid.*

48 *Ibid.*, pp. 4–5.

49 George Lyman Kittredge (ed.), *The Tempest* (Boston, Ginn, 1939), p. xix; Novak (ed.), *Works*, X, pp. 328–43.

50 'Preface to *The Tempest*', in *Works*, X, p. 4.

51 Hume misses the irony in the dedication to Davenant and therefore concludes that in the preface '[the faculty of] judgment is rated highly' ('Dryden on Creation', p. 297). For another literal reading, see Edmond, *Rare Sir William Davenant*, pp. 198–9.

52 'Preface to *The Tempest*', in *Works*, X, p. 4.

53 *Dramatick Poesie*, in *Works*, XVII, p. 64.

54 'Preface to *Tyrannick Love*', in *Works*, X, p. 111.
55 *Ibid.*, p. 112.
56 John Harrington Smith and Dougald MacMillan (eds), *Works*, VIII, p. 285.
57 'Preface to *Gondibert*' [1650], in *Critical Essays*, ed. Spingarn, II, p. 17.
58 *Ibid.*, pp. 2, 4.
59 Although the supernatural is not immediately present in the poem, there are three instances in which reference is made to folk superstition: that a dead hero rules a star; that dreams may be prophetic; and that, when placed near an evil character, emeralds change colour. For another interpretation of these references, see David F. Gladish (ed.), *Gondibert* (Oxford, Clarendon Press, 1971), p. 289.
60 *Poetics*, in *Aristotle's Theory of Poetry*, ed. Butcher, p. 101.
61 *Discourses*, p. 38.
62 *Poetics*, in *Aristotle's Theory of Poetry*, ed. Butcher, pp. 95–7.
63 Butcher (trans. and ed.), *Aristotle's Theory of Poetry*, p. 173.
64 'Preface to *Tyrannick Love*', in *Works*, X, p. 112.
65 *Ibid.*, p. 109.
66 Dryden's treatment of religion, as Jean H. Hagstrum notes, is not without its 'ironies and incongruities'. See *Eros and Vision: The Restoration to Romanticism* (Evanston, Northwestern University Press, 1989), pp. 113–14.
67 'Prologue to *Tyrannick Love*', in *Works*, X, p. 114.
68 *Ibid.*
69 'Preface to *Tyrannick Love*', in *Works*, X, pp. 111–12. *Eludit gyro* etc. (*Aeneid* XI.695; trans. Watson).

CHAPTER SIX
Varieties of comic experience (1671)

1 Derek Hughes, *Dryden's Heroic Plays* (Lincoln, Nebraska, University of Nebraska Press, 1981), p. 38.
2 'Prologue to *The Wild Gallant*', in *Works*, VIII, p. 6.
3 'Epilogue to *The Wild Gallant* Reviv'd', in *Works*, VIII, p. 90. Pepys noted the same problem in the original version (23 February 1663, *Diary*, IV, p. 56).
4 16 August 1667, *Diary*, VIII, p. 387. Oddly, he also commends the wit of the play.
5 'Prologue to *Sir Martin Mar-all*', in *Works*, IX, p. 208.
6 Although Samuel Johnson found much in it to be 'judicious and profound', the preface has not especially interested Dryden's later critics and biographers. A summary of its major themes can be found in Moore, *The Nobler Pleasure*, pp. 88–95; Maximillian E. Novak (ed.), *Works*, X, pp. 444–9. Robert D. Hume interprets the play, but only in passing, as a blunt dismissal of low comedy (*Development of English Drama*, p. 277). For Robert Markley, whose remarks are also quite brief, it is an altogether more complex work, ostensibly 'intended to shore up [Dryden's] credentials as a satirist in the Jonsonian tradition', but actually designed to deflect the ideological challenge posed by the witty dialogue of *An Evening's Love* (*Two-Edg'd Weapons: Style and Ideology in the Comedies of Etherege, Wycherley, and Congreve* (Oxford, Clarendon Press, 1988), pp. 94–5).
7 Dryden's plays through 1670 include the following: tragi-comedies – *The Rival Ladies* (1664), *Secret Love* (1668), *The Tempest* (1670); comedies – *Sir Martin Mar-all* (1668), *The Wild Gallant* (1669); heroic plays – *The Indian Queen* (1665), *The Indian Emperour*

(1667), *Tyrannick Love* (1670). The near symmetry in his dramatic output remains striking even if we add to the list plays performed but not published before 1671. These works include a comedy, *An Evening's Love* (1668; 1671), and a heroic play, *The Conquest of Granada, Part One* (1670; 1672).

8 For a discussion of wit and humour in Fletcher, Jonson and Shakespeare, see the following: Wallis, *Fletcher, Beaumont, and Company*; James E. Savage, *Ben Jonson's Basic Comic Characters and Other Essays* (Hattiesburg, Miss., University and College Press of Mississippi, 1973); Lawrence Babb, *The Elizabethan Malady: A Study of Melancholia in English Literature from 1580 to 1642* (East Lansing, Michigan State College Press, 1951); C. L. Barber, *Shakespeare's Festive Comedy* (Princeton, Princeton University Press, 1959).

9 Norman N. Holland, *The First Modern Comedies: The Significance of Etherege, Wycherley, and Congreve* (Cambridge, Mass., Harvard University Press, 1959), pp. 20–7. See also Rose A. Zimbardo, *A Mirror to Nature: Transformations in Drama and Aesthetics, 1660–1732* (Lexington, Kentucky, University Press of Kentucky, 1986), pp. 62–4.

10 'Epilogue to *The Wild Gallant* Reviv'd', in *Works*, VIII, p. 91.

11 See 'To the Right Honourable, John, Earl of Mulgrave', in *Works*, XII, p. 154.

12 Every century has had its own favourite term for what the Restoration knew as comedy of wit. In the eighteenth century, it was genteel comedy; in the nineteenth, comedy of manners; in the twentieth, high comedy. See Bateson, 'Contributions', pp. 89–93.

13 In several of the later dedications literary criticism far outstrips compliment. Such works are not in fact dedications at all. As Dryden suggests they are prefaces addressed to a single person. See, for example, 'Discourse concerning ... Satire', in *Works*, IV, pp. 3, 15–16. See also the 'Preface to *The Spanish Fryar*', in *Works*, XIV, p. 103. For evidence that Dryden eventually finds ways to assert his independence even within the dedications, see Griffin, *Literary Patronage*, pp. 76–96.

14 'Preface to *An Evening's Love*', in *Works*, X, p. 202.

15 Following a Restoration convention, neither Dryden nor Shadwell mentions each other by name. Dryden may not refer exclusively to Shadwell; nor Shadwell, to Dryden. Nevertheless, it has never been doubted that each, in the main, is the target of the other's remarks. For a history of their quarrel, see Oden (ed.), *Dryden and Shadwell*, pp. vi–xxii.

16 'Preface to *The Sullen Lovers*' [1668], in *Critical Essays*, ed. Spingarn, II, p. 150.

17 *Dramatick Poesie*, in *Works*, XVII, p. 57.

18 'Preface to *The Sullen Lovers*', in *Critical Essays*, ed. Spingarn, II, pp. 150–1.

19 *Ibid.*

20 *Ibid.*, p. 150.

21 'Preface to *An Evening's Love*', in *Works*, X, pp. 205–6.

22 *Ibid.*, pp. 205, 207, 209.

23 'Prologue to *The Tempest*', in *Works*, X, p. 6. For Dryden's earlier views on Jonson and Fletcher, see *Dramatick Poesie*, in *Works*, XVII, pp. 56–8.

24 'Preface to *An Evening's Love*', in *Works*, X, p. 202.

25 This phrase appears in the *Essay of Dramatick Poesie* (in *Works*, XVII, p. 57).

26 Though implied in the 'Preface to *An Evening's Love*', this view is more clearly stated in the 'Defence of the Epilogue' (1672). See 'Defence of the Epilogue', in *Works*, XI, pp. 217–18.

27 'Preface to *An Evening's Love*', in *Works*, X, pp. 203, 205, 212. In an earlier discussion of low comedy, Dryden had made the same points. See 'Defence of An Essay', in *Works*, IX, pp. 5–6.

28 'Preface to *An Evening's Love*', in *Works*, X, pp. 209–10 *et passim*.

29 The background studies I consulted on 'wit' include the following: S. L. Bethell, 'Gracián, Tesauro, and the Nature of Metaphysical Wit', *The Northern Miscellany of Literary Criticism*, I (1953), 19–40; Gerald Webster Chapman (ed.), *Literary Criticism in England: 1660–1800* (New York, Alfred A. Knopf, 1966), pp. 151–62; J. A. Cuddon, *A Dictionary of Literary Terms*, rev. edn (New York, Doubleday, 1976); Ernst Robert Curtius, *European Literature and the Latin Middle Ages*, trans. Willard R. Trask (New York, Harper and Row, 1953), pp. 273–301; Alastair Fowler, *Conceitful Thought: The Interpretation of English Renaissance Poems* (Edinburgh, Edinburgh University Press, 1975); Thomas H. Fujimura, *The Restoration Comedy of Wit* (Princeton, Princeton University Press, 1952), pp. 16–38; G. M. A. Grube, *The Greek and Roman Critics* (Toronto, University of Toronto Press, 1965); C. S. Lewis, *Studies in Words* (London, Cambridge University Press, 1960), pp. 86–110; Joseph A. Mazzeo, 'Metaphysical Poetry and the Poetic of Correspondence', *Journal of the History of Ideas*, 14 (1953), 221–34; Joseph A. Mazzeo, 'A Seventeenth-Century Theory of Metaphysical Poetry', *Romanic Review*, 42 (1951), 245–55; Forrest G. Robinson, *The Shape of Things Known: Sidney's Apology in Its Philosophical Tradition* (Cambridge, Mass., Harvard University Press, 1972); Stuart M. Tave, *The Amiable Humorist: A Study in the Comic Theory and Criticism of the Eighteenth and Early Nineteenth Centuries* (Chicago, University of Chicago Press, 1960); Dale Underwood, *Etherege and the Seventeenth-Century Comedy of Manners*, Yale Studies in English, vol. 135 (New Haven, Yale University Press, 1957), pp. 94–110; W. L. Ustick and H. H. Hudson, 'Wit, "Mixt Wit", and the "Bee in Amber"', *Huntington Library Bulletin*, 8 (1935), 103–30; Geoffrey Walton, *Metaphysical to Augustan: Studies in Tone and Sensibility in the Seventeenth Century* (London, Bowes and Bowes, 1955), pp. 13–22; George Williamson, *The Proper Wit of Poetry* (Chicago, University of Chicago Press, 1961).

30 *Certain Eclogues*, quoted in Chapman (ed.), *Literary Criticism in England*, p. 154.

31 *Every man out of his Humour*, in *Ben Jonson*, II, p. 459 *et passim*.

32 *Human Nature, or the Fundamental Elements of Policy*, in *The English Works of Thomas Hobbes*, ed. William Molesworth (1850; rpt. Aalen, Scientia Verlag, 1962), IV, p. 55.

33 *Leviathan*, ed. C. B. Macpherson (Baltimore, Penguin, 1968), pp. 134–5.

34 'Preface to Homer', in *Critical Essays*, ed. Spingarn, II, p. 70.

35 During the second half of the seventeenth century, so far as many contemporaries were concerned, literature helped set the context in which political activity took place, and not the other way around. For Davenant, the Civil War was made possible by the absence of a properly constituted heroic poem or great national epic ('Preface to *Gondibert*', in *Critical Essays*, ed. Spingarn, II, pp. 33–53). For Sprat, men who immoderately pursue the 'Ornaments of speaking' are rendered incapable of sound political judgment and hence are easily seduced into rebellion (*History*, pp. 111–13). For Hobbes himself, 'Divines' who copy 'the example of … Poets, ancient and modern', and who therefore claim 'to speak by inspiration', are seditious: they are responsible for the 'subversion or disturbance of the Common-wealths' in which they live ('Answer to Davenant's "Preface"', in *Critical Essays*, ed. Spingarn, II, pp. 58–9). For an entirely different reading of remarks such as these, see Steven Zwicker, *Lines of Authority: Politics and English Literary Culture, 1649–1689* (Ithaca, New York, Cornell University Press, 1993), pp. 17–36.

36 *History*, pp. 413–16. The interest in reforming wit has long been seen as part of a campaign against enthusiasm – religious, political, philosophical. See, for example, George Williamson, 'The Restoration Revolt Against Enthusiasm', in *Seventeenth-Century*

Contexts, pp. 202–39. (First published in *Studies in Philology*, 30 (1930), 571–603.) Some of the inadequacies in the approach – for example, the failure to recognize that the reformers are often indistinguishable from those whom they attack – have been pointed out in Michael Cyril William Hunter, *John Aubrey and the Realm of Learning* (New York, Science History Publications, 1975); McKeon, *Politics and Poetry*, pp. 20–3; Vickers, 'Royal Society and Prose Style', pp. 1–76.

37 'An account', in *Works*, I, p. 53.
38 *Ibid.*
39 *Ibid.*, pp. 53–4.
40 *Dramatick Poesie*, in *Works*, XVII, pp. 28–30. *Totum triduum* etc. (*Eunuch* II.i; my trans.)
41 *Ibid.*
42 *Ibid.*, p. 30.
43 *Institutio Oratoria*, trans. H. E. Butler (Loeb Classical Library, 1921), II, p. 439. I owe to Professor John C. Nelson the observation that Dryden might have learned as much about wit from Castiglione's *The Book of the Courtier* as from Quintilian's *Institutio*.
44 *Ibid.*, pp. 447, 449.
45 *Ibid.*, pp. 451, 455, 457, 463.
46 *Ibid.*, pp. 445, 493.
47 *Ibid.*, pp. 453, 455.
48 *Ibid.*, pp. 441, 469, 471, 485.
49 *Ibid.*, pp. 467, 469, 471.
50 *Ibid.*, pp. 441, 443.
51 'Preface to *An Evening's Love*', in *Works*, X, p. 205.
52 Curtius, *European Literature*, p. 294; Spingarn (ed.), *Critical Essays*, I, p. xxxviii.
53 *Bartholomew Fair*, in *Ben Jonson*, VI, p. 19. The added segment of the stage direction is taken from one of the variant readings listed in the edition.
54 S. L. Bethell, 'Nature of Metaphysical Wit', pp. 23–4, 26–30.
55 *Dramatick Poesie*, in *Works*, XVII, pp. 11, 53, 60.
56 Curtius, *European Literature*, pp. 293–4.
57 On the seventeenth-century poetic of correspondence, see Mazzeo, 'Metaphysical Poetry', pp. 228–34. For an interesting qualification of Mazzeo's argument, see Ernest B. Gilman, *The Curious Perspective: Literary and Pictorial Wit in the Seventeenth Century* (New Haven, Yale University Press, 1978), pp. 69–75.
58 'The Sunne Rising' [1632], in *The Poems of John Donne*, ed. H. J. C. Grierson (London, Oxford University Press, 1933), p. 11.
59 *An Evening's Love*, in *Works*, X, pp. 271–2.
60 *Marriage à-la-Mode*, in *Works*, XI, p. 259.
61 *A Short View of the Immorality and Profaneness of the English Stage* [1698], in *Critical Essays*, ed. Spingarn, III, pp. 253–6.
62 For an interpretation that stresses the dismal isolation of the characters, see Derek Hughes, 'The Unity of Dryden's *Marriage à-la-Mode*', *Philological Quarterly*, 61 (1982), 125–42.
63 'Defence of the Epilogue', in *Works*, XI, p. 213.
64 'Preface to *An Evening's Love*', in *Works*, X, p. 206. Dryden appears to have won the debate with Shadwell. Within five years, Shadwell was practising, and perhaps even advocating, a form of mixed drama. See 'To the Most Illustrious Prince, William, Duke of Newcastle', in *The Virtuoso* [1676], ed. Marjorie Hope Nicolson and David Stuart Rodes (Lincoln, Nebraska, University of Nebraska Press, 1966), p. 3. See also Brian

Corman, 'Thomas Shadwell and the Jonsonian Comedy of the Restoration', in *From Renaissance to Restoration: Metamorphoses of the Drama,* ed. Robert Markley and Laurie Finke (Cleveland, Bellflower Press, Case Western Reserve University, Department of English, 1984), pp. 127–150.

65 'Preface to *An Evening's Love*', in *Works,* X, p. 207. Rose A. Zimbardo, however, believes that each level of the plot represents another stage in the scale of being. See *A Mirror to Nature,* pp. 36–75.
66 'Preface to *An Evening's Love*', in *Works,* X, p. 204.
67 See, for instance, Novak (ed.), *Works,* X, p. 446.
68 'Epilogue to the University of Oxford', in *Works,* I, pp. 147–8. The Epilogue was first spoken in 1673.
69 'Preface to *An Evening's Love*', in *Works,* X, p. 204.
70 *Ibid.,* p. 203.
71 Dryden borrows Hobbes's theory of laughter (*Leviathan,* p. 125); but he applies it, unlike Hobbes himself, only to laughter produced by farce.
72 'Preface to *An Evening's Love*', in *Works,* X, pp. 203–4, 209.
73 *Ibid.,* pp. 209–10.
74 *Ibid.,* p. 209.
75 'A Dialogue on Dramatic Poetry', in *Selected Essays: 1917–1932* (New York, Harcourt Brace, 1932), p. 33. (First published as 'A Dialogue on Poetic Drama', in *Of Dramatick Poesie ... Preceded by a Dialogue on Poetic Drama* (London, Frederick Etchells and Hugh Macdonald), 1928.) For additional statements on the morality of Restoration comedy, see the following: Robert D. Hume, 'The Myth of the Rake in "Restoration Comedy"', in *The Rakish Stage: Studies in English Drama, 1660–1800* (Carbondale, Southern Illinois University Press, 1983), pp. 138–75 (first published in *Studies in the Literary Imagination,* 10 (1977), 25–55); Dudley Miles, 'Morals of the Restoration', *Sewanee Review,* 24 (1916), 105–14; P. F. Vernon, 'Marriage of Convenience and the Moral Code of Restoration Comedy', *Essays in Criticism,* 12 (1962), 370–87. For a survey of other views of Restoration comedy, see John T. Harwood, *Critics, Values, and Restoration Comedy* (Carbondale, Southern Illinois University Press, 1982).
76 'Preface to *The Sullen Lovers*', in *Critical Essays,* ed. Spingarn, II, p. 148. For a discussion of Dryden's other detractors, see Novak (ed.), *Works,* X, p. 464.
77 'Preface to *An Evening's Love*', in *Works,* X, pp. 210–2. When he calls the poet a 'maker', Dryden actually uses the Greek term.
78 *Ibid.,* pp. 210–1.
79 *Ibid.*
80 *Ibid.,* pp. 212–13.
81 12 July 1827, *Specimens of the Table Talk* [1835], in *The Complete Works of Samuel Taylor Coleridge,* ed. W. G. T. Shedd (New York, Harper, 1853), VI, p. 293; *On the Principles of Genial Criticism concerning the Fine Arts* [1814], in *Criticism: The Major Texts,* p. 365.

CHAPTER SEVEN
The heroic play (1672)

1 Dryden's occasional disparagement of his talent for comedy has been taken far too literally: once again, his irony has been lost. The 'Preface to *An Evening's Love*' (1671) is hardly the work of a man uncertain of his gifts. Moreover, he would not have proclaimed to his audience that his comedies were not worth reading.

281

2 *The Language of Tragedy* (New York, Columbia University Press, 1947), p. 155.

3 Letter to Dr. Bohun, *c.* January 1671, quoted in *Works*, XI, p. 411.

4 For an example of a contemporary attack on heroic drama, see *The Censure of the Rota* [1673], in *Drydeniana*, V, pp. 1–21. Also, see Eric Rothstein, *Restoration Tragedy: Form and the Process of Change* (Madison, University of Wisconsin Press, 1967), pp. 24–47.

5 *The Rehearsal*, ed. D. E. L. Crane (Durham, North Carolina, University of Durham Press, 1976), p. 66.

6 For a short summary of twentieth-century criticism on the heroic play, see Michael W. Alssid, *Dryden's Rhymed Heroic Tragedies: A Critical Study of the Plays and of Their Place in Dryden's Poetry*, Salzburg Studies in English Literature, Poetic Drama, no. 7 (Salzburg, Universität Salzburg, 1974), II, 23–48.

7 *Ideas of Greatness: Heroic Drama in England* (New York, Barnes and Noble, 1971), p. 3. Also, see Derek Hughes, *Dryden's Heroic Plays* (Lincoln, Nebraska, University of Nebraska Press, 1981), p. 3n.

8 Claude Rawson, 'Beyond the Mexique Bay', rev. of *The Indian Queen*, by John Dryden and Henry Purcell, *Times Literary Supplement*, 24 February 1984, p. 192. Also, see Harley Granville-Barker, *On Dramatic Method* (1931; rpt. New York, Hill and Wang, 1956), pp. 133–57.

9 There are a number of exceptions. For a discussion of Dryden's narrative language, see Alssid, *Dryden's Rhymed Heroic Tragedies*, II, pp. 256–74. For some suggestive remarks on Dryden's relationship to Ariosto, see Irvin Ehrenpreis, *Acts of Implication: Suggestion and Covert Meaning in the Works of Dryden, Swift, and Austin* (Berkeley, University of California Press, 1980), pp. 20–34.

10 'To the Reader', in *The Dramatic Works in the Beaumont and Fletcher Canon*, ed. Fredson Bowers *et al.* (Cambridge, Cambridge University Press, 1972), III, p. 497.

11 Letter to Ormonde, 23 January 1662, in *The Dramatic Works of Roger Boyle*, ed. William Smith Clark II (Cambridge, Mass., Harvard University Press, 1937), I, p. 23. Orrery's description was probably encouraged by Caroline practice. William Cartwright's *The Royal Slave* (1639), a serious play with a happy ending, was called a 'Tragi-Comedi' on the title page of every edition. That Cartwright regarded his drama as a tragi-comedy is further suggested by the following lines from one of the two prologues: 'We hope here's none inspir'd from late damn'd bookes, / Will sowre it [*The Royal Slave*] into Tragedy with their lookes'. See 'Prologue to the University', in *The Plays and Poems of William Cartwright*, ed. C. Blackmore Evans (Madison, Wisconsin, University of Wisconsin Press, 1951), p. 196.

12 'To the Reader', in *The Dramatic Works of Sir William D'Avenant*, ed. James Maidment and W. H. Logan (1872; rpt. New York, Russell and Russell, 1964), III, p. 257. For a history of the term in the Restoration, see W. S. Clark, 'The Definition of the "Heroic Play" in the Restoration Period', *Review of English Studies*, 8 (1932), 437–44.

13 'To the Right Honourable the Earl of Clarendon', in *Works*, II, [i].

14 *Ibid.*

15 'To … Roger Earl of Orrery', in *Works*, VIII, pp. 98–9; *Dramatick Poesie*, in *Works*, XVII, p. 68. Dryden dedicated *The Rival Ladies* to Orrery; they seem to have been in correspondence; and Dryden was almost certainly familiar with his literary views.

16 'Answer to Davenant's "Preface"' [1650], in *Critical Essays*, ed. Spingarn, II, p. 55.

17 *Dramatick Poesie*, in *Works*, XVII, p. 75.

18 'Of Heroique Playes', in *Works*, XI, p. 10.

19 'An account', in *Works*, I, p. 54. Robert D. Hume believes that Dryden continued to

equate the two genres until the 'Grounds of Criticism in Tragedy' (1679). See *Dryden's Criticism*, pp. 213–14.

20 'Defence of *An Essay*', in *Works*, IX, p. 6; 'Preface to *Tyrannick Love*', in *Works*, X, p. 112.

21 'Of Heroique Playes', in *Works*, XI, pp. 9–10.

22 *Cavalier Drama*, pp. 41, 59. A number of Harbage's conclusions about Caroline drama have been called in question by Kevin Sharpe, who argues for the intellectual dignity of the plays. See *Criticism and Compliment: The Politics of Literature in the England of Charles I* (Cambridge, Cambridge University Press, 1987).

23 To those who find Dryden's handling of literary history inadequate, C. K. Stead provides the perfect rejoinder:

> It is not in fact the literary historian who can radically alter our perspective on literary history. He sees too many exceptions to commit himself to the broad sweep; and his evaluations are usually tentative and always relative ... The literary historian's tasks most often prove to be menial. He follows behind the major critic, confirming, completing, complaining, correcting ('Eliot, Arnold, and the English Poetic Tradition', in *The Literary Criticism of T. S. Eliot: New Essays*, ed. David Newton-De Molina (London, Athlone Press, 1977), p. 191).

24 'To the ... Earl of Clarendon', in *Works*, II, [ii].

25 Smith and MacMillan (eds), in *Works*, VIII, pp. 285–6.

26 Cornell March Dowlin, *Sir William Davenant's 'Gondibert'*, Ph.D. diss. University of Pennsylvania (Philadelphia, privately printed, 1934), pp. 89–90. Though unpublished, Dowlin's work remains important, one frequently cited in studies of Davenant. See also Edward J. Dent, *Foundations of English Opera* (1928; rpt. New York, Da Capo Press, 1965), pp. 68–9; Harbage, *Cavalier Drama*, p. 186.

27 'Of Heroique Playes', in *Works*, XI, p. 8.

28 On the staging of *The Siege of Rhodes*, see Richard Southern, *Changeable Scenery: Its Origin and Development in the British Theatre* (London, Faber and Faber, 1952), pp. 109–23.

29 *The Diary of John Evelyn*, ed. E. S. de Beer (Oxford, Clarendon Press, 1955), III, p. 229. De Beer thinks it likely that Evelyn refers not to *The Siege of Rhodes* but to a later work, *The History of Sir Francis Drake* (1659). The two works, in any event, are of a similar type. And they affected a contemporary playgoer like Aubrey in a similar way:

> Being freed from imprisonment, because Playes (*scil.* Tragedies and Comoedies) were in those Presbyterian times scandalous, he [Davenant] contrives to set up an Opera *stylo recitativo* ... It began at Rutland howse in Charter-house-yard; next at the Cock-pitt in Drury-Lane, where were acted very well, *stylo recitativo*, Sir Francis Drake, and the Siege of Rhodes. It did affect the Eie and eare extremely. The first brought Scenes in fashion in England; before, at playes, was only a Hanging (*Brief Lives*, ed. Oliver Lawson Dick, 3rd edn (London, Secker and Warburg, 1958), p. 88).

See also Philip Parsons, 'Restoration Tragedy as Total Theatre', in *Restoration Literature: Critical Approaches*, ed. Harold Love (London, Methuen, 1972), pp. 42–3. Although most scholars are in agreement that there was no *ballet de corps* in *The Siege of Rhodes*, there are indications in the text that some dancing did take place.

30 'Restoration Tragedy', in *Restoration Literature*, ed. Love, p. 36.

31 *The First Dayes Entertainment at Rutland House*, in *Works*, I, p. 345. Although these lines are spoken by Diogenes, who condemns public entertainments, they are consistent with Davenant's own views.

32 *The Play-house to be Lett*, in *Works*, II, p. 72. Before the Restoration, to avoid trouble with the authorities, Davenant did not call his work a play. He variously referred to it as an 'opera', a 'maske', a 'Representation'. See Arthur H. Nethercot, *Sir William D'Avenant: Poet Laureate and Playwright-Manager* (Chicago, University of Chicago Press, 1938), pp. 308–9.

33 'Of Heroique Playes', in *Works*, XI, p. 9.

34 *The Royal Slave*, in *Plays and Poems*, p. 239.

35 *The Siege of Rhodes*, in *Works*, II, p. 8.

36 'Of Heroique Playes', in *Works*, XI, p. 9.

37 *Cavalier Drama*, p. 212.

38 'Of Heroique Playes', in *Works*, IX, p. 10.

39 'To the Reader', in *Dramatic Works*, III, p. 234.

40 'Of Heroique Playes', in *Works*, IX, p. 9.

41 'Preface to *Gondibert*', in *Critical Essays*, ed. Spingarn, II, pp. 1–6. For a different interpretation, see Sharpe, *Criticism and Compliment*, p. 101.

42 'Preface to *Gondibert*', in *Critical Essays*, ed. Spingarn, II, p. 7.

43 *Ibid.*, pp. 33–50; Sharpe, *Criticism and Compliment*, pp. 102–7.

44 'Preface to *Gondibert*', in *Critical Essays*, ed. Spingarn, II, pp. 14, 51.

45 *Ibid.*, pp. 12–14. When engaged in compliment, Dryden holds a similar position. See 'To His Royal Highness the Duke', in *Works*, XI, pp. 2–6.

46 'Preface to *Gondibert*', in *Critical Essays*, ed. Spingarn, II, pp. 1–2.

47 Spingarn (ed.), *Critical Essays*, I, pp. xxvii–xxxviii.

48 *Ibid.*, pp. 4, 17.

49 Philip Bordinat and Sophia B. Blaydes, *Sir William Davenant* (Boston, Twayne, 1981), pp. 86–7; Dowlin, *Davenant's 'Gondibert'*, pp. 86–9.

50 'Of Heroique Playes', in *Works*, XI, p. 9. See also Dent, *Foundations of English Opera*, pp. 65–9.

51 Ellen Rosand, *Opera in Seventeenth-Century Venice: The Creation of a Genre* (Berkeley, University of California Press, 1991), p. 60; Peter H. Nurse, *Classical Voices: Studies of Corneille, Racine, Molière, Mme de Lafayette* (Totowa, New Jersey, Rowman and Littlefield, 1971), pp. 16–20.

52 *Literary Criticism in the Italian Renaissance*, II, p. 1004.

53 Dowlin, *Davenant's 'Gondibert'*, pp. 77–83.

CHAPTER EIGHT
The heroic play (concluded)

1 'Of Heroique Playes', in *Works*, XI, p. 9. As Arthur H. Nethercot observes, Davenant's subsequent work developed in the direction of 'full-bodied drama'. See *Sir William D'Avenant*, p. 335.

2 'Of Heroique Playes', in *Works*, XI, p. 10. *Le Donne* etc. (*Orlando Furioso* I.1–2; trans. Waldman).

3 *Dryden's Heroic Drama*, pp. 12–15.

4 'Of Heroique Playes', in *Works*, XI, p. 16; also, see 'To His Royal Highness the Duke', in *Works*, XI, pp. 6–7.

5 'Of Heroique Playes', in *Works*, XI, p. 12.

6 Hume, *Development of English Drama*, pp. 273–4; Winn, *John Dryden*, pp. 146–8.

7 Dowlin, *Davenant's 'Gondibert'*, p. 94.

8 *Dramatick Poesie*, in *Works*, XVII, p. 70; 'Defence of *An Essay*', in *Works*, IX, pp. 5–7; 'An account', *Works*, I, p. 54. In a number of ways, Dryden warns us not to expect an exhaustive treatment of the subject. For instance, he calls 'Of Heroique Playes' 'a short account'.

9 For a discussion of Renaissance criticism on the *Furioso*, see Weinberg, *Literary Criticism in the Italian Renaissance*, II, pp. 954–1073. See also Henry Knight Miller, *Henry Fielding's 'Tom Jones' and the Romance Tradition*, ELS Monograph Series, no. 6 (Victoria, University of Victoria, 1976), pp. 7–21.

10 As one Italian critic, Lionardo Salviati, succinctly stated: 'This [alleged] difference between romance and epic is nonexistent' (*Degli Accademici della Crusca difesa dell' Orlando Furioso dell' Ariosto* ..., quoted in and trans. Weinberg, *Literary Criticism in the Italian Renaissance*, II, p. 1004. For a further discussion of the equation of the romance with the epic in sixteenth- and seventeenth-century criticism, see Trusten Wheeler Russell, *Voltaire, Dryden, and Heroic Tragedy* (1946; rpt. New York, AMS Press, 1966).

11 For an interpretation that stresses Dryden's indebtedness to the epic, and not the romance, see Richard Law, 'The Heroic Ethos in John Dryden's Heroic Plays', *Studies in English Literature*, 23 (1983), 389–98.

12 For a different interpretation of the impact of the French romance on the heroic play, see Hughes, *Dryden's Heroic Plays*, pp. 3–4.

13 Alfred Harbage also emphasizes continuity and development. See *Cavalier Drama*, pp. 41, 59, 212.

14 'Of Heroique Playes', in *Works*, XI, p. 10.

15 *Ibid.*

16 *The Allegory of Love* (London, Oxford University Press, 1938), p. 302.

17 Graham Hough, *A Preface to 'The Faerie Queen'* (New York, Norton, 1963), pp. 25–6.

18 *Ibid.*, p. 26.

19 'To ... Roger Earl of Orrery', in *Works*, VIII, p. 95.

20 *Poetics*, in *Aristotle's Theory of Poetry and Fine Art*, ed. Butcher, p. 107.

21 According to Laura Brown, Dryden 'complicate[s]' or 'soften[s]' '[t]he rigid evaluative hierarchy that governs form' in *The Siege of Rhodes* (*English Dramatic Form, 1660–1700: An Essay in Generic History* (New Haven, Yale University Press, 1981), p. 4). But it is difficult to conceive of any hierarchic pattern, however loosely drawn, that can accommodate Dryden's heroic action.

22 *The Language of Tragedy*, p. 158.

23 Lanfranco Caretti, quoted in 'Ariosto Approached', rev. of *Orlando Furioso*, trans. Sir John Harrington, ed. Robert McNulty, *Times Literary Supplement*, 6 October 1972, p. 1196. On the 'fortuitous ... conclusion' of *The Conquest of Granada*, see Brown, *English Dramatic Form*, p. 16.

24 *Discourses*, p. 78.

25 The position grows out of his earlier defence of tragi-comedy (*Dramatick Poesie*, in *Works*, XVII, pp. 46–7), to which we are all but referred ('Of Heroique Playes', in *Works*, XI, p. 10). Dryden's relationship to Tasso is discussed in John C. Sherwood, 'Dryden and the Critical Theories of Tasso', pp. 351–9.

26 *The Indian Queen*, in *Works*, VIII, p. 188.

27 *Ibid.*, p. 198.

28 'To His Royal Highness the Duke', in *Works*, XI, p. 6.

29 On the lack of development in Dryden's heroes, see Brown, *English Dramatic Form*, pp. 15–18.
30 *The Rise of Romance* (New York, Oxford University Press, 1971), p. 30.
31 Roger Sherman Loomis, 'Morgain la fée and the Celtic goddesses', quoted in Vinaver, *Rise of Romance*, p. 86.
32 On the instability of Ariosto's characters, see Daniel Javitch, 'Rescuing Ovid from the Allegorizers', in *Ariosto 1974 in America*, ed. Aldo Scaglione (Ravenna, Longo, 1976), p. 93.
33 *Orlando Furioso*, trans. Guido Waldman (New York, Oxford University Press, 1974), p. 103.
34 'Ariosto Approached', p. 1196. See also Daniel Javitch, 'Cantus Interruptus', *Modern Language Notes*, 95 (1980), 66–80.
35 *The Indian Queen*, in *Works*, VIII, p. 187.
36 *The Conquest of Granada, Part One*, in *Works*, XI, p. 56.
37 Kirsch, *Dryden's Heroic Drama*, p. 108.
38 *The Conquest of Granada, Part Two*, in *Works*, XI, p. 172.
39 *Riposta a M. Giouambattista Pigna*, quoted in Weinberg, *Literary Criticism in the Italian Renaissance*, II, p. 959.
40 *The Indian Queen*, in *Works*, VIII, p. 194.
41 *The Conquest of Granada, Part Two*, in *Works*, XI, p. 170.
42 *Tyrannick Love*, in *Works*, X, pp. 187–8.
43 *The Conquest of Granada, Part Two*, in *Works*, XI, pp. 114–15.
44 Rudolf Gottfried (ed.), *Ariosto's 'Orlando Furioso'*, trans. Sir John Harrington (Bloomington, Midland-Indiana University Press, 1971), pp. 18–19.
45 *Tyrannick Love*, in *Works*, X, pp. 136–7.
46 On the relationship of the heroic plays to the satires, see Jefferson, 'Aspects of Dryden's Imagery', in *Dryden's Mind and Art*, ed. King, pp. 39–42.
47 'To His Royal Highness the Duke', in *Works*, XI, p. 6; 'Of Heroique Playes', in *Works*, XI, p. 16.
48 'Of Heroique Playes', in *Works*, XI, pp. 13–14.
49 *The Indian Queen*, in *Works*, VIII, p. 220.
50 *The Indian Emperour*, in *Works*, IX, p. 83.
51 *Tyrannick Love*, in *Works*, X, p. 176.
52 *The Conquest of Granada, Part One*, in *Works*, XI, p. 52.
53 'Of Heroique Playes', in *Works*, XI, pp. 11–13; Hough, *Preface*, pp. 34–5. For an interpretation that stresses the importance of the supernatural in the design of the plays, see Jack M. Armistead, 'Dryden and the Occult as Dramatic Code: *Tyrannick Love*', *Papers on Language and Literature*, 24 (1988), 367–83.
54 *Dryden's Heroic Drama*, p. 106.
55 'Of Heroique Playes', in *Works*, XI, p. 18.

CHAPTER NINE
Sweeping of the stakes (1672)

1 'Epilogue to *The Conquest of Granada, Part II*', in *Works*, XI, p. 201.
2 *Ibid*.
3 For reactions to the 'Defence', see the following: *The Censure of the Rota* [1673], in *Drydeniana*, V, pp. 4–21; Gerard Langbaine, *An Account of the English Dramatick Poets* [1691], in *Critical Essays*, ed. Spingarn, III, pp. 113–16; George Saintsbury, *A History*

of English Criticism (New York, Dodd Mead, 1911), pp. 123–4; Hume, *Dryden's Criticism*, pp. 95–6.

4 Hoyt Trowbridge, 'Dryden on the Elizabethans', in *From Dryden to Jane Austen*, p. 11. (First published as 'Dryden's "Essay on the Dramatic Poetry of the Last Age"' in *Philological Quarterly*, 22 (1943), 240–50.) Trowbridge follows W. P. Ker, who believes that the '"Defence" was omitted in some copies of the second edition [of *The Conquest of Granada*], and in later editions' (*Essays of John Dryden*, I, p. lxxiv). The 'Defence', however, did appear in the third edition and was not omitted until the fourth. See Hugh Macdonald, *John Dryden: A Bibliography of Early Editions and of Drydeniana* (Oxford, Clarendon Press, 1939), p. 109.

5 'Defence of the Epilogue', in *Works*, XI, pp. 216–17.

6 *Ibid.*, p. 217. Dryden also attributes the new 'refinement' in poetry to the improved social standing of poets. In the preceding age, authors did not 'keep the best company'. With the possible exception of Ben Jonson, they were, none of them, 'conversant in Courts'. In contrast, Restoration poets have immediate 'access' to Charles and his courtiers, who serve them as models, patrons and judges ('Defence of the Epilogue', in *Works*, XI, pp. 215–17). The dependence of great literature on good breeding and court life is a subject to which Dryden will frequently return, though never with greater emphasis than in the 'Discourse concerning ... Satire' (1693). On this aspect of the 'Discourse', see John Fowler, 'Dryden and Literary Good-breeding', in *Restoration Literature*, ed. Love, pp. 227–8.

7 'Defence of the Epilogue', in *Works*, XI, pp. 207–11.

8 *Ibid.*, pp. 205, 207.

9 *Ibid.*, p. 211.

10 *Ibid.*, pp. 212, 215, 217.

11 *Ibid.*, p. 215.

12 *Ibid.*, pp. 206–7.

13 *Ibid.*, pp. 203–4, 216–17.

14 *Ibid.*, pp. 206–7.

15 *Dramatick Poesie*, in *Works*, XVII, pp. 55–6.

16 'Defence of the Epilogue', in *Works*, XI, p. 213.

17 *Ibid.*, pp. 206–10, 212–15, 217–18. For an interpretation that stresses the 'defensive' and apologetic nature of Dryden's argument, its 'recoil' from the very epilogue it tries to defend, see Jennifer Brady, 'Dryden and Negotiations of Literary Succession and Precession', in *Literary Transmission and Authority: Dryden and Other Writers*, ed. Earl Miner and Jennifer Brady (Cambridge, Cambridge University Press, 1993), pp. 35–7.

18 *Of Dramatick Poesie* (1668; rpt. Menston, Scholar Press, 1969), p. 48.

19 *Dramatick Poesie*, in *Works*, XVII, p. 56.

20 The heroic plays were nevertheless attacked in two anonymous, contemporary works, *The Censure of the Rota* (1673) and *The Friendly Vindication of Mr. Dryden* (1673), for violating the rules set down in the 'Defence'. Dryden briefly defended himself in the dedication of *The Assignation* (1673), and more detailed rebuttals were made in his behalf in *Mr. Dreyden Vindicated* (1673) and *A Description of the Academy of the Athenian Virtuosi* (1673).

21 For a list of the critical terms which Dryden introduced into English, see Barbara M. H. Strang, 'Dryden's Innovations in Critical Vocabulary', *Durham University Journal*, 51 (1959), 114–23.

22 For a further discussion of the chronology of Dryden's essays, see above, p. 43.

CHAPTER TEN
The classical moment (1673–1679)

1 The many troubles besetting Dryden at this time are discussed in McFadden, *Dryden: The Public Writer*, pp. 139–65.

2 On the quarrel with Settle, see Monk and Novak (eds), *Works*, XVII, pp. 387–400. On the Rose Alley attack, see Winn, *John Dryden*, pp. 325–9.

3 In 'The Authors Apology for Heroique Poetry; and Poetique Licence' (1677), Dryden celebrates the epic as 'the greatest work of humane Nature' (in *Works*, XII, p. 88). But in doing so he seems merely to be carried away by his own argument: he would defend the epic against those who 'condemn' it. In the middle period taken as a whole, including the essays he wrote after the 'Apology', his preference remained with tragedy. He did not in fact change his mind until his third period. For a discussion of his later reversal, see below, p. 178.

4 'Prologue to *Aureng-Zebe*', in *Works*, XII, p. 159.

5 'Epilogue to *Aureng-Zebe*', in *Works*, XII, p. 249.

6 'Authors Apology', in *Works*, XII, p. 88. As his distinction between important and unimportant rules suggests, nowhere in his middle period does Dryden endorse the arguments put forth in the *Essay of Dramatick Poesie* by Crites and Lisideius. Indeed, in his middle phase, the positions represented by those two, positions founded upon the 'scrupulous' observance of all rules, are ridiculed mercilessly (see 'Preface to *All for Love*', in *Works*, XIII, pp. 12–13).

Clearly, Robert D. Hume would disagree with me. According to Hume, in the 'Preface to *Troilus and Cressida*', Dryden 'appears as obsessed with the unity of place ... as ever Crites was' (*Dryden's Criticism*, p. 213; and see also Pechter, *Dryden's Classical Theory*, pp. 60–1).

The comparison of Dryden and Crites, however, does not hold. Crites wants a play to be staged on a single spot of ground ('the Scene ought to be continu'd through the Play, in the same place where it was laid in the beginning'). But if there must be a change, it should not occur 'in the middle of an Act' (*Dramatick Poesie*, in *Works*, XVII, pp. 18–19). Dryden's position in his middle period is very different. In accordance with his current practice, he would allow a change within an act, though he would allow only one. Within an act, there is to be 'no leaping from Troy to the Grecian Tents, *and thence back again*' ('Preface to *Troilus and Cressida*', in *Works*, XIII, p. 226; italics added). In any event, since he takes up and drops the subject in a single sentence, albeit a long one, he hardly 'appears obsessed with unity of place'.

7 'Authors Apology', in *Works*, XII, pp. 90–7.

8 'Preface to *All for Love*', in *Works*, XIII, p. 18.

9 'Preface to *Oedipus*', in *Works*, XIII, pp. 116–17.

10 'To the Right Honourable Robert, Earl of Sunderland', in *Works*, XIII, p. 224.

11 For a significant exception, see Grube, *The Greek and Roman Critics*, pp. 340–2.

12 On Dryden's use of the Boileau translation, see Aden, 'Dryden and Boileau', p. 498. Although analogues to *On the Sublime* can be found in his early criticism, there is no evidence that Dryden had read Longinus before 1674. See Paul H. Fry, 'Dryden's Earliest Allusion to Longinus', *English Language Notes*, 19:1 (1981), 22–4; Alfred Rosenberg, *Longinus in England bis zum Ende des 18. Jahrhunderts* (Berlin, Mayer und Müller, 1917), p. 20. The existence of these analogues helps, of course, to explain Dryden's later enthusiasm for *On the Sublime*.

13 *On the Sublime*, trans. W. Rhys Roberts (Cambridge, Cambridge University Press, 1899), p. 57.
14 *Ibid.*, pp. 47, 53, 61.
15 *Ibid.*, p. 57.
16 *Ibid.*, pp. 145, 147.
17 *Ibid.*, pp. 79, 81.
18 *Ibid.*, pp. 43, 45.
19 *Ibid.*, p. 57.
20 *Ibid.*, p. 43.
21 It has long been known that, in the eighteenth century, the influence of Longinus helped bring about the rejection of the classical rules. More recently, it has been argued that the rejection actually began in the late seventeenth century, almost as soon as *On the Sublime* was widely read. But this interpretation appears to be based upon a backward reading of history. Longinus may have encouraged seventeenth-century critics in their hatred of pedantry, but he also inspired a renewed commitment to the rules by revealing them as the source of emotional and imaginative power. Such was his effect on Dryden and Rymer; such was his effect on Boileau. For discussion of Longinus as a revolutionary force on classicism, see the following: Théodore A. Litman, *Le Sublime en France: 1660–1714* (Paris, A. G. Nizet, 1971); W. G. Moore, 'Boileau and Longinus', *French Studies*, 15 (1975), 52–62; Wimsatt and Brooks, *Literary Criticism*, pp. 284–5.

For discussion of Longinus as a sustaining force on classicism, see the following: Jules Brody, *Boileau and Longinus* (Geneva, E. Droz, 1958), pp. 100–4; Samuel Holt Monk, *The Sublime: A Study of Critical Theories in XVIII-Century England* (1935; rpt. Ann Arbor, Ann Arbor–University of Michigan Press, 1960), pp. 26, 44; Gordon Pocock, *Boileau and the Nature of Classicism* (Cambridge, Cambridge University Press, 1980), pp. 121–2, 247–8. For my further discussion of his influence on Dryden, see above, pp. 163–71. For the opposite point of view, see Fry, *Reach of Criticism*, pp. 87–124; George Watson, 'Dryden's First Answer to Rymer', *Review of English Studies*, n.s. 14 (1963), 17–23.
22 Rymer's early criticism is discussed in Curt A. Zimansky (ed.), *The Critical Works of Thomas Rymer* (New Haven, Yale University Press, 1956), pp. xx–xxvii. Dryden first mentions *The Tragedies of the Last Age* (issued in 1677, though with '1678' on its title page) in a letter to the Earl of Dorset (*Letters*, pp. 13–14). In the 'Heads of an Answer to Rymer', a set of private notes written in his presentation copy of *The Tragedies of the Last Age*, Dryden explores possible answers to the book. On the significance of these notes, which were set down late in 1677, see Hume, *Dryden's Criticism*, pp. 102–23.
23 *The Literary Critics*, p. 54; Watson (ed.), *'Of Dramatick Poesy'*, I, pp. 195, 238. The same argument has also been put forth, though not quite so baldly, by critics and scholars so very different as Earl Miner, James Sutherland, Maximillian E. Novak and James Anderson Winn. See Miner, 'Mr. Dryden and Mr. Rymer', in *Philological Quarterly*, 54 (1975), 139–44; Sutherland, *English Literature*, p. 397; Novak (ed.), *Works*, XIII, pp. 504–5; Winn, *John Dryden*, p. 304.
24 As Rymer does not attack the *Essay of Dramatick Poesie* directly in *The Tragedies of the Last Age*, so Dryden with equal civility refrains from directly attacking Rymer. The absence of hostility is not, as Watson believes, a sign of caution ('Dryden's First Answer', p. 22). For all its tack and avoidance of direct confrontation, the 'Grounds' remains, as Zimansky observes, the only 'real answer' to Rymer in the seventeenth century (*Critical Works*, p. 194). Cf. Hume, *Dryden's Criticism*, pp. 119–20.

25 On the impact of Longinus on French criticism, see the following: Brody, *Boileau and Longinus*; H. F. Brooks, 'Guez de Balzac: Eloquence and the Life of the Spirit', *L'Esprit Créateur*, 15 (1975), 59–78; R. C. Knight, *Racine et La Grèce*, 2nd edn (Paris, A. G. Nizet, 1974); Litman, *Le Sublime en France*.

26 *The Tragedies of the Last Age*, in *Critical Works*, pp. 21, 29, 75.

27 'Preface to *Troilus and Cressida*', in *Works*, XIII, p. 228. In his extended and generally excellent discussion of Dryden's theories of imitation David Bruce Kramer leaps over the essays of the late 1670s, and he therefore misses the Longinian influence on Dryden's conception of poetic borrowing (*The Imperial Dryden*, pp. 63–138). The change in Dryden's views, which he dates from the 1690s, actually occurred almost a decade and a half earlier.

28 'The Grounds of Criticism in Tragedy', in *Works*, XIII, p. 232.

29 *Ibid.*, pp. 232–3.

30 *Ibid.*, p. 243.

31 *Ibid.*

32 *Ibid.*, p. 248. In his first period, Dryden had conceived of the 'Soul of Poetry' in different terms. See *Dramatick Poesie*, in *Works*, XVII, p. 44.

33 'The Grounds', in *Works*, XIII, p. 233.

34 These terms are taken from *Dramatick Poesie*, in *Works*, XVII, p. 55.

35 John C. Sherwood ('Dryden and the Rules: The Preface to *Troilus and Cressida*', *Comparative Literature*, 2 (1950), 75, 80–1) underestimates the influence of Longinus. For an opinion comparable to my own, see Rosenberg, *Longinus in England*, p. 28.

36 'The Grounds', in *Works*, XIII, pp. 239–40.

37 'Preface to *Troilus and Cressida*', in *Works*, XIII, p. 225.

38 *Ibid.*, p. 226.

39 *Ibid.*

40 'The Grounds', in *Works*, XIII, pp. 244–7.

41 *Ibid.*, p. 238.

42 *Ibid.*, pp. 240–1, 246. See also 'Preface to *Troilus and Cressida*', in *Works*, XIII, pp. 227–8.

43 *Ibid.*, p. 231.

44 See, for example, the discussion of Richard II 'led in Triumph through the Streets of London' ('Preface to *Troilus and Cressida*', in *Works*, XII, p. 246).

45 *On the Sublime*, p. 61.

46 'The Grounds', in *Works*, XIII, p. 245.

47 *Life of Dryden*, pp. 181–2, 192–4.

CHAPTER ELEVEN
The great tradition (1680–1700)

1 John Barnard, 'Dryden, Tonson, and the Subscriptions for the 1697 *Virgil*', *Papers of the Bibliographical Society of America*, 57 (1963), 129–51.

2 René Bray, *La Formation de la Doctrine Classique en France* (1927; rpt. Paris, Nizet, 1961), p. 37.

3 'Of the Three Unities' [1660], in *The Continental Model: Selected French Critical Essays of the Seventeenth Century, in English Translation*, ed. Scott Elledge and Donald Schier, rev. edn (Ithaca, Cornell University Press, 1970), p. 109. In the *Essay of Dramatick Poesie*

(in *Works*, XVII, p. 26) Eugenius borrows Corneille's example, but only to use it for a very different purpose: to prove that the Ancients failed to observe the unity of time properly.

4 *Ibid.*, p. 115.
5 E. B. O. Borgerhoff, *The Freedom of French Classicism* (Princeton, Princeton University Press, 1950), pp. 235–45.
6 *The Characters, or the Manners of the Age* [1688–94], in *The Works of M. de La Bruyère* (London, 1752), I, pp. 41–2.
7 *The Art of Poetry* [1674], trans. Sir William Soames and John Dryden, in *Works*, II, p. 152.
8 'To the Most Honourable John, Lord Marquess of Normanby', in *Works*, V, p. 322.
9 *Ibid.*, p. 287.
10 *Ibid.*, pp. 303–4.
11 'Preface to *Sylvæ*', in *Works*, III, p. 14.
12 'To the Reader', in *Works*, III, p. 122.
13 'Preface to *Fables*', in '*Of Dramatic Poesy*', II, p. 278.
14 'To the Right Honourable, My Lord Radcliffe', in *Works*, IV, pp. 366–7.
15 'Preface to *Fables*', '*Of Dramatic Poesy*', II, p. 281.
16 'Discourse concerning ... Satire', in *Works*, IV, p. 11.
17 'To My Dear Friend Mr. Congreve ...', in *Works*, IV, p. 432. For an interpretation that stresses Dryden's later ambivalence towards the idea of progress, see Achsah Guibbory, 'Dryden's View of History', *Philological Quarterly*, 52 (1973), 197–204.
18 'To ... John, Lord Marquess of Normanby', in *Works*, V, p. 270.
19 'A Parallel of Poetry and Painting', in *Works*, XX, pp. 70–1.
20 'Preface to *Cleomenes*', in *Works*, XVI, p. 171. See also 'To the Right Honourable James Earl of Salisbury' [the dedication of *Love Triumphant*, 1694], in *Works*, XVI, p. 171. Cf. 'To Sir Godfrey Kneller', in *Works*, IV, p. 466.
21 'Discourse concerning ... Satire', in *Works*, IV, pp. 68–9. Dryden later reworked the details of his identification of Aeneas with Augustus. See Maurer (ed.), in *Works*, XX, p. 315.
22 The 'Life of Lucian', which was not published until after Dryden's death, was probably written in 1696.
23 'Preface to *Albion and Albanius*', in *Works*, XV, p. 3.
24 'To the Right Honourable the Earl of Albingdon', in *Works*, III, p. 233.
25 'Preface to *Sylvæ*', in *Works*, III, pp. 17–18. Cf. Abraham Cowley, 'Preface to *Poems*' [1656], in *Critical Essays*, ed. Spingarn, II, p. 86.
26 For a discussion of the 'Discourse', see below, pp. 223–30.
27 'Discourse concerning ... Satire', in *Works*, IV, p. 88.
28 'Preface to *Albion and Albanius*', in *Works*, XV, p. 4.
29 'Preface to *Sylvæ*', in *Works*, III, p. 18. *nequeo dicere* etc. (Juvenal, *Satire VII*.56; trans. by Noyes). Dryden freely adapts the text to his purpose.
30 'To ... the Earl of Albingdon', in *Works*, III, pp. 231–2.
31 That Dryden translated no plays remains a striking fact, even if one grants that he did not have complete freedom in his choice of subjects.
32 'Preface to *Sylvæ*', in *Works*, III, pp. 3–4.
33 'Postscript to the Reader', in *Works*, VI, pp. 807–8.

CHAPTER TWELVE
The Battle of the Books (1680–1700)

1 *Dramatick Poesie*, in *Works*, XVII, p. 55. On Dryden's handling of the literary character of an author, see Jean Hagstrum, *Samuel Johnson's Literary Criticism* (Minneapolis, University of Minnesota Press, 1952), pp. 38–41.
2 'Preface to *Ovid's Epistles*', in *Works*, I, pp. 114–15.
3 *Ibid.*, pp. 115, 117–18.
4 This phrase is taken from T. R. Steiner, *English Translation Theory: 1650–1800* (Amsterdam, Van Gorum, 1975), p. 28.
5 'Preface to *Ovid's Epistles*', in *Works*, I, p. 118.
6 *Ibid.*, pp. 118–19.
7 On the development of Dryden's theory of translation, see Steiner, *English Translation Theory*, pp. 27–31.
8 'Preface to *Ovid's Epistles*', in *Works*, I, p. 119.
9 *Ibid.*, p. 109.
10 *Ibid.*, p. 111.
11 *Ibid.*, pp. 109, 111.
12 *Ibid.*, p. 111.
13 *Ibid.*, pp. 112, 114.
14 *Ibid.*, pp. 113–14.
15 *Ibid.*, p. 112.
16 *Ibid.*, p. 113.
17 *Ibid.*, pp. 111–2.
18 'An account', in *Works*, I, pp. 53–4.
19 *Biographia Literaria*, ed. James Engell and W[alter] Jackson Bate, vol. VII, pt 2 of *The Collected Works of Samuel Taylor Coleridge* (Princeton, Princeton University Press, 1983), pp. 115–16.
20 'Preface to *Ovid's Epistles*', in *Works*, I, pp. 109–10. On anti-Augustanism in the Restoration, see Howard D. Weinbrot, *Augustus Caesar in 'Augustan' England* (Princeton, Princeton University Press, 1978). Cf. Howard Erskine-Hill, *The Augustan Idea in English Literature* (London, Edward Arnold, 1983). The irreverent discussion of Augustus looks forward to *Absalom and Achitophel* (1681), where Charles's altogether 'diviner Lust' is described with much verve.
21 'Preface to *Ovid's Epistles*', in *Works*, I, pp. 111, 113.
22 *Ibid.*, pp. 112–13.
23 Daitches, *Critical Approaches*, p. 216.
24 'Preface to *Ovid's Epistles*', in *Works*, I, p. 118.
25 On the history of the character as a literary genre, see Benjamin Boyce, *The Theophrastan Character in England to 1642* (Cambridge, Mass., Harvard University Press, 1947); David Nichol Smith (ed.), *Characters from the Histories and Memoirs of the Seventeenth Century* (Oxford, Clarendon Press, 1918), pp. ix–lii. An adequate account of the role of the character in literary criticism has yet to be written.
26 There has been little or no discussion of Dryden's place in the history of literary biography. See, for example, the following: Richard D. Altick, *Lives and Letters: A History of Literary Biography in England and America* (New York, Alfred A. Knopf, 1965); Martine Watson Brownley, 'Johnson's *Lives of the English Poets* and Earlier Traditions of the Character Sketch in England', in *Johnson and His Age*, ed. James Engell, Harvard

University Studies, no. 12 (Cambridge, Mass., Harvard University Press, 1984), 29–53; Robert Halsband, 'The "Penury of English Biography" before Samuel Johnson', in *Biography in the 18th Century*, ed. J. D. Browning *et al.*, Publications of the McMaster University Association for 18th Century Studies, no. 8 (New York, Garland, 1980), 112–27.

27 The dating of the Quarrel between the Ancients and Moderns has been variously conceived. On the Quarrel as originating in the Quattrocento, see Hans Baron, 'The Querelle of the Ancients and the Moderns as a Problem for Renaissance Scholarship', *Journal of the History of Ideas*, 20 (1959), 3–22; on the Quarrel as a constant in history, see Curtius, *European Literature*, pp. 251–5.

28 *An Essay upon the Ancient and Modern Learning*, in *Critical Essays*, ed. Spingarn, III, pp. 64–5. In my discussion of the controversy, I am very much indebted to Joseph M. Levine, *The Battle of the Books: History and Literature in the Augustan Age* (Ithaca, Cornell University Press, 1991). I have also found useful John R. Clark, *Form and Frenzy in Swift's 'Tale of a Tub'* (Ithaca, Cornell University Press, 1970), pp. 83–115; Gilbert Highet, *The Classical Tradition: Greek and Roman Influences on Western Literature* (New York, Oxford University Press, 1949), pp. 262–88; Hippolyte Rigault, *Histoire de la Querelle des Anciens et des Modernes* (Paris, 1836).

29 *Ancient and Modern Learning*, in *Critical Essays*, ed. Spingarn, III, p. 65.

30 *Reflections upon Ancient and Modern Learning* (London, 1694), pp. 311–12.

31 On the significance of Bentley's work, see Levine, *Battle of the Books*, pp. 47–83.

32 The group known as the Christ Church Wits included, among others, Francis Atterbury, Charles Boyle, and William King. On their role in the Battle, see Levine, *Battle of the Books*, pp. 52–5.

33 It is generally believed that, while he often debated the relative merits of the Ancients and Moderns, Dryden showed no interest in the quarrel over learning. See, for instance, Levine, *Battle of the Books*, pp. 272–7; Watson (ed.), '*Of Dramatic Poesy*', II, 177.

34 Dryden, however, did know Atterbury, and he does refer to him in a manuscript advertisement for the *Virgil*. See Ward (ed.), *Letters*, p. 172.

35 On the composition of these works, see A. C. Guthkelch and D. Nicol Smith (eds), *A Tale of a Tub, to which is added The Battle of the Books and The Mechanical Operation of the Spirit*, 2nd edn (Oxford, Clarendon Press, 1958), pp. xliii–li.

36 Irvin Ehrenpreis, *Swift: The Man, His Works, and the Age* (Cambridge, Mass., Harvard University Press, 1962), I, pp. 186–7; Ricardo Quintana, *The Mind and Art of Jonathan Swift* (1936; rpt. Gloucester, Mass., Peter Smith, 1963), pp. 85–6.

37 Swift's views on learning resemble those of the early humanists, for whom the rigorous application of philological principles was subordinate to aesthetic and moral concerns. His position is nicely expressed in the rebuke delivered by Scaliger – the elder Scaliger, that is, not the younger – in *The Battle of the Books* (in *A Tale of a Tub …*, p. 252). On the transformations which classical scholarship underwent beginning in the late sixteenth century, and of which Swift disapproved, see E. J. Kenney, *The Classical Text: Aspects of Editing in the Age of the Printed Book* (Berkeley, University of California Press, 1974), pp. 1–74. For some necessary qualifications of Kenney's argument, see Anthony Grafton, *Defenders of the Text: The Traditions of Scholarship in an Age of Science* (Cambridge, Mass., Harvard University Press, 1991).

38 Edward Rosenheim, *Swift and the Satirist's Art* (Chicago, University of Chicago Press, 1963), pp. 88, 205–6.

39 *A Tale of a Tub*, in *A Tale of a Tub …*, p. 69. *Tommy Potts* is a chapbook tale based on

the legend of Fair Rosamond. As Frank H. Ellis suggests, Dryden may be saddled with the work on the basis of his having written an 'epilogue ... for a stage version of the same legend'. See 'Notes on *A Tale of a Tub*', *Swift Studies*, 1 (1986), 10.

40 *A Tale of a Tub*, in *A Tale of a Tub*..., p. 147. On Bentley's real passion for tools of reference, see Miriam K. Starkman, *Swift's Satire on Learning in 'A Tale of a Tub'* (Princeton, Princeton University Press, 1950), pp. 96–7. In his enthusiasm, Bentley was not alone. To the existence of epitomes and 'Abridgements', William Wotton attributed much of the success of the Moderns (*Reflections upon Ancient and Modern Learning*, pp. 332–40).

41 *A Tale of a Tub*, in *A Tale of a Tub* ..., p. 69.

42 *Ibid.*, pp. 130–1. Scott found much in the late essays to like, but he too complained about Dryden's interest in scholarship, especially in the 'Discourse':

> In that treatise [the 'Discourse'], our author exhibits a good deal of that sort of learning which was in fashion among the critics; and, I suspect, was contented rather to borrow something from them, than put himself to the trouble of compiling more valuable materials. Such is the disquisition concerning the origin of the word *Satire*, which is chiefly extracted from Casaubon, Dacier, and Rigault (*Life of Dryden*, p. 319).

The reaction remains quite common, though not undisputed. For a favourable estimate of Dryden's scholarship, see Howard Weinbrot, 'The Achievement of Dryden's "Discourse"', in *Eighteenth-Century Satire: Essays on Text and Context from Dryden to Peter Pindar* (Cambridge, Cambridge University Press, 1988), pp. 1–8.

43 *A Tale of a Tub*, in *A Tale of a Tub*..., p. 94. Dryden may be absent from the list of critics because the narrator has momentarily taken over his identity and is to be imagined as speaking in his name. In any event, we know that Swift associated Dryden with tradition-building from the hilarious episode in *The Battle of the Books* where Dryden insists on his kinship to Virgil.

44 'Discourse concerning ... Satire', in *Works*, IV, p. 45. For an analysis of the structure of the 'Discourse', see below, pp. 223–8.

45 *A Tale of a Tub*, in *A Tale of a Tub*..., pp. 102–3.

46 *Ibid.*, p. 98.

47 *Swift's Satire of Learning*, p. 102.

48 *A Dissertation upon the Epistles of Phalaris*, in *The Works of Richard Bentley*, ed. Alexander Dyce (1836; rpt. New York, AMS Press, 1966), I, p. 334. The quotation is taken from the revised and expanded argument which Bentley published in 1699, the so-called 'Second Dissertation'.

49 'Discourse concerning ... Satire', in *Works*, IV, pp. 33–6. *Satira quidem* etc. (*Institutio Oratoria*, x.i.93; Loeb trans.).

50 Dryden never attacked Temple directly. In 1692, however, he wrote slightingly of Temple's friend Saint-Évremond, with whose criticism Temple's had much in common. See 'A Character of Saint-Evremond', *Works*, XX, pp. 8–11.

51 *A Tale of a Tub*, in *A Tale of a Tub*..., p. 7.

CHAPTER THIRTEEN
A critic and scholar (1680–1700)

1 *Dramatick Poesie*, in *Works*, XVII, pp. 20–1, 28–30.

2 'A Character of Polybius and His Writings', in *Works*, XX, p. 23.

3 'The Life of Plutarch', in *Works*, XVII, p. 248.

4 *Ibid.*, p. 267.

5 On Dryden's handling of his sources, see Maurer (ed.), *Works*, XX, pp. 431–5.

6 Watson (ed.), '*Of Dramatic Poesy*', II, p. 1. See also Levine, *Battle of the Books*, p. 274.

7 'Life of Plutarch', in *Works*, XVII, p. 275.

8 *Ibid.*, pp. 247–8.

9 'Discourse concerning ... Satire', in *Works*, IV, p. 28. The Delphin edition of Juvenal ('the *Dauphin's Juvenal*') was edited by Ludovicus Prateus (Louis Desprez). For a discussion of the accomplishments of all five men, see John Edwin Sandys, *A History of Classical Scholarship*, 3rd edn (1920; rpt. New York, Hafner, 1964), II; Frost (ed.), *Works*, IV, pp. 543–4. Dryden's first explicit and direct praise of textual scholarship appears in *Religio Laici* (1682), where he pays tribute to the Biblical criticism of Richard Simon (in *Works*, II, p. 116). For another interpretation of Dryden's reaction to Simon's work, see Harth, *Dryden's Thought*, p. 197.

10 'Discourse concerning ... Satire', in *Works*, IV, p. 49.

11 *Ibid.*, p. 54.

12 *Ibid.*, p. 45.

13 *Ibid.*, p. 28. See also Peter E. Medine, Introduction to *De Satyrica Graecorum Poesi & Romanarum Satirica*, by Isaac Casaubon (1605; rpt. Delmar, New York, Scholars' Facsimiles and Reprints, 1972), pp. x–xii. For a modern classicist's views on the early history of satire, see C. V. Van Rooy, *Studies in Satire and Related Literary Theory* (Leiden, E. J. Brill, 1965), pp. 1–29.

14 'Discourse concerning ... Satire', in *Works*, IV, p. 32.

15 *Ibid.*, p. 34.

16 *Ibid.*, pp. 29, 36–7.

17 *Ibid.*, p. 37.

18 *Ibid.* Throughout the 'Discourse', Dryden is inconsistent in his spelling of 'satire'. He recognizes that it 'ought to be with *i* and not with *y*; to distinguish its true derivation from *Satura*, not from *Satyrus*' ('Discourse concerning ... Satire', in *Works*, IV, pp. 48–9). But having so often written 'satyre' for 'satire', he does not think it worth the trouble to set the error right. Correct spelling is, he thinks, a French affectation.

19 *Ibid.*, pp. 39–41.

20 *Ibid.*, p. 42.

21 *Ibid.*, p. 36.

22 *Ibid.*, p. 40.

23 *Ibid.*

24 *Ibid.*, pp. 42–3. Dryden's 'Proposition' has stood up fairly well. The satire of Ennius seems indeed to have been inspired by Greek literature, though not so much by Old Comedy as by the poetry and prose of Hellenistic times. See Van Rooy, *Studies in Satire*, p. 34.

25 On Dryden's use of previous scholarship and translations, see Frost (ed.), *Works*, VI, pp. 857–70.

26 'Dryden's Latin Scholarship', in *Essential Articles*, ed. Swedenberg, p. 401. (First published in *Modern Philology*, 40 (1943), 241–55.) For other defences of Dryden's scholarship against the traditional charge of inadequate preparation and carelessness, see Frost, 'More About Dryden as Classicist', in *John Dryden*, pp. 146–52; Hammond, 'Figures of Horace', in *Horace Made New*, pp. 127–30.

27 'To ... John, Lord Marquess of Normanby', in *Works*, V, p. 275.

28 *Ibid.*, p. 309. Perhaps the complaint was not entirely new. In *Religio Laici* (1682), Dryden had glanced at '*Country-Curates*' who silently appropriate the Biblical scholarship of others. See *Religio Laici*, in *Works*, II, p. 116.

29 See, for example, Zwicker, *Politics and Language*, pp. 67–8, 178–9.

30 It has been said that Dryden invented the idea of a 'Confederacy' against Virgil. But Virgil's authority at the time, if not in danger of being overthrown, was nonetheless sharply questioned. See the anonymous *Verdicts of the Learned concerning Virgil's and Homer's Heroic Poems* (London, 1697).

31 'Reflections upon the French Translators', in *Miscellaneous Essays* (London, 1692), p. 185.

32 *Ibid.*, p. 186.

33 *Ibid.*, p. 188.

34 'Character of Saint-Evremond', in *Works*, XX, pp. 9–10. For reasons that are unclear, Dryden wrote only the concluding pages of the essay. His collaborator has not been identified. On Dryden's relations with Saint-Évremond, see John Aden, 'Dryden and Saint-Evremond', *Comparative Literature*, 6 (1954), 232–9.

35 'To ... John, Lord Marquess of Normanby', in *Works*, V, p. 288.

36 *Ibid.*

37 *Ibid.*, p. 290.

38 *Ibid.*, p. 309.

39 *Ibid.*, pp. 312–13. *Dum pelago* etc. (*Aeneid* IV.52; trans. by Noyes).

40 René Le Bossu, *Traité du Poëme Epique* (Paris, 1675), pp. 66–7, 69–71; Jean Regnauld de Segrais, *Traduction de l'Eneide de Virgile* (Paris, 1668), p. 7.

41 The passage deserves to be quoted at length:

> [W]e must confess that *Æneas* was none of the greatest Hero's, and that *Virgil* was sensible of it himself. But what cou'd he do? The *Trojan* on whom he was to build the *Roman* Empire, had been already vanquish'd; he had lost his Country, and was a Fugitive ... Since therefore he cou'd make no more of him in Valour, he resolved not to give him that Vertue, as his Principal, but chose another, which was Piety. 'Tis true this latter, in the Composition of a Hero, was not altogether so shining as the former; but it intitled him more to the favour of the Gods, and their Protection, in all his undertakings: And, which was the Poets chiefest aim, made a nearer Resemblance betwixt *Æneas* and his Patron *Augustus Cæsar,* who, above all things, lov'd to be flatter'd for being Pious, both to the Gods and his Relations ('Character of Saint-Evremond', in *Works*, XX, p. 9).

42 'To ... John, Lord Marquess of Normanby', in *Works*, V, pp. 280–1.

43 The first position has been stated best by William J. Cameron ('John Dryden's Jacobitism', in *Restoration Literature*, ed. Love, pp. 277–308); the second, by Zwicker (*Politics and Language*, pp. 177–88).

44 'To ... John, Lord Marquess of Normanby', in *Works*, V, pp. 282–3. *genus irritabile* etc. (II Epistles ii; trans. by Noyes).

45 See, for example, Zwicker, *Politics and Language*, pp. 197–205. The *Virgil* contains a series of plates which illustrate scenes from the *Aeneid*. Each plate bears the name and crest of a subscriber to the volume, and Zwicker argues that, in the matching up of plate with buyer, Dryden may have found a means of distributing rewards and punishments. See *Politics and Language*, pp. 190–6.

46 Virgil, *Æneidos VI*, in *Opera*, ed. Carolus Ruaeus, 2nd edn (Paris, 1682), p. 549. *Hic quibus* etc. (*Aeneid* VI.608–11; Loeb trans.). The edition from which I quote is the one

which Dryden preferred.

47 *Virgil's Æneis*, in *Works*, V, p. 556.
48 The allusion to Mary has been noted frequently. See, for instance, Cameron, 'John Dryden's Jacobitism', in *Restoration Literature*, ed. Love, pp. 290–1.
49 *Virgil's Æneis*, in *Works*, V, p. 343.
50 For an analysis of the passage, see Winn, *John Dryden*, pp. 487–8.
51 Letter to Tonson, *c.* January 1695, in *Letters*, p. 80.
52 'Postscript to the Reader', in *Works*, V, p. 810.
53 'Notes and Observations on Virgil's Works in English', in *Works*, VI, p. 820.
54 *Ibid.*, p. 830.
55 *Dryden's 'Aeneid' and Its Seventeenth Century Predecessors* (Manchester, Manchester University Press, 1960), p. 261.
56 'To ... John, Lord Marquess of Normanby', in *Works*, V, pp. 303–4.
57 'Notes and Observations', in *Works*, VI, p. 820.
58 *Ibid.*, p. 813.
59 *Ecloga IV*, in *Opera*, p. 36.
60 *Virgil's Pastorals*, in *Works*, V, p. 97.
61 'Notes and Observations', in *Works*, VI, pp. 811–2.
62 *Ibid.*, p. 812.
63 *Ibid.* For an example of Dryden's conjectural emendations, see 'Notes and Observations', in *Works*, VI, p. 832.
64 T. E. Page (ed.), *Bucolica et Georgica* (London, Macmillan, 1898), pp. 148–9. Cf. Robert Coleman (ed.), *Eclogues* (Cambridge, Cambridge University Press, 1977), p. 148.
65 'Notes and Observations', in *Works*, VI, p. 821. As Frost points out, 'Howard translated the fourth, not the sixth, Aeneid and supplied no notes. Dryden may have been remembering Howard's heavily annotated translation of Statius' *Achilleis*' (*Works*, VI, p. 1120).
66 'Notes and Observations', in *Works*, VI, pp. 812, 814. Dryden's insistence on the value of informal, social discourse in the development of scholarship is, no doubt, a protest against the attempt by the learned to make the study of the ancient world their exclusive domain. On the institutions which had grown up to support the scholar and to keep the outsider at bay, see Anne Goldgar, *Impolite Learning: Conduct and Community in the Republic of Letters, 1680–1750* (New Haven, Yale University Press, 1995).
67 *The Dunciad*, in *The Poems of Alexander Pope*, ed. John Butt (New Haven, Yale University Press, 1963), pp. 777–8. On Pope and the new learning, see Levine, *Battle of the Books*, pp. 181–244.
68 Seventeenth-century antiquarianism is discussed in David C. Douglas, *English Scholars: 1660–1730*, 2nd edn (London, Eyre and Spottiswoode, 1951). See also Graham Parry, *The Trophies of Time: English Antiquarians of the Seventeenth Century* (Oxford, Oxford University Press, 1995).
69 On the emendations, see William L. Alderson and Arnold C. Henderson, *Chaucer and Augustan Scholarship*, University of California Publications, English Studies, no. 35 (Berkeley, University of California Press, 1970), 57–62. My discussion of Dryden and Chaucer is much indebted to this work.
70 Alderson and Henderson, *Chaucer and Augustan Scholarship*, p. 68.
71 Letter to Pepys, July 1699, in *Letters*, p. 115.
72 On the scholarly resources available to Dryden, see Alderson and Henderson, *Chaucer and Augustan Scholarship*, pp. 15–52.
73 It is interesting to note that, when he returned to the translation of Ovid in the late

1690s, Dryden took the trouble to consult the Delphin edition of Ovid's works, which had been published since he had last worked on the poet. See Bottkol, 'Dryden's Latin Scholarship', in *Essential Articles*, ed. Swedenberg, pp. 416, 423.

74 'Preface to *Fables*', in *'Of Dramatic Poesy'*, II, pp. 270, 289.

CHAPTER FOURTEEN

The modern temper (1693–1700)

1 According to Alvin B. Kernan (*The Plot of Satire* (New Haven, Yale University Press, 1965), pp. 6–7), Dryden's purpose in the 'Discourse' is to celebrate ancient satire. In his history of satire, Dryden does indeed dwell upon the Ancients, but only to demonstrate afterwards the superiority of the Moderns. A similar strategy underlies Neander's comparison of the Elizabethan and Restoration dramatists in the *Essay of Dramatick Poesie*. See above, pp. 49–52.

2 When in the dedication of the *Essay of Dramatick Poesie* Dryden addressed him, Sackville had the courtesy title Lord Buckhurst. He was created Earl of Middlesex in 1675, and succeeded his father as Earl of Dorset in 1677. See Frost (ed.), *Works*, IV, p. 527.

3 On the relationship Dryden establishes between himself and Dorset, see David Bywaters, *Dryden in Revolutionary England* (Berkeley, University of California Press, 1991), pp. 134–6.

4 'Discourse concerning … Satire', in *Works*, IV, p. 3. In his study of Vespasian, to which Dryden alludes, Suetonius stresses the emperor's kindness and forbearance, the virtues which in his comparison of the two men, Dryden attributes also to Dorset. See *Lives of the Caesars*, trans. J. C. Rolfe, rev. edn (Loeb Classical Library, 1951), II, pp. 305–9.

5 'Discourse concerning … Satire', in *Works*, IV, p. 23. Dryden was no doubt encouraged to look back on his career by the appearance in the 1690s of many makeshift collections of his poems and plays. See Macdonald, *John Dryden: A Bibliography*, p. 146.

6 'Discourse concerning … Satire', in *Works*, IV, pp. 13–15.

7 *Ibid.*, pp. 19–23.

8 Dryden takes on all the commentators, but his work may have been designed to compete specifically with André Dacier's essay 'Préface sur les satires d'Horace, où l'on explique l'origine & le progrès de la satire des Romains' (1687), which furnished Dryden with his title and which was translated into English in 1692. On Dacier's influence and importance, see Howard D. Weinbrot, *The Formal Strain: Studies in Augustan Imitation and Satire* (Chicago, University of Chicago Press, 1969), pp. 60–4.

9 'Discourse concerning … Satire', in *Works*, IV, pp. 36–48. On Dryden's alleged preference for formal verse satire, see William Frost, 'Dryden's Theory and Practice of Satire', in *Dryden's Mind and Art*, King, ed. pp. 194–5.

Narrative verse satire was first identified by Quintilian as a separate kind of satire. Whether it was invented by Publius Terentius Varro, who was born in 82 B.C. and after whom it is named, or the invention of Menippus of Gadara, who lived in the first half of the third century B.C., has never been settled. The works of both men, with the exception of a few fragments, have been completely lost. Quintilian opted for Menippus; Dryden, following Casaubon, preferred Varro:

> [H]e [Varro] Entitled his own Satires *Menippean*: Not that *Menippus* had written any Satires, (for his were either Dialogues or Epistles) but that *Varro* imitated his Style, his Manner, and his Facetiousness ('Discourse concerning … Satire', in *Works*, IV, p. 47).

298

10 'Discourse concerning ... Satire', in *Works*, IV, pp. 6, 11–2. Dryden's concern with the Christian virtues has been found 'unconvincing, coming as it does from the author of *Absalom and Achitophel* and *Mac Flecknoe*' (Bywaters, *Dryden in Revolutionary England*, p. 141). Between the satires and the 'Discourse', however, there lies the significant fact of his conversion. The full literary ramifications of that event – its encouragement, for instance, of a new flexibility – have yet to be studied.

11 'Discourse concerning ... Satire', in *Works*, IV, pp. 51, 53. In writing of Persius, Dryden may also have had in mind John Oldham, another young satirist, on whom he had passed a similar judgment ten years earlier. See 'To the Memory of Mr. Oldham', in *Works*, II, p. 175.

12 'Discourse concerning ... Satire', in *Works*, IV, pp. 65–9, 72. Cf. Bywaters, *Dryden in Revolutionary England*, pp. 145–6.

13 'Discourse concerning ... Satire', in *Works*, IV, p. 50.

14 *Ibid.*, pp. 50, 69. Though there were some precedents for it on the Continent, the method was indeed new in England. See Howard D. Weinbrot, *Alexander Pope and the Traditions of Formal Verse Satire* (Princeton, Princeton University Press, 1982), pp. 22–5.

15 'Discourse concerning ... Satire', in *Works*, IV, pp. 51, 55–6, 64.

16 *Ibid.*, p. 48. Leon Guilhamet's view of satire as 'a borrower of forms', is closer to Dryden's than Guilhamet allows. See *Satire and the Transformation of Genre* (Philadelphia, University of Pennsylvania Press, 1987), pp. 1–17.

17 Dryden's rules are always treated as if they were designed exclusively for formal verse satire, but it is hard to see why they do not also apply to Varronian satire. It is in this section of the essay, after all, that Dryden invokes as explanatory models *Absalom and Achitophel* and Boileau's *Lutrin*.

18 Guilhamet finds Dryden's idea of unity in the 'Discourse' perversely restrictive. In the 1670s Dryden had rejected the mixing of comedy and tragedy in the drama; as a corollary, according to Guilhamet, he now rejects the mixing of topics in satire (*Satire and the Transformation of Genre*, p. 5). Dryden, however, does allow subjects to be mixed in satire. And he justifies the practice with an argument he had used much earlier when he sanctioned the mixing of plots in tragi-comedy. In his views on unity and multiplicity in satire, he hearkens back not, as Guilhamet argues, to the 'Preface to *Oedipus*' (1679), but to the *Essay of Dramatick Poesie* (1668):

> Their [French] Plots are single, they carry on one design ... : Our Playes, besides the main design, have under plots or by-concernments, of less considerable Persons, and Intrigues, which are carried on with the motion of the main Plot: as they say the Orb of the fix'd Stars, and those of the Planets, though they have motions of their own, are whirl'd about by the motion of the *primum mobile*, in which they are contain'd: that similitude expresses much of the *English* Stage: for if contrary motions may be found in Nature to agree; if a Planet can go East and West at the same time; one way by virtue of his own motion, the other by the force of the first mover; it will not be difficult to imagine how the under Plot, which is onely different, not contrary to the great design, may naturally be conducted along with it (*Dramatick Poesie*, in *Works*, XVII, pp. 46–7).

> [A] Perfect Satire ... ought only to treat of one Subject; to be confind'd to one particular Theme; or, at least, to one principally. If other Vices occur in the management of the Chief, they shou'd only be transiently lash'd, and not be insisted on, so as to make the Design double: As in a Play of the *English* Fashion, which we call a *Tragecomedy*, there is to be but one main Design: And tho' there

be an Under-plot, or Second Walk of Comical Characters and Adventures, yet they are subservient to the Chief Fable, carry'd along under it, and helping to it … Thus the *Copernican* Systeme of the Planets makes the Moon to be mov'd by the motion of the Earth, and carry'd about her Orb, as a Dependant of hers … ('Discourse concerning … Satire', in *Works*, IV, p. 79).

Although they refer to different cosmologies – one to the Ptolemaic, the other to the Copernican – and have a slightly different emphasis, the two passages are remarkably similar.

19 Cf. 'To … Mr. Congreve', in *Works*, IV, p. 432.

20 Like Johnson, some modern critics are troubled by Dryden's praise of Dorset. But they should not be. The tradition of panegyric encouraged the writer to move easily back and forth between the facts of an individual life and an ideal. The very extravagance of Dryden's praise is designed to discourage a literal reading.

21 *The Satires of Decimus Junius Juvenalis … Together with the Satires of Aulus Persius Flaccus*, in *Works*, IV, p. 91.

22 'Discourse concerning … Satire', in *Works*, IV, pp. 87–9.

23 On the conventions of Roman satire, see the following: Robert C. Elliott, *The Power of Satire: Magic, Ritual, Art* (Princeton, Princeton University Press, 1960), pp. 113–16; Ulrich Knoche, *Roman Satire*, trans. Edwin S. Ramage (Bloomington, Indiana University Press, 1976); Lucius R. Shero, 'The Satirist's *Apologia*', *Classical Studies*, series no. II, University of Wisconsin Studies in Language and Literature, no. 15 (Madison, University of Wisconsin Press, 1922), pp. 148–67. Dryden's interest in the *apologia* motivates, and even justifies, an aspect of the 'Discourse' that has puzzled most commentators: the long digression on the epic poem.

24 'Discourse concerning … Satire', in *Works*, IV, p. 59.

25 *Ibid.*, p. 60.

26 *Ibid.*, p. 8.

27 *Ibid.*, p. 10.

28 *Ibid.*, p. 87.

29 *Ibid.*, p. 28.

30 'Preface to *Fables*', in '*Of Dramatic Poesy*', II, p. 278.

31 *Ibid.*, p. 271. I cannot agree with Paul H. Fry that Dryden's reference to Hobbes's theory of association is 'the key passage in the "Preface"' (*Reach of Criticism*, p. 103). The preface is centred not on a psychology of creation but on a view of literary tradition. The phrase 'thrid of my discourse' invokes not so much Hobbes's 'TRAYNE of Imaginations' as it does the tapestry metaphor of the writer of romance. On this traditional metaphor, see Susan Perry Alexander, 'The Poet's Craft: The Tapestry Metaphor for Poetry in Ariosto and Spenser', Ph.D. diss. Columbia University, 1982.

32 'Preface to *Fables*', in '*Of Dramatic Poesy*', II, p. 270.

33 *Ibid.*, p. 275.

34 Cedric D. Reverend II, *Dryden's Final Poetic Mode: The 'Fables'* (Philadelphia, University of Pennsylvania Press, 1988), pp. 6–7. Cf. Fry, *Reach of Criticism*, pp. 93–8.

35 'Preface to *Fables*', in '*Of Dramatic Poesy*', II, p. 289.

36 *Ibid.*

37 *Ibid.*, p. 287.

38 *Ibid.*

39 *Ibid.*, p. 274.

40 *Ibid.*, pp. 271–2, 278, 286.

41 *Ibid.*, pp. 279–80.
42 *Ibid.*, p. 290.
43 *Ibid.*, p. 270. Zwicker points out that themes of tradition and family are also pervasive both in the dedication of *Fables* and in two of the original poems Dryden included in the collection (*Politics and Language*, pp. 160–4).
44 'Preface to *Fables*', in '*Of Dramatic Poesy*', II, p. 275.
45 The Preface is not, as Fry contends, 'deliberately cast in a nonanalytic mode' (*Reach of Criticism*, p. 99). It is filled with argument, inference and example. Indeed, if he omits supporting detail, Dryden generally takes care to insist that he could supply it if he would. See 'Preface to *Fables*', in '*Of Dramatic Poesy*', II, pp. 271, 276, 278.
46 *Ibid.*, pp. 271, 289.
47 *Ibid.*, pp. 277, 280, 282.
48 *Ibid.*, p. 280.
49 *Ibid.*, p. 284.
50 *Ibid.*, p. 287.
51 *Ibid.*, p. 289.
52 *Ibid.*, p. 281.
53 *Ibid.*, p. 287.
54 *Ibid.*, p. 286.
55 *Ibid.*, pp. 282–3.
56 *Ibid.*, pp. 281, 286.
57 *Ibid.*, pp. 277–8.
58 *Ibid.*, p. 284.
59 *Ibid.*, pp. 290–1.
60 *Ibid.*, p. 280.
61 *Ibid.*, pp. 284–5.
62 *Ibid.*, p. 272.
63 *Ibid.*, p. 273.
64 *Ibid.*
65 *Ibid.*, p. 271.
66 *Ibid.*, p. 288.
67 *Ibid.*, p. 289. *facile est* etc. (source unknown; trans. by Noyes).
68 *Ibid.*, p. 270.
69 *Ibid.*, p. 291. When he was actually Poet Laureate, Dryden could argue that, on the basis of his royal patent, he was Chaucer's successor in the post: in the document Chaucer was named as the first laureate. Now that he has lost the post, he claims that he is still Chaucer's successor, but as the latter's true (or spiritual) son and heir.
70 *Ibid.*, pp. 273–4.
71 *Ibid.*, p. 293.
72 *Ibid.*, p. 291.
73 *Ibid.*, p. 285.
74 *Ibid.*, p. 293.
75 'Discourse concerning ... Satire', in *Works*, IV, pp. 70–1. On Dryden's extension of the concept of raillery to prose polemic, see 'Life of Lucian', in *Works*, XX, pp. 221–2.
76 'Preface to *Fables*', in '*Of Dramatic Poesy*', II, pp. 291–2.
77 *Ibid.*, p. 292.
78 *Ibid.*, p. 293.
79 *Ibid.*, pp. 272–3. Cf. 'To ... Roger Earl of Orrery', in *Works*, VIII, p. 95.

CHAPTER FIFTEEN
Evaluations

1 'Discourse concerning ... Satire', in *Works*, IV, p. 4.
2 *Ibid.*, pp. 4–5.
3 Hoyt Trowbridge, 'Dryden on the Elizabethans', in *From Dryden to Jane Austen*, p. 5. (First published as 'Dryden's "Essay on the Dramatic Poetry of the Last Age"' in *Philological Quarterly*, 22 (1943), 240–50.)
4 James Kinsley and Helen Kinsley (eds), *Dryden: The Critical Heritage* (New York, Barnes and Noble, 1971), pp. 4–5, 16.
5 'Life of Dryden', in *Lives*, I, p. 418.
6 *Ibid.*, p. 370. The moral basis of the *Lives* is discussed in Paul Fussell, *Samuel Johnson and the Life of Writing* (New York, Harcourt Brace, 1971), pp. 255–78. See also K. J. H. Berland, 'Johnson's Life-Writing and the *Life of Dryden*', *The Eighteenth-Century: Theory and Interpretation*, 23 (1982), 197–218. Cf. Greg Clingham, 'Another and the Same: Johnson's Dryden', in *Literary Transmission*, ed. Miner and Brady, pp. 123–32.
7 'Life of Dryden', in *Lives*, I, pp. 400–1.
8 *Ibid.*, p. 412.
9 *Ibid.*, p. 415; see also 'Life of Butler', in *Lives*, I, p. 217.
10 'Life of Dryden', in *Lives*, I, p. 413.
11 *Ibid.*, p. 417.
12 Throughout the 'Life of Dryden', Johnson restates Dryden's *obiter dicta* and frequently applies to Dryden statements which Dryden applies to other writers. (In the 'Life', for example, Johnson applies to Dryden the latter's own statement about poets who 'boast ... how little time their works have cost them'.) See Dryden, 'Preface to *Fables*', in '*Of Dramatic Poesy*', II, p. 273; Johnson, 'Life of Dryden', in *Lives*, I, p. 348.
13 'Life of Dryden', in *Lives*, I, p. 418. On Dryden's influence on Johnson's habit of viewing 'literary works as marriages ... of dichotomous elements', see Robert DeMaria, Jr., 'Johnson's Form of Evaluation', *Studies in English Literature*, 19 (1979), 502–3.
14 George Birkbeck Hill cites many of the parallels in his edition of the *Lives*. They have not, however, been taken into account in any discussion of the 'Life of Dryden'. Indeed, Johnson has been celebrated for his originality and genius precisely where he is most dependent upon Dryden's self-criticism. For examples of this praise, see Kinsley and Kinsley (eds), *Dryden: The Critical Heritage*, p. 16; Maximillian E. Novak, 'Johnson, Dryden, and the Wild Vicissitudes of Taste', in *The Unknown Samuel Johnson*, ed. John J. Burke, Jr. and Donald Kay (Madison, University of Wisconsin Press, 1983), pp. 55, 57; Catherine N. Parke, 'Imlac and Biographical Thinking', in *Domestick Privacies: Samuel Johnson and the Art of Biography*, ed. David Wheeler (Lexington, Kentucky, University of Kentucky Press, 1987), p. 99.
15 *The Critical and Miscellaneous Prose Works of John Dryden* ... (London, 1800), I, pp. i–ii.
16 Dryden's works were of longstanding interest to Johnson. The personal library that Johnson brought to (or assembled at) Oxford University in 1728 contained three of Dryden's translations: the Juvenal, the Virgil, and the Chaucer. In the first edition of the *Dictionary* (1755), he turned to Dryden for 11,310 quotations; and in the fourth edition (1773), he added another 91. Of these quotations, a number were taken directly from the critical prose: for example, 12 from the 'Preface to *Ovid's Epistles*', 102 from the 'Discourse concerning ... Satire' and 74 from the 'Preface to *Fables*'. On these points, see Samuel Johnson, *A Dictionary of the English Language*, CD-ROM, Cambridge,

Cambridge University Press, 1996; Aleyn Lyell Reade, *Johnsonian Gleanings* (1928; rpt. New York, Octagon Books, 1968), V, pp. 27–30, 225; Weinbrot, *The Formal Strain*, p. 69. I am grateful to Professor Weinbrot for reminding me of some of these facts.

17 'Preface to *Fables*', in '*Of Dramatic Poesy*', II, p. 272.

18 'Life of Dryden', in *Lives*, I, p. 397.

19 *Ibid.*, p. 459.

20 'Postscript to the Reader', in *Works*, VI, p. 807.

21 'Life of Dryden', in *Lives*, I, p. 419.

22 *Ibid.*

23 'To ... Roger Earl of Orrery', in *Works*, VIII, p. 100.

24 'Preface to *Ovid's Epistles*', in *Works*, I, p. 118.

25 'Life of Dryden', in *Lives*, I, pp. 422–3.

26 'To ... John, Lord Marquess of Normanby', in *Works*, V, p. 329.

27 *Ibid.*, p. 330.

28 'Preface to *Ovid's Epistles*', in *Works*, I, pp. 114–18.

29 'Life of Dryden', in *Lives*, I, pp. 421–2. For Johnson's earlier, and essentially similar, views on the same subject, see *Idler 69*, in '*The Idler*' *and* '*The Adventurer*', ed. W[alter] J[ackson] Bate *et al.*, vol. 2 of *The Yale Edition of the Works of Samuel Johnson* (New Haven, Yale University Press, 1963), pp. 214–17.

30 'Discourse concerning ... Satire', in *Works*, IV, p. 88.

31 'Preface to *Fables*', in '*Of Dramatic Poesy*', II, p. 270.

32 Johnson gives the sense of Cowley, but not Cowley's language. See Cowley, 'Preface to *Pindaric Odes*', in *Complete Works*, II, p. [4].

33 'To ... Lord Radcliffe', in *Works*, IV, p. 370.

34 'Imlac and Biographical Thinking', in *Domestick Privacies*, p. 99. The point is restated, with minor changes, in Catherine N. Parke, *Samuel Johnson and Biographical Thinking* (Columbia, Missouri, University of Missouri Press, 1991), p. 138.

35 See above, pp. 241–2.

36 'Life of Dryden', in *Lives*, I, pp. 225–6. Johnson abandons Dryden's navigational image for a commercial metaphor. It should be noted that Dryden also sometimes thinks of literary activity as a form of trade or manufacturing. See 'To ... John, Lord Marquess of Normanby', in *Works*, V, p. 336.

37 Scott, *Life of Dryden*, pp. 51–2; Saintsbury, *A History of English Criticism*, pp. 110–29; Watson, *The Literary Critics*, pp. 59–60; Watson (ed.), '*Of Dramatic Poesy*', I, pp. v–xvii; Kirsch, *Dryden's Heroic Drama*, pp. 3–4; Arthur C. Kirsch (ed.), *Literary Criticism of Dryden*, pp. ix–xvii.

38 Hume, *Dryden's Criticism*; Pechter, *Dryden's Classical Theory*; Engell, *Forming the Critical Mind*, pp. 15–43. The dismissive tendency inherent in the approach is made manifest in the conclusions of David Hopkins:

> Much of Dryden's early criticism is designed, directly or indirectly, to defend or justify his own dramatic practice and that of his contemporaries. Since that practice was itself usually prompted by the need to follow and create fashion rather than by more artistic motives, it is perhaps not surprising that a great deal of the criticism associated with it seems, from a later vantage-point, to have dated badly. Whereas the best critical writing of Pope, Johnson or Coleridge, for all the initial unfamiliarity of its idiom, can be seen on closer inspection to bear on those central questions which inevitably recur to readers of literature in all periods, Dryden's early criticism seems, for all the attractiveness of its manner, for the most part

narrowly of its time, its best insights coming in incidental observations (which often bear on the general workings of the human mind) rather than in the main body of its literary judgements (*John Dryden*, p. 46).

39 'The Metaphysical Poets', in *Selected Essays: 1917–1932*, p. 247. In the year or so prior to the original publication of the essay in the *Times Literary Supplement* on 20 October 1921, Eliot was immersed in the reading of Dryden. See Letter to Lytton Strachey, 17 February 1920, in *The Letters of T. S. Eliot: 1898–1922*, ed. Valerie Eliot (San Diego, Harcourt Brace Jovanovich, 1988), p. 367. Eliot's first essay on Dryden, a review of Mark Van Doren's study, was published in the *Times Literary Supplement*, 9 June 1921, pp. [361]–2. On Eliot's interest in Dryden, see Ronald Bush, *T. S. Eliot: A Study in Character and Style* (New York, Oxford University Press, 1983), pp. 114–15; Engell, *Forming the Critical Mind*, pp. 38–40; David Macaree, 'T. S. Eliot and John Dryden: A Study in Relationship', *English Studies in Canada*, 13:1 (1987), 35–48.

40 'Andrew Marvell', in *Selected Essays*, p. 259; 'The Metaphysical Poets', in *Selected Essays*, pp. 247–8. (The Marvell essay was first published in *Times Literary Supplement*, 31 March 1921, [201]–2.)

41 For a different account of the source of Eliot's theory, see C. K. Stead, 'Eliot, Arnold, and the English Poetic Tradition', in *Literary Criticism of T. S. Eliot*, ed. Newton-De Molina, pp. 184–206.

42 'Andrew Marvell', in *Selected Essays*, p. 260; 'John Dryden', in *Selected Essays*, pp. 273–4; 'The Metaphysical Poets', in *Selected Essays*, p. 247.

43 *The Use of Poetry and the Use of Criticism: Studies in the Relationship of Criticism to Poetry in England* (London, Faber and Faber, 1933), p. 84.

44 *John Dryden: The Poet, the Dramatist, the Critic* (New York, Terence and Elsa Holliday, 1932), p. 52. Cf. 'Andrew Marvell', in *Selected Essays*, pp. 260–1.

45 *John Dryden*, p. 64.

46 *Ibid.*, p. 56.

47 *Ibid.*, pp. 22–3.

48 James Sutherland, *The English Critic* (London, H. K. Lewis, 1953), pp. 5–7, 18.

49 W[alter] Jackson Bate, *The Burden of the Past and the English Poet* (London, Chatto and Windus, 1971), pp. 45–6.

50 William Hazlitt, 'On Gusto', in *The Round Table*, ed. F. J. S. (London, J. M. Dent, 1951), pp. 72–89; William Hazlitt, 'On Poetry in General', in *Lectures on the English Poets*, ed. A. R. Waller (London, J. M. Dent, 1951), pp. 1–18.

51 Matthew Arnold, 'Maurice de Guérin', in *The Complete Prose Works of Matthew Arnold*, ed. R. H. Super (Ann Arbor, University of Michigan Press, 1962), III, pp. 13–16, 30, 33–6.

52 *John Dryden*, p. 42.

53 'Preface to *All for Love*', in *Works*, XIII, pp. 12–13.

Bibliography

EDITIONS OF DRYDEN'S WORKS

Beurline, L. A., and Fredson Bowers (eds), *John Dryden: Four Comedies*, Chicago, University of Chicago Press, 1967.
——, *John Dryden: Four Tragedies*, Chicago, University of Chicago Press, 1967.
Boulton, James T. (ed.), *Of Dramatick Poesie*, London, Oxford University Press, 1967.
Hammond, Paul, and David Hopkins (eds), *The Poems of John Dryden*, 4 vols proposed, London, Longman, 1995–.

Ker, W. P. (ed.), *Essays of John Dryden*, 2 vols, Oxford, Clarendon Press, 1900.
Kinsley, James (ed.), *The Poems of John Dryden*, 4 vols, Oxford, Clarendon Press, 1958.
Malone, Edmond (ed.), *The Critical and Miscellaneous Prose Works of John Dryden*, 3 vols in 4, London, 1800.
Noyes, George R. (ed.), *The Poetical Works of Dryden*, rev. edn, Boston, Houghton Mifflin, 1950.
Of Dramatick Poesie, 1668; rpt. Menston, Scholar Press, 1969.
Scott, Sir Walter (ed.), *The Works of John Dryden*, 18 vols, London, 1808, rev. George Saintsbury, London, 1882–92.
Swedenberg, H. T., Jr, *et al.* (eds), *The Works of John Dryden*, 20 vols proposed, Berkeley, University of California Press, 1956–.Ward, Charles E. (ed.), *The Letters of John Dryden, with Letters Addressed to Him*, Durham, North Carolina, Duke University Press, 1940.
Watson, George (ed.), *'Of Dramatic Poesy' and Other Critical Essays*, 2 vols, London, J. M. Dent, 1962.

SECONDARY SOURCES

Aden, John M., 'Dryden and Boileau: The Question of Critical Influence', *Studies in Philology*, 50 (1953), 491–509.
——, 'Dryden and the Imagination: The First Phase', *PMLA*, 74 (1959), 28–40.
——, 'Dryden and Saint-Evremond', *Comparative Literature*, 6 (1954), 232–9.
Aden, John M. (comp.), *The Critical Opinions of John Dryden: A Dictionary*, Nashville, Vanderbilt University Press, 1963.
Allen, Ned Bliss, *The Sources of John Dryden's Comedies*, 1935; rpt. New York, Gordian Press, 1967.
Alssid, Michael W., *Dryden's Rhymed Heroic Tragedies: A Critical Study of the Plays and of Their Place in Dryden's Poetry*, 2 vols, Salzburg Studies in English Literature, Poetic Drama, no. 7, Salzburg, Universität Salzburg, 1974.
Amarasinghe, Upali, *Dryden and Pope in the Early Nineteenth Century: A Study of Changing Literary Taste, 1800–1830*, Cambridge, Cambridge University Press, 1962.
Archer, Stanley, 'The Persons in *An Essay of Dramatic Poesy*', *Papers on Language and Literature*, 2 (1966), 305–14.
Armistead, Jack M., 'Dryden and the Occult as Dramatic Code: *Tyrannick Love*', *Papers on Language and Literature*, 24 (1988), 367–83.

Arundell, D. D. (ed.), *Dryden and Howard: 1664–1668*, Cambridge, Cambridge University Press, 1929.

Atkins, G. Douglas, *The Faith of John Dryden: Change and Continuity*, Lexington, Kentucky, University Press of Kentucky, 1980.

Barbeau, Anne T., *The Intellectual Design of John Dryden's Heroic Plays*, New Haven, Yale University Press, 1970.

Barnard, John, 'Dryden, Tonson, and the Subscriptions for the 1697 *Virgil*', *Papers of the Bibliographical Society of America*, 57 (1963), 129–51.

Bately, Janet M., 'Dryden's Revisions in the *Essay of Dramatic Poesy*: The Preposition at the End of the Sentence and the Expression of the Relative', *Review of English Studies*, n.s., 15 (1964), 268–82.

Björk, Lennart, 'The "Inconsistencies" of Dryden's Criticism of Shakespeare', *Anglia*, 91 (1973), 427–35.

Bohn, William E., 'The Development of John Dryden's Literary Criticism', *PMLA*, 22 (1907), 56–139.

Bredvold, Louis I., *The Intellectual Milieu of John Dryden: Studies in Some Aspects of Seventeenth-Century Thought*, University of Michigan Publications, Language and Literature, no. 12, Ann Arbor, University of Michigan Press, 1934.

Burke, Helen, '*Annus Mirabilis* and the Ideology of the New Science', *ELH*, 57 (1990), 307–34.

Bywaters, David, *Dryden in Revolutionary England*, Berkeley, University of California Press, 1991.

Cohen, Ralph, 'John Dryden's Literary Criticism', in *New Homage to John Dryden*, Los Angeles, William Andrews Clark Memorial Library, 1983, pp. 61–85.

Cubbage, Virginia, 'The Reputation of John Dryden: 1700–1779', Ph.D. diss. Northwestern University, 1944.

Davie, Donald, 'Dramatic Poetry: Dryden's Conversation Piece', *Cambridge Journal*, 5 (1952), 553–61.

Drydeniana, 14 vols, New York, Garland Publishing, 1974–6.

Ehrenpreis, Irvin, *Acts of Implication: Suggestion and Covert Meaning in the Works of Dryden, Swift, and Austin*, Berkeley, University of California Press, 1980.

Elias, Richard Lane, 'Dryden's Restoration Criticism', Ph.D. diss. Temple University, 1978.

Eliot, T. S., *John Dryden: The Poet, the Dramatist, the Critic*, New York, Terence and Elsa Holliday, 1932.

Erskine-Hill, Howard, 'John Dryden', in *Dryden to Johnson*, ed. Roger H. Lonsdale, London, Barrie and Jenkins, 1971, pp. 23–57.

Fowler, Alastair, 'That Great Neglected Poet: The "Silent Graces" and Moral Authority of Dryden's Verse', rev. of *The Poems of John Dryden*, ed. Paul Hammond, *Times Literary Supplement*, 7 July 1995, pp. 3–4.

Freedman, Morris, 'Milton and Dryden on Rhyme', *Huntington Library Quarterly*, 24 (1961), 337–44.

——, 'Milton and Dryden on Tragedy', in *English Writers of the Eighteenth Century*, ed. John H. Middendorf, New York, Columbia University Press, 1963, pp. 158–71.

Frost, William, *Dryden and the Art of Translation*, Yale Studies in English, no. 128, New Haven, Yale University Press, 1955.

——, *John Dryden: Dramatist, Satirist, Translator*, New York, AMS Press, 1988.

Fry, Paul H., 'Dryden's Earliest Allusion to Longinus', *English Language Notes*, 19:1 (1981), 22–4.

Guibbory, Achsah, 'Dryden's View of History', *Philological Quarterly*, 52 (1973), 197–204.

Haley, David B., *Dryden and the Problem of Freedom: The Republican Aftermath, 1649–1680*, New Haven, Yale University Press, 1997.

Hall, James M., *John Dryden: A Reference Guide*, Boston, G. K. Hall, 1984.

Hamilton, K. G., *John Dryden and the Poetry of Statement*, East Lansing, Michigan State University Press, 1969.

Hammond, Paul, 'The Circulation of Dryden's Poetry', *Papers of the Bibliographical Society of America*, 86 (1992), 379–409.

——, 'Figures of Horace in Dryden's Literary Criticism', in *Horace Made New: Horatian Influences on British Writing from the Renaissance to the Twentieth Century*, ed. Charles Martindale and David Hopkins, Cambridge, Cambridge University Press, 1993, pp. 127–47.

——, 'Flecknoe and *Mac Flecknoe*', *Essays in Criticism*, 35 (1985), 315–29.

——, *John Dryden: A Literary Life*, New York, St. Martin's Press, 1991.

Harth, Phillip, *Contexts of Dryden's Thought*, Chicago, University of Chicago Press, 1968.

Hoffman, Arthur W., *John Dryden's Imagery*, Gainesville, University of Florida Press, 1962.

Hopkins, David, *John Dryden*, Cambridge, Cambridge University Press, 1986.

Hughes, Derek, *Dryden's Heroic Plays*, Lincoln, Nebraska, University of Nebraska Press, 1981.

——, 'The Unity of Dryden's *Marriage à-la-Mode*', *Philological Quarterly*, 61 (1982), 125–42.

Hume, Robert D., *Dryden's Criticism*, Ithaca, Cornell University Press, 1970.

——, 'Dryden on Creation: "Imagination" in the Later Criticism', *Review of English Studies*, n.s., 21 (1970), 295–314.

Huntley, Frank L[ivingston], *On Dryden's 'Essay of Dramatic Poesy'*, University of Michigan Contributions in Modern Philology, no. 16, Ann Arbor, University of Michigan Press, 1951.

——, 'The Unity of John Dryden's Dramatic Criticism', Ph.D. diss. University of Chicago, 1941.

Jensen, H. James (comp.), *A Glossary of John Dryden's Critical Terms*, Minneapolis, University of Minnesota Press, 1969.

King, Bruce, *Dryden's Major Plays*, Edinburgh, Oliver and Boyd, 1966.

King, Bruce (ed.), *Dryden's Mind and Art*, Edinburgh, Oliver and Boyd, 1969.

Kinsley, James, and Helen Kinsley (eds), *Dryden: The Critical Heritage*, New York, Barnes and Noble, 1971.

Kirsch, Arthur C., *Dryden's Heroic Drama*, Princeton, Princeton University Press, 1965.

Kirsch, Arthur C. (ed.), 'Introduction', *Literary Criticism of Dryden*, Lincoln, Nebraska, University of Nebraska Press, 1966, pp. ix–xvii.

Kramer, David Bruce, *The Imperial Dryden: The Poetics of Appropriation in Seventeenth-Century England*, Athens, Georgia, University of Georgia Press, 1994.

Latt, David J., and Samuel Holt Monk, *John Dryden: A Survey and Bibliography of Critical Studies, 1895–1974*, Minneapolis, University of Minnesota Press, 1976.

Law, Richard, 'The Heroic Ethos in John Dryden's Heroic Plays', *Studies in English Literature*, 23 (1983), 389–98.

LeClercq, Richard V., 'The Academic Nature of the Whole Discourse of *An Essay of Dramatic Poesy*', *Papers on Language and Literature*, 8 (1972), 27–38.

——, 'Corneille and *An Essay of Dramatic Poesy*', *Comparative Literature*, 22 (1970), 319–27.

Bibliography

Lees, F. N., 'John Dryden', in *From Dryden to Johnson*, ed. Boris Ford, Baltimore, Pelican Books, 1965, pp. 97–113.

Macaree, David, 'T. S. Eliot and John Dryden: A Study in Relationship', *English Studies in Canada*, 13:1 (1987), 35–48.

Macdonald, Hugh, *John Dryden: A Bibliography of Early Editions and of Drydeniana*, Oxford, Clarendon Press, 1939.

Mace, Dean T., 'Dryden's Dialogue on the Drama', *Journal of the Warburg and Cortauld Institutes*, 25 (1962), 87–112.

McFadden, George, 'Dryden and the Numbers of His Native Tongue', in *Essays and Studies in Language and Literature*, ed. Herbert H. Petit, Duquesne Studies, Philological Series, no. 5, Pittsburgh, Duquesne University Press, 1964, 87–109.

——, *Dryden: The Public Writer, 1660–1685*, Princeton, Princeton University Press, 1978.

——, 'Dryden's "Most Barren Period" – and Milton', *Huntington Library Quarterly*, 24 (1960), 283–96.

McKeon, Michael, *Politics and Poetry in Restoration England: The Case of Dryden's 'Annus Mirabilis'*, Cambridge, Mass., Harvard University Press, 1975.

MacLachlan, Christopher, 'Dryden, Truth, and Nature', *British Journal of Aesthetics*, 20 (1980), 153–9.

Miner, Earl, *Dryden's Poetry*, 1967; rpt. Bloomington, Indiana University Press, 1971.

——, 'Mr. Dryden and Mr. Rymer', *Philological Quarterly*, 54 (1975), 137–51.

——, 'Renaissance Contexts of Dryden's Criticism', *Michigan Quarterly Review*, 12 (1973), 97–115.

Miner, Earl (ed.), *John Dryden*, 1972; rpt. Athens, Ohio, Ohio University Press, 1975.

Miner, Earl, and Jennifer Brady (eds), *Literary Transmission and Authority: Dryden and Other Writers*, Cambridge, Cambridge University Press, 1993.

Moore, Frank Harper, *The Nobler Pleasure: Dryden's Comedy in Theory and Practice*, Chapel Hill, University of North Carolina Press, 1962.

Oden, Richard (ed.), *Dryden and Shadwell*, Delmar, New York, Scholars' Facsimiles and Reprints, 1977.

Osborn, James M., *John Dryden: Some Biographical Facts and Problems*, rev. edn, Gainesville, University of Florida Press, 1965.

Pechter, Edward, *Dryden's Classical Theory of Literature*, London, Cambridge University Press, 1975.

Pendlebury, B. J., *Dryden's Heroic Plays: A Study of the Origins*, 1923; rpt. New York, Russell and Russell, 1967.

Proudfoot, L., *Dryden's 'Aeneid' and Its Seventeenth Century Predecessors*, Manchester, Manchester University Press, 1960.

Ramsay, Paul, *The Art of John Dryden*, Lexington, Kentucky, University of Kentucky Press, 1969.

——, *The Lively and the Just: An Argument for Propriety*, University of Alabama Studies, no. 15, [Tuscaloosa, Alabama], University of Alabama Press, 1962.

Rawson, Claude, 'Beyond the Mexique Bay', rev. of *The Indian Queen*, by John Dryden and Henry Purcell, *Times Literary Supplement*, 24 February 1984, p. 192.

Reverand, Cedric D. II, 'Dryden's "Essay of Dramatic Poesie": The Poet and the World of Affairs', *Studies in English Literature*, 22 (1982), 375–93.

——, *Dryden's Final Poetic Mode: The 'Fables'*, Philadelphia, University of Pennsylvania Press, 1988.

Russell, Trusten Wheeler, *Voltaire, Dryden, and Heroic Tragedy*, 1946; rpt. New York, AMS Press, 1966.

Salvaggio, Ruth, *Dryden's Dualities*, English Language Studies Monograph Series, no. 29, Victoria, British Columbia, University of Victoria Press, 1983.

Schilling, Bernard N. (ed.), *Dryden: A Collection of Critical Essays*, Englewood Cliffs, New Jersey, Prentice-Hall, 1963.

Scott, Sir Walter, *The Life of Dryden*, ed. Bernard Kreissman, Lincoln, Nebraska, Bison-University of Nebraska Press, 1963.

Selden, R[aman], 'Hobbes, Dryden, and the Ranging Spaniel', *Notes and Queries*, n.s., 20 (1973), 388–90.

Sherwood, John C., 'Dryden and the Critical Theories of Tasso', *Comparative Literature*, 28 (1966), 351–9.

——, 'Dryden and the Rules: The Preface to the *Fables*', *Journal of English and Germanic Philology*, 52 (1953), 13–26.

——, 'Dryden and the Rules: The Preface to *Troilus and Cressida*', *Comparative Literature*, 2 (1950), 73–83.

——, 'Precept and Practice in Dryden's Criticism', *Journal of English and Germanic Philology*, 68 (1969), 432–40.

Sherwood, Margaret, *Dryden's Dramatic Theory and Practice*, 1898; rpt. New York, Russell and Russell, 1966.

Smith, David Nicol, *John Dryden*, London, Cambridge University Press, 1950.

Strang, Barbara M. H., 'Dryden's Innovations in Critical Vocabulary', *Durham University Journal*, 51 (1959), 114–23.

Swedenberg, H. T., Jr (ed.), *Essential Articles for the Study of John Dryden*, Hamden, Connecticut, Archon Books, 1966.

Thale, Mary, 'Dryden's Critical Vocabulary: The Imitation of Nature', *Papers on Language and Literature*, 2 (1966), 315–36.

Thorpe, Clarence DeWitt, 'The Psychological Approach in Dryden', in *The Aesthetic Theory of Thomas Hobbes*, University of Michigan Publications in Language and Literature, no. 18, Ann Arbor, University of Michigan Press, 1940, pp. 189–220.

Trowbridge, Hoyt, *From Dryden to Jane Austen: Essays on English Critics and Writers, 1660–1818*, Albuquerque, University of New Mexico Press, 1977.

Van Doren, Mark, *John Dryden: A Study of His Poetry*, rev. edn, Bloomington, Indiana University Press, 1960.

Waith, Eugene, *The Herculean Hero in Marlowe, Chapman, Shakespeare, and Dryden*, London, Chatto and Windus, 1962.

Ward, Charles E., *The Life of Dryden*, Chapel Hill, University of North Carolina Press, 1961.

Williamson, George, 'Dryden as Critic', *University of California Chronicle*, 32 (1930), 71–6.

Watson, George, 'Dryden's First Answer to Rymer', *Review of English Studies*, n.s., 14 (1963), 17–23.

Winn, James A., *John Dryden and His World*, New Haven, Yale University Press, 1987.

——, *'When Beauty Fires the Blood': Love and the Arts in the Age of Dryden*, Ann Arbor, University of Michigan Press, 1992.

Winn, James A. (ed.), *Critical Essays on John Dryden*, New York, G. K. Hall, 1997.

Wykes, David, *A Preface to Dryden*, London, Longman, 1977.

Young, Kenneth, *John Dryden: A Critical Biography*, London, Sylvan Press, 1954.

Zwicker, Steven N., *Politics and Language in Dryden's Poetry: The Arts of Disguise*, Princeton, Princeton University Press, 1984.

BACKGROUND WORKS

Adolph, Robert, *The Rise of the Modern Prose Style*, Cambridge, Mass., M. I. T. Press, 1968.

Aguzzi-Barbagli, Danilo, '*Ingegno, Acutezza*, and *Meraviglia* in the Sixteenth-Century Great Commentaries to Aristotle's *Poetics*', in *Petrarch to Pirandello: Studies in Italian Literature in Honour of Beatrice Corrigan*, ed. Julius A. Molinaro, Toronto, University of Toronto Press, 1973, pp. 73–93.

Alderson, William L., and Arnold C. Henderson, *Chaucer and Augustan Scholarship*, University of California Publications, English Studies, no. 35, Berkeley, University of California Press, 1970.

Alexander, Susan Perry, 'The Poet's Craft: The Tapestry Metaphor for Poetry in Ariosto and Spenser', Ph.D. diss. Columbia University, 1982.

Alssid, Michael W., *Thomas Shadwell*, New York, Twayne, 1967.

Altick, Richard D., *Lives and Letters: A History of Literary Biography in England and America*, New York, Alfred A. Knopf, 1965.

'Ariosto Approached', rev. of *Orlando Furioso*, trans. Sir John Harrington, ed. Robert McNulty, *Times Literary Supplement*, 6 October 1972, 1195–6.

Ariosto, Ludovico, *Orlando Furioso*, trans. Guido Waldman, New York, Oxford University Press, 1974.

Arnold, Matthew, *The Complete Prose Works of Matthew Arnold*, ed. R. H. Super, vol. III, Ann Arbor, University of Michigan Press, 1962.

Atkins, J. W. H., *English Literary Criticism: 17th and 18th Centuries*, London, Methuen, 1951.

——, *Literary Criticism in Antiquity*, Cambridge, Cambridge University Press, 1934.

Aubrey, John, *Brief Lives*, ed. Oliver Lawson Dick, 3rd edn, London, Secker and Warburg, 1958.

Auerbach, Erich, *Mimesis*, trans. William R. Trask, Princeton, Princeton University Press, 1953.

Babb, Lawrence, *The Elizabethan Malady: A Study of Melancholia in English Literature from 1580 to 1642*, East Lansing, Michigan State College Press, 1951.

Bacon, Francis, *The Advancement of Learning*, ed. G. W. Kitchin, London, J. M. Dent, 1915.

Baker, Herschel, *The Wars of Truth*, Cambridge, Mass., Harvard University Press, 1952.

Barber, C. L., *Shakespeare's Festive Comedy*, Princeton, Princeton University Press, 1959.

Baron, Hans, 'The Querelle of the Ancients and the Moderns as a Problem for Renaissance Scholarship', *Journal of the History of Ideas*, 20 (1959), 3–22.

Bate, W[alter] Jackson, *The Burden of the Past and the English Poet*, London, Chatto and Windus, 1971.

——, *From Classic to Romantic: Premises of Taste in Eighteenth-Century England*, 1946; rpt. New York, Harper Torchbooks–Harper and Row, 1961.

Bate, Walter Jackson (ed.), *Criticism: The Major Texts*, New York, Harcourt Brace, 1952.

Bateson, F. W., 'Contributions to a Dictionary of Critical Terms, I, Comedy of Manners', *Essays in Criticism*, 1 (1951), 89–93.

Beaumont, Francis, and John Fletcher, *The Dramatic Works in the Beaumont and Fletcher Canon*, ed. Fredson Bowers *et al.*, 10 vols proposed, Cambridge, Cambridge University Press, 1966–.

Beljame, Alexandre, *Men of Letters and the English Public in the Eighteenth Century*, 2nd edn, ed. Bonamy Dobrée, trans. E. O. Lorimer, London, Kegan Paul, Trench, and Trubner, 1948.

Bell, Walter George, *The Great Fire in 1666*, London, John Lane, 1920.

——, *The Great Plague in London in 1665*, London, John Lane, 1924.

Bentley, Gerald Eades, *Shakespeare and Jonson: Their Reputations in the Seventeenth Century Compared*, 2 vols, Chicago, University of Chicago Press, 1945.

Bentley, Richard, *The Works of Richard Bentley*, ed. Alexander Dyce, 2 vols, 1836; rpt. New York, AMS Press, 1966.

Berland, K. J. H., 'Johnson's Life-Writing and the *Life of Dryden*', *The Eighteenth Century: Theory and Interpretation*, 23 (1982), 197–218.

Bethell, S. L., 'Gracián, Tesauro, and the Nature of Metaphysical Wit', *The Northern Miscellany of Literature*, 1 (1953), 19–40.

Bond, Donald F., 'Distrust of the Imagination in English Neo-Classical Criticism', *Philological Quarterly*, 14 (1935), 54–69.

Bordinat, Philip, and Sophia B. Blaydes, *Sir William Davenant*, Boston, Twayne, 1981.

Borgerhoff, E. B. O., *The Freedom of French Classicism*, Princeton, Princeton University Press, 1950.

Boulton, James T. (ed.), *Johnson: The Critical Heritage*, New York, Barnes and Noble, 1971.

Bowra, C. M. *From Virgil to Milton*, London, Macmillan, 1945.

Boyce, Benjamin, *The Theophrastan Character in England to 1642*, Cambridge, Mass., Harvard University Press, 1947.

Boyle, Roger [Orrery], *The Dramatic Works of Roger Boyle*, 2 vols, ed. William Smith Clark II, Cambridge, Mass., Harvard University Press, 1937.

Brand, Charles Peter, *Torquato Tasso: A Study of the Poet and of His Contribution to English Literature*, Cambridge, Cambridge University Press, 1965.

Bray, René, 'Honnête homme', in *Dictionnaire Des Lettres Françaises: Le Dix-Septième Siècle*, ed. Cardinal Georges Grente, Paris, Arthème Fayard, 1954.

——, *La Formation de la doctrine classique en France*, 1927; rpt. Paris, Nizet, 1961.

Brereton, Geoffrey, *French Tragic Drama in the Sixteenth and Seventeenth Centuries*, London, Methuen, 1973.

Brody, Jules, *Boileau and Longinus*, Geneva, E. Droz, 1958.

Brooks, H. F., 'Guez de Balzac: Eloquence and the Life of the Spirit', *L'Esprit Créateur*, 15 (1975), 59–78.

Brown, Laura, *English Dramatic Form, 1660–1760: An Essay in Generic History*, New Haven, Yale University Press, 1981.

Brownley, Martine Watson, 'Johnson's *Lives of the English Poets* and Earlier Traditions of the Character Sketch in England', in *Johnson and His Age*, ed. James Engell, Harvard University Studies, no. 12, Cambridge, Mass., Harvard University Press, 1984, pp. 29–53.

Bullitt, John, and W[alter] J[ackson] Bate, 'Distinctions Between Fancy and Imagination in Eighteenth-Century English Criticism', *Modern Language Notes*, 60 (1945), 8–15.

Bunyan, John, *The Miscellaneous Works of John Bunyan*, ed. Roger Sharrock *et al.*, 12 vols proposed, Oxford, Clarendon Press, 1976–.

Burke, John J. Jr, and Donald Kay (eds), *The Unknown Samuel Johnson*, Madison, University of Wisconsin Press, 1983.

Burke, Peter, *The Fortunes of the Courtier: The European Reception of Castiglione's 'Cortegiano'*, Cambridge, Polity Press, 1995.

Bury, J. B., *The Idea of Progress*, London, Macmillan, 1920.

Bush, Douglas, *English Literature in the Earlier Seventeenth Century*, 2nd edn, Oxford, Clarendon Press, 1966.

Bush, Ronald, *T. S. Eliot: A Study in Character and Style*, New York, Oxford University Press, 1983.

Butcher, S. H. (trans. and ed.), *Aristotle's Theory of Poetry and Fine Art*, corrected 4th edn, 1911; rpt. New York, Dover Books, 1951.

Cartwright, William, *The Plays and Poems of William Cartwright*, ed. C. Blackmore Evans, Madison, University of Wisconsin Press, 1951.

Casaubon, Isaac, *De Satyrica Graecorum Poesi et Romanarum Satirica*, ed. Peter E. Medine, 1605; rpt. Delmar, New York, Scholars' Facsimiles and Reprints, 1972.

Castiglione, Baldassare, *The Book of the Courtier*, trans. Charles S. Singleton, New York, Anchor-Doubleday, 1959.

Chapman, Gerald Webster (ed.), *Literary Criticism in England: 1660–1800*, New York, Alfred A. Knopf, 1966.

Cicero, *De Oratore*, ed. E. W. Sutton and H. Rackham, 2 vols, Loeb Classical Library, 1942.

Clark, A. F. B., *Boileau and the French Classical Critics in England: 1660–1830*, 1925; rpt. New York, Russell and Russell, 1965.

Clark, Donald Lemen, *Rhetoric in Greco-Roman Education*, New York, Columbia University Press, 1957.

Clark, John R., *Form and Frenzy in Swift's 'Tale of a Tub'*, Ithaca, Cornell University Press, 1970.

Clark, W. S., 'The Definition of the "Heroic Play" in the Restoration Period', *Review of English Studies*, 8 (1932), 437–44.

Coleridge, Samuel Taylor, *Biographia Literaria*, ed. James Engell and W[alter] Jackson Bate, vol. VII, pt. 2 of *The Collected Works of Samuel Taylor Coleridge*, Princeton, Princeton University Press, 1983.

——, *The Complete Works of Samuel Taylor Coleridge*, ed. W. G. T. Shedd, 7 vols, New York, Harper, 1853.

Corman, Brian, 'Thomas Shadwell and the Jonsonian Comedy of the Restoration', in *From Renaissance to Restoration: Metamorphoses of the Drama*, ed. Robert Markley and Laurie Finke, Cleveland, Bellflower Press, Case Western Reserve University, Department of English, 1984, pp. 127–50.

Corneille, Pierre, *The Chief Plays of Corneille*, trans. Lacy Lockert, Princeton, Princeton University Press, 1957.

——, *Writings on the Theatre*, ed. H. T. Barnwell, Oxford, Basil Blackwell, 1965.

Cowley, Abraham, *The Complete Works in Verse and Prose of Abraham Cowley*, ed. Alexander B. Grosart, 2 vols, 1881; rpt. New York, AMS Press, 1967.

Cuddon, J. A., *A Dictionary of Literary Terms*, rev. edn, New York, Doubleday, 1976.

Curtis, M. H., *Oxford and Cambridge in Transition: 1558–1642*, Oxford, Clarendon Press, 1959.

Curtius, Ernst Robert, *European Literature and the Latin Middle Ages*, trans. Willard R. Trask, New York, Harper and Row, 1953.

Dacier, André, *Oeuvres d'Horace*, 10 vols, Paris, 1681–89.

Daitches, David, *Critical Approaches to Literature*, London, Longmans Green, 1956.

Davenant, Sir William, *The Dramatic Works of Sir William D'Avenant*, ed. James Maidment and W. H. Logan, 2 vols, 1872; rpt. New York, Russell and Russell, 1964.

——, *Gondibert*, ed. David F. Gladish, Oxford, Clarendon Press, 1971.

——, *The Works of Sir William Davenant*, 2 vols, 1673; rpt. New York, Benjamin Blom, 1968.

Demaria, Robert, Jr, 'Johnson's Form of Evaluation', *Studies in English Literature*, 19 (1979), 501–14.

Dennis, John, *The Critical Works of John Dennis*, ed. Edward Niles Hooker, 2 vols, Baltimore, John Hopkins Press, 1939–43.

Dent, Edward J., *Foundations of English Opera*, 1928; rpt. New York, Da Capo Press, 1965.

De Sola Pinto, Vivian, *Restoration Carnival*, London, Folio Society, 1954.

Dobrée, Bonamy (ed.), *Five Heroic Plays*, London, Oxford University Press, 1960.

——, *Restoration Comedy: 1660–1720*, Oxford, Oxford University Press, 1924.

Donne, John, *The Poems of John Donne*, ed. H. J. C. Grierson, London, Oxford University Press, 1933.

Douglas, David C., *English Scholars, 1660–1730*, 2nd edn, London, Eyre and Spottiswoode, 1951.

Dowlin, Cornell March, *Sir William Davenant's 'Gondibert', Its Preface, and Hobbes's Answer: A Study in English Neo-Classicism*, Ph.D. diss. University of Pennsylvania, 1932, Philadelphia, privately printed, 1934.

Dunn, Kevin, *Pretexts of Authority: The Rhetoric of Authorship in the Renaissance Preface*, Stanford, Stanford University Press, 1994.

Edmond, Mary, *Rare Sir William Davenant*, New York, St. Martin's Press, 1987.

Ehrenpreis, Irvin, *Swift: The Man, His Works, and the Age*, 3 vols, Cambridge, Mass., Harvard University Press, 1962–83.

Elias, A. C., Jr, *Swift at Moor Park: Problems in Biography and Criticism*, Philadelphia, University of Pennsylvania Press, 1982.

Eliot, T. S., *The Letters of T. S. Eliot: 1898–1922*, ed. Valerie Eliot, San Diego, Harcourt Brace Jovanovich, 1988.

——, *Selected Essays: 1917–1932*, New York, Harcourt Brace, 1932.

——, *The Use of Poetry and the Use of Criticism: Studies in the Relationship of Criticism to Poetry in England*, London, Faber and Faber, 1933.

Elkin, Peter Kinsley, *The Augustan Defense of Satire*, Oxford, Clarendon Press, 1973.

Elledge, Scott, 'Cowley's Ode *Of Wit* and Longinus on the Sublime: A Study of One Definition of the Word *Wit*', *Modern Language Quarterly*, 9 (1948), 185–98.

Elledge, Scott, and Donald Schier (eds), *The Continental Model: Selected French Critical Essays of the Seventeenth Century*, Ithaca, Cornell University Press, 1970.

Elliott, Robert C., *The Power of Satire: Magic, Ritual, Art*, Princeton, Princeton University Press, 1960.

Ellis, Frank, 'Notes on *A Tale of a Tub*', *Swift Studies*, 1 (1986), 9–14.

Engell, James, *Forming the Critical Mind: Dryden to Coleridge*, Cambridge, Mass., Harvard University Press, 1989.

Erskine-Hill, Howard, *The Augustan Idea in English Literature*, London, Edward Arnold, 1983.

Etherege, Sir George, *Letters of Sir George Etherege*, ed. Frederick Bracher, Berkeley, University of California Press, 1974.

Evelyn, John, *The Diary of John Evelyn*, ed. E. S. de Beer, 6 vols, Oxford, Clarendon Press, 1955.

Fletcher, Harris Francis, *The Intellectual Development of John Milton*, 2 vols, Urbana, University of Illinois Press, 1961.

Foss, Michael, *The Age of Patronage: The Arts in Society, 1660–1750*, Ithaca, Cornell University Press, 1971.

Fowler, Alastair, *Conceitful Thought: The Interpretation of English Renaissance Poems*, Edinburgh, Edinburgh University Press, 1975.

Fry, Paul H., *The Reach of Criticism: Method and Perception in Literary Theory*, New Haven, Yale University Press, 1983.

Fujimura, Thomas H., *The Restoration Comedy of Wit*, Princeton, Princeton University Press, 1952.

Fussell, Paul, *Samuel Johnson and the Life of Writing*, New York, Harcourt Brace, 1971.

Gallaway, Francis, *Reason, Rule, and Revolt in English Classicism*, 1940; rpt. Lexington, Kentucky, University of Kentucky Press, 1966.

Gaunt, William, *Court Painting in England from Tudor to Victorian Times*, London, Constable, 1980.

Gaw, Allison, 'Tuke's *Adventures of Five Hours*, in Relation to the "Spanish Plot" and to John Dryden', in *Studies in English Drama*, ed. Allison Gaw, Publications of the University of Pennsylvania, Series in Philology, no. 14, Philadelphia, University of Pennsylvania, 1917.

Gerbert, Clara (ed.), *An Anthology of Elizabethan Dedications and Prefaces*, 1933; rpt. New York, Russell and Russell, 1966.

Gilman, Ernest B., *The Curious Perspective: Literary and Pictorial Wit in the Seventeenth Century*, New Haven, Yale University Press, 1978.

Goldgar, Anne, *Impolite Learning: Conduct and Community in the Republic of Letters, 1680–1750*, New Haven, Yale University Press, 1995.

Gottfried, Rudolf (ed.), 'Introduction', *Ariosto's 'Orlando Furioso'*, trans. Sir John Harrington, Bloomington, Midland-Indiana University Press, 1971, pp. 9–20.

Grafton, Anthony, *Defenders of the Text: The Traditions of Scholarship in an Age of Science*, Cambridge, Mass., Harvard University Press, 1991.

Granville-Barker, Harley, *On Dramatic Method*, 1931; rpt. New York, Hill and Wang, 1956.

Griffin, Dustin, *Literary Patronage in England, 1650–1800*, Cambridge, Cambridge University Press, 1996.

Grube, G. M. A., *The Greek and Roman Critics*, Toronto, University of Toronto Press, 1965.

Guilhamet, Leon, *Satire and the Transformation of Genre*, Philadelphia, University of Pennsylvania Press, 1987.

Hagstrum, Jean H., *Eros and Vision: The Restoration to Romanticism*, Evanston, Northwestern University Press, 1989.

——, *Samuel Johnson's Literary Criticism*, Minneapolis, University of Minnesota Press, 1952.

Halsband, Robert, 'The 'Penury of English Biography' before Samuel Johnson', in *Biography in the 18th Century*, ed. J. D. Browning *et al.*, Publications of the McMaster University Association for 18th Century Studies, no. 8, New York, Garland, 1980, pp. 112–27.

Hamilton, Anthony, *Count Gramont at the Court of Charles II*, trans. Nicholas Deakin, London, Barrie and Rockliff, 1965.

Hanning, Robert W., and Donald Rosand (eds), *Castiglione: The Ideal and the Real in Rennaissance Culture*, New Haven, Yale University Press, 1983.

Hanzo, Thomas, *Latitude and Restoration Criticism*, Anglistica, no. 12, Copenhagen, Rosenkilde and Bagger, 1961.

Harbage, Alfred, *Cavalier Drama: An Historical and Critical Supplement to the Study of the Elizabethan and the Restoration Stage*, 1936; rpt. New York, Russell and Russell, 1964.

Harwood, John T., *Critics, Values, and Restoration Comedy*, Carbondale, Southern Illinois University Press, 1982.

Hathaway, Baxter, *Marvels and Commonplaces: Renaissance Literary Criticism*, New York, Random House, 1968.

Haydn, Hiram Collins, *The Counter-Renaissance*, 1950; rpt. New York, Atheneum, 1960.

Hazlitt, William, *Lectures on the English Poets*, ed. A. R. Waller, London, J. M. Dent, 1951.

——, *The Round Table*, ed. F. J. S., London, J. M. Dent, 1951.

Heath, James, *A Brief Chronicle of the Late Intestine VVar in the Three Kindoms of England, Scotland and Ireland...*, 2nd impression, London, 1663.

Hedbäck, Ann-Mari (ed.), *Sir William Davenant, The Siege of Rhodes: A Critical Edition*, Studia Anglistica Upsaliensa, no. 14, Uppsala, Almqvist and Wiksell, 1973.

Henn, T. R., *Longinus and English Criticism*, Cambridge, Cambridge University Press, 1934.

Herrick, Marvin T., *Comic Theory in the Sixteenth Century*, 1950; rpt. Urbana, University of Illinois Press, 1964.

——, *The Poetics of Aristotle in England*, New Haven, Yale University Press, 1930.

——, *Tragi-comedy: Its Origin and Development in Italy, France, and England*, Urbana, University of Illinois Press, 1955.

Heylbut, Rose, *English Opinions of French Poetry: 1660–1750*, 1923; rpt. New York, AMS Press, 1966.

Hill, Geoffrey, *The Enemy's Country: Words, Contexture, and Other Circumstances of Language*, Stanford, Stanford University Press, 1991.

Hobbes, Thomas, *The English Works of Thomas Hobbes*, ed. William Molesworth, vol. I, 1850; rpt. Aalen, Scientia Verlag, 1962.

——, *Leviathan*, ed. C. B. Macpherson, Baltimore, Penguin, 1968.

Holland, Norman N., *The First Modern Comedies: The Significance of Etherege, Wycherley, and Congreve*, Cambridge, Mass., Harvard University Press, 1959.

Hollier, Denis (ed.), *A New History of French Literature*, Cambridge, Mass., Harvard University Press, 1989.

Hope, Quentin Manning, *Saint-Evremond: The Honnête Homme as Critic*, Bloomington, Indiana University Press, 1962.

Horace, *Satires, Epistles, and Ars poetica*, Loeb Classical Library, 1929.

Hotson, Leslie, *The Commonwealth and Restoration Stage*, Cambridge, Mass., Harvard University Press, 1928.

Hough, Graham, *A Preface to 'The Faerie Queen'*, New York, W. W. Norton, 1963.

Howard, Sir Robert, *The Dramatic Works of Sir Robert Howard*, London, 1722.

Hughes, Leo, *A Century of English Farce*, Princeton, Princeton University Press, 1956.

Hume, Robert D., *The Development of English Drama in the Late Seventeenth Century*, Oxford, Clarendon Press, 1976.

——, *The Rakish Stage: Studies in English Drama, 1660–1800*, Carbondale, Southern Illinois University Press, 1983.

Hume, Robert D., and Judith Milhous, 'Dating Play Premières from Publication Data, 1660–1700', *Harvard Library Bulletin*, 22 (1974), 374–405.

Hunter, Michael Cyril William, *John Aubrey and the Realm of Learning*, New York, Science History Publications, 1975.

Hutton, Ronald, *The Restoration: A Political and Religious History of England and Wales, 1658–1667*, Oxford, Oxford University Press, 1985.

Irving, William Henry, *The Providence of Wit in the English Letter Writers*, Durham, North Carolina, Duke University Press, 1955.

Jack, Ian, *Augustan Satire: Intention and Idiom in English Poetry, 1660–1750*, 1952; rpt. London, Oxford University Press, 1966.

Jackson, Wallace, *Immediacy: The Development of a Critical Concept from Addison to Coleridge*, Amsterdam, Rodopi, 1973.

Jackson, Wallace, *The Probable and the Marvelous: Blake, Wordsworth, and the Eighteenth-Century Critical Tradition*, Athens, Georgia, University of Georgia Press, 1978.

Javitch, Daniel, 'Cantus Interruptus', *Modern Language Notes*, 95 (1980), 66–80.

——, *Poetry and Courtliness in Renaissance England*, Princeton, Princeton University Press, 1978.

——, 'Rescuing Ovid from the Allegorizers', in *Ariosto 1984 in America*, ed. Aldo Scaglione, Ravenna, Longo, 1976, pp. 97–107.

Jenkins, Ralph Eugene, 'Some Sources of Samuel Johnson's Literary Criticism', Ph.D. diss. University of Texas, 1969.

Jensen, H. James, 'A Note on Restoration Aesthetics', *Studies in English Literature*, 14 (1974), 317–26.

Johnson, Samuel, *A Dictionary of the English Language*, CD-ROM, Cambridge, Cambridge University Press, 1996.

——, *'The Idler' and 'The Adventurer'*, ed. W[alter] J[ackson] Bate *et al.*, vol. I of *The Yale Edition of the Works of Samuel Johnson*, New Haven, Yale University Press, 1963.

——, *Lives of the English Poets*, ed. George Birkbeck Hill, 3 vols, 1905; rpt. New York, Octagon Press, 1967.

Jones, J. R., *Country and Court: England, 1658–1714*, Cambridge, Mass., Harvard University Press, 1978.

Jones, Richard Foster, *Ancients and Moderns: A Study of the Rise of the Scientific Movement in Seventeenth-Century England*, St. Louis, Washington University Press, 1961.

——, 'Science and Criticism in the Neo-Classical Age of Literature', *Journal of the History of Ideas*, 1 (1940), 381–412.

——, 'Science and English Prose Style in the Third Quarter of the Seventeenth Century', *PMLA*, 45 (1930), 997–1009.

Jonson, Ben, *Ben Jonson*, ed. C. H. Herford and Percy and Evelyn Simpson, 11 vols, Oxford, Clarendon Press, 1925–52.

Juvenal, *Juvenal and Persius*, ed. G. G. Ramsay, Loeb Classical Library, 1940.

Kelso, Ruth, *The Doctrine of the English Gentleman in the Sixteenth Century*, University of Illinois Studies in Language and Literature, no. 14, Urbana, University of Illinois Press, 1929.

Kennedy, George Alexander, *Quintilian*, New York, Twayne, 1969.

Kenney, E. J., *The Classical Text: Aspects of Editing in the Age of the Printed Book*, Berkeley, University of California Press, 1974.

Kernan, Alvin B., *The Plot of Satire*, New Haven, Yale University Press, 1965.

Knight, R. C., *Racine et La Grèce*, 2nd edn, Paris, A. G. Nizet, 1974.

Knoche, Ulrich, *Roman Satire*, trans. Edwin S. Ramage, Bloomington, Indiana University Press, 1976.

Kroll, Richard, *The Material Word: Literate Culture in the Restoration and Early Eighteenth Century*, Baltimore, Johns Hopkins University Press, 1991.

Krutch, Joseph Wood, *Comedy and Conscience after the Restoration*, New York, Columbia University Press, 1949.

La Bruyère, [Jean] de, *The Characters, or the Manners of the Age* [1688–94], in *The Works of M. de La Bruyère*, 2 vols, London, 1752.

Lanham, Richard A., *The Motives of Eloquence: Literary Rhetoric in the Renaissance*, New Haven, Yale University Press, 1976.

Le Bossu, René, *Traité du Poëme Épique*, Paris, 1675.

Levine, Joseph M., *The Battle of the Books: History and Literature in the Augustan Age*, Ithaca, Cornell University Press, 1991.

Lewis, C. S., *The Allegory of Love*, London, Oxford University Press, 1938.

——, *English Literature in the Sixteenth Century, Excluding Drama*, Oxford, Clarendon Press, 1954.

——, *Studies in Words*, London, Cambridge University Press, 1960.

Litman, Théodore A., *Le Sublime en France: 1660–1714*, Paris, A. G. Nizet, 1971.

Loftis, John, *The Spanish Plays of Neoclassical England*, New Haven, Yale University Press, 1973.

Longinus, *On the Sublime*, trans. W. Rhys Roberts, Cambridge, Cambridge University Press, 1899.

Lord, George de Forest *et al.* (eds), *Poems on Affairs of State: Augustan Satirical Verse, 1660–1714*, Vols I–III, New Haven, Yale University Press, 1963–8.

Love, Harold (ed.), *Restoration Literature: Critical Approaches*, London, Methuen, 1972.

Lynch, Kathleen, *The Social Mode of Restoration Comedy*, 1926; rpt. New York, Biblo and Tannen, 1965.

Maguire, Nancy Klein, *Regicide and Restoration: English Tragicomedy, 1660–1671*, New York, Cambridge University Press, 1992.

Mahoney, John L., *The Whole Internal Universe: Imitation and the New Defense of Poetry, 1660–1830*, New York, Fordham University Press, 1985.

Mallinson, G. J., *The Comedies of Corneille*, Manchester, Manchester University Press, 1984.

Markley, Robert, *Two Edg'd Weapons: Style and Ideology in the Comedies of Etherege, Wycherley, and Congreve*, Oxford, Clarendon Press, 1988.

Marks, Emerson R., *Relativist and Absolutist: The Early Neoclassical Debate in England*, New Brunswick, New Jersey, Rutgers University Press, 1955.

Marshall, Geoffrey, *Restoration Serious Drama*, Norman, University of Oklahoma Press, 1975.

Marshall, W. Gerald (ed.), *The Restoration Mind*, Newark, Delaware, University of Delaware Press, 1997.

Martin, Peter, *Edmond Malone, Shakespearean Scholar: A Literary Biography*, Cambridge, Cambridge University Press, 1995.

Mazzeo, Joseph A., 'Metaphysical Poetry and the Poetic of Correspondence', *Journal of the History of Ideas*, 14 (1953), 221–34.

——, 'A Seventeenth-Century Theory of Metaphysical Poetry', *Romanic Review*, 42 (1951), 245–55.

Miles, Dudley, 'Morals of the Restoration', *Sewanee Review*, 24 (1916), 104–14.

Miller, G. M., *The Historical Point of View in English Literary Criticism from 1570–1770*, Anglistische Forschungen, no. 35, Heidelberg, C. Winter, 1913.

Miller, Henry Knight, *Henry Fielding's 'Tom Jones' and the Romance Tradition*, ELS Monograph Series, no. 6, Victoria, British Columbia, University of Victoria, 1976.

Milton, John, *Complete Poetry and Major Prose*, ed. Merritt Y. Hughes, New York, Odyssey Press, 1957.

Molière [Jean-Baptiste Poquelin], *The Works of Mr. de Molière*, trans. John Ozell, vol. I, 1714; rpt. New York, Benjamin Blom, 1967.

Monk, Samuel Holt, *The Sublime: A Study of Critical Theories in XVIII-Century England*, 1935; rpt. Ann Arbor, Ann Arbor–University of Michigan Press, 1960.

Moore, W. G., 'Boileau and Longinus', *French Studies*, 15 (1975), 52–62.

Morrah, Patrick, *Restoration England*, London, Constable, 1979.

Mumby, Frank A., and Ian Norrie, *Publishers and Booksellers*, rev. 5th edn, London, Jonathan Cape, 1974.

Murphy, James J. (ed.), *Renaissance Eloquence: Studies in the Theory and Practice of Renaissance Rhetoric*, Berkeley, University of California Press, 1983.

Nelson, Robert J., *Corneille: His Heroes and Their Worlds*, Philadelphia, University of Pennsylvania Press, 1963.

Nethercot, Arthur H., *Sir William D'Avenant: Poet Laureate and Playwright-Manager*, Chicago, University of Chicago Press, 1938.

Nevo, Ruth, *The Dial of Virtue: A Study of Poems on Affairs of State in the Seventeenth Century*, Princeton, Princeton University Press, 1963.

Newton-De Molina, David (ed.), *The Literary Criticism of T. S. Eliot: New Essays*, London, Athlone Press, 1977.

Nicoll, Allardyce, *A History of Restoration Drama: 1660–1700*, rev. 4th edn, vol. I of *A History of English Drama: 1660–1900*, Cambridge, Cambridge University Press, 1952.

Noyes, Robert Gale, *Ben Jonson on the English Stage: 1660–1776*, 1935; rpt. New York, Benjamin Blom, 1966.

Nurse, Peter H., *Classical Voices: Studies of Corneille, Racine, Molière, Mme de Lafayette*, Totowa, New Jersey, Rowman and Littlefield, 1971.

Ogg, David, *England in the Reign of Charles II*, 2 vols, 2nd edn, Oxford, Oxford University Press, 1956.

Oliver, H. J., *Sir Robert Howard (1628–1698): A Critical Biography*, Durham, North Carolina, Duke University Press, 1963.

Otis, Brooks, *Ovid as an Epic Poet*, 2nd edn, Cambridge, Cambridge University Press, 1970.

——, *Virgil: A Study in Civilized Poetry*, Oxford, Clarendon Press, 1963.

Ovid, *'Heroides' and 'Amores'*, ed. Grant Showerman, Loeb Classical Library, 1914.

——, *Metamorphoses*, ed. Frank Justas Miller, 2 vols, 2nd edn, Loeb Classical Library, 1921.

Parke, Catherine N., *Samuel Johnson and Biographical Thinking*, Columbia, Missouri, University of Missouri Press, 1991.

Parry, Graham, *The Trophies of Time: English Antiquarians of the Seventeenth Century*, Oxford, Oxford University Press, 1995.

Patterson, Annabel, *Marvell and the Civic Crown*, Princeton, Princeton University Press, 1978.

Payne, Deborah C., *Patronage, Professionalism, and the Marketplace of Restoration Theatre, 1660–1685*, forthcoming.

Pepys, Samuel, *The Diary of Samuel Pepys*, ed. Robert Latham and William Matthews, 11 vols, Berkeley, University of California Press, 1970–83.

Pinto, Vivian De Sola, *Restoration Carnival: Five Courtier Poets*, London, Folio Society, 1954.

——, *Sir Charles Sedley, 1639–1701: A Study in the Life and Literature of the Restoration*, New York, Boni and Liveright, 1927.

Piper, David, *The Image of the Poet: British Poets and Their Portraits*, Oxford, Clarendon Press, 1982.

Piper, William Bowman, *The Heroic Couplet*, Cleveland, Case Western University Press, 1969.

Plutarch, *The Parallel Lives*, ed. Bernadotte Perrin, 11 vols, Loeb Classical Library, 1914–26.

Pocock, Gordon, *Boileau and the Nature of Classicism*, Cambridge, Cambridge University Press, 1980.

Pooley, Roger, 'Language and Loyalty: Plain Style at the Restoration', *Literature and History*, 6 (1980), 2–18.

——, 'Plain and Simple: Bunyan and Style', in *John Bunyan, Conventicle and Parnassus: Tercentenary Essays*, ed. N. H. Keeble, Oxford, Clarendon Press, 1988, pp. 91–111.

Pope, Alexander, *The Poems of Alexander Pope*, ed. John Butt, New Haven, Yale University Press, 1963.

Prior, Moody, *The Language of Tragedy*, New York, Columbia University Press, 1947.

Pottle, Frederick A., *The Idiom of Poetry*, rev. edn, Bloomington, Indiana University Press, 1963.

Purver, Margery, *The Royal Society: Concept and Creation*, Cambridge, Mass., M. I. T. Press, 1967.

Quintana, Ricardo, *The Mind and Art of Jonathan Swift*, 1936; rpt. Gloucester, Mass., Peter Smith, 1963.

Quintilian, *Institutio Oratoria*, ed. H. E. Butler, 4 vols, Loeb Classical Library, 1921.

Reade, Aleyn Lyell, *Johnsonian Gleanings*, 9 vols, 1928; rpt. Octagon Books, 1968.

Rebhorn, Wayne A., *Courtly Performances: Masking and Festivity in Castiglione's Book of the Courtier*, Detroit, Wayne State University Press, 1978.

Rigault, Hippolyte, *Histoire de la querelle des anciens et des modernes*, Paris, 1836.

Robinson, Forrest G., *The Shape of Things Known: Sidney's Apology in Its Philosophical Tradition*, Cambridge, Mass., Harvard University Press, 1972.

Robinson, Michael F., *Opera Before Mozart*, 1966; rpt. New York, Apollo-William Morrow, 1967.

Rosand, Ellen, *Opera in Seventeenth-Century Venice: The Creation of a Genre*, Berkeley, University of California Press, 1991.

Rose, Sister Anthony, *The Jeremy Collier Stage Controversy: 1689–1726*, 1937; rpt. New York, Benjamin Blom, 1966.

Rosenberg, Alfred, *Longinus in England bis zum Ende des 18. Jahrhunderts*, Berlin, Mayer und Müller, 1917.

Rosenheim, Edward, *Swift and the Satirist's Art*, Chicago, Chicago University Press, 1963.

Rothstein, Eric, *Restoration Tragedy: Form and Process of Change*, Madison, University of Wisconsin Press, 1967.

Rymer, Thomas, *The Critical Works of Thomas Rymer*, ed. Curt A. Zimansky, New Haven, Yale University Press, 1956.

Saint-Evremond, Charles de Marguetel de Saint Denis de, *Miscellaneous Essays*, London, 1692.

Saintsbury, George, *A History of English Criticism*, New York, Dodd Mead, 1911.

Sandys, John Edwin, *A History of Classical Scholarship*, 3rd edn, 3 vols, 1920; rpt. New York, Hafner, 1964.

Sasek, Lawrence A., *The Literary Temper of the English Puritans*, 1961; rpt. New York, Greenwood Press, 1969.

Savage, James E., *Ben Jonson's Basic Comic Characters and Other Essays*, Hattiesburg, Miss., University and College Press of Mississippi, 1973.

Savile, George [Halifax], *Complete Works*, ed. J. P. Kenyon, Baltimore, Penguin, 1969.

Schilling, Bernard N. (ed.), *Essential Articles for the Study of English Augustan Backgrounds*, Hamden, Connecticut, Archon Books, 1961.

Segrais, Jean Regnauld de, *Traduction de l'Eneide de Virgile*, Paris, 1668.

Shadwell, Thomas, *The Complete Works of Thomas Shadwell*, ed. Montague Summers, 5 vols, London, Fortune Press, 1927.

Shadwell, Thomas, *The Virtuoso*, ed. Marjorie Hope Nicolson and David Stuart Rodes, Lincoln, Nebraska, University of Nebraska Press, 1966.

Shakespeare, William, *Romeo and Juliet*, ed. George Lyman Kittredge, rev. Irving Ribner, Lennox, Mass., Xerox College Publishing, 1968.

——, *The Tempest*, ed. George Lyman Kittredge, Boston, Ginn, 1939.

Sharp, Robert Lathrop, *From Donne to Dryden: The Revolt Against Metaphysical Poetry*, 1940; rpt. Hamden, Connecticut, Archon Books, 1964.

Sharpe, Kevin, *Criticism and Compliment: The Politics of Literature in the England of Charles I*, Cambridge, Cambridge University Press, 1987.

Shero, Lucius R., 'The Satirist's *Apologia*', *Classical Studies*, series no. II, University of Wisconsin Studies in Language and Literature, no. 15, Madison, University of Wisconsin Press, 1922, 148–67.

Sidney, Sir Philip, *Sir Philip Sidney*, ed. Katherine Duncan-Jones, New York, Oxford University Press, 1989.

Singleton, Marion White, *God's Courtier: Configuring a Different Grace in George Herbert's 'Temple'*, Cambridge, Cambridge University Press, 1987.

Smith, G. Gregory, *Elizabethan Critical Essays*, 2 vols, Oxford, Clarendon Press, 1904.

Smith, John Harrington, *The Gay Couple in Restoration Comedy*, Cambridge, Mass., Harvard University Press, 1948.

Sorelius, Gunnar, *The Giant Race Before the Flood: Pre-Restoration Drama on the Stage and in the Criticism of the Restoration*, Studia Anglistica Upsaliensia, no. 4, Uppsala, Almqvist and Wiksell, 1966.

Southern, Richard, *Changeable Scenery: Its Origin and Development in the British Theatre*, London, Faber and Faber, [1952].

Spenser, Edmund, *The Poetical Works of Edmund Spenser*, ed. J. C. Smith and E. De Selincourt, London, Oxford University Press, 1912.

Spingarn, J. E., *Literary Criticism in the Renaissance*, 1889; rpt. New York, Harcourt Brace, 1963.

Spingarn, J. E. (ed.), *Critical Essays of the Seventeenth Century*, 3 vols, 1908–9; rpt. Bloomington, Indiana University Press, 1957.

Sprague, Arthur Colby, *Beaumont and Fletcher on the Restoration Stage*, 1926; rpt. New York, Benjamin Blom, 1965.

Sprat, Thomas, *History of the Royal Society*, ed. Jackson I. Cope and Harold Whitmore Jones, St. Louis, Washington University Press, 1958.

Starkman, Miriam K., *Swift's Satire on Learning in 'A Tale of a Tub'*, Princeton, Princeton University Press, 1950.

Steiner, T. R., *English Translation Theory, 1650–1800*, Amsterdam, Van Gorum, 1975.

Stephens, James, *Francis Bacon and the Style of Science*, Chicago, University of Chicago Press, 1975.

Suetonius, *Lives of the Caesars*, trans. J. C. Rolfe, rev. edn, vol. II, Loeb Classical Library, 1951.

Sutherland, James, *The English Critic*, London, H. K. Lewis, 1953.

——, *English Literature of the Late Seventeenth Century*, Oxford, Clarendon Press, 1969.

——, 'The Impact of Charles II on Restoration Literature', in *Restoration and Eighteenth-Century Literature: Essays in Honor of Alan Dugald McKillop*, ed. Carroll Camden, Chicago, University of Chicago Press, 1963, pp. 251–63.

——, *On English Prose*, Toronto, University of Toronto Press, 1957.

——, 'Prologues, Epilogues, and Audience in the Restoration Theatre', in *Of Books and Humankind: Essays and Poems Presented to Bonamy Dobrée*, ed. John Butt, London, Routledge and Kegan Paul, 1964, pp. 37–54.

Swedenberg, H. T., Jr, *The Theory of the Epic in England: 1660–1800*, University of California Publications in English, no. 15, Berkeley, University of California Press, 1944.

Swift, Jonathan, *A Tale of a Tub, to which is added The Battle of the Books and The Mechanical Operation of the Spirit*, ed. A. C. Guthkelch and D. Nicol Smith, 2nd edn, Oxford, Oxford University Press, 1958.

Tasso, Torquato, *Discourses on the Heroic Poem*, trans. Mariella Cavalchini and Irene Samuel,

Oxford, Clarendon Press, 1973.

——, *Jerusalem Delivered*, trans. Edward Fairfax, ed. John Charles Nelson, New York, Capricorn Books, 1963.

Tave, Stuart M., *The Amiable Humorist: A Study in the Comic Theory and Criticism of the Eighteenth and Early Nineteenth Centuries*, Chicago, University of Chicago Press, 1960.

Terence, *Terence*, ed. John Sargeaunt, 2 vols, Loeb Classical Library, 1912.

Thormählen, Marianne, *Rochester: The Poems in Context*, Cambridge, Cambridge University Press, 1993.

Trimpi, Wesley, *Ben Jonson's Poems: A Study of the Plain Style*, Stanford, Stanford University Press, 1962.

Tuke, Sir Samuel, *The Adventures of Five Hours*, ed. A. E. H. Swaen, Amsterdam, Swets and Zeitlinger, 1927.

Underwood, Dale, *Etherege and the Seventeenth-Century Comedy of Manners*, Yale Studies in English, vol. 135, New Haven, Yale University Press, 1957.

Ustick, W. L., and H. H. Hudson, 'Wit, "Mixt Wit," and the "Bee in Amber",' *Huntington Library Bulletin*, 8 (1935), 103–30.

Van Lennep, William (ed.), *The London Stage, 1660–1800, Part I: 1660–1700*, intro. Emmet L. Avery and Arthur H. Scouten, Carbondale, Southern Illinois University Press, 1965.

Van Rooy, C. V., *Studies in Satire and Related Literary Theory*, Leiden, E. J. Brill, 1965.

Verdicts of the Learned concerning Virgil's and Homer's Poems, London, 1697.

Vernon, P. F., 'Marriage of Convenience and the Moral Code of Restoration Comedy', *Essays in Criticism*, 12 (1962), 370–87.

Vickers, Brian, 'The Ingredients of a Romance', rev. of *The Novel in Antiquity*, by Thomas Hagg, *Times Literary Supplement*, 20 April 1984, p. 427.

——, 'The Royal Society and English Prose Style: A Reassessment', in *Rhetoric and the Pursuit of Truth: Language and Change in the Seventeenth and Eighteenth Centuries*, Los Angeles, William Andrews Clark Memorial Library, 1985.

Villiers, George [Buckingham], *The Rehearsal*, ed. D. E. L. Crane, Durham, North Carolina, University of Durham Press, 1976.

Vinaver, Eugène, *The Rise of Romance*, New York, Oxford University Press, 1971.

Virgil, *Bucolica et Georgica*, ed. T. E. Page, London, Macmillan, 1898.

——, *Eclogues, Georgics, Aeneid*, trans. H. Rushton Fairclough, rev. edn, 2 vols, Loeb Classical Library, 1934.

——, *Opera*, ed. Carolus Ruaeus, 2nd edn, Paris, 1682.

——, *Eclogues*, ed. Robert Coleman, Cambridge, Cambridge University Press, 1977.

Waith, Eugene M., *Ideas of Greatness: Heroic Drama in England*, New York, Barnes and Noble, 1971.

——, *The Pattern of Tragicomedy in Beaumont and Fletcher*, 1952; rpt. Hamden, Connecticut, Archon Books, 1969.

Wallis, Lawrence B., *Fletcher, Beaumont, and Company: Entertainers to the Jacobean Gentry*, New York, King's Crown Press, 1947.

Walton, Geoffrey, 'Seventeenth-Century Ideas of Wit', in *Metaphysical to Augustan: Studies in Tone and Sensibility in the Seventeenth Century*, London, Bowes and Bowes, 1955, pp. 13–22.

Watson, George, *The Literary Critics: A Study of English Descriptive Criticism*, Baltimore, Penguin, 1962.

Wedgwood, C[icely] V[eronica], *Seventeenth-Century English Literature*, London, Oxford University Press, 1950.

Weinberg, Bernard, *A History of Literary Criticism in the Italian Renaissance*, 2 vols, Chicago, University of Chicago Press, 1961.

Weinbrot, Howard D., *Alexander Pope and the Traditions of Formal Verse Satire*, Princeton, Princeton University Press, 1982.

——, *Augustus Caesar in 'Augustan' England*, Princeton, Princeton University Press, 1978.

——, *Britannia's Issue: The Rise of British Literature from Dryden to Ossian*, Cambridge, Cambridge University Press, 1993.

——, *Eighteenth-Century Satire: Essays on Text and Context from Dryden to Peter Pindar*, Cambridge, Cambridge University Press, 1988.

——, *The Formal Strain: Studies in Augustan Imitation and Satire*, Chicago, University of Chicago Press, 1969.

Wellek, René, *The Rise of English Literary History*, Chapel Hill, University of North Carolina Press, 1941.

Wellek, René, and Alvaro Ribiero (eds), *Evidence in Literary Scholarship: Essays in Memory of James Marshall Osborn*, Oxford, Clarendon Press, 1979.

Welsted, [Leonard], *A Dissertation Concerning the Perfection of the English Language...*, in *Epistles, Odes, &c. Written on Several Subjects...*, London, 1724.

Wheeler, David (ed.), *Domestick Privacies: Samuel Johnson and the Art of Biography*, Lexington, Kentucky, University of Kentucky Press, 1987.

Wilcox, John, *The Relation of Molière to Restoration Comedy*, 1938; rpt. New York, Benjamin Blom, 1964.

Wiley, Autrey Nell (ed.), *Rare Prologues and Epilogues: 1642–1700*, 1940; rpt. Port Washington, New York, Kennikat Press, 1970.

Wilkins, Ernest Hatch, *A History of Italian Literature*, rev. edn, Cambridge, Mass., Harvard University Press, 1974.

Wilkinson, L. P., *Ovid Surveyed*, Cambridge, Cambridge University Press, 1962.

Willey, Basil, *The Seventeenth-Century Background: Studies in the Thought of the Age in Relation to Poetry and Religion*, 1935; rpt. New York, Anchor-Doubleday, 1953.

Williamson, George, *The Proper Wit of Poetry*, Chicago, University of Chicago Press, 1961.

——, *The Senecan Amble: A Study in Prose Form from Bacon to Collier*, Chicago, University of Chicago Press, 1951.

——, *Seventeenth-Century Contexts*, Chicago, University of Chicago Press, 1970.

Wilmot, John [Rochester], *The Letters of John Wilmot, Earl of Rochester*, ed. Jeremy Treglown, Chicago, University of Chicago Press, 1980.

Wilson, John Harold, *The Court Wits of the Restoration: An Introduction*, Princeton, Princeton University Press, 1948.

——, *The Influence of Beaumont and Fletcher on Restoration Drama*, Columbus, Ohio, Ohio State University Press, 1928.

Wimsatt, William K., Jr, and Cleanth Brooks, *Literary Criticism: A Short History*, New York, Alfred A. Knopf, 1957.

Wing, Donald, *Short-Title Catalogue of Books Printed in England, Scotland, Ireland, Wales, and British America and of English Books Printed in Other Countries: 1641–1700*, 3 vols, New York, Columbia University Press, 1945–51.

Wordsworth, William, *The Prelude: 1799, 1805, 1850*, ed. Jonathan Wordsworth *et al.*, New York, W. W. Norton, 1979.

Wotton, William, *Reflections upon Ancient and Modern Learning*, London, 1694.

Zimbardo, Rose A., *A Mirror to Nature: Transformations in Drama and Aesthetics, 1660–1732*, Lexington, Kentucky, University Press of Kentucky, 1986.

Zwicker, Steven N., *Lines of Authority: Politics and English Literary Culture, 1649–1689*, Ithaca, Cornell University Press, 1993.

Index

'JD' refers to John Dryden. Unless otherwise noted, all works of literature cited are by JD. Major sections under 'Dryden, John' include 'characteristics', 'as critic', 'life and career', 'personas', 'selected readings by', 'views on', and 'as writer'. His writings are treated under separate headings, as are sections of individual works: prefaces, prologues and so on. An 'i' after a page reference indicates an illustration. An 'n.' after a page reference indicates a note and is followed by the note number.

English antiquarianism 220
English critical theory 15
English criticism, break with Aristotelianism
117
English literary traditions 13, 160
English literature, influence of *The Courtier* on
28, 264n.21, 264n.32
English plays 46, 50, 51
English playwrights 39–40
Ennius, Quintus 207–8
Entertainment at Rutland House (Davenant,
1657) 125
epic poetry 223
Aristotle's views on 62
compared with tragedy 121
distinguished from historical poems 69
English genius for 223
identification with romance 130, 285n.10
JD's views on 109, 178, 179, 288n.3
language permissible in 70
purpose of 122
relationship to heroic plays 124
similarity to drama 121
stages in JD's understanding of 120–3
epic poets 122
epigraph to *An Essay of Dramatick Poesie*
(1668) 45
the epilogue, history of 23, 24
'Epilogue to *The Adventures of Five Hours*'
(Tuke, 1663) 35
'Epilogue to *Aureng-Zebe*' (1676) 158–9
subject discussed in, integration of character
and dialogue 159
'Epilogue to *The Conquest of Granada, Part II*'
(1672) 146
see also 'The Defence of the Epilogue'
'Epilogue to *The Rehearsal*' (Buckingham,
1672) 119
'Epilogue to *Tyrannick Love*' (1672) 29–30
'Epilogue to the University of Oxford' (1673)
114–15
'Epilogue to *The Wild Gallant,* as it was first
acted' (1663; 1669) 267n.54
'Epilogue to *The Wild Gallant* Reviv'd' (1669)
100
Epistles of Phalaris 194, 195, 196
Erasmus, Desiderius 226
An Essay of Dramatick Poesie (1668) 43–60
characters in 44
circumstances of composition 43, 269n.1
context for later criticism 80
context for 'Prologue to *Secret Love*' 74, 75
description of 2
form of 58–9
intentions in 45
JD's accomplishments in 61
JD's evaluation of 85, 241–2
JD's persona in 60–1
levels of meaning in 44–5

place in JD's criticism 43
reception of 81–4, 251
reflections of divided Court tastes 27
revision of 1684 152
sources and analogues of 44, 270n.15,
271n.52, 272n.56
as statement of ideals and purpose 52
structure of 43–4
style of 44, 59
subjects discussed in: *The Adventures of Five
Hours* 35; blank verse vs rhyme 53–5;
central argument 51; comic wit 109;
current literary scene 45–6; English
literary tradition 241; equation of epic
and drama 121–2; French drama 58–9;
JD's debt to Fletcher 130; the just and
the lively 46, 49, 50, 90; Quarrel of the
Ancients and Moderns 46–9; Roman wit
201; self-sufficiency of English drama
50–1; Shakespeare's plays 17–18, 50, 53;
tragi-comedy 49–50
summary of 147
see also Crites; 'A Defence of *An Essay of
Dramatick Poesie*'; Eugenius; Lisideius;
Neander; 'To ... Charles Lord Buckhurst'
'An Essay on Satire' (Mulgrave, 1679; 1689)
157
essays: *see* critical essays
*An Essay upon the Ancient and Modern
Learning* (Temple, 1690) 194
see also Temple, Sir William
Etherege, Sir George 102
Eugenius (character in *An Essay of Dramatick
Poesie*) 44, 201
allusion to laws of comedy 58
complaints against Ancients 49
views on modern drama 48
views on progress in playwrighting 47
views on wit 109–10
Euripides 174, 199
Evelyn, John 125
Evelyn, Mary 119
An Evening's Love (1671) 101–2, 112
Everyman Out of His Humour (Jonson, 1600)
108
examen, uses of 50, 270n.31
Examen Poeticum (1693) 183
subject discussed in: theory of translation 250

Fables Ancient and Modern (1700) 183
see also 'Preface to *Fables Ancient and
Modern*'
Fairfax, Thomas, 3rd Baron 178
false sublime 20, 163
fancy 70
see also imagination; wit
farce 100, 104, 114–15
Felltham, Owen (also Feltham) 249
Fénelon, François de la Mothe 175

Speroni, Sperone 71
Spingarn, J. E. 128
Sprat, Thomas 58–9, 66, 108–9, 279n.35
stage directions, in heroic plays 144–5
Starkman, Miriam 199
The State of Innocence (1677) 157
Statius, Publius Palpinius 62, 132
Stead, C. K. 283n.23
structure (or architectonics)
  in literature of the just 12
  in literature of the lively 12
style, contents of 168
the sublime (literary excellence) 161, 162–3
Suetonius (Gaius Suetonius Tranquillus) 298,
  298n.4
Sunderland, Robert Spencer, 2nd Earl of 160
the supernatural 132, 145
  see also the marvellous
Surrey, Henry Howard, Earl of 28
suspension of disbelief 88
Swift, Jonathan 2
  attacks on JD 195–6
  attacks on JD's scholarship 197
  The Battle of the Books 196
  beliefs of 200, 220, 293n.37
  causes of disagreements with JD 200
  'A Digression concerning Criticks' (Swift,
    1704) 197–9
  views on the Moderns 196
  see also A Tale of a Tub
syntax, faulty 149

Tacitus, Publius Cornelius 44
A Tale of a Tub (Swift, 1704) 195–7
  argument of 196
  see also 'A Digression concerning Criticks';
    'Introduction to *The Tale of a Tub*'
Tasso, Torquato 11, 95–6, 116, 137
taste, as basis of literary judgment 82
technical terms, uses of in poetry 68
The Tempest (Davenant and Dryden, 1667) 90,
  91–2, 93
  see also 'Preface to *The Tempest*'; 'Prologue to
    The Tempest'
Temple, Sir William 194, 196, 200
Terence (Publius Terentius Afer) 109
Tesauro, Emanuele 111
theatrical companies 263n.12
Theocritus 217
theology, JD's analogy from 85
third manner (JD's, 1680–1700)
  characteristics of 22, 33
  learned style of 199
third period (JD's, 1680–1700)
  attention to lesser genres in 180–1
  autobiography in 184–5
  categorization of authors in 183
  changes in JD's classicism in 173
  characteristics of 172

flexibility in 182
focus on the epic in 179
JD's views on tragedy in 178
JD's views on tragi-comedy in 179
JD's views on unities of time in 178
major developments in 222
overview of 172–3
reconciliation of principles of first and middle
  periods in 186
shift in emphasis in character sketches in 191
summary of 172–3, 182
translations written during 209
views on French criticism in 176
views on French literature in 173
views on the just and the lively in 14
  see also criticism (JD's), in third period
Thraxalla (fict.) 138
the three unities (action, place, time): *see* unity
  (JD on)
Tibullus, Albius 188, 191
time: *see* unity, of time
'To … Charles Lord Buckhurst (dedication of
  An Essay of Dramatick Poesie, 1668)
  44–5, 60, 241–2
  see also Dorset, Charles Sackville, Lord
  Buckhurst, 6th Earl of; *An Essay of
  Dramatick Poesie*
'To the Earl of Abindgon' (dedication of
  Eleonora, 1692)
  subject discussed in: panegyric 180
'To … James, Duke of Monmouth' (dedication
  of *Tyrannick Love,* 1670) 94
  see also preface to *Tyrannick Love; Tyrannick
  Love*
'To … John Lord Marquess of Normanby'
  (dedication of the *Æneis,* 1697) 209–15
  reception of 210
  scholarship in 210
  strengths of 210
  subjects discussed in: Aeneas as epic hero
    211; defence of Virgil 210; JD's methods
    of translation 248; originality in poetry
    176–7; time period covered by the *Aeneid*
    212–13; Virgil's aims in the *Aeneid* 213
  see also Æneis
'To Lord Clifford' (dedication of the *Pastorals,*
  1697) 180
'To … Lord Radcliffe' (dedication of *Examen
  Poeticum,* 1693) 177, 193, 250
'To the Memory of Mr. Oldham' (1684) 24,
  299n.11
'To the Metropolis of Great Britain'
  (dedication of *Annus Mirabilis,* 1667) 63,
  64
  self-presentation in 65
  subject discussed in: inhabitants of London
    65
  see also 'An [A]ccount of the ensuing Poem';
    Annus Mirabilis

340